LOVE ON THE ROCKS

LORI ROTSKOFF

LOVE

MEN, WOMEN, AND ALCOHOL IN

ON THE

POST-WORLD WAR II AMERICA

ROCKS

The University of North Carolina Press   Chapel Hill & London

The paper in this book meets the guidelines for
permanence and durability of the Committee on
Production Guidelines for Book Longevity of the
Council on Library Resources.

Library of Congress
Cataloging-in-Publication Data
Rotskoff, Lori.
Love on the rocks : men, women, and alcohol in post–
World War II America / by Lori Rotskoff.
    p. cm. — (Gender and American culture)
Includes bibliographical references and index.
ISBN 0-8078-2728-2 (cloth: alk. paper)
ISBN 0-8078-5402-6 (pbk.: alk. paper)
    1. Alcoholism—United States—History—20th century.
2. Drinking of alcoholic beverages—United States—
History—20th century. 3. Alcoholics—United States—
Family relationships—History—20th century.
4. Alcoholics—Rehabilitation—United States—History—
20th century. 5. Sex role—United States—History—20th
century. I. Title. II. Gender & American culture
HV5292 .R68 2002
394.1'3'09730904—dc21   2002002093

TO MY PARENTS

Judi and Ken Rotskoff

CONTENTS

ACKNOWLEDGMENTS

After working on this project for so long, I am happy to recognize those who have aided my efforts. I have accumulated many debts—personal and professional—that I am eager to acknowledge.

My interest in American cultural history was sparked while I was an undergraduate at Northwestern University, where I had the privilege of studying with Karen Halttunen. An outstanding teacher, mentor, and friend, she has continued to offer me wise counsel over the past decade. Her careful reading of my manuscript improved my prose immeasurably.

This book originated in a seminar paper and, later, a dissertation I wrote as a graduate student in the American Studies program at Yale University. Jean-Christophe Agnew first encouraged me to pursue this project, and at times he seemed to understand better than I did why it was worth pursuing. I am grateful for his unflagging interest in my topic and for his willingness to share invaluable insights about the writing of cultural history. Nancy F. Cott has been a most reliable and encouraging mentor; I thank her not only for the model of her own teaching and scholarship but also for the sound advice and helpful criticism she has offered along the way. Michael Denning's perceptive responses to early drafts greatly enriched this study and led me to ask new, fresh questions of my material.

Many friends and colleagues at Yale, including Elspeth Brown, Julia Ehrhardt, Catherine Gudis, Jeff Hardwick, Marina Moskowitz, and Rebecca Schreiber, offered intelligent advice and support, especially during our dissertation writing years. I have benefited greatly from Ann Fabian's perceptive reading of my work, as well as her abiding friendship.

As fellow panelists at academic conferences, Elayne Rapping, Katherine Chavigny, and Trysh Travis shared their research findings and ideas in ways that have enriched my own endeavors. In their capacity as commentators and panel chairs, several people have read and commented on earlier drafts of my chapters, including Harry Marks, Rima Apple, Nancy Tomes, David Musto, and Scott Haine. Over the years my conversations with Michelle McClellan on the history of alcohol and gender (and more recently on the challenges of combining academic work and child-rearing) have been especially valuable.

A number of people, including Caroline J. Acker, Sarah W. Tracy, and Ron Roizen, helped me to sharpen my arguments, correct factual errors, and understand better how my work fits into the scholarship on the history of alcohol. John W. Crowley generously shared his knowledge and offered support and suggestions at nearly every stage, including the final draft of the manuscript. David Kyvig's thoughtful comments also improved the book.

A number of people aided me in my research efforts. Barbara Miller, chief archivist at the Al-Anon archives, was especially helpful during my stay in Virginia Beach. She happily shared her knowledge of the fellowship's history and responded with alacrity to my research requests. My thanks go to Frank Mauser and others at the Alcoholics Anonymous archives in New York City for allowing me access to published sources. I am also grateful to Joan K. Jackson, who enlightened me about aspects of the history of alcoholism that I would not have otherwise learned. Rarely are historians fortunate enough to meet the subjects about whom they are writing, and to find them to be encouraging guides as well.

For financial support I gratefully acknowledge the Woodrow Wilson Foundation, for granting me a Mellon Fellowship in the Humanities; Yale University, for awarding me an Enders research grant; and the American Historical Association, for awarding me an Albert J. Beveridge research grant.

My editor at the University of North Carolina Press, Chuck Grench, has made publishing this book a pleasure, and I thank him for his confidence in my project. I also thank Ron Maner, Amanda McMillan, and many others at UNC Press who helped make this publication a reality.

Debts of longer standing I owe to my parents, Judi and Ken Rotskoff, who have encouraged me in my educational endeavors since I was a child. Their emotional and material support, not to mention their continuing faith in my abilities, helped me to see this project through. With joy I dedicate this book to them.

My husband, Michael Canter has been a loving and loyal partner since we met during our college years. Many times he cheerfully tolerated my spending an entire weekend in front of the computer or engaged me in lively discussions about my analysis or my research. I am grateful for his enthusiastic support of my work—my teaching as well as my writing—

over the years I have devoted to this project. But most of all I thank him for being my constant companion in *life*.

I extend my last, but certainly not least, words of gratitude to my sons, Benjamin and Elijah. Each child's impending birth served as a natural deadline and heightened the sense of clarity and focus I needed to complete this project at various stages. Every day they shift my attention from women and men in the past to the nitty-gritty realities of family life in the present—and to happy, hopeful thoughts about the future.

LOVE ON THE ROCKS

INTRODUCTION

In 1929 Ella Boole, social reformer and president of the Woman's Christian Temperance Union (WCTU), published a book chronicling the history of American women in the temperance movement. Imploringly titled *Give Prohibition Its Chance*, the book offered an impassioned argument supporting the law that had banned the sale of liquor for a decade. Like her more famous predecessor Frances Willard (who presided over the WCTU from the 1870s through the 1890s), Boole claimed that women and children had been the greatest victims of drink in the past, and that they would suffer most if national Prohibition were repealed. An outspoken defender of the Eighteenth Amendment, Boole believed that Prohibition was helping to safeguard the moral sanctity, financial health, and general happiness of the American family. Boole lambasted the saloon as a "social evil" that turned respectable workingmen into drunken brutes. Before Prohibition, she wrote, "it was the home that suffered . . . the women and children who did without necessary food and clothing . . . the wife and mother who listened until midnight for the staggering footsteps of her drunken husband or son."[1] Still rooted in an ideology of domesticity that entrusted Protestant, middle-class, white women with ensuring the moral solvency of the home, the WCTU of the 1920s viewed "King Alcohol" as an inherently addictive substance that would debilitate even the most well-intentioned imbibers. According to the WCTU, social and legal coercion was required to "protect" the family when tactics of moral suasion and public education failed.[2] Though the WCTU was not alone in shaping the politics of temperance (indeed, the male-dominated Anti-Saloon League was ultimately more instrumental in securing national Prohibition by 1919), its gendered, moralistic vision of alcohol consumption held sway through the early decades of the twentieth century.

By the 1950s, however, religious female reformers had lost the influence they once wielded with respect to the politics of drink. By midcentury the sentimental temperance tale of the forlorn family had exhausted its cultural currency, its descriptive power to stir the hearts and minds of readers. Within public debates over alcohol consumption, the voices of evangelical reformers were muffled by other social groups who engendered new ways of understanding and treating chronic inebriety. Soon after the repeal of Prohibition in 1933, the public discourse on excessive drinking was no longer structured as a wet-versus-dry debate over legal proscription; rather, it stemmed from the concerns of doctors, psychiatrists, social workers, and lay therapists—a diverse body of experts whose claims to authority were rooted not in a mission of moral uplift but in privileged access to scientific knowledge, spiritual insight, or therapeutic technique.

Various groups of scientific, medical, and self-credentialed authorities replaced an essentially moralistic view of overindulgence as a *sin* with a modern, therapeutic conception of excessive drinking as a *sickness*. While some physicians viewed alcohol addiction as a disease as early as the eighteenth century, before 1930 the strong cultural influence of temperance reformers prevented a thorough medicalization of habitual drunkenness in society at large.[3] Between the 1930s and 1960s, however, a new consensus took shape as "traditional moralistic interpretations . . . were abandoned in favor of a 'scientific' or medical view according to which the chronic drunkard is [treated as] the victim of a physiological or psychological aberration."[4] Certainly moral and religious judgments were not effaced entirely from new understandings of alcoholism. But during the mid-twentieth century, experts increasingly defined the overconsumption of alcohol as a medical and psychological problem that rendered certain people subjects for scientific scrutiny, diagnosis, and therapy. Out of this professional and ideological terrain emerged the modern paradigm of "alcoholism" as an illness, or pathology. Forming what historians have retrospectively called an "alcoholism movement," these authorities aimed to treat people with drinking problems and to heighten public awareness about problem drinking.[5]

One such expert was Thelma Whalen, a Texas social worker who worked in an alcoholism treatment hospital in the years following World War II. In 1953—exactly twenty years after the repeal of Prohibition—Whalen published an article titled "Wives of Alcoholics: Four Types Observed in a Family Service Agency." Over the course of her professional career as a family caseworker, Whalen counseled dozens of women married to alcoholic men, and she discovered "striking similarities" among them. Countering the notion that the alcoholic's wife was a passive victim of circumstances beyond her control, Whalen claimed that women facilitated their husbands' inebriety. "The wife of an alcoholic is not simply the object of mistreatment in a situation which she had no part in creating," Whalen wrote. In the "sordid sequence of marital misery" that plagues the alcoholic family, she argued, the wife is "an active participant in the creation of the problems which ensue."[6] For Whalen, then, alcoholism was a problem interwoven in the fabric of troubled relations between husbands and wives.

Whalen's diagnosis of the alcoholic's spouse was a far cry from the image of the "drunkard's wife" prevalent a century earlier. Shunning the rhetoric of religion and morality, post–World War II experts on the alcoholic family spoke the language of social science, psychiatry, and above all, therapy. No longer a passive victim or an "innocent bystander" in the midst of domestic upheaval, the spouse in the social worker's estimation was implicated in the "marital misery" she endured. Whereas Ella Boole portrayed the desolate wife to symbolize the threat men's drinking posed to *all* women, Whalen assumed that drinking was problematic only in particular households: those inhabited by individuals who could be diagnosed as "alcoholics." Rather than militating for legislation that would affect the access of an entire society to alcohol, midcentury experts targeted women whose lives were directly affected by drinking. Rather than try to stop all men from drinking, they exhorted individual women to scrutinize their personal responses to men's drinking, to focus inwardly on their own marriages and psyches.

During the post–World War II era, psychiatric social workers such as Thelma Whalen were not alone in viewing alcoholism in terms of marital relationships. Other public health advocates located alcoholism in the domestic sphere, in the private homes of women and men. Between 1940 and the early 1960s Whalen's article was one of dozens of scientific studies that focused on the wives and marriages of alcoholics. At the same time Alcoholics Anonymous (AA), a not-for-profit "fellowship" dedicated to the treatment and recovery of compulsive drinkers, created an institutional context for such concerns. From its beginning in 1935 AA encouraged members' spouses to participate informally in the organization's program of ritual disclosure, spiritual rebirth, and mutual support. Like many credentialed authorities, AA members believed that families could play a major role in perpetuating—or arresting—an alcoholic's drinking. In 1951 Lois Wilson, the wife of AA cofounder Bill Wilson, officially established the Al-Anon Family Groups, which encouraged wives to follow the same Twelve Step program used by alcoholics themselves. The founders of AA and Al-Anon believed that women could improve their own and their husbands' lives by creating an emotional and spiritual climate conducive to sobriety.

Following the transition from the temperance reform literature to the publications of postwar alcoholism experts, in this book I investigate important connections among alcohol consumption, gender roles, and family life from the 1910s through the 1960s, with an emphasis on the post–World War II period. In essence I explore the *engendering* of alcoholism as a psychological and bodily illness in the mid-twentieth century. I use the word "engender" here in a double sense: first, to denote the formation of new institutions and forms of therapy associated with the alcoholism movement. These include communities of academic experts (especially those affiliated with the Yale Center for Studies on Alcohol, established in 1940); psychiatrists and social workers at alcoholism treatment hospitals and mental health facilities across the nation; public relations organizations; and the fellowships of AA and the Al-Anon Family Groups. These groups shaped perceptions of alcoholism through publications in scholarly journals and mass-circulation magazines, inspirational self-help or "recovery" literature; published works of fiction; and commercial films and television programs.

Second, and just as significantly, this term refers to matters of gender and the family. As suggested in the historical vignettes above, over the course of U.S. history citizens have perceived excessive drinking primarily as a *masculine* indulgence. One continuity from the turn of the century through the 1950s rested in the perception that most heavy drinkers, and hence most alcoholics, were men. This assumption influenced the alcoholism paradigm in the 1940s and 1950s, when the term "alcoholic" usually meant "male alcoholic." Sex-ratio statistics varied slightly, but most authorities agreed that women comprised approximately one-sixth of all alcoholics. When experts did focus on women's drinking, they noted it specifically, highlighting the unusual status of female alcoholics.[7] These gendered presuppositions also informed the lay therapists who founded AA, a fact reflected in the predominantly white, middle-class, male membership of the organization during its early decades.[8] At the same time nondrinking spouses in an alcoholic marriage were usually wives. When the Al-Anon Family Groups were officially organized, they welcomed members of both sexes, but the overwhelming majority of participants were women.

Because assumptions of sexual difference were so thoroughly embedded in the alcoholism paradigm, ideas about excessive alcohol intake provide a revealing window through which to observe the construction of gender identities for both men and women. Discourses of alcoholism reflected and reshaped ideologies of gender, helping to define norms of proper and "healthy" masculinity and femininity. Historian Elizabeth Lunbeck's analysis of psychiatrists in the 1910s and 1920s applies to later decades as well: "Gender conflict, real and rhetorical, shaped day-to-day practice and colored psychiatrists' and social workers' reflections upon it. It was encoded in the categories that ordered their observations, sometimes overtly . . . and sometimes silently." Lunbeck's study focuses on how psychiatrists developed concepts of "normal" manhood and womanhood while mining the prosaic realm of their subjects' day-to-day lives. In their efforts "to aid the common man and woman to deeper, practical insights into everyday life," early-twentieth-century psychiatrists created a discourse of "normalizing judgments" about gender. Later alcohol specialists, concerned as they were with pathological deviations from the "normal," nonetheless incorporated normative ideas about gender in their conceptions of alcoholic men and their nonalcoholic spouses.[9]

The gendered trajectory from temperance reform to alcoholism moves from a richly documented and well-traveled domain to a territory that historians are just beginning to visit. Though several studies have illuminated the domestic politics of nineteenth-century and Progressive Era temperance reform, we know little about the history of the "alcoholic marriage" in the decades following repeal. And while historians and sociologists have examined the organizational structures, therapies, and public relations efforts of alcohol experts in the mid-twentieth century, few have paid attention to the crucial role of gender and family ideology in the construction of alcoholic identities.[10] In order fully to understand public debates over Prohibition, cultural depictions of normative or excessive drinking, and therapeutic ideas about alcoholism, we need to view this history through the lens of gender and investigate the most intimate social arenas affected by cultures of drink and sobriety.

The overlapping topics of drinking and alcoholism offer fresh insights for students of American cultural history. Recent studies have addressed the theme of alcoholism in American cinema, fiction, and vernacular narrative. These studies are often nuanced and compelling, and they begin to highlight the significance of drink in U.S. society.[11] But the cultural history of alcohol consumption in the twentieth century—one that situates rituals of drink and sobriety within a broad context of historical change—is only beginning to be written. By focusing on relationships among drinking, gender, and family life, we can gain a new perspective on crucial developments in U.S. history, including the Great Depression of the 1930s, the social reconstruction of the home front after World War II, and the impact of the Cold War on domestic culture in the 1950s and 1960s. The history of alcoholism sheds new light on how gender roles, especially those associated with breadwinning and homemaking, marriage and parenthood, intersected with larger transformations on a national and even global scale.

The topics of drinking and alcoholism provide a unique opportunity to investigate the family as a mutable social institution and ideological creation. Historian Stephanie Coontz defines the family as a sphere that offers access to the production and consumption of society's resources. As she writes, the family "provides people with an explanation of their rights and obligations that helps link personal identity to social role. At the same time, [it] constitutes an arena where people can affect their rights and obligations, . . . a place where people can resist assignment to their social roles or attempt to re-negotiate those roles." Drawing on work by anthropologists and feminist theorists, Coontz cautions that we cannot construct a precise definition of "the family" because what a given culture defines as a family varies across time and space. But conceptualizing the family as an arena in which members define and contest their roles as providers, managers, and consumers of emotional and material resources permits us to explore the complex relationships between family and society as they have changed over time.[12]

Applying this theoretical framework to family history, historians argue that the dominant pattern of family life in the United States changed markedly during the decades surrounding the turn of the twentieth century, and especially after the 1920s. To summarize a complex historical argument, the rise of a bureaucratic, corporate social order based on mass production and consumption ushered in a new family system that redefined Americans' expectations of family life. Characterized by a cult of privacy, the "new familialism" increased the family's importance as a site of personal expression and emotional well-being. Rather than simply providing a peaceful haven from the stresses of the public sphere—an ideological function assigned to the Victorian nuclear family during the nineteenth century—the modern family was expected to generate psychic fulfillment and excitement for its members, to "provide a whole alternative world of satisfaction and intimacy." Twentieth-century Americans not only retained elements of the Victorian "family as refuge," but they also viewed the family as a kind of "encounter group" in which their deepest personal longings could be expressed and achieved. In short, Americans heightened their psychic demands on domestic life, idealizing the nuclear family as a realm of profound emotional fulfillment as well as a site of social reproduction.[13]

The new familialism that emerged during the early twentieth century reached its apotheosis during the post–World War II era. By midcentury, as the memory of the hardships of the Depression began to fade and the wartime economy of scarcity was converted into a thriving consumer economy, unprecedented numbers of Americans were investing themselves, emotionally and financially, in a vision of privatized, nuclear family life. In the aftermath of World War II millions of Americans—at the behest of educators, advertisers, government officials, and producers of popular culture—subscribed to an ascendant domestic ideology that revised traditional familial values for the Cold War era. The dominant ideal of the white, middle-class, nuclear family was based on strictly divided gender roles: a husband was supposed to provide for his wife and children through his status as breadwinner while a wife worked primarily as a homemaker, consumer, and family caretaker. Amidst the anxieties surrounding the unleashing of atomic energy, political antagonism abroad, and anticommunist hysteria at home, government and industry harnessed family ideology to a national effort aimed at achieving global economic and political supremacy. Narratives in mass-circulation magazines, movies, television shows, and other cultural forms aligned the suburban nuclear family with happiness, affluence, and other blessings of U.S. citizenship. As historian Elaine Tyler May summarizes, the legendary family of the late 1940s and 1950s promised "to fulfill virtually all its members' personal needs through an energized and expressive personal life."[14]

Of course these idealized representations of gender and family life were, after all, prescriptions and not descriptions of how most Americans actually behaved. It is clear that too much emphasis on the stereotypical white, middle-class, suburban family oversimplifies a more complex historical picture and overlooks racial, ethnic, and other cultural variations in domestic arrangements. Historians have too often misunderstood the dominant family ideology itself, ignoring the ambiguities and internal contradictions inherent in prevailing postwar discourses.[15] For many individuals who tried to conform to dominant ideals, family life often fell short of inflated expectations. As men and women heightened their demands of domestic life, the distance between family ideals and realities could be great indeed; as Stephanie Coontz writes, "No sooner did the idea appear that the family should be the source of all emotional satisfaction than the rage for failing to meet those emotional needs welled up against it."[16] If scholars have painted a broad picture of domestic ideology in the post–World War II period, they have only just begun to delineate the tensions that lay embedded within the postwar domestic consensus— tensions that belied the family's mythic promise as a site of psychic and material well-being for men and women alike. While producers of popular culture crafted endless depictions of the "happy" 1950s family and experts tried to mold Americans into "well-adjusted" households, an undercurrent of anxiety and unhappiness ran through domestic culture. Even fervent proponents of conventional family patterns conceded that family life was fraught with problems.[17]

Yet the darker underside of domestic life during the mid-twentieth century remains largely uncovered. Cultural anthropologists have long noted that a central function of the modern American family is to provide "nurturance," defined not simply as the shelter and nourishment required for physical survival but also as a "certain kind of relationship" that entails enduring affection, love, and emotional support.[18] Debates about alcoholism provide a rich opportunity to examine ideologies of family life because alcoholism so often signifies the family's *failure* to meet cultural standards of nurturance. Literally and symbolically, habitual drinking interferes with patterns of caregiving among husbands, wives, and children, calling into question the roles and responsibilities of drinkers and nondrinkers alike. Through the subject of alcoholism we can probe the anthropological argument that the symbolic meanings of the idealized family "are often best illuminated by explicating their opposites."[19] Discourses of diseased, dysfunctional, or deviant families do not merely target certain groups or households as special objects of attention and rehabilitation; they also shape and reinforce norms of successful family life for the rest of society.

The shift from temperance narratives to marital dramas of alcoholism highlights the changing relationship between family and society from the turn of the twentieth century through the Cold War era. When alcohol consumption was politicized as a social problem during the Prohibition era, female temperance advocates pursued a maternalist politics of domesticity that proclaimed that women's unique sensibilities gave them special authority to reform society, and especially to improve the lives of women and children. For proponents of Prohibition the root causes of domestic disintegration lay not in the private realm of the family itself but in society at large. Temperance linked women's private roles to organized, public activity; family problems associated with drunkenness were imagined *as* social problems that required social and legal solutions.[20] But during the mid-twentieth century, alcoholism experts reversed this formulation. Rather than protecting the family from dangerous external forces and substances, they viewed the family itself as the site where alcoholism originated. In a time when heightened avowals of idealized family life channeled the optimism of post–World War II America, the family was especially vulnerable as a scapegoat when social trends threatened visions of security and progress. With the engendering of alcoholism as a family disease, Americans increasingly viewed alcoholism as a family problem. Despite or, more likely, because of the fact that representations of the family were used to symbolize U.S. security in a threatening Cold War context, families were often blamed as the source of problems that plagued society at large.

Exploring the gendered history of drink and sobriety also highlights the changing relationship between alcohol and class affiliation. Not only did drinking narratives reimagine the connection between manly indulgence and familial success; they also reflected a shift in the position of the "problem drinker" on the hierarchical ladder of social class. While dry activists believed that alcohol endangered all potential drinkers, regardless of economic status, the fight for Prohibition targeted the urban, working-class barroom as the main site of moral decay. The typical drunkard in the prohibitionist's imagination was a workingman who spent his modest wages treating himself and others to drinks after a hard day of manual labor. During the saloon era (roughly from 1870 to 1920) masculine rituals of intemperance were was seen as threatening to families of all classes. But by the 1940s the quintessential drinker had metamorphosed from the laboring saloon-goer to the middle- or upper-middle-class businessman, a salaried manager or professional who drank at men's clubs, in cocktail lounges, or at home. On the silver screen and the printed page, in psychiatrists' offices and at AA-sponsored meetings, the modern alcoholic was increasingly perceived as a respectable yet beleaguered professional or bureaucrat, a man who enjoyed a measure of social and financial stability before alcoholism took its toll. Often he resided in the suburbs of a major metropolitan area or in a middle-class section of a small city. Although experts, like temperance crusaders, believed that *anyone* could become a habitual drinker, the customs and problems of white, middle- and upper-class drinkers increasingly set the terms of public discourse on alcohol-related issues. Certainly, working-class styles of drinking persisted after repeal, but they did not arouse public consternation as they did during the saloon era.

On a related note the paradigm shift from temperance to alcoholism entailed both changes and continuities with respect to racial and ethnic identification. During the saloon era tavern clienteles were generally comprised of immigrants or their second-generation descendants of European ethnicity. Many dry reformers focused specifically on the habits of Irish, German, or Slavic saloon regulars, and some comments in their literature amounted to thinly veiled ethnic slurs. In the South segregated saloons attracting African American drinkers incurred the wrath of reformers who feared racial violence as well as drink-induced disorder. But by and large, northern and midwestern reformers did not emphasize racial or ethnic differences and generally treated all saloon-goers with equal contempt.[21] Later most proponents of the alcoholism movement downplayed or ignored racial differences in drinking patterns. While some sociologists focused on the drinking habits of particular ethnic groups, the alcoholic in the modern expert's imagination was usually figured as white—sometimes explicitly but more often implicitly. The racialized identity of alcoholic men dovetailed with their increasingly middle-class, suburban, professional affiliation. On a representational level, white characters in movies, novels, and advertisements signified the typical drinker's racial background; in the realm of therapeutic practice, treatment facilities and the AA fellowships attracted an overwhelmingly white population (at least during the period covered here).[22] This study's focus on the construction of white, middle-class manhood and womanhood (and secondarily on white working-class masculinity) is thus itself an artifact of the dominant culture being addressed.

This book offers a historical narrative encompassing several cultural trajectories: a shift from a moralistic to a medicalized view of chronic drunkenness; a new, widespread acceptance of "social drinking" as a desirable recreational activity; a change in the social location of the alcoholic drinker and his family; and a symbolic inversion from the threaten*ed* to the threaten*ing* family as a primary locus of scientific and popular concern. These vectors of historical change are interrelated. The transition from sin to sickness exemplifies what previous writers have called "the triumph of the therapeutic ethos," a worldview that heralds the pursuit of individual well-being, bodily health, and psychological satisfaction as life's ultimate goal. For several decades scholars have linked the rise of therapeutic culture to the growth and consolidation of the American middle class and, specifically, to the needs of a new professional-managerial class that arose amidst the bureaucratic expansion of corporate capitalism during the decades surrounding the turn of the twentieth century.[23] Recently Joel Pfister has exhorted fellow cultural historians to explore more fully the therapeutic realm as a "symptom of vaster historical transformations" involving the formation of racial, gender, and especially class identity. "Why," he asks, "have many members of the middle and upper classes so enthusiastically preoccupied themselves with—assigned such meaningfulness and fascination to—notions of the self, the family, and the body" that center on interpersonal conflicts? Histories of psychological life, he argues, must address how therapeutic ideas function in the formation of white, middle- and upper-class identities, affirming "their social superiority or potency by elevating the cultural value of anxiety, sexual conflicts, and familial tensions." Pfister suggests that these classes "resignified anxiety as affirmation, emotional turmoil as subjective potency, and familial ambivalence as psychological capital. Curiously, class identity often came to entail not only a 'psychological' preoccupation with oneself and with others, but also a measure of suffering."[24] The twin topics of drinking and alcoholism provide a novel "case study" for this kind of cultural history.

Cultures of drink, temperance, and sobriety have long served as arenas for the creation and negotiation of social identity. The phrase "culture of drink" refers to the physical setting, social rituals, and cultural meanings of a particular drinking style or situation. It encompasses questions of who drinks, when and where drinking occurs, what beverages are consumed, how drinkers understand their motivations to drink, and how drinkers pursue relationships with fellow drinkers (and often with nondrinkers as well). "Temperance culture" refers to the writings and experiences of reformers and other groups who aimed to limit or banish drinking on philosophical, moral, or political grounds. The term "culture of sobriety," finally, signifies a social and ideological realm in which people are defined (or define themselves) as problematic drinkers and struggle self-consciously to restrict their alcohol consumption.

In all of these cultural milieus, drinkers and nondrinkers forge, sustain, endanger, or sever social connections with drinkers and nondrinkers alike. Americans use rituals of drink and sobriety to manage emotions and mediate personal relationships. Many of these relationships are familial, such as the bond between husband and wife or parent and child; others involve connections among neighbors, friends, acquaintances, employers, colleagues, subordinates, and even strangers. *Love on the Rocks* illustrates how the narratives and rituals of drink, temperance, and sobriety have provided men and women with meaningful and historically specific ways to understand the creation or dissolution of social bonds, both inside and outside the domestic domain.

Of the social bonds affected by cultures of drink and sobriety, marriage is among the most significant. The institution of marriage has long inscribed assumptions about the rights and obligations accorded to men and women by virtue of their sex and marital status. During the postwar period marriage was the bedrock of the prevailing white, middle-class, domestic ideal. To be perceived as a normative family in the eyes of the dominant culture required, first and foremost, a marital union between a husband and a wife. Indeed, in 1940 the Census Bureau classified family data into three types. The first, called the normal family, had a male head living with his wife (with or without other household members or children). Although the other two types recognized the existence of other male-headed families and female-headed households, respectively, this federal bureau echoed strong currents in popular culture that prescribed marriage between a dominant male and a subordinate female as the favored, normal arrangement.[25]

Ideas about drink and alcoholism invite us to consider marriage as a crucial site of gender formation, defined as the dynamic social process by which *both* genders are formed, reshaped, and contested in relation to each other.[26] Indeed, to uncover the social and emotional history of family life requires that we examine the historical definition of gender for men and women alike. Implicitly and explicitly, cultures of drink and sobriety offered lessons in "proper" or "healthy" gender-role performance. Both husbands and wives in an alcoholic marriage were figured as failures, unable to meet the gendered expectations of the new familialism. While drink advocates after the repeal of Prohibition depicted moderate drinking as consistent with successful gender identification for men (and increasingly for women as well), cultures of sobriety maintained that alcoholism contributed to gendered failure, and they encouraged abstinence as the only route to domestic rehabilitation.

In large part, then, this book tells the story of two complementary figures in American culture: the sober husband and the supportive wife.

As representations of successful manhood and womanhood, these dual ideals functioned as cultural models or exemplars for Americans confined in an alcoholic marriage. The very notion of sobriety is defined by an *absence* of drinking; one who has never consumed alcohol regularly, while literally living an alcohol-free lifestyle, is not usually perceived as a "sober" individual. Thus the figure of the sober husband was implicitly compared with drinking men and with his former drinking self.[27] During his transition from active drinking to recovery, the sober husband participated in several social realms, each with its specific moral, material, and affective economy: the masculine culture of drink, the gendered fellowship of AA, and the nuclear family unit. Furthermore, a husband's involvement in each of these realms was viewed in terms of its effects on his wife. The figure of the alcoholic's wife was shaped, in part, by general norms of the wife's domestic role but also by her troubled relationship with an alcoholic man. While her husband's participation in homosocial moral economies threatened her own marital success, she, too, was exhorted to act in gender-specific ways to restore family harmony. Invoking images of sober husbands and supportive wives sheds new light on patterns of material and emotional exchange that characterized family and community life for millions of Americans in the twentieth century.

A few words on the scope of this book are in order. As a cultural history of men, women, and alcohol consumption from the 1930s through the 1960s (with an emphasis on the immediate postwar decades), this study focuses primarily on how drinking and sobriety affected marital roles and relationships. To the extent that expectations for married couples with children also entailed norms of parenthood—ideas about being a "good" father or mother—this book touches on issues related to child-rearing. But specific topics such as parent-child relationships in alcoholic homes, the socialization of children and teenagers with regard to drinking, and the transmission of alcoholism from generation to generation are addressed only briefly. (In 1957 Al-Anon founded its Alateen branch for the adolescent children of alcoholics, which adapted the fellowship's mission to the needs of young people. By the 1970s Alateen had attracted significant numbers of participants and published its first hardcover book in 1973.) Furthermore, this is not a book about women alcoholics. Although several chapters address changing patterns of social drinking among women as well as men, and while women's experiences of alcoholism are mentioned at times for comparative purposes, this subject is distinct and complex enough to warrant historical treatment in its own right.[28] Finally, for historical reasons mentioned above, the drinking experiences of African Americans and other racial and ethnic groups are not central to the story told here. There is much more to learn about the history of alcoholism, gender, and the family, and I hope that other scholars and writers will address and answer the many significant questions that remain.

Chapter 1, "Cultures of Drink in Prohibition and Post-Repeal America," explores the politics of Prohibition through the lenses of gender and class, relating temperance reform to ideals of manhood and womanhood in the early twentieth century. It also investigates the annulment of Prohibition as a watershed moment in the normalization of social drinking during a time when men and women of all social classes coped with the exigencies of recession and war. As social drinking became identified with normative ideals of masculinity, habitual drunkenness could be more readily pathologized as a malady, setting the stage for the alcoholism movement.

Chapter 2, "Engendering the Alcoholic," focuses on the gendered assumptions that informed the alcoholism paradigm in scientific literature and popular films. While convivial drinking became more accepted among normal middle-class men (and increasingly among women as well), experts came to view *excessive* consumption as a sign of inadequate masculine identity. Their pronouncements, moreover, were part of a broader crisis in men's roles, especially the gender destabilization and class anxiety wrought by the erosion of breadwinning during the Great Depression and the wrenching social transformations on the home front during and after World War II.

Chapter 3, "Alcoholics Anonymous and the Culture of Sobriety," addresses the role of the mutual-help movement in shaping alcoholic identities. By midcentury AA had become the nation's best-known treatment program for habitual drinkers, an association of locally based groups whose members meet voluntarily to counteract a common affliction in their lives.[29] Emphasizing the gendered and familial dimensions of sobriety during AA's early decades, this chapter argues that AA originated an ideal of "sober manhood" that mediated between competing roles and responsibilities demanded of most male members. Moving beyond the realm of elite experts, this chapter considers the historical agency of drinkers themselves in the creation of an alcoholic culture.

Chapter 4, "The Dilemma of the Alcoholic Marriage," shows how normative ideas about the roles of women as well as men were embedded in the alcoholism paradigm. This chapter addresses how Al-Anon members enacted multiple roles as wives, mothers, homemakers, and often wage earners and shows how their experiences shaped the ideal of the supportive wife of the alcoholic. The development of Al-Anon offers an especially clear lens into the cultural history of white, middle-class marriage in postwar America. Through diagnoses of the alcoholic marriage, professional and lay experts supported a vision of domestic life based on self-sufficient male providers and dependent female homemakers; in so doing, they developed therapeutic sanctions against deviance from dominant gender ideologies.

Chapter 5, "Drink and Domesticity in Postwar America," analyzes various cultures of drink in the post–World War II period, a time when broad ranks of Americans not only became more conscious of alcoholism but also melded alcohol more fluidly into the whirl of social life. In turn, the acceptance of alcoholic beverages in middle-class and cosmopolitan society shaped how filmmakers, writers, and other cultural producers used alcoholism as a metaphor for other problems endemic to the Cold War domestic suburban milieu. Drawing on fiction, film, advertising, and other documents of "cocktail culture," this chapter links problem drinking, and addiction more generally, to themes of consumerism, materialism, and family life in the 1950s and beyond.

Ultimately this book considers the metaphorical significance of alcoholism in mid-twentieth-century America and underscores the extent of the changes in perceptions of drinking over the course of several decades. Yet the shift from temperance reform to the alcoholism movement also contained continuities that meshed with broader contours of gender and family history. From the early 1900s through the post–World War II era, dominant norms of masculinity and femininity divided the social, economic, and emotional responsibilities of the nuclear family along gender lines. Domestic ideology dovetailed with consumer capitalism to perpetuate the ideals of the independent male breadwinner and the subordinate female caretaker. As the United States steered itself through the successive crises of depression, war, and cold war, these ideals accommodated and absorbed new social realities while retaining their power to prescribe the terms of acceptable behavior. For both temperance advocates in the 1910s and therapeutic experts in the 1950s, a husband's alcohol consumption could signify the family's ability—or conversely, its inability—to partake of national plenty, to thrive during hard times, and to convert men's income into sustenance for women and children. Though their solutions to familial distress varied greatly, both groups perpetuated and redefined a normative gender system that assigned men and women different natures, capacities, and roles based on sex. The history of alcoholism thus encourages us to recognize ideological continuities as well as differences over a span of time that is frequently segmented. By investigating this history, we can better grasp the cultural implications of alcohol consumption in our nation's recent past.

1

CULTURES OF DRINK IN PROHIBITION AND POST-REPEAL AMERICA

DISSOLUTE MANHOOD AND THE
RITUALS OF INTEMPERANCE

In 1913 at age thirty-six, the novelist Jack London published his autobiographical novel *John Barleycorn*. Centering on his encounters with alcohol and his fellow drinkers, London offered a personal chronicle of excessive drinking and a vivid account of the saloon culture that defined recreational life for working-class men of his day. London situated alcohol consumption in the context of the work and leisure of laboring men, especially in the saloons, or "poorman's clubs," of an urbanizing nation. For London, drinking was a profoundly social act. As a youth he drank not because he liked the taste or intoxicating effects of alcohol, but to share in the conviviality that seemed magically to swirl around liquor. The desire for alcohol, London wrote, "is cultivated in social soil." "All drinkers begin socially. . . . When I thought of alcohol, the connotation was fellowship. When I thought of fellowship, the connotation was alcohol. Fellowship and alcohol were Siamese twins. They always occurred linked together."[1]

Indeed, the saloon was the quintessential site where men encountered the camaraderie of drink, and historians have long relied on London's evocative descriptions to reimagine saloon-goers' rituals of intemperance. The subculture of the saloon was central to the formation of gender identity for its male patrons. It helped forge a definition of manliness predicated on a rejection of familial obligations and the creation of strong social bonds among men. The saloon was a major site of a working-class "bachelor subculture" in which men of various ethnic backgrounds (including married men who were not literally bachelors) spent their leisure time in the company of other men. Scorning the domesticating influence of women, the bachelor subculture celebrated an ethic of male solidarity and reciprocity.[2] The avid saloon-goer epitomized "dissolute manhood," one of two opposing constructions of manhood that vied for allegiance in the early twentieth century. Dissolute masculinity defined the untrammeled, pleasure-seeking male as the epitome of manliness. Even among those who renounced dissipated manhood for its alternative, the "respectable" manhood of the married breadwinner, "the grown man's jealously guarded right to drink with his mates was the most common and most contested adult holdover from the youthful masculinist ethos."[3] London's *John Barleycorn* was a testament to both the pleasures and the pitfalls of dissolute manhood.

London was among the first modern writers to idealize intoxication as a mode of cultural iconoclasm and to glorify alcohol as a preservative of virility.[4] Paradoxically, however, his narrative also included a passionate—if unlikely—plea for the passage of Prohibition. For even while he depicted the saloon as a robustly masculine arena, London expressed his desire that alcohol be rendered illegal. Personifying spirituous beverages with a reference to the grain used in brewing beer, London portrayed "John Barleycorn" as a deceptive seducer of "healthy, normal boys," a beguiling yet harmful inveigler who eroded the healthy vitality of those he ensnared. Ultimately London concluded that alcohol "poisons" the "social man-impulses" of unwitting youth, yet men would continue to drink as long as saloons existed to lure them.

London's skepticism toward alcohol developed relatively late in his short life, deepening as his dependence on drink exacerbated his suffering from depression. In *John Barleycorn* London dramatized the ill effects of alcoholic excess on mind and body.[5] Yet throughout the narrative London depicted liquor as an animating source of virility, an irony that rendered John Barleycorn all the more insidious yet did not diminish the author's nostalgia for his youthful debauchery. "Drink was the badge of manhood," he exclaimed. "Wherever life ran free and great, there men drank. Romance and adventure seemed always to go down the street locked arm in arm with John Barleycorn." Drinkers were "the livest, keenest men . . . the more comradely men, the more venturous, the more individual." In the saloons, he recalled, "men talked with great voices, laughed great laughs, and there was an atmosphere of greatness."[6] The underlying logic of *John Barleycorn* figured the habitual drinker as the manliest of men, one who enjoyed "a homosocial intimacy with other men that exists nowhere outside the world of the bottle."[7]

The saloon was a predominantly masculine domain; most customers were males seeking the fellowship of other men of similar age and economic standing. Many were immigrants, and most were skilled or unskilled laborers loyal to the working-class districts in which they lived and toiled. In addition to bonding in the workplace, workers forged a sense of class identity during their leisure hours, which were often passed in the familiar surroundings of the neighborhood saloon. Replacing the "kitchen trade" of older domestic grog shops (where women congregated with men as sellers and consumers of liquor), saloons emerged as leisure spaces clearly distinct from the home. Although female customers were sometimes welcome in saloons, until 1920 most watering holes were committed to male exclusivity.[8]

Catering to the various ethnic subcultures that comprised the working-class population, saloons provided facilities and services seldom available anywhere else. More than simply a place to drink, the saloon supplied visitors with food, water, toilet facilities, newspapers, and even banking services. At the saloon men could catch up on neighborhood gossip, hear the latest political news, or exchange information about job prospects. As a "workingman's club" it offered companionship and diversion.[9] According to one observer saloon-goers "found relaxation of various kinds, such as billiards and pool, cards and gambling, music and dancing." They "found respite and refreshment from the taxing toil of the day. . . . There was an aching need, a real demand for the rest and change of thought found in the saloon." In short, saloons catered "in a hundred ways to the social and political needs of men."[10]

How did the saloon become a bastion of maleness? More than simply a place where men congregated free from the constraints and demands of wives or mothers, the saloon allowed men to forge an alternative set of social relationships, creating a "sympathetic company of peers." And rather than simply relaxing inhibitions or promoting conviviality, alcohol served as an *agent* of social bonds, tangibly (if evanescently) forging links among men who drank together.[11]

Saloon culture revolved around the custom of treating. Reciprocal treating rituals, rooted in an ethic of mutuality and solidarity, create a democratic gift economy among drinkers at a bar. According to custom each drinker must treat other saloon patrons to a "round" of drinks; after consuming drinks purchased by others, one must pay a collective debt to the group. As the drinking continues, the group coheres as long as enough men agree to pay the bill in turn. Treating rituals exemplify what anthropologists call a circular system of gift giving. In such a system goods are circulated within specific "gift communities," where they leave a trail of interconnected relationships in their path. Treating is defined by obligation: the obligation to give, the obligation to receive, and the obligation to treat in return.[12] Thus alcohol's connection to manly camaraderie stemmed not merely from its intoxicating effects but from its status as a digestible gift. By allowing men to declare solidarity with kin, neighbors, and passers-by, treating rituals turned the saloon into an internal democracy in which "all who could safely enter received equal treatment and respect."[13] Although saloon-going was a solitary experience for some, for most it was a group activity, a symbol of egalitarianism, a way to participate in local community life.[14]

Jack London recalled his own emerging awareness of drinking rituals, and his account suggests that the acts of purchasing and exchanging drinks were as significant as consumption itself. While London's first drinking companions were fellow sailors aboard a whaling schooner, in saloons he refined his knowledge of treating behavior. As he wrote, "It was not until I . . . got ashore in the congregating places of men, where drink flowed, that the buying of drinks for other men, and the accepting of drinks from other men, devolved upon me as a social duty and a manhood rite." For London winning "manhood's spurs" meant submitting to a gift economy in which money was subordinate to the treating system. Earlier London had been a "thrifty, close-fisted boy" who stretched his meager earnings by "pinching and saving" every nickel. But his new friends "were magnificently careless of money, calling up eight men to drink whisky at ten cents a glass." Before he learned the tacit rules of exchange, he allowed a fellow seaman to treat several times before reciprocating. His initiation into the culture of drink thus entailed humiliation: "*I had let him buy six drinks and never once offered to treat*," he recalled. "I could feel myself blushing with shame . . . and buried my face in my hands. And the heat of my shame burned up my neck and into my cheeks and forehead." He soon realized that if he wanted to enjoy manly camaraderie, he had to part ways with thrift: "Which was it to be? I was aware that I was making a grave decision. I was deciding between money and men, between niggardliness and romance. Either I must throw overboard all my old values of money and look upon it as something to be flung about wastefully, or I must throw overboard my companionship with those men whose peculiar quirks made them care for strong drink." Faced with this dilemma, he decided that "money no longer counted. It was comradeship that counted."[15] In his conversion from an economy of scarcity to an economy of excess, London repudiated a sturdy work ethic as much as he embraced the alcohol-laced realm of leisure.[16] In "deciding between money and men," countless saloon regulars chose the latter.

Yet London was only partly right when he asserted that "money no longer counted" in the saloon. Although he renounced acquisitiveness, he still needed hard currency to put drinks into circulation. While the treating system was not reducible to the logic of market exchange, the saloon *was* a commercial institution, and liquor was a commodity to be bought and sold. Although men transformed their cash earnings into intoxicating, liquid gifts for themselves and others, their money had a different meaning for the saloon-keepers who profited thereby. As London noted, saloons were "always warm and comfortable," but they "were not charitable institutions. A man could not make a lounging place of a saloon without occasionally buying something over the bar."[17] Economist Thorstein Veblen even described treating as a working-class form of "conspicuous consumption," in which participants gained status by demonstrating their ability to spend freely.[18]

So as much as treating finessed the commercialized aspects of saloon patronage, workingmen had limited funds, and their expenditure on drink bore implications for spending *outside* the saloon. Indeed, spending money on drink could limit men's participation in the realm of commercialized, heterosocial leisure. As a young man London also sought the company of women, a desire that conflicted with his commitment to saloon life. London described how he once spent a whole week's wages in one "short evening" and had to survive the rest of the week without so much as a dime for carfare. Such a predicament, he explained, forced him and a friend "to break an engagement with two girls from West Oakland with whom [they] were attempting to be in love. . . . Like many others financially embarrassed, [they] had to disappear for a time from the gay whirl—at least until Saturday night pay-day."[19] London found that the masculine culture of drink could compete with a concurrent desire to date women. As courtship rituals increasingly required men to pay for refreshments and entertainment, saloon prerogatives often kept men from treating women to a night on the town. Thus the bachelor subculture could delay a heterosexual man's transition to marriage; for men who planned eventually to marry, balancing male-centered and heterosocial leisure could prove a difficult task indeed.[20]

Moreover, alcohol bestowed on London a badge of manliness that male-female sociability simply could not confer. As historian George Chauncey convincingly argues, men of the bachelor subculture achieved a "manly" identity primarily through their interactions with other men. Sexual prowess with women was an important sign of manliness; it mattered, however, not simply because it proved a man's ability to dominate women but because it reflected one's *relative* masculinity compared to other men. Saloons, poolrooms, boxing rings, and gambling dens provided sites in which men performed their gendered identity as manly men, engaging in rituals and contests through which they enacted their virility. "Even as they celebrated their masculine camaraderie and commitment to fraternity," Chauncey writes, men "constantly had to prove their manhood." Heavy drinking, then, was one way in which working-class men could "perform" their manhood in the company of other men. The ability to treat and to hold one's liquor signaled that a man could compete successfully with his peers; paradoxically, out of such leisurely competition emerged feelings of manly solidarity.[21]

Of course Jack London was not the only commentator to link alcohol and masculinity. In 1931 author Travis Hoke exclaimed that the tavern's shiny brass rail "was more than a footrest; it was a symbol of masculinity emancipate, or manhood free to put its feet on something." Others noted that treating served as a "ritual of masculine renewal" similar to body building and competitive sports.[22] Excessive drinking especially was seen as a hallmark of manhood. Thorstein Veblen, expounding on his theory of conspicuous consumption, remarked that "infirmities induced by overindulgence are among some peoples freely recognised [*sic*] as manly attributes."[23] Another observer noted that drinking large amounts of straight liquor could help one "uphold a reputation as a he-man, no matter what happened to the lining of the stomach." The idea of competitive yet companionable drinking was "to stay even with one's drinking partners in terms of quantity, monetary outlay, and degree of intoxication."[24] Even psychiatrists charged with treating chronic drunkards were loath to condemn their patients' behavior outright because they believed that drinking was often central to a man's gender identity. Mental health practitioners respected the manly prerogatives of saloon culture and realized "that a touch of dissipation might figure among the qualities that made a man's reputation." While they recognized habitual drunkenness as a problem, they did not believe that drinking always indicated serious pathology, because it blended so seamlessly into workingmen's daily lives.[25]

Saloons thus epitomized working-class masculinity in the late nineteenth and twentieth centuries, but this does not mean that drinking was accepted only within the working class. While the majority of saloongoers were laborers and modest wage earners, London claimed that well-known "reporters, editors, lawyers, and judges" frequented local bars, putting a "seal of social approval on the saloon."[26] Middle-class and affluent men who drank generally imbibed at home, in expensive hotels, at upscale restaurants, or in private clubs. While the saloon was often described as the "poor man's club," it also makes sense to regard the upper-class private men's club as a "rich man's saloon." Well-heeled businessmen and professionals regaled themselves at posh hotel bars and other elegant establishments that featured original artwork, fancy carpets, and elaborate furnishings. London, for his part, recalled his first evening at a men's club in San Francisco, a place he entered only after he achieved literary success. Seated in a leather chair, London was bewildered by the menu of liqueurs, highballs, and brands of scotch. Upper-class drinkers, he learned, enjoyed beverages vastly different from the "poor men's drinks" of "cheap beer and cheaper whisky." Club members did not engage in treating rituals as often as their working-class counterparts, but they did partake in dinnertime toasts, which had a similar group-bonding effect.[27]

No doubt these different drinking styles and milieus distinguished men of different social backgrounds and inflected men's experience of masculinity with distinctive class and ethnic accents. Turn-of-the-century cities featured a range of drinking establishments catering to different clienteles. Young male clerks were attracted to small, stand-up lunchrooms, while corporate leaders wined and dined at semiprivate restaurants. Other bars in downtown districts drew groups of politicians or journalists. Some taverns, patronized by immigrants from specific nations or regions, remained tenaciously ethnocentric, while other establishments appealed to more diverse crowds of men as they darted to and from work.[28] The cocktail culture embraced by well-to-do men in the early twentieth century was thus quite different from the "beer-and-whiskey world of saloongoers."[29] Drinking could connote the cosmopolitan respectability of affluent men as surely as saloon rituals conferred virility on working-class drinkers. In upscale cabarets and clubs, drinking helped to define a genteel version of dissolute manhood, one that shunned saloon treating rituals and drunken comportment yet celebrated worldly pleasures pursued apart from the domestic sphere.[30]

Solidly middle-class males had a more ambivalent relationship to the culture of drink. Many such men drank at home or during business activities, but often with more restraint than regular saloon patrons. In the nineteenth century many middle-class men were members of fraternal lodges. Although most fraternal orders officially banned liquor, many provided amenable drinking spaces for those who wished to imbibe. Lodges unable to afford their own buildings often met in the back rooms or second-story halls of saloons. For men with upwardly mobile class aspirations, however, the trick was to maintain a balance between sociability and intoxication. Drunken comportment was not publicly acceptable; one drank to enjoy oneself or to be sociable—but only in moderation. Fraternizing in their leisure hours, professionals and businessmen made valuable career contacts, but too much drinking could hinder success in the white-collar workplace.[31]

Accordingly, men in the middling ranks were least likely to socialize in drink-dominated settings. Historians have offered a plausible (if generalized) argument about why middle-class men used alcohol less often as a medium of sociability. As economic and social pressures stripped laboring men of control in the workplace, workers sought relaxation and self-expression in the saloon. Affluent men, I would add, were secure in their status; social drinking threatened neither their pocketbooks nor their ability to advance business interests. Middle-class men, however, were salaried employees and self-employed proprietors who experienced economic insecurity in the decades surrounding the turn of the century. Temperance had long been a cardinal bourgeois virtue, one that helped to ensure one's foothold in the respectable middle classes. Middle-class men relieved pressure "mainly through the creation of an intense family life" and regarded the "drinking-cum-fellowship among classes above and below as an expression of indiscipline." Emulating neither the saloon-goer's treating rituals nor the club member's champagne tastes, midlevel employees could not afford to waste money better used as a hedge for future advancement. Also, many believed that drinking clouded the businessman's mind.[32] With aspirations beyond the working class, yet without the financial cushion enjoyed by the elite, they tended not to orient their social lives around drink—if they did not shun it altogether.

These scenarios suggest that competing notions of manhood—dissolute and respectable—corresponded not only to stages in a man's life cycle (bachelorhood vs. marriage) but often, generally speaking, to class identity. I am not implying that all men fell into one, clearly demarcated social class or that bourgeois husbands never socialized with men in their leisure hours. Like all cultural constructions of class and gender identity, these labels represent contested, changeable categories of social existence. Furthermore, people's experiences of social identity are more fluid and ambiguous than such labels imply. (*John Barleycorn*, for example, suggests as much. London's narrator moves from the life of a low-paid sailor to that of a respected novelist. After years of debauchery he decides to marry, and he comes to prefer drinking alone rather than in groups.) But to a great extent, dissolute and respectable manhood connoted different states of mind, varying sets of values, and alternative lifestyles. If individual men felt pulled between these two poles of identity, the tension that resulted only underscored the cultural distance between them.

Drinking rituals helped to define these contrasting models of gendered selfhood. For many men, frequent indulgence in alcohol was part and parcel of dissolute manhood and its rejection of familial imperatives. Of all the settings in which Americans drank spirituous beverages, the saloon most powerfully encouraged men to derive manly identity from flowing taps of beer and whiskey. In the all-male club or elegant hotel bar, the consumption of aperitifs or sparkling wine signaled class exclusivity as well as the prerogatives of gender. Both settings, despite their differences, allowed men of similar economic station to mingle on equal terms, share information, and spend time away from domestic responsibilities. The ideal of the respectable breadwinner, on the other hand, rested less comfortably with homosocial drinking and mitigated against excessive consumption. Among bourgeois men who worked industriously to secure their financial status, occasional or restrained drinking—in public or at home—was often acceptable. Yet for many adherents of respectable manhood, abstinence remained a virtue, at least until the repeal of Prohibition.

Indeed, from the mid-nineteenth century through at least the 1910s the dominant middle-class social order *opposed* the masculine culture of drink in both its working- and upper-class guises. To a great extent Prohibition can be interpreted as a referendum against the moral economies of sociability that cohered among drinking men. Some drys were motivated by class and ethnic biases and focused their animosity on certain groups, while others demonized alcohol as an addictive substance that corrupted all drinkers.[33] Accordingly, scholars have interpreted Prohibition in two seemingly contradictory ways. First, it is seen as an effort by temperance reformers to eliminate the specific public drinking culture of the saloon. This interpretation holds that dry reformers worked symbolically to inscribe particular configurations of class, ethnic, and religious hierarchy upon the body politic; the antisaloon movement stemmed from reformers' desire to impose a moral code on laboring men who threatened bourgeois notions of discipline and order. The saloon became a metaphor for the dislocations accompanying urbanization, industrialization, and immigration; Prohibition was inseparable from the class prejudices, nativism, and anti-Catholicism of many old-stock reformers. Yet at the same time most reformers believed that *anyone* could succumb to the ravages of drink, regardless of gender or social station; that was why drys sought to ban the liquor trade outright. Reformers detested the substance of alcohol, not just the saloon, scorning consumption by the rich as well as the modest. Thus, second, temperance is seen as a moral crusade that vilified all modes of drinking as harmful and all habitual drinkers as sinful. While the social *effects* of Prohibition were most palpable in certain communities, the legal *intention* of Prohibition aimed to bring all citizens under the sway of dry ideology.[34] In any case, whether they emphasized the drinker's social inferiority or the drink's sinful influence, reformers believed that Prohibition would restore civic virtue and shield all citizens from the tyranny of drink.

This goal—to protect future generations from the destructive effects of alcohol—was London's own objective in writing his narrative. The author's love of alcoholic conviviality was eventually overshadowed by a "new and most diabolical complication." As he began to drink alone, for the intoxicating effect, he developed a "ghastly" drinking habit. As London wrote, "I had the craving at last, and it was mastering me. . . . My brain could not think the proper thoughts because continually it was obsessed with the one thought that across the room in the liquor cabinet stood John Barleycorn."[35] Dissolute manhood had offered many pleasures, but as London pursued his writing career and began his marriage to his wife, Charmian, alcoholic excess proved more limiting than liberating.[36] Formerly one of the heartiest supporters of the drinking culture, London came to feel that Americans would be better off without it. In saloons men convened to "drink like men," but too much drinking could prove dangerous and bring those same men to ruin.[37] Alarmed by the symbolic and material damage associated with intemperance, temperance reformers mounted an unprecedented challenge to dissolute manhood and the cultures of drink in which it flourished.

RIGHTEOUS WOMANHOOD AND THE POLITICS OF TEMPERANCE

Distanced from female temperance activists by life experience as well as gender, Jack London was an unlikely proponent of "home protection," a reform platform that aimed to improve women's and children's lives through the politics of alcohol. As one who suffered personally from addiction, London was motivated by impulses different from those compelling members of the Woman's Christian Temperance Union (WCTU), one of the nation's most influential reform organizations since its founding in 1874. Yet his conclusion to *John Barleycorn* resembled propaganda produced by the organization. "The women are the true conservators of the race," London wrote. "The women know. They have paid an incalculable price of sweat and tears for man's use of alcohol. . . . They will legislate for the babes of boys yet to be born; and for the babes of girls, too, for they must be the mothers, wives, and sisters of these boys."[38] London's reference to female temperance activists summarized the gendered politics of the WCTU. In 1913, the same year London published *John Barleycorn*, the WCTU's national president, Anna Gordon, sent a petition to the House of Representatives "praying for the passage of the joint resolution providing for a referendum to the states on National Constitutional Prohibition." This appeal, Gordon wrote, came from "a host of home-loving women who . . . have wrought marvelously for the moral and spiritual advancement of [their] country."[39] Beholden to an evangelical reform tradition that entrusted bourgeois women with ensuring the moral solvency of the home, Gordon and her supporters viewed alcohol as a worrisome threat to family life. Employing a maternalist rhetoric of home protection, the WCTU argued that abstinence would safeguard the health and happiness of the American family.[40]

Against men's rituals of intemperance, then, righteous women pursued the politics of temperance. Like all temperance reformers, the Protestant, middle-class women of the WCTU waged a symbolic as well as literal crusade against "Demon Rum." Unlike London, most female reformers were motivated not so much by private histories of suffering as by a broader set of concerns about family that crystallized around the issue of alcohol. Alcohol highlighted women's vulnerable position within the male-dominated family and made it possible to address that vulnerability in symbolic terms. Casting their struggle as a conflict between righteousness and sin, hearth and tavern, genteel feminine influence and wanton masculine indulgence, middle-class women found in temperance a means to defend their general interests as wives and mothers. For just as the WCTU regarded all men as potential victims of drink, so, too, did it envision all women as potential victims of male drinkers. According to reformers the coercive power of federal law was needed to defend the family from sinful male excess when moral suasion and civic education failed. The WCTU did not challenge the family's patriarchal structure, but it did seek to lessen the liabilities women faced by virtue of their sexual subordination. Male abstinence would force men to channel their financial and emotional resources into the home.[41]

At the heart of many reform narratives stood the pathetic figure of the drunkard's wife. In temperance tale after temperance tale, dry ideologues symbolized the social costs of drink through depictions of women and children "ruined" by besotted men. Reformers capitalized on images of marital misery for more than a century. As one writer observed in 1930, "The prime symbol of the Prohibition campaign, from 1830 to 1930, [had] been the picture of the drunkard's wife. Here the argument against liquor was strongest."[42] One reformer told the story of a woman from an "old, respectable Virginia family" who "unfortunately married a man who soon developed an appetite for liquor." Her husband abandoned her and her three children in "a poor tenement in one of the poorest quarters of the city." Like other deserted wives she faced "woe, misery, privation, neglect, want, pinching poverty, and disgrace."[43] Another tract, published in 1915, featured the "True Story of One Woman's Life," in which a "wan woman, with dark, sad eyes" spoke to a crowd of girls in order to dissuade them from marrying drinking men. "To marry a drunkard is the crown of all misery. . . . I have gained the fearful knowledge at the expense of happiness, sanity, almost life itself. . . . Girls, it is you I wish to rescue from the fate that overtook me. Do not blast your lives as I have blasted mine; do not be drawn into the madness of marrying a drunkard."[44]

Female temperance reformers deployed the symbol of the drunkard's wife throughout the nineteenth century. During the antebellum era fearful wives were first used as metaphors by reformers seeking to combat family violence. Victorian sexual attitudes differentiated between the sexual natures of men and women: the ideal woman was expected to be passionless and pure, while men were seen as lustful and weak in self-control. Beliefs in male brutishness and female purity informed temperance ideology: men's drinking further unleashed their "animal passions," while innocent women fell prey to husbands' brutish behavior.[45] By the 1850s political activism in the temperance movement dovetailed with new ideas about women's rights. For early feminists Susan B. Anthony and Elizabeth Cady Stanton, temperance brought to the surface women's latent rage against their reliance on irresponsible or abusive men, and they used the image of the "helpless, outraged, hungry" wife to formulate a radical argument in favor of divorce. Believing that suppressed female anger could be channeled into feminist activism, Stanton and Anthony found in the drunkard's wife a symbol of women's abject status in marriage. As Stanton boldly proposed in 1852, "Let no woman remain in the relation of wife with the confirmed drunkard. . . . Let us . . . modify the laws affecting marriage, and the custody of children, that the drunkard shall have no claims on either wife or child."[46]

But more conservative temperance reformers refused to advocate divorce for drunkards' wives, and Stanton and Anthony parted company with the (far more numerous) women who would later comprise the WCTU. In the mid-nineteenth century radical critiques of marriage were a threat to dominant gender ideologies. Most evangelical reformers, committed to principles of Christian morality and female subordination, aimed to protect the marital bond, not encourage its dissolution. Thus from the mid-1870s through the first decades of the twentieth century the WCTU eschewed feminists' radical criticism of female dependency and focused instead on reforming male behavior. "Women of the WCTU," historian Elizabeth Pleck writes, "seemed more concerned with uplifting men than with raising the status of women. They believed in a marriage not of equals but of respectables, headed by a worthy husband, with his wife, an acquiescent subordinate, at his side." The WCTU endorsed the traditional, home-centered woman. It aimed to curb the worst abuses of the marital status quo rather than change women's status or the institution of marriage altogether.[47]

The symbolic aspects of the WCTU's crusade are worth underscoring again. Although the WCTU sought tangible results—the literal banishment of alcohol—its members politicized liquor to assuage a host of anxieties experienced by all women, not just those directly victimized by drink. Indeed, many women whose husbands were not drunkards were also ill treated and abandoned. Because married women were economically dependent on men and lacked equal political and legal rights, their status was determined by that of their husbands. A drunken husband was particularly threatening to a powerless woman's existence. Given their acceptance of traditional gender roles, WCTU members translated their concerns into a maternalist politics of domesticity that protected their interests as guardians of the hearth. Female temperance activists believed that their moral sensibilities gave them the authority to reform society and especially to improve women's and children's lives. Whether petitioning to shut down saloons, testifying before legislators, or organizing prayer meetings, reformers linked women's private roles to organized, public activity.[48] By attacking alcohol as the root cause of domestic disintegration, the WCTU imagined drink-induced family problems as *social* problems requiring social and legal solutions.

Ultimately temperance efforts culminated in the passage of national Prohibition. By the late 1910s reformers had successfully challenged the cultures of drink that bubbled in the saloons, bars, and clubs of a modernizing nation. Their crusade emerged out of a complex welter of social and cultural factors; dry politics were defined as much by class, ethnic, and regional differences as by conflicts marked along gender lines. But despite the multiple facets of social identity that conjoined in the prism of temperance reform, to a great extent Prohibition can be viewed as a mandate against men's drinking and against the common conflation of drink with masculinity. Prohibitionists often characterized the typical victim of Demon Rum as a middling, drinking man whose intemperance severed his obligations to family and industry. Prohibitionists exempted no man—whether single or married, working class or wealthy, Protestant or Catholic—from a definition of manhood premised on fiscal responsibility and domestic authority. By linking liquor with the degeneracy of men, families, and society at large, prohibitionists found in the rituals of drink a raison d'être for temperance laws. Although dry legislation would not completely sever the connections among drinking, treating, and masculinity, it did weaken those associations, in large part by driving the saloon underground and limiting men's (especially working-class men's) access to liquor.

Alarmed by the resources "squandered" among saloon-going men, righteous reformers wrestled with the tension between dissolute and respectable manhood and found the latter far more worthy of their support. A vote for Prohibition not only dampened the free exchange of spirituous beverages; it also indicated support for a particular vision of marriage, leisure, and family life. In large part the conflict between dissolute and respectable manhood shaped the battle between wets and drys. Ultimately the Eighteenth Amendment represented an (albeit partial and temporary) attempt to define each ideal in relation to the consumption or nonconsumption of alcohol. At least through the mid-1920s the hegemony of dry reformers stemmed not only from claims about the effects of drink but from their success in defining dissolute manhood as sinful and deviant. Defining respectable manhood as *the* prevailing manly ideal, reformers engendered Prohibition as a powerful sanction against men's deviance from that norm.

How did prohibitionists portray the respectable, breadwinning husband, the ideal against which they measured the drunkard and found him so inferior? For temperance reformers ideal manhood differed sharply from the hard-drinking, working-class masculinity rendered in *John Barleycorn*. In 1889 WCTU president Frances Willard offered her "opinion of men," claiming that happily married men "have a delicacy, a brotherly considerateness, a homelikeness of character and manner, quite unmistakable." Contrasting the domesticated husband with the saloon-going bachelor, Willard wrote that "the man with the one woman that he loves, and who loves him . . . with happy children at his knee, and an unselfish purpose in his soul, is as far removed from his self-centered, squandering, dissatisfied brethren as is the light-house keeper from the ship-wrecked crew." As she elaborated, the man who renounced "wicked self-indulgence" for the "sanctities of fatherhood" and family-centered leisure "shall be seen to exceed all others to which a manly spirit can attain." Moreover, the home-loving man deserved praise because he voluntarily succumbed to domestic influence: "A thousand motives, prejudices, and conventions hedge women into homes, but men, with all the world to choose from, *choose* the home."[49] For Willard the ideal man not only abstained from drink; he also renounced manly camaraderie in order to spend time with his nuclear family.

Recorded in her memoirs, Frances Willard's paean to domesticated men was part of a larger cultural development: the emergence of "masculine domesticity" in the late nineteenth and early twentieth centuries. The ideal of masculine domesticity reshaped male gender identity for middle-class men and encouraged them to seek meaning and happiness within the private sphere as well as the workplace. Various experts, including psychiatrists and child-rearing advisers as well as reformers, exhorted men to balance virility and aggressiveness with a heightened interest in domestic matters. This new mode of manhood, which stressed men's roles as husbands and fathers, was part of a more general redefinition of domestic life that entailed the rise of "companionate marriage," which altered relationships between husbands and wives; sufficient job security for middle-class men, which allowed them to devote more time to home affairs; and the expansion of suburbs, which created a spatial context for a more intense form of family life.[50]

Adherence to masculine domesticity required a shift in men's use of leisure time. Certainly many middle-class men spent time in male-dominated clubs and organizations during off-work hours. But husbands were expected to devote more attention to home and family, and the emphasis was on mutual obligation within the domestic sphere. It is significant that this new middle-class ethos took shape during the same decades that working-class men solidified the recreational rituals of saloon culture. While many married saloon-goers believed that strong family ties and domestic stability were desirable goals, working-class men generally did not embrace companionate marriage. Indeed, pub regulars sought the companionate ideal in male peer groups, not at home, and maintained a more traditional form of marriage that emphasized male prerogative and female subservience.[51]

Masculine domesticity also entailed implicit prescriptions for manly work. In the bourgeois family a man's primary domestic obligation was economic: to provide wages or a salary earned at a respectable trade, business, or profession. Of course breadwinning had been a cardinal component of male gender identity, for working-class and middle-class men, throughout the nineteenth century. Work experiences and work culture have long played central roles in the formation of men's self-conception, especially as industrialization eroded the corporate household economy and hurled men into the rough-and-tumble world of competitive capitalism. The ideology of breadwinning defined men first and foremost as earners. To achieve middle-class status the respectable breadwinner needed to succeed in the workplace, but the fruits of his labors were best enjoyed at home.[52] Domesticated manhood and breadwinning were two sides of the same coin.

While unfettered or dissolute masculinity was defined in opposition to men's domestic responsibilities, respectable or domestic manhood derived from a man's obligations to family. The breadwinning ideal lionized the dutiful husband and father who parlayed his earnings into a source of status at home. Men would feel beholden to their families, but they also gained authority from their roles as hard-working providers. Middle-class wives expected more intimacy and cooperation from husbands, but such expectations often translated into more subtle forms of male dominance in the household. In this way the "new" masculinity reshaped patriarchal relations and redefined domestic life in the early twentieth century. On one hand, masculine domesticity softened the boundaries between gender spheres, enlarging the realm of activity that men and women shared. But on the other hand, it maintained a gender-based division of labor within the middle class, legitimating male prerogatives at home and in society.[53]

Furthermore, in the half-century after 1880 male breadwinning became increasingly intertwined with the burgeoning consumer culture that was transforming American society. In the decades surrounding the turn of the century the orientation of U.S. economic and cultural life shifted from the production to the consumption of material goods.[54] This transformation entailed the growth of advertising, marketing, product design, and credit industries; the expansion of department stores and mail order catalogs; the rise of middle-class purchasing power; and the development of a therapeutic "consumer ethos" that validated personal pleasure and self-gratification. As brokers and businessmen created a mass market for the goods produced by industrial capitalism, "commodity consumption emerged as a way of life, a basic force that shaped American culture."[55] By the 1920s more and more Americans were measuring men's success in terms of the level of household consumption they could support. Especially among men in white-collar occupations, incomes were used to purchase an increasing array of goods and services.[56]

Unlike the homosocial economy of the saloon, the ideal middle-class family of the 1910s and 1920s channeled men's time and energy into the home. In contrast many working-class husbands clung to traditional marital norms that required men to provide financially for their dependents yet allowed them to venture out in their leisure hours. Such men rejected a nuclear family life that exhausted the male breadwinner's emotional and material resources. Of course relationships among drinking patterns, social class, and manly identity were complex. Not all working-class husbands embraced saloon conviviality, and among those who did, only a minority drank so heavily or habitually that their families suffered grave consequences.[57] Likewise not all aspirants to middle-class respectability adhered to norms of companionate marriage or consumerist breadwinning. But as contrasting *ideals* of gender and family life, dissolute and respectable manhood shaped how vast numbers of men—and women—experienced work, leisure, marriage, and domestic affairs.

One can argue that the conflict between these different gender ideologies fanned the flames of the temperance crusade. Channeling their distrust of dissolute manhood into a broad assault on the liquor industry, dry reformers succeeded (at least temporarily) in prohibiting the manufacture and sale of intoxicating beverages. Sparked by the indignation of righteous womanhood, prohibitionists rallied against the industries and institutions most notoriously affiliated with dissolute manhood: brewery and barroom, distillery and dramshop. Embedded in liquor legislation were deeply held convictions about the obligations that men owed to women and families. Insofar as virile masculinity had been intertwined with convivial drinking, reformers invoked alternative models of manhood to supplant fraternal loyalty with domestic fealty. Throughout the 1920s drys believed that Prohibition was improving the lives of American families—morally, socially, and economically.

As long as Demon Rum was demonized as a grave social threat, the traditional gendered order seemed to mandate the Eighteenth Amendment. But as the 1920s gave way to the 1930s, repeal advocates began to sway public opinion against Prohibition, arguing that it caused problems worse than those it was intended to eliminate: a black market in liquor, organized crime, urban violence, and a general disrespect for law. The enforcement of Prohibition proved daunting for federal officials, as an underground network of rumrunners furnished speakeasies and other illicit establishments with a free-flowing supply of bootlegged liquor. Over time such unlawful behavior weakened the prohibitionists' political power. In 1933 antiprohibitionists overturned the Eighteenth Amendment and ushered in a new set of norms about drinking, leisure, and domestic life that affected Americans of all social classes.

DEPRESSION, WAR, AND THE
RISE OF SOCIAL DRINKING

The Great Depression sounded the death knell of national Prohibition. Although relatively few citizens suffered a direct loss in the stock market crash of 1929, the Wall Street debacle sparked an economic fiasco of such major proportions that not many Americans escaped the hardships it engendered. Banks began to fail, resulting in a nationwide collapse of the banking system by 1932. Employers trimmed dividends, curtailed spending, and fired workers. By 1933 more than one-quarter of the population was out of work. In its longevity and severity the Depression of the 1930s was worse than any other economic upheaval in U.S. history. As one historian observed, the Depression "brought fear, uncertainty and destitution to substantial portions of the white middle class that had begun to taste moderate affluence in the previous decade. . . . And it left scars, upon both the physical environment and the mental landscapes of the men, women, and children who endured it. For those between the ages of five and forty-five when the stock market crashed, the Great Depression was the transforming event of a lifetime."[58]

As the nation focused on solving its monumental economic dilemma, the battle over liquor paled in significance. With the federal government facing a crisis of political faith and financial instability, politicians searched for new ways to raise tax revenues and increase consumption on a national level. Large numbers of powerful Americans abandoned their support of Prohibition and joined the repeal movement. As the Depression worsened, repealers began to shift public opinion. During Prohibition, some analysts estimated, Americans had spent approximately $36 billion on bootlegged liquor, and the government had not earned a dime of tax money from it. Although President Herbert Hoover was a staunch prohibitionist, antiliquor influence plummeted in the federal government in the early years of the Depression. After Franklin Delano Roosevelt campaigned openly on a wet platform and enjoyed his first victory in 1932, repeal itself was almost anticlimactic. On April 7, 1933, wine and beer were declared legal. On December 5 of the same year, the Eighteenth Amendment was officially repealed, rendering the production and sale of alcoholic beverages permissible once again.[59]

Advocates for repeal quickly capitalized on the Depression when formulating their arguments. A rejuvenated liquor industry would not only increase state and federal tax revenues; it would also provide thousands of new jobs. As unemployment skyrocketed, this argument had particularly strong appeal. By the nadir of the Depression in 1933 the cultural image of the "forgotten man" had become common in the American popular imagination. Out of a job, in need of money, and forsaken by the corporate world and the federal government, the forgotten man lost the familial authority and manly self-confidence he formerly enjoyed as an employed wage earner. The figure of the forgotten man made an especially poignant appearance through national radio (which by the mid-1930s had become the most influential form of mass media), and it was invoked by none other than President Franklin D. Roosevelt himself. In April 1932 FDR delivered a radio address in which he argued for a series of government programs "that built from the bottom up and not from the top down; that put their faith once more in the forgotten man at the bottom of the economic pyramid."[60] The opportunity to revive long-stagnant beverage industries was cast as an opportunity to remember thousands of forgotten men.

By the mid-1930s prorepeal businessmen were citing evidence to prove that new alcohol policies were benefiting the economy. One such writer published a pamphlet titled *The Effect of Repeal on Industrial Recovery*, a spirited defense of spirituous beverages. Considering new job openings in industries ranging from distilling and retailing to hotel service and advertising, he claimed that repeal had put approximately 1 million people back to work, fully one-fourth of the total number of jobless Americans who found new employment by 1935. Industrial sectors that supplied raw materials and infrastructure watched profits rise by twenty times from 1933 to 1934, an increase attributed primarily to repeal. Given the new demand for glass bottles, in the glass industry alone repeal "meant employment for 16,000 more men and an increase in payroll of $16 million." Farmers, railroad personnel, waiters, and even musicians (with new opportunities to perform in restaurants and clubs) all benefited. Manufacturers of paper, steel, lumber, and trucks applauded repeal. In the final analysis, many wets concluded, repeal had "put billions of dollars into extra circulation in legitimate business channels, provided re-employment, . . . lessened crime, and put hundreds of millions of dollars into Government . . . treasuries."[61]

The Great Depression was the final catalyst for the demise of Prohibition, but the social effects of repeal extended far beyond any role it played in improving the nation's dire economic situation. Repeal marked a turning point in U.S. history, not simply because of its unprecedented role in overturning a constitutional amendment, but because it symbolized a major shift in cultural values and behavior. With repeal the worldview espoused by temperance reformers suffered an unprecedented blow. Before the demise of the Eighteenth Amendment, federal legislation had codified (at least on paper) a vision that equated moral respectability and civic responsibility with abstinence from drink. Repeal advocates aimed to

convince broad ranks of Americans to abandon this worldview, to interpret indulgence in alcohol and other "minor vices" not as deviant or sinful
behavior but as a normal part of life. By and large, repealers eliminated
social disapproval from drinking. After 1933 manufacturers of alcoholic
beverages campaigned to persuade the public that their business was cred-
itable; that drinking took place in respectable places, including the home;
and that women as well as men could drink with no risk to their health or
reputation. By the late 1940s the alcoholic beverage industries and other
wet spokespersons had succeeded remarkably in this effort.[62]

Yet the normalization of drink as a respectable form of consumption
began long before repeal. As mentioned above, abstinence was not the
only model of alcohol consumption available to Americans who considered themselves to be genteel, reputable citizens. Although drinking behaviors varied among men of different classes, the restrained consumption
of alcohol in private and semiprivate settings was often acceptable. Furthermore, despite the common view of drinking as a masculine activity,
men were not alone in their alcohol consumption. Due in large part to
reformers' vociferous crusade against liquor, public debates at the time—
as well as historians' accounts in retrospect—have emphasized the masculine cultures of drink in working-class saloons and, less often, in upper-
class clubs. But large numbers of respectable American women did drink,
often with anonymous frequency.[63] Contrary to the dry belief that most
women were inherently abstemious, many Victorian women drank alcohol in the form of patent medicines and other supposedly curative tonics.
They also drank moderately at home, with meals, and at banquets and
weddings. Arbiters of domestic entertainment spilled much ink on topics
such as how to pair wine with food at a luncheon, how to display glassware
for after-dinner cordials, and when to serve champagne at a soiree. But
while alcohol was a valued element in many Victorian social events, it did
not dominate sociability as it did within saloons.[64]

During the nineteenth century this heterosocial model of moderate,
refined alcohol consumption was pursued only in private domains. Until
1900 alcohol helped to define a division between women's and men's recreational spheres. Respectable women rarely entered public male drinking spaces, while men drinking at home did so in a realm of female
authority.[65] It is ironic, however, that while temperance reformers inched
closer to their goal of Prohibition, the acceptance of public drinking in
mixed company grew stronger. While dry rhetoric emphasized the dangers of male saloon attendance, heterosocial drinking was actually increas-

ing after the turn of the century. This development was part of a more general transformation in urban recreation: the commercialization of public amusements. By the 1910s new sites of commodified leisure, such as cabarets, movie palaces, and dance halls, were attracting large crowds of pleasure-seekers. Unlike the saloon, such places were patronized by men and women together, and they hailed from a range of social classes and ethnic groups. Some of these new establishments served alcohol. But even those not associated with alcohol consumption facilitated an overall blending of male and female worlds, which further normalized mixed-sex drinking in places where it did occur.[66]

Paradoxical though it may seem, heterosocial drinking continued during Prohibition, especially among affluent Americans and youth. This was due in large part to the wording of the Eighteenth Amendment, which proscribed the transportation and sale of intoxicating beverages but did not outlaw private consumption per se. Thus while temperance reformers succeeded in their primary goal of dismantling the public drinking culture of the saloon, they did not prevent people from drinking in their own homes or in illicit speakeasies.[67] The total per capita consumption of alcohol decreased during Prohibition, but for persons with access to stockpiled or bootlegged liquor, drinking continued to define sociability, albeit in new ways. For many, alcohol remained a part of fashionable hospitality, a trend noted in 1930 by one journalist who observed that "the American bar, supposed to have been cut root and branch from our life by the Eighteenth Amendment, has merely been transplanted into the home."[68]

The home, in turn, provided the setting for a new American institution in the 1920s: the cocktail party. Given the poor quality of illicit alcohol during Prohibition, cocktails gained in popularity, in part because melding spirits with other liquids "helped disguise the fact that the scotch one was drinking had been aged for hours instead of years." Instructing readers how to prepare juleps, eggnogs, and martinis, home entertainment guides equated mixed drinks with conviviality and gracious hospitality. With witty titles such as *Giggle Water*, *The Saloon in the Home*, and *Wet Drinks for Dry People*, cocktail manuals winked self-consciously yet dismissively at the law of the land. Moreover, they facilitated the feminization, or domestication, of drink. Cocktails tamed alcohol's threatening connotations, as sugar, soda water, fruit juice, and garnishes softened the effects of straight liquor: "The cocktail provided hard liquor, but softened, feminized enough to remove hard liquor's most opprobrious male associations. Women who would never think of consuming straight gin could ask for a dry martini without fearing for their reputations. The cocktail provided a neatly packaged, suitably disguised, fashionably dressed shot of liquor."[69] Signifying a style of consumption removed from the saloon's aggressively masculine atmosphere, mixed drinks epitomized an avantgarde, heterosocial culture of leisure.

Ironically, then, Prohibition facilitated the popularity of social drinking, which in turn contributed to the rise in anti-Prohibition sentiment by the late 1920s. One of Prohibition's intended results, the elimination of the saloon, bore an unintended consequence. By decreasing the amount of public drunkenness among men, it removed the most visible and notorious drinkers from the collective consciousness, allowing for the glamorization of more restrained drinking among middle-class folk who considered themselves respectable. The increasing numbers of female drinkers also undermined the gendered assumptions of wet and dry opponents that had structured public debates on alcohol. The image of a fashionable lady drinking with men flagrantly opposed reformers' depictions of a dry American womanhood victimized by drink. Drinking women contradicted the basic temperance belief that liquor was inherently dangerous and that women would naturally set an example for men through their own abstinence.[70]

The growing numbers of middle- and upper-class women who accepted moderate drinking helped fuel the campaign for repeal. In the late 1920s a number of politically astute women joined the repeal movement, challenging the WCTU's equation of women and Prohibition. Led by socialite and political fundraiser Pauline Morton Sabin, they opposed temperance reformers' belief in women's innate dryness by forming the Women's Organization for National Prohibition Reform (WONPR) in 1929. WONPR members supported general prorepeal arguments based on civil liberties and economics, but they rooted their critique of Prohibition in a maternalist ideology appropriated, ironically enough, from the WCTU. The WONPR adopted the rhetoric of home protection but emphasized the *failure* of Prohibition to preserve the sanctity of American homes. Along with other repeal groups, the WONPR supported Franklin D. Roosevelt in the 1932 presidential election.[71]

Two cultural aspects of the normalization of social drinking are worth emphasizing here. First, the WONPR equated its cause with modernity during a time when many people were preoccupied with all things modern. While the WCTU remained associated with Victorian morality and evangelical reform, repeal women cultivated a secular, fashionable image. By the late 1920s, living a modish lifestyle meant accepting alcohol as part of the social landscape. Contemporary observer Frederick Lewis Allen noted that "up-to-date people" viewed prohibitionists as either modern-day Puritans ("blue-nosed, ranting spoilsports") or stifled Victorians ("old ladies with bustles and inhibitions"). For the avant garde, "it was better to be modern . . . and sophisticated, and smart, to smash conventions and to be devastatingly frank. And with a cocktail glass in one's hand it was easy at least to be frank."[72] Pauline Sabin's persona further associated repeal with modernity. Upscale magazines such as *Vogue*, which often referred to "smart" women's moderate drinking, portrayed Sabin as sophisticated and confident in the public world.[73] Sabin and other WONPR members epitomized the image of the New Woman in the 1920s: a free-thinking, intelligent, yet feminine woman who combined marriage and mother-hood with pursuits outside the home.[74] By the end of the decade fewer women identified with dry ideology, a trend reflected in the WONPR's claim that its total membership exceeded the WCTU's in 1931.[75] In the 1920s, sentimental temperance narratives replete with hopeless male drunkards and long-suffering wives seemed increasingly anachronistic.

A second factor that facilitated repeal lay in the erosion of public support for dry views of alcohol as a substance. Repeal advocates believed that alcohol *could* be consumed safely, in moderation. As social drinking gained acceptance, fewer citizens viewed alcohol as inherently threatening to all drinkers. Whereas dry reformers rejected any scenario other than complete abstinence, wets "did not consider alcohol dangerous in and of itself—or at least not dangerous enough to warrant federal prohibition."[76] Restrained drinking belied the dry depiction of liquor as an evil substance that hurled all drinkers down a dangerous slippery slope. In this sense repeal marked the triumph of social or moderate drinking—as a cultural model and mode of behavior—over the ideal of abstinence.[77]

On one hand, then, repeal reinforced social trends that had been evolv-ing since Prohibition was enacted. But on the other hand, repeal also engendered change. Americans could now drink openly, without the self-conscious flouting of convention that had characterized illicit consump-tion. Whereas Prohibition colored the act of drinking in shades of re-bellion, after repeal alcohol melded into the dominant culture. This change was best symbolized by President Roosevelt, whose well-known martini rituals endowed the cocktail hour with an "official sanction."[78] As one writer reflected, after repeal "came the era of frankness. The world was in a state of economic depression but the human mind, at least, was free. . . . The new cocktail lounge, tavern, or supper club was in a contemporary mode. It had comfort, allure, fashion. . . . Alcohol was in good standing again."[79]

In 1939 writer Frederick Lewis Allen penned a sequel to his study of popular mores during the 1920s, and it included a vivid account of the "tremendous" changes that swept the nation in 1933. According to Allen, "Hotels and restaurants blossomed with cocktail lounges and taprooms and bars, replete with chromium fittings, mirrors, bright-colored modern furniture, Venetian blinds, [and] bartenders taken over from the speakeasies." Architects and interior decorators, eager to apply principles of modern industrial design to commercial spaces, brought "bright color and simplified furniture" to cocktail lounges and restaurants, "with the odd result that throughout the nineteen-thirties most Americans instinctively associated modernist decoration with eating and drinking." Pancake houses started purveying Manhattans and old-fashioneds; business executives no longer needed to hide bottles of scotch in their golf bags; and "so many bright new bars appeared along the city streets that drinking seemed to have become not only respectable but ubiquitous."[80]

In the 1930s merchandisers placed alcoholic beverages squarely in the public's gaze and grasp. Beer, wine, and liquor manufacturers padded the pages of newspapers and magazines with enticing advertisements. The serial *Vanity Fair*, for example, printed six full pages of ads for spirits in December 1933, the very month repeal was enacted. By September 1935 more than 20 percent of the display advertising in the *New York Times* was devoted to wine and liquor ads. At first middlebrow publications such as *American Magazine* refused hard liquor ads but stated that beer drinking was "thoroughly consistent with true temperance and decent living." Yet within a year the same magazine carried an ad for Four Roses whiskey.[81] According to one economist who measured the total revenue spent on radio and print advertising in 1940, the category of alcoholic beverages stood fifth on the list of high expenditures. In the newspapers, ads for intoxicating beverages were exceeded only by automobile and grocery promotions. Outdoor advertising, billboards, and point-of-purchase displays promoted beer, wine, and liquor in countless public and retail spaces.[82]

New marketing symbols, from the sophisticated cocktail lounge to cold canned beer (first available in the 1930s), reinforced the ideal of social drinking in polite company. What occurred was nothing less than a full-scale campaign to normalize and domesticate drinking among Americans of all social classes. In contrast to the working-class associations of saloon drinking, the post-repeal campaign promoted the view that alcohol consumption was a badge of status and affluence. In the 1930s print advertising continued to depict drinking—and especially the consumption of cocktails—as a sign of social distinction. In January 1934 the Biltmore Hotel in New York was promoting a sophisticated Cocktail Hour in its elegant Madison Room. A Golden Wedding Whiskey ad of 1935 encouraged consumption "at swank bars and hotels. . . . At the homes of friends. . . . At the busiest liquor stores."[83] Another ad published in *Life* described vermouth drinkers as cosmopolitan: "You won't have to talk about the continent for people to know you've traveled—if you call for Martini and Rossi," explained the ad, complementing an illustration of glistening highball glasses ready for the taking by a group of tuxedo-clad middle-aged men.[84] During a decade when working-class tavern-goers no longer preoccupied the imagination of the dominant cultural order, such advertisements celebrated the expanding cocktail culture of middle- and upper-class drinkers.[85]

The world of urban nightlife also changed in the wake of repeal, as new modes of entertainment initially created by affluent urbanites were adapted to larger middle-class audiences. During the 1920s the association of the nightclub with illegal alcohol and organized crime gave it an unsavory reputation. But during the Depression a new kind of establishment, the theater-restaurant, concentrated on a broader audience than that served by exclusive hotels and clubs. While a wealthy café society expanded, many club owners reduced their prices, hosted spectacular shows, and competed with movie houses, theaters, and ballrooms for middle-class patronage. Alcohol was usually served at these places, but the drinking was often more restrained than it had been in the saloons and speakeasies of past eras. Floor shows, music, and dancing—not alcohol per se—were billed as the primary lures. This trend, moreover, was not limited to big cities. From Seattle to Salt Lake City, from Akron to Albany, nightclubs "went public" after repeal, attracting crowds across the class spectrum.[86]

Hollywood movies also celebrated the new permissiveness toward imbibing. The infamous Hays Production Code of 1934, which prohibited filmmakers from screening lustful embraces and other overtly sexual actions, inaugurated one of the most effective attempts to censor popular culture according to strict standards of Christian morality. But while clergymen and motion picture moguls were busy banning "morally objectionable" content on the grounds of sex (and, less often, violent crime), restrictions on drinking were abandoned.[87] During an era when censors were so vigilant about policing popular films, the relatively lax policy toward drinking reflected the increasing acceptance of alcohol in society at large.

Exemplifying this trend was a series of popular films starring Myrna Loy and William Powell: the *Thin Man* films, which combined the genres of comedy and mystery crime thriller. The first film, titled *The Thin Man*, was released in 1934, one year after repeal and two years after Dashiell Hammett published the detective novel on which the screenplay was based. The central characters are an affluent married couple named Nick and Nora Charles, who inhabit a swank, spacious Manhattan apartment. The plot revolves around a mysterious murder that the Charleses happen upon during the course of their daily life. In the first film the daughter of a wealthy family friend appeals to Nick when she discovers that her father, who has been consorting with a mercenary mistress, has vanished. In response Nick becomes a whimsical detective, attending parties and cabarets where he can mingle with people he suspects are involved in the man's disappearance. The appeal of these films lies in the witty repartee and humorous exchanges among Nick, Nora, and their eccentric acquaintances. The films are not somber murder mysteries but lighthearted parodies of both serious crime drama and the lifestyle of the cosmopolitan elite.

Moreover, the *Thin Man* films are permeated with drinking scenes. In the 1934 movie Nick and Nora are almost always consuming alcohol: at lunch, at parties, and in bed before retiring. Drinking defines the couple's upscale social position and happy-go-lucky attitude toward life, including their effort to find the dead man's killer. Drinking also helps to shape the film's humor. At one point Nora unabashedly orders five drinks from a bar waiter so she can "keep up" with her husband; in another scene Nick encourages guests at a party to "eat, drink, and be merry." Walking around with a silver cocktail tray, he announces that "tomorrow may bring sorrow, so tonight let us be gay." Another scene shows Nora waking up in the morning complaining of a hangover. But soon after she is depicted wearing a robe and holding an ice bag to her head, she is elegantly dressed and having a grand time drinking with Nick once again. The main characters appear cheerful and giddy—and never too intoxicated to respond to clues that may solve their murder mystery. Alcohol even figures into the film's amusing detective plot. At the end Nick and Nora host a dinner party, getting their high-rolling suspects drunk enough and their tongues loose enough, to expose the criminals in their midst.[88]

After fourteen years of Prohibition, *The Thin Man* celebrated the return of licit alcohol with a humorous and exaggerated vengeance. Certainly the sheer excess of the couple's drinking spoofed the decadent extremism pursued by a minority of drinkers. But despite its gently satirical tone, the film nonetheless condoned drinking as a sign of worldly sophistication. While the viewer would be hard pressed to define Nick and Nora's consumption as moderate, at no time are they seriously depicted as problem drinkers. Nora's headache and Nick's occasional stumbling are part of the film's humor, benign results of the characters' festive, fashionable lifestyle. Their drinking may be excessive, but it is excessive in the way that a caricature is exaggerated: for comic effect. Drinking, the *Thin Man* implied, could be a boon to romantic marriage, a source of fun and excitement, a tonic to the sorrows of the Depression era. Nora's hangover notwithstanding, the film offered audiences anything but a sobering message about drinking.

It is worth underscoring the difference between the celebration of cocktail culture in *The Thin Man* and the temperance tracts of earlier decades. During Prohibition, drys pitted men's mutual participation in saloon culture *against* their domestic obligations. Every dollar spent on a round of drinks was a dollar squandered from the family economy. But when films and advertisements portrayed drinking among avant-garde devotees of the good life, they contradicted traditional narratives of men's drinking as a threat to women's familial interests. In *The Thin Man* Nick Charles was just as apt to treat his wife to martinis as he was his male friends and associates, and drinking was depicted as an enhancement rather than a detriment to marital relations. Nora, in effect, became "one of the boys," joining her husband and other fun-loving couples in rituals of heterosocial drinking.

Of course such movies had great promotional value for the beer and liquor industries of the 1930s. Despite the increase of liquor advertising in print, the alcoholic beverage industry agreed *not* to advertise on the radio, a compromise in the face of political pressure that post-repeal promotions would go too far. This was a significant concession, given radio's huge popularity at the time, but films such as *The Thin Man* supplied indirect advertising and promoted the alluring mystique of the cocktail. Indeed, the *Thin Man* films were not the only movies to glamorize drinking during the Depression years. According to writer Joseph Lanza, "A ritual cocktail scene was often the rule rather than the exception for many dramas and comedies" produced during the 1930s. On the silver screen "the cocktail evolved from a universal symbol of licentiousness into one of class and civility. It served as a combination stage prop and narrative crutch to guide both actors and viewers during some of modern America's most trying years."[89]

A second example of the glamorization of alcohol was the 1934 musical film *Murder at the Vanities*. The movie featured Danish actor Carl Brisson as a suspect in a double murder and Victor McLaglen as the detective on the trail of justice. As the mystery-detective plot thickens, the film digresses to include an extravagant song-and-dance number in which the protagonist sports a top hat and tails while crooning to a group of stylishly dressed women. The title of his song is "Cocktails for Two," and the lyrics summarize the era's new celebration of heterosocial drinking:

No longer slinking
Respectably drinking
Like civilized ladies and men.

As Brisson sings, each woman sits in front of an intimate candlelit table, accompanied by two drinks while awaiting her turn to dance.[90] In the "Cocktails for Two" scene social drinking was invoked to remedy otherwise grim situations.[91] During the Depression, drinking promised psychological release and emotional escape as well as economic profit. Seeking a temporary respite from reality, viewers enjoyed films featuring splashy songs, dreamy love plots, and fantastic sets that honored the fleeting pleasures of life. Cocktails—in actuality and on the silver screen—could function as a tonic to lift people's spirits during hard times.

In promotional and cinematic depictions of civilized drinking, liquor was no longer a bone of contention in dramas of sexual antagonism between hard-drinking husbands and long-suffering wives. Perhaps a lifestyle based on heterosocial leisure or companionate marriage—as imagined by filmmakers and advertisers—dampened men's desires to blow off steam in all-male pubs or clubs. Why escape from women in pursuit of relaxation when one could invite them in on the fun? Although repeal by no means eliminated male-dominated drinking spaces, new forms of leisure rendered traditional temperance narratives based on gender conflict all the more irrelevant. As cocktail culture domesticated drink, liquor lost much of its power to symbolize women's vulnerability as a sex, as it had during the nineteenth and early twentieth centuries.

Furthermore, shifts in gender roles during the Depression era may have made the older temperance plot seem even more anachronistic. Temperance tracts depicted polarized familial interests and a domestic realm in which the rightful needs of women and children were ignored by self-indulgent men. But as the masculine identity of the forgotten man suffered new blows, Americans focused more on bolstering the authority of men and less on promoting the distinct interests of women. In many cultural, political, and intellectual realms people expressed anxiety about the Depression in explicitly gendered terms.[92] New Deal policies, for example, focused on reviving full employment and financial solvency *for men*. Public debates raged about the propriety of married women's gainful employment; employed wives were commonly seen as a threat to men's prerogatives as family providers. New Deal ideologues subordinated the goal of sexual equality to that of family security, which could ostensibly be achieved by restoring men's gainful employment. Moreover, policy makers and social commentators aimed to bolster men's psychological as well as financial well-being.[93] In the words of one federal official, during the Depression jobless "men actually go to pieces. They lose the respect of their wives, sons and daughters because they lose respect for themselves, even though they have broken no laws and . . . their deportment as fathers and neighbors continues to be above reproach."[94] Men who derived their identity from the ability to "finance" family life experienced joblessness as a humiliating failure.[95]

Given the disruption the Depression caused to traditional gender norms, Americans were quick to embrace reassuring images that buttressed men's self-identity *as* men. Therefore they may have been less likely to support an ideology that dismissed drinking, a conventional sign of masculine prerogative. In such a context, perhaps, stories lamenting the neglect of women had less cultural resonance. In the face of gender crisis many artists and writers aimed to reduce rather than exacerbate gender conflict within marriage. For example, commissioners of public art sponsored by the New Deal favored murals of sturdy frontier husbands and wives working together in rural settings. Endorsing the "comradely ideal," such pictures invoked the frontier as a metaphor for democracy and economic vitality; images of the pioneer family represented security and unity in the face of adversity.[96] This spirit of harmony contradicted narratives that hinged on marital discord. Perhaps depictions of happy-go-lucky couples swilling cocktails represented a leisure-time equivalent to the shared labor portrayed in these public artworks. Realities of the Depression era brought strife to many households. But in popular culture, images of marital conviviality allowed viewers vicariously to experience domestic tranquility.

The alacrity with which producers of popular culture created celebratory images of social drinking indicates just how far the traditional evangelical worldview had declined by the time of repeal. As the voices of temperance reformers were dampened, moderate or social drinking became acceptable in mainstream society and even signified upward mobility and social prestige among the middle and upper classes. As cosmopolitan, mixed-sex drinking supplemented masculine drinking styles in the popular imagination, those who would cast drinking as a threat to the modern American family were swimming against strong cultural currents.

When the 1930s gave way to the 1940s, the nation's economy had rebounded somewhat, but the Depression still cast a pall over the social landscape. In retrospect repeal had not improved the economy as significantly as wet advocates had predicted. As the prospect of U.S. involvement in World War II became more certain, citizens began to focus on their nation's security in the global order. Many believed, correctly, that the war effort would finally shake the country out of its long economic malaise. The Depression may have energized the campaign for repeal, but during World War II the effectiveness of wet public relations efforts reached new heights.[97]

When the United States entered the war after the bombing of Pearl Harbor in 1941, liquor industry leaders feared a resurgence of prohibitionist sentiment—and rightly so. They could not forget that in 1917 World War I had provided the ultimate advantage for temperance reformers when Congress curtailed liquor production for the duration of the war. As early as 1936 wet factions cautioned that "if some national emergency (war, for example) developed into national hysteria," drys would take advantage of the situation and reinstate prohibitionist measures. In the early 1940s dry politicians hoped that World War II would breathe new life into their campaign; many pushed for strict federal liquor controls. The exigencies of war provided temperance advocates with a fresh set of rationales.[98]

The primary argument in favor of stricter wartime regulations centered on the nation's ability to fight successfully. A clear example can be found in a speech given in 1942 by George Barton Cutten, president of Colgate University. As he proclaimed, "We are at war. Alcohol and war do not mix any better than alcohol and gasoline." If the nation was "serious" about defeating its overseas enemies, it needed to steer clear of a "national drunken debauch." "A sober nation with the morale born of clear thinking, determination and courage can eventually defeat Hitler and the Japs," Cutten proclaimed, "but a drunken nation will travel through the Slough of Despond to inevitable danger of defeat." Another dry spokesperson argued that "effective preparedness" was "negatived" [*sic*] by the sale of alcohol in the current "hour of national emergency." Nothing less than the viability of U.S. democracy was at stake, and the risk that drinking posed to the war effort was not worth any benefits it provided.[99]

As drys argued, the continued sale of beverage alcohol would drain the country's precious economic resources and weaken the supply of industrial alcohol needed for war matériel. With so many staple products—including milk, meat, and gasoline—subject to strict rationing, how could the liquor industry justify the sale of an unnecessary, unwholesome product except in the name of selfish greed? As Cutten noted, "When sugar is being rationed and grain is wanted by a starving world, it is noteworthy to observe that in 1940, 2,000,000 tons of grain were used for alcoholic beverages."[100]

Moreover, they contended, free access to beer and liquor would weaken soldiers and civilians alike. The sober purpose of the war effort literally required a sober population that would not allow frivolity to interfere with production on the home front. Also, if alcohol was available to soldiers on army bases, the skill and judgment of the nation's fighting troops would be impaired. "The morale that comes out of a bottle is not the morale to put into a battle," Cutten cautioned. "No officer gave a wrong command because he remained sober." This reference to morale coming out of a bottle acknowledged the fact that homosocial drinking had long been a source of male bonding, a situation that military leaders certainly aimed to promote among the expanding ranks of GIs. But drys aimed to deflate gendered rhetoric that might be used to promote wet efforts. "If to counterbalance its disastrous effects, alcohol could add one jot or tittle of courage, ability, skill or manhood," wrote Cutten, "we might be willing to sacrifice in order to increase morale." But in his view drinking was "destructive and annihilating."[101] Dry leaders thus urged the War Department to rescind regulations permitting the sale of beer on military bases at home and abroad.[102]

Yet the most influential military leaders disagreed with the dry position. Top officials, including Secretary of War Henry Stimson, voiced strong opposition to a 1941 Senate bill that aimed to "remove liquor from the workshop of the American Army, Navy and Air Force." While dry advocates asked sarcastically if their nation was fighting to "make the world safe for the liquor traffic," federal officials argued that prohibition would damage the esprit de corps necessary to win the war. Military leaders argued that restrictions against beer would create resentment among soldiers and that prohibition would not prevent soldiers from drinking anyway. Moreover, they allayed fears of debauchery by praising U.S. troops in the press for their responsible drinking. Though distilleries were converted to war production in 1942, breweries were allowed to make beer for consumption at home and overseas. Even hard liquor manufacturers were allowed to produce beverage alcohol during brief "liquor holidays" in 1944 and 1945. In the end wartime prohibitionists did not prevail. Lawmakers ignored dry demands and enlisted "the liquor industry in the war effort in order to raise revenue, provide vital combat materials, and boost military and civilian morale."[103]

The beer industry, for its part, depicted beer as an inevitable part of the wartime scene. The chairman of the Brewing Industry Foundation boasted that his enterprise "endeavored to meet the highest obligations of good citizenship and to deserve the trust and confidence that the American people have placed in beer as a beverage of moderation and as an aid to the national morale."[104] Beer sales, in fact, increased more than 50 percent per capita from 1940 to 1945. Indeed, the fears of would-be prohibitionists that army bases would become recruiting grounds for beer and liquor interests were not as overwrought as they might have seemed. One brewery spokesperson heralded the establishment of army camps as "a chance for brewers to cultivate a taste for beer in millions of young men who will eventually constitute the largest beer-consuming section of our population."[105]

Popular opinion also ran against the renewal of restrictions on alcohol. One survey in 1941 indicated that voters ranked a new national prohibition law the least acceptable of fourteen possible constraints that the wartime government might impose. Widespread drinking among GIs also reinforced the wet cause, and many people believed that soldiers would have ignored restrictions anyway.[106] Furthermore, government officials and industry promoters employed rhetorical strategies to enhance the public's acceptance of drinking. Among the most effective of these lay in the use of the term "moderation." During the repeal campaign, wets touted the idea of moderation to justify a legal beverage trade. If this concept was useful in enacting repeal, it proved even more significant in bolstering wartime alcohol policies. As quoted above, the beer industry extolled its product as a "beverage of moderation." Military personnel used similar terms; army psychiatrist Merrill Moore, for example, assured the public that "drinking in moderation" posed no threat to military life.[107] The assumption that most people drank moderately helped solidify the wets' hegemony in society at large. Allowing and even encouraging restrained drinking by soldiers and civilians, politicians and businessmen precluded another wartime prohibition law.

As advertisements in popular magazines reveal, the beer industry not only positioned its product as a soothing refreshment; it included beer as part of the very raison d'être of the nation's war involvement. In September 1944, as the war was winding down, the Brewing Industry Foundation placed an ad in *Life* depicting two men conversing over a smoky outdoor barbecue pit. One of the men wears a chef's hat and kitchen gloves and is flipping steaks on the grill while a smiling woman serves a tray of filled pilsner glasses in the background. The image is meant to represent the daydream of a navy serviceman writing a letter home. "Boy did those grilled steaks used to taste swell," he remarks as he fondly recalls a moment from his prewar past. Under the image and caption the ad copy editorializes on the "small familiar pleasures" that justified the sailor's wartime service. "All over the world today . . . men away from home . . . fighting a war to help preserve the things they've left behind . . . are thinking of things like this," notes the ad. Backyard steak suppers, friendly games of horseshoes, and "the right to enjoy a refreshing glass of beer" were among the "little things" that added up to "home," the most important thing U.S. soldiers were fighting for in the first place. "Wholesome and satisfying, how good it is . . . as a beverage of moderation after a hard day's work . . . with good friends . . . with a home-cooked meal."[108]

This ad reveals strong cultural links among drinking, domesticity, and Americans' understanding of their wartime participation. Indeed, it exemplifies how citizens perceived their political obligations during World War II in terms of *private* motivations and goals. Soldiers' willingness to fight and sacrifice for their country stemmed in large part from the desire for a rewarding domestic life, a consumerist private sphere filled with goods and conveniences. According to historian Robert Westbrook, "Proponents of the war openly attempted . . . to exploit private obligations in order to convince Americans to serve the cause of national defense." These allegiances—"to families . . . to friends, and generally, to an 'American Way of Life' defined as a rich (and richly commodified) private realm of experience—were tirelessly invoked in the campaign to mobilize Americans for World War II and formed the centerpiece of the propaganda produced by the state and its allies in Hollywood, the War Advertising Council, and elsewhere."[109] Depicting beer as part and parcel of a promised postwar world filled with bountiful domestic pleasures, the Brewing Industry Foundation further normalized alcohol consumption, rendering it as patriotic and as American as Uncle Sam himself.

Sometimes advertisements for hard liquor invoked themes of civilian patriotism. Like so many ads during the war, one for Seagram's Five Crown whiskey aimed not only to sell liquor but also to persuade readers to buy war bonds in support of the war effort. Its cartoon illustration features five men who personify qualities of Seagram's liquor: body, lightness, flavor, richness, and smoothness. Four of the cartoon figures hold war bonds in their hands and utter such nonsensical proclamations as "I'm flavor—requesting More War Bond investing!" and "I'm Smoothness—commending more Victory Lending." The largest figure, symbolizing the whiskey's robust "body," holds a spear to the back of yet another character, a cartoon rendition of Adolf Hitler bearing the label "toughness." Below a poem exhorting readers to "sock away a tenth of [their] pay" in war bonds, the ad copy proclaims that "Seagram keeps the toughness out . . . blends extra pleasure in." In a bizarre, even audacious way, the ad implied that drinking whiskey was as patriotic an act as buying war bonds, and that defeating Hitler's "tough" armies would enable Americans to enjoy the pleasures of such a "smooth" blended whiskey.[110] On one hand, the Seagram's ad deployed the War Advertising Council's strategy to encourage civilians to spend less money and make short-term sacrifices for the future good of the nation. On the other hand, however, the enjoyment of whiskey was portrayed as a lasting prerogative, even during a time of strict rationing.

In contrast to wartime prohibitionists, such ads envisioned no conflict between alcohol consumption and the war effort. Indeed, they implied that drinking was a fundamental right of U.S. citizens. Through advertising, public relations, political lobbying, and other strategies the beer and liquor industries ensured that the United States would fight a "wet war" at home and abroad. Indeed, the government's permissive wartime stance stemmed in large part from the formidable influence of these industries.[111]

DRINK, GENDER, AND SOCIABILITY
IN THE 1930S AND 1940S

The decades surrounding repeal witnessed the domestication of drink, a melding of masculine and feminine drinking styles that rendered alcohol consumption acceptable among broad ranks of middle-class Americans. Mixed-sex speakeasies replaced the all-male saloon during Prohibition, resulting in new forms of heterosocial leisure that involved and sometimes revolved around drinking. However, the argument that gender "was no longer essential, or even significant, to alcohol use itself" is overstated. In fact, heterosocial leisure did not eclipse masculine cultures of drink entirely. The persistence of exclusive masculine drinking rituals, as well as attitudes toward *men's* drinking, specifically, continued to infuse debates and practices regarding drinking and alcoholism through the post–World War II period. The turn-of-the-century saloon may have disappeared, but long-standing associations between manly self-expression and alcoholic indulgence continued to shape popular views and experiences of drinking.[112]

According to some contemporary observers the acceptance of women quaffing in public was still tenuous in the 1940s. As sociologist Herbert Bloch noted in the *American Scholar* in 1949, "Drinking between the sexes [was] a relatively belated development in American social evolution." While many post–World War II bars witnessed the "free commingling of the sexes in repartee and bibulousness," most citizens were reluctant to "accept women as the full equal drinking partners of men." Observing contemporary advertising trends, Bloch found that many liquor ads portrayed "wholesome and respectable" women, but rarely did they depict them "actually in the drinking act itself." Given that "drinking as a recreational practice [had] been almost wholly masculine-dominated" for more than a century, Bloch was not surprised to discover pockets of abiding intolerance toward women's drinking.[113]

Other social scientists also qualified their remarks about the rise in women's social drinking. One 1946 study explained that Americans could be divided into three categories: regular drinkers (who consumed alcohol more than three times a week), occasional drinkers, and abstainers. The study found that 17 percent of the sampled adult population were regular drinkers; 48 percent were occasional drinkers, and 35 percent never drank at all. But these figures were not evenly distributed by gender. "Of the male population 75 percent drink, as do 56 percent of the women, but three times as many men as women were classified as 'regular' drinkers." So despite the "narrowing of the gap between the sexes in respect to drinking," by the mid-1940s men were still more likely to drink, and to drink more often, than their female counterparts. The authors concluded that "at the moment, drinking has an uncertain and changing status. While fewer people perhaps now regard it as a sin, it has not yet achieved the universal respectability of well-established patterns of social behavior." Indeed, the decades after repeal were a time of transition—and often confusion—regarding attitudes toward drinking. Lingering concerns about the respectability of drinking were consistent with a persistent consumption gap between the sexes.[114]

Furthermore, the demise of Prohibition marked the return of male exclusivity in many taverns. In urban working-class neighborhoods far removed from the urbane nightclub, repeal revived traditional masculine drinking patterns. Though historians have not explored this development in depth, New York journalist Pete Hamill has written a memoir that vividly evokes this chapter in the history of drink. His autobiography of childhood and youth, *A Drinking Life*, recounts his experiences growing up in Brooklyn during the 1930s and 1940s. Hamill's father, an Irish immigrant factory worker, spent his free time in a local bar called Gallagher's, which Pete first entered as a young boy. His recollections, so reminiscent of Jack London's prose in *John Barleycorn*, are worth quoting at length:

> One Sunday, when I was almost eight, [my father] said to me, Come on, McGee. I walked with him up to the corner and for the first time entered the tight, dark, amber-colored, wool-smelling world of a saloon. . . . In I went behind him, to stand among the stools and the gigantic men, overwhelmed at first by the sour smell of dried beer, then inhaling tobacco smells, the toilet smell, the smell of men. The place had been a speakeasy during Prohibition, and the men still entered through the back door. It was supposed to be a restaurant, but . . . nobody was ever there, except a few quiet women, who could not get service in the bar-room proper. In that room, the men were jammed together at a high three-sided bar, talking, smoking, singing, laughing, and drinking. . . . There was no television then, so they made their own entertainment.[115]

Gallagher's was a place where colorful, sugar-laced cocktails were as rare as women, a place where men convened to drink like men. Recalling the rough, turn-of-the-century saloons of Jack London's literary imagination, Hamill's words should quell any notion that Prohibition severed the link between drink and manly conviviality.

Away at overnight camp, Hamill tasted his first experience drinking in a peer group setting, a time that marked his first conscious feeling that he was "moving toward becoming a man." That summer Hamill "was converted to the creed of machismo," and "drinking was a crucial part" of his awakening virility. By the time he was in high school, Hamill was frequenting the neighborhood bars. "I didn't know it at the time," he remarks, "but I had entered the drinking life. Drinking was part of being a man. Drinking was an integral part of sexuality, . . . the sacramental binder of friendships . . . the reward for work, the fuel of celebration, the consolation for death or defeat."[116] More than three decades after London wrote his autobiographical novel—one that he hoped would hasten a future in which boys would no longer regard drinking as a sign of manhood—Pete Hamill learned precisely the same lesson his predecessor had learned in the late nineteenth century.

Contemporary observers also shed light on working-class drinking patterns. During the Depression, sociologists participated in federally funded efforts to document virtually all aspects of social life in the United States, and commercialized leisure was no exception.[117] For example, Northwestern University professor Arthur J. Todd oversaw an extensive survey of recreation in Chicago. Sponsored by the Works Progress Administration, Todd and his fieldworkers compiled data about facilities ranging from amusement parks and bowling alleys to movie theaters and circuses. They devoted an entire chapter to "retail liquor establishments and cabarets," which assessed the development of drinking parlors from the pre-Prohibition era to 1937. The old-time saloon had disappeared. But "what substitute, if any, has arisen to take its place?" Todd asked. Without masking his personal biases, he noted that while "the term saloon is no longer used . . . it is generally agreed that in most instances its successor the modern tavern has been no improvement over the saloon of 1918." Citing reports by the Juvenile Protective Association, Todd noted that taverns in "less respectable neighborhoods" offered entertainment that appealed to working-class men, including gambling, "indecent dancing," and prostitution. Although post-repeal taverns attracted young female patrons in search of excitement, neighborhood taprooms continued to attract "old-timers who recall[ed] the bar and brass-rail days of the pre-prohibition era."[118] Many taverns had a room adjacent to the barroom designed to serve women and mixed-sex groups. But the barroom itself, he discovered, retained a masculine atmosphere.

For other sociologists, too, long-standing assumptions about working-class male drinkers held fast. In 1945 John Dollard published "Drinking Mores of the Social Classes," a brief article in which he distinguished among six social levels in U.S. society. Fully one-third of the population fell into a category he labeled the "upper-lower class," which designated "poor but honest folk; the working element." In contrast to the "ignorant, shiftless" masses of the "lower-lower class" (who accounted for 25 percent of the population), "upper-lower class" persons drank frequently, yet with "some occupational restraints." As members of the "chief labor group," he explained, working-class men drank mostly at home and in taverns. Differentiating between the masculine drinking styles of middle-class men and the "upper-lower class," Dollard explained that the latter did "not have the 'drink like a gentleman' taboo." Workingmen, he found, often become "openly aggressive when drinking because they have not been trained to exercise the control of aggression that is demanded of those at the top." Among the "lowest" class of Americans, he argued, drinking was the least restrained. "Both men and women drink, although usually not in mixed groups." Men, in particular, engaged in "Saturday-night-to-Monday-morning binges, without much social control."[119] Despite his implicit class condescension, Dollard shared with Jack London a view of aggressive, robust manhood.

Liquor advertisements during the 1930s reflected the coexistence of masculine and heterosocial drinking cultures. On one hand, advertisers knew that women shoppers actually bought most of the packaged beer, wine, and liquor sold for home consumption. Both the beer can and the supermarket were new in the 1930s, and to the extent that women functioned as family purchasers during the Depression, they played a major role in moving alcoholic merchandise from store shelves to home refrigerators and liquor cabinets. Thus some ads featured images of women (or cropped illustrations of manicured female hands) serving drinks in a domestic setting. The domestication of drink entailed making women feel comfortable in the presence of alcohol, whether or not they drank themselves.

But on the other hand, while some ads pictured women holding champagne or mixed drinks, most portrayed drinking as a masculine indulgence. This was especially true of advertisements for packaged spirits, which combined appeals to elite class status with assumptions about manhood. In the Martini and Rossi vermouth ad mentioned above, all of the human figures illustrated were men. So, too, with a Hennessy cognac ad from 1938 that featured four tuxedo-attired men drinking and smoking cigars in a men's club. Another brandy ad claimed that Martell cognac was "the socially correct liqueur of gentlemen." Immediately after repeal Four Roses whiskey evoked the manly associations of the saloon era with an image of a ruddy, rifle-toting man celebrating a bird hunt with a shot of whiskey "as rich and satisfying as a platter of canvasback duck, as mellow as an October afternoon in the woods, [and] as dependable" as the hunting dog at his feet. "Ever since Repeal," the copy read, "I've been hunting for that kind of old-fashioned whiskey." It was similar to another ad printed in 1937. Surrounded by drawings of men horseback riding, fishing, and shooting arrows, the ad copy declared, "Sportsmen all over the world seem to prefer John James [whiskey]. It's hearty, robust, mellow—a man's drink."[120] With their references to hunting and the rugged outdoors, these ads registered a style of masculinity different from that symbolized by brandy-swirling club members. Yet both ad types portrayed alcohol, and especially straight liquor, as an essential part of life and leisure for upwardly mobile (or thus aspiring) men.

That many such ads graced the pages of *Fortune* magazine, which targeted the (temporarily beleaguered) ranks of salaried managers, brokers, and other businessmen, underscores the fact that working-class men were not the only men to engage in homosocial drinking during this period. Many writers commented on the drinking habits of professionals and corporate managers. In the advertising profession, for example, account executives and copy writers often conducted business in restaurants, bars, or clubs, where they could consume a three-martini lunch while planning strategies or negotiating deals. According to one advertising man, "Among and between clients and agencies, drinking plays a salubrious and beneficial part, so long as the individuals are the lucky nine out of ten to whom alcohol is not a poison. A few highballs unstuff the stuffed shirts, relieve the tension, bring . . . relief to a tough job, help get an O.K."[121] Another writer even used the phrase "alcoholic professions" to denote certain fields, such as public relations, sales, and real estate, in which alcohol mediated transactions between buyers and sellers, brokers and clients. Describing the dealings of advertising executives, he noted that "you just about have to drink in agency work. Luncheons are a favorite time for conferences and . . . they're always wet. I've known a lot of smart fellows in advertising and publicity, but if they've got any tendency toward alcoholism they're not smart to stay in the business." Sales-men, too, learned that success lay in being a "good fellow—and being a good fellow seems to mean drinking with the other guy till he practically passes out and signs your order."[122]

Novelist Henry Beetle Hough offered a more detailed account of cor-porate drinking practices. In 1954 Hough penned a book on behalf of an anonymous friend about the friend's life as an alcoholic. The narrator had been an advertising executive in New York City for many years, and Hough illustrated his former white-collar milieu as follows:

There are fine restaurants in the mid-town district . . . and at the noon hour, a general interval stretching from twelve to three, one may meet an engaging lot of successful men having their cocktails at these bars. . . . Someone may speak of the ritual drinking of the American business man. Well, here it is, not only of the business man but of the artist and lawyer and writer as well. . . . The extension of the so-called lunch hour . . . makes it possible for much pleasant and useful talk to be exchanged, for the transaction of business, the approval or disapproval of ideas and hopes. The softening up of prospects, the cementing of reputations and relationships, and so on.

According to men of the professional-managerial class, "Drinking was good for business." Hough's narrator reported that "almost everyone drank, as if alcohol were a catalytic agent in the presence of which all the urgent reactions in the ferment of advertising would take place more advantageously." The material accoutrements of drink, "the accessories of liquor [that] gleamed in the windows of expensive shops—many varieties of crystal glasses, jiggers and bar spoons and bottle-openers of brightest chrome or silver," lent a "special atmosphere" to the businessman's bibu-lous rituals.[123]

It is not surprising that sociologist John Dollard also weighed in on the subject of drinking among middle-class and wealthy Americans. Con-tinuing his categorization according to class, he described the drinking behavior of the "upper-middle class"—those "nice, morally respectable people with some wealth" who fell below the upper class but above the working- and lower-middle classes on the social spectrum. He found that unlike the upper-class women of both "old money" and "nouveau riche" families, women of the upper-middle class rarely drank. Within this stratum, which represented 10 percent of the population, "men drank at social occasions, at their poker games and at casual gatherings in friends' houses." Dollard also found that drinking was "not customary in mixed groups" among people of this social rank. Although Dollard, writing in 1945, paid little attention to masculine drinking in business or quasi-professional settings, his observations support the notion that men of various class backgrounds drank together in same-sex groups.[124]

Print advertisements reveal that liquor continued to play a role in masculine networks of gift exchange. One ad for G&W Spirits referred to rituals of reciprocity that invoked yet departed from saloon treating customs. Printed in the December 1937 issue of *Time*—at the height of the holiday season—the ad featured G&W bourbon, scotch, gin, and rye as "gift-worthy" liquors. Although women were the primary purchasers of gifts exchanged among relatives and friends, this ad explicitly targeted men as participants in commercialized Christmas rituals.[125] Under the headline "This Christmas be sure you Give Wisely" is a picture of a bald, middle-aged man, dressed in a coat and tie, looking into a mirror and holding a hairbrush. With a bewildered look on his face, he peers down toward the brush, which bears a card labeled "To Father." A well-meaning son had selected an inappropriate gift for his hairless father. But as the ad implied, such problems could be avoided by giving bottles of liquor instead. Under the image was a list of "gift-worthy persons" who would presumably enjoy receiving G&W: family members, including brothers-in-law and grandfathers; friends and acquaintances, such as a "college chum" or a "man-who-did-you-a-favor"; and "those who serve you," including a barber, the elevator man, a janitor, or an "employee (male)." Significantly, all twenty-seven possible gift recipients were either assumed to be male or identified as such. After repeal the packaged liquor trade created more opportunities for sellers to promote bottled spirits as tangible tokens of gratitude or affection. While different from the camaraderie of tavern treating, holiday gift exchange represented another way in which American men used liquor to mediate social relationships.

Furthermore, the arrival of World War II created new settings for all-male drinking. During the war years the largest percentage of nonelderly American men congregated in the armed services. Historians estimate that more than 16 million soldiers were sent overseas to fight.[126] Far away from mothers, wives, sisters, and sweethearts, GIs stationed on military bases forged new social ties among fellow draftees, predominantly other men. We have seen how military leaders justified the continued sale of alcoholic beverages, especially beer, by invoking the importance of camaraderie and morale among the troops. At least for the duration of the war, then, millions of men drank in homosocial groups practically by default.

On the home front, journalists constructed a gendered symbol of heroism and patriotism in celebration of the wartime soldier. To generate public support for the war, government propaganda and the media characterized the typical GI as an emblem of strength, integrity, and bravery. The mythologized soldier was both ordinary and exceptional. War reporters wrote that GI's were "just ordinary American boys . . . friendly and enthusiastic and sensible . . . who fought well when the going was good." But the average soldier, comfortable with guns and machines, was also an outstanding athlete who fought courageously, even "savagely," when his country depended on it. Presenting a militaristic version of manly identity and citizenship, the soldier was a figure on whom the entire country could rely for national security. As represented by military officials, moderate drinking coexisted easily with this cultural symbol of youthful, hardy manhood. The dual image of young men casually drinking beer during their off-hours, yet aggressively battling during moments of crisis, invoked complementary constructions of masculinity designed to enhance the public's faith in its male protectors.[127]

The normalization of drinking during the 1930s and early 1940s occurred within a range of recreational cultures, including the urbane nightclub, the at-home cocktail party, the so-called three-martini lunch, the military canteen, and the neighborhood tavern. Although heterosocial drinking gained acceptance in American recreational life, it did not entirely efface the special status of drinking as a male activity. From the living room to the cocktail lounge, settings for heterosocial drinking supplemented and sometimes competed with traditional male drinking bastions, but they did not replace them altogether. Like the mixed company in which they were often consumed, cocktails may have domesticated hard liquor, but hard liquor itself retained its gendered connotations as a masculine beverage. In fact, since alcohol was styled as a concomitant of work and leisure for men of various classes and occupations, it is possible that the general acceptance of liquor also enhanced the status of drinking among men *as a group*. Some men may have *also* drunk in the company of women. But such occasions had a different cultural meaning than, say, a night at the bar "with the boys" or a round of drinks with one's clients or associates.

In the decades after repeal, moderate drinking continued to play a role in shaping masculine identity. To the extent that men rooted their sense of manhood in rituals of male camaraderie, alcohol continued to lubricate social interaction, strengthening bonds among men. Such was the case, certainly, with men who frequented neighborhood bars or who drank while serving in the military. To the extent that ideals of manhood were premised on married men's privileged status within the family unit, social drinking could signify a combination of career success, domestic authority, and even marital companionship. Among working-class men drinking was still strongly linked to patterns of sociability and neighborhood affiliation. But it is equally significant that an increase in alcohol consumption among all classes of men—and women—meant that Americans no longer associated convivial drinking primarily with traditional saloon culture.

The decades following repeal thus witnessed a fundamental shift in the cultural history of drinking. As the voices of dry crusaders were eclipsed by liquor tycoons, advertisers, and movie producers who glamorized social drinking, fewer middle-class Americans equated moral respectability with abstinence. In fact, the wet campaign to normalize drinking involved a redefinition of the term "temperance" itself. No longer used to signify abstinence, the word came to denote moderation, drinking that was restrained, responsible, and above all, relaxing. Moderate or social drinking as a category or level of consumption was a relative concept, defined in relation to what it was *not*: it was not habitually excessive drinking, nor was it seen to cause major personal problems for the drinker. After Prohibition, drinking became acceptable in mainstream society, often signifying conspicuous consumption, upscale leisure, and social prestige.

But what about drinkers who were anything *but* moderate? How was their drinking defined in the post-repeal era? And how did their families fare? By the mid-1930s such questions were posed—and answered—not by evangelical social reformers hot with rage against the saloon but by a diverse group of professional experts who engendered the modern alcoholic.

2 ENGENDERING THE ALCOHOLIC

Recorded in the pages of *Life* magazine is telling evidence of the central place of alcohol in post-repeal American culture. In May 1946 *Life* published an eleven-page, illustrated feature titled "Liquor: Current Studies in Medicine and Psychiatry Are Bringing Enlightenment to the 30,000 Year-Old Problem of Drinking." Judging from the subtitle of the piece (which was comprised of six individual, related sections) readers would expect the article to focus on physical and psychological afflictions associated with heavy drinking as well as therapies for treating "problem" drinkers. But in fact only several paragraphs focus on such matters; most of the feature depicts drinking in a celebratory light. According to author Francis Wickware, drinking was a normal, even salubrious activity for most Americans. "Of the estimated 50,000,000 drinkers in the U.S.," he wrote, "all but a fraction use alcohol moderately and . . . regularly because it makes them feel better and more appreciative of themselves and their fellows. . . . Taken for purposes of social relaxation or as a gustatory adjunct, alcohol never has damaged anyone." Wickware conceded that "the habitual heavy drinker who neglects his diet and general health is more susceptible to . . . disease than a nondrinker." But by and large, he claimed, temperate drinkers were as healthy as their abstaining counterparts, and they suffered fewer stomach ulcers besides.[1]

Moreover, he implied, they had more fun. In a section called "Famous U.S. Bars," Wickware described five celebrated watering holes, ranging from imitation "old-time taverns" in Denver and Chicago to "glittery, modernistic palaces" in Los Angeles. Photographs of well-dressed men and women illustrated the sophisticated ambience enjoyed by patrons of such establishments. Another section explained how ten alcoholic beverages were manufactured. From wine and whiskey to bourbon and brandy, *Life* educated readers on the makings of their favorite spirits. The feature's most practical—and no doubt most popular—section was a two-page color spread of thirty cocktail recipes. Relatively staid drinks like the martini and the old-fashioned were portrayed alongside exotic concoctions such as the Singapore sling and the sloe gin fizz. Illustrations of the various potables depicted no fewer than ten kinds of glassware, including shallow champagne saucers and slim highballs. Overall the article glamorized the colorful cocktail as a key ingredient in a cosmopolitan social life.

More than a decade after the demise of Prohibition, *Life* magazine glorified alcohol as a "tension reliever" and social lubricant. In this article, and in scores of advertisements that filled the magazine's pages, liquor signified entertainment and enjoyment for the average consumer. Actual consumption patterns show that *Life* was reporting on a trend already taking hold in U.S. society. In 1934 (the year of the first *Thin Man* film) per capita consumption of wine, beer, and spirits was almost one gallon; by 1946 it had doubled to slightly more than two gallons. Although total alcohol consumption was much lower in the mid-1930s than it had been before Prohibition (and, in fact, the early-twentieth-century level of intake was not reached again until around 1970), the rapid, short-term increase during the 1940s must have seemed significant to Americans at the time.[2] *Life* magazine played a part in encouraging drinking, especially among persons who identified with the white, socially mobile, middle-class population that *Life*'s editors implicitly imagined their readers to comprise.[3] On one hand, then, the celebratory tone of *Life*'s tribute to alcohol matched the exultant mood of the nation in the immediate aftermath of World War II. After many years facing the hardships of recession and war, citizens in 1946 had much to celebrate: the triumph of the Allies over fascism abroad and the elimination of wartime exigencies at home. In this context *Life* heralded the contribution of liquor to a national feeling of jubilation. Problem drinkers there might be, but their problems would not detract from the pleasures of drink for most Americans.

Yet on the other hand, the problem drinker, "the habitual heavy drinker" mentioned in Wickware's article, was significant nonetheless. Indeed, if we want to understand the cultural history represented by *Life*'s tribute to drink, we should not dismiss too quickly the more serious, cautious message conveyed in its title. Rather than focus exclusively on the glamorous bars and cocktail recipes—aspects on which the author, and no doubt most readers, lavished their attention—we might ponder why Wickware and his editor chose to highlight the more negative side of drinking at the outset. The first paragraph of the article lauded the U.S. public for evincing more concern about the "serious and complicated disease of alcohol addiction." There, Wickware praised both doctors and the media for dispelling prejudice and superstition about habitual drinking and for moving the subject of alcoholism "out of the realm of morals" and into the more appropriate "sphere of psychiatry and medicine."[4]

What, after all, did moderate drinking entail? In order for the concept to function as more than a descriptive label for social behavior (such as a glass of wine at dinner or drinking that did not lead to intoxication) and to connote, instead, a positive stance regarding the free exchange and consumption of alcohol, the ideal of moderation required a cultural counterpoint. Indeed, the word "moderate" is a relative term, designating a realm between two extremes. The *American Heritage Dictionary* defines the adjective as "within reasonable limits; not excessive or extreme" or "of medium or average quantity, quality, or extent." Moderate consumption occupied a middle ground between total abstinence and chronic drunkenness. Whereas prohibitionists depicted excess to justify abstinence as a standard, wets relied on the notion of excessive or problem drinkers to legitimate the concept of social drinking. In order to portray most people's drinking as normal, antiprohibitionists needed a deviant standard against which to measure that normality.

Expressed within *Life*'s feature story, then, were two related models of alcohol consumption: social drinking, which the author viewed as beneficial to individual and social welfare, and alcoholism, a serious disease afflicting a minority of drinkers. While the overall article celebrated the former, it did so by constructing both paradigms of drinking, which depended on one another for their respective definitions. Furthermore, it offered an implicit argument about the relationship between the two consumption models: social drinking did not necessarily lead to alcoholic drinking, while the overindulgence of some individuals did not call into question the propriety of most drinkers to consume with relative restraint.[5] Certainly not all Americans agreed with this latter point, and other writers offered different points of view.[6] For our purposes, however, the *Life* feature is significant not only for the specific moral and political stance it conveyed toward social drinking but, more generally, because it reflected a new set of parameters within which most Americans, regardless of their particular attitudes toward drinking, were beginning to understand alcohol consumption and its attendant problems.

What distinguished a problem drinker from a social drinker who imbibed at a party, a bar, or a backyard barbecue? How did Americans come to recognize and identify the alcoholics in their midst? How did they understand the causes of excessive drinking? And how did their ideas reflect the specific historical circumstances in which they were engendered? Whereas *Life* emphasized the milieu of the social drinker and portrayed alcoholism as a distinct, if related, medical problem, this chapter reverses the emphasis, discussing the history of alcoholic identities in a broader context of American drinking behavior and social change.

In the aftermath of World War II, social critics as well as magazine journalists noted a shift in popular views of habitual drunkenness. Sociologist Herbert Bloch, writing in the *American Scholar* in 1949, remarked that the growing ranks of "social drinkers" were yielding greater numbers of "excessive pathological drinkers." Of particular interest to him was the stark difference between contemporary and traditional views of chronic drunkenness:

> No longer does John Barleycorn constitute a moral problem, a reprehensible degenerate and an object of scorn or pity to the good ladies of the Temperance Union. *Instead, he is now a sick man—a mighty sick man.* The celebrated target of the pulpits now becomes a matter of scientific concern and analytical vivisection to the psychiatrist, the sociologist, the physiologist and the medical profession. He now enjoys moral impunity, but no longer scientific disinterest and detachment. . . . His metamorphosis has been similar to the belated respectability accorded other social problems and diseases, such as syphilis and gonorrhea, which, lifted from the previous perspective of moral opprobrium, now fall within the province of a scientifically enlightened interest.[7]

As Bloch observed, while Americans were adjusting to their post-Prohibition lifestyles, a well-funded, diverse cohort of researchers and public health educators engendered a new model of habitual drunkenness (alcoholism) and a new category of subjective identity (the alcoholic). As reformers and politicians lost the power to shape alcohol policy in the United States, other professional groups gained newfound cultural influence. The new authorities were physicians, psychiatrists, social workers, and lay therapists—medical and mental health experts who brought new concerns and therapeutic techniques to bear on matters that had preoccupied temperance activists only two decades earlier. In the process they disseminated a modern paradigm of habitual drunkenness as a malady rather than a moral transgression.[8] The new paradigm located the source of addiction not in alcohol per se but in the body and mind of the individual who drank intemperately.[9]

In effect, experts displaced the traditional view of habitual drinking as a sin with a modern notion of overconsumption as an illness. Certainly, physicians treated inebriates as patients and regarded compulsive drinking as a matter of "scientifically enlightened interest" long before observers in the 1940s found their therapies worthy of note. The notion of alcohol addiction as a disease did not originate in the twentieth century; in fact, the first medical diagnosis of inebriety in the United States was offered in 1785 by physician Benjamin Rush. But given the influence enjoyed by dry politicians and reformers in shaping ideas (and laws) about alcohol, earlier attempts at medicalization, such as the inebriate asylum movement, were circumscribed within relatively narrow professional domains. A number of nineteenth-century physicians posited biological explanations for chronic drunkenness and developed institutional methods of treatment, but their movement remained on the fringes of both medicine and charity work and had all but collapsed by the time Prohibition was enacted.[10]

The post-repeal revival of the medical model did not entirely efface moralistic attitudes toward drunkenness, but the emerging disease concept of the 1930s and 1940s represented a significant break with the evangelical worldview of dry reformers. The disease concept was an "organizing metaphor" or "governing image"—a new way to talk about alcohol problems outside traditional wet-dry rhetoric. "The rise of a disease concept of alcoholism," one historian has explained, "was based more on its metaphorical utility as a slogan than on its scientific validity. Its ascendance was more one of declaration than of scientific conclusion." On an individual basis it provided a new way for excessive drinkers to understand their vulnerability to alcohol. On a broader social level it signaled a shift in the types of institutions and individuals who aimed to solve alcohol-related problems.[11]

Previous scholars have explored how a small band of researchers and campaigners recast popular attitudes toward excessive drinking in the mid-twentieth century. Bruce Holley Johnson coined the term "alcoholism movement" to denote the overlapping organizations dedicated to research, treatment, and public relations in the field. Important individuals who revived the disease concept included E. M. Jellinek, an influential biostatistician who coordinated the Yale Center for Studies on Alcohol, founded in 1940, and Marty Mann, a savvy publicist who founded the National Committee for Education on Alcoholism (NCEA) in 1944. What united these groups into a movement, Johnson argues, was their concerted effort to promote a scientific model of drunkenness and a humanitarian view of the problem drinker as a sick person. The NCEA publicized the disease concept through mass-circulation magazines, radio interviews, and educational campaigns targeting social workers, clergymen, doctors, and even film producers.[12]

Robin Room, a leading scholar on the history and sociology of alcoholism, has focused on why post-repeal activists adopted an exclusive interest in alcoholism, abandoning a wider array of social problems related to drinking. While acknowledging the influence of Alcoholics Anonymous and the beer and liquor industries in promoting the disease concept, Room emphasized scientific researchers' success in attaining institutional and financial support. Sociologist Ron Roizen has also aimed to explain the alcoholism movement's success. His work concerns the engine of social change: "How did we . . . get from the temperance paradigm and its rich and varied complements of conceptual focuses and social-action corollaries to the alcoholism paradigm and its equally rich but very different complements?" he asks. Roizen focused on various political and economic developments of the 1930s that laid the material groundwork for new cultural attitudes toward drinking and alcoholism.[13]

But we know much less about the *cultural* transformation itself. Psychiatrists, public health workers, and other writers produced a voluminous literature designed to identify, characterize, and treat the alcoholic, that "mighty sick man" who metamorphosed from the drunken degenerate he once was. While it is important to understand the social and political environment in which the alcoholism movement fashioned a new concept of alcoholic identity, historians have not adequately explored the cultural implications of that identity. In order to understand the shift from temperance to alcoholism, we need to examine the language and imagery Americans used to characterize and explain the excessive drinkers in their midst.

Moreover, we need to assess the shift from moral judgment to medical diagnosis in a new light. Previous historians have tended to privilege the work of scientific experts, a relatively small group of individuals who wielded great influence. As an explanatory framework, the transformation from sin to sickness provides an apt conceptualization for the study of alcoholism. It is a perfect example of what historians call the "triumph of the therapeutic sensibility," or "therapeutic ethos," a constellation of cultural values that validates the pursuit of personal well-being, health, and psychic security as life's highest goal.[14] The alcoholism paradigm *did* originate in psychiatric, scientific, and other therapeutic circles, and it would be dubious to explore this history without considering the writings of medical and psychological experts.

As with all writings penned by educated, elite authorities, however, the scientific literature on alcoholism reveals as much, if not more, about the professional concerns and social identities of the experts as it does about their alcoholic subjects, not to mention the uses and perceived abuses of alcohol in society at large. To situate alcoholism in a broad historical context, we need to ask, Was the paradigm itself a response to social developments that had little directly to do with drinking? What social changes and cultural anxieties did the new diagnostic narratives of alcoholism address (or perhaps obscure)? When did the pronouncements of experts begin to resonate in popular culture, and why did they gain influence when they did? What was the relationship between alcoholism and changing patterns of work and family life in this period?

In reevaluating the shift from temperance ideology to alcoholism, we might recognize a seemingly obvious yet significant continuity: the habitual drinker, in both paradigms, is usually male. In 1949, when the *American Scholar* defined the alcoholic as a mighty sick man, the subject's gender identification was not simply a case of universal usage to denote the word "person." Just as dry reformers and politicians enacted Prohibition primarily as a referendum against men's drinking and against the common conflation of drink with masculinity, so, too, did the alcoholism movement incorporate assumptions of sexual difference into its vision of habitual drunkenness.

As experts began to define the alcoholic in the language of science, they produced empirical data that corroborated long-standing perceptions of drinking as a manly indulgence. For example, in formulating his classic statement of the disease model, prominent Yale scientist E. M. Jellinek assumed the alcoholic to be a man and did not employ data on women alcoholics. In 1948 *Newsweek* magazine quoted Jellinek, claiming that "there are 750,000 alcoholics of both sexes . . . and the women among them are distinctly in the minority."[15] When Yale physiologist Howard Haggard wrote that alcoholism "centers on the illness of a man," he meant this literally; later in the same article he claimed that "the proportion of men and women who drink to excess" in the United States was one woman to six men.[16] Another expert, psychiatrist Abraham Myerson, agreed that "it is fair to specify men" when referring to most alcoholics; his research revealed that "alcoholic addiction [was] seven times more prevalent among men than . . . among women."[17] As we shall see, such overt references to gender were supported by many implicit assumptions about the sex of the alcoholic drinker.[18]

Indeed, there is a discrepancy between the gendering of alcoholism and the acceptance of heterosocial drinking after repeal. Given the normalization of public drinking among men *and* women, it may seem puzzling that experts viewed alcoholism primarily as a male affliction. Indeed, some observers argued hyperbolically that women's social drinking was causing female alcoholism rates to skyrocket.[19] But leading experts, Jellinek included, countered that most women drinkers drank moderately. In their view men were more likely to cross the line into pathological excess. Making sense of this contradiction requires understanding the *limits* of mixed-sex drinking. The rise of heterosocial drinking explains much about the ideological triumph of moderation by the early 1940s, but it does not explain the gendering of the alcoholism model at the same time. Long-standing perceptions of drinking as a masculine activity lingered in the post-repeal decades, and they bore significant implications for the alcoholism model. From the 1930s into the post–World War II era, Americans relied on and reshaped ideologies of manhood to distinguish between normal and problem drinkers. Traditional ideas about alcoholic excess and its threat to male vitality and familial well-being were not abandoned but, rather, reformulated. For despite the domestication of drink, Americans continued to view habitual drinking as wholly incompatible with the things moderate drinking was intended to enhance: pleasant sociability, career advancement, social prestige, and marital compatibility. In formulating new ideas about alcoholism, a pathology of consumption that could never be domesticated, Americans not only drew boundaries between normal and problem drinkers; they also reinscribed divisions between healthy and pathological gender identity.[20] Furthermore, they replaced images of rowdy saloon-goers and "skid-row bums" with depictions of beleaguered, besotted businessmen and bureaucrats, registering new concerns about the typical problem drinker's class affiliation.

While the disease paradigm was gendered with masculine accents, female drinkers were by no means ignored. Some experts even believed that alcoholism among women was increasing during the 1940s. But the disease concept itself was premised on notions of drinking as a manly activity, and "alcoholism was constructed as an elastic category, enabling psychiatrists to interpret alcoholism in either men or women as a problem of gender identity."[21] When psychiatrists did consider female alcoholics, they applied the same rhetoric of pathology to women as they did to men. As a result they considered women alcoholics to be especially sick: first, because they engaged in deviant drinking behavior and, second, because that behavior was seen as a masculine neurosis. Even in the relatively few studies of women drinkers, experts assumed a priori that alcoholism was linked to issues of masculine sex-role identity.[22] This book's focus on male drinkers reflects the fact that experts at the time tended to treat women alcoholics separately, basing their pronouncements on theories originally designed to apply specifically to men.

DIAGNOSING THE ALCOHOLIC MAN

In the United States the foundational books and articles about alcoholism were published between 1935 and 1945. In 1940 E. M. Jellinek and other members of the Yale Center began publishing the *Quarterly Journal of Studies on Alcohol*, the first scholarly journal in the field since the demise of the *American Journal of Inebriety* in 1914. Three years later Jellinek organized the first annual Yale summer session on alcohol studies to inform interested citizens about current research. The lectures from the 1944 session, given by physiologists, social workers, ministers, economists, and other professionals, were reprinted in a book titled *Alcohol, Science, and Society*. Among the most important texts of the alcoholism movement, it sold over 50,000 copies and was reprinted four times between 1945 and 1952.[23]

Psychoanalysts, however, were the first twentieth-century writers to advance a medical interpretation of chronic drunkenness. An article by German psychiatrist Karl Abraham published in 1908 and translated into English in 1926 was the first instance in which "alcoholism" was used in scientific literature to refer not simply to the physical effects of drinking but to habitual drinking behavior itself. Abraham and other psychoanalysts sought a term free of the moralistic or pre-Freudian connotations of "drunkenness," "inebriety," or "dipsomania." By 1915 a few American psychiatrists had used the term "alcoholism," but it did not appear in lay publications until the 1930s. The word "alcoholic" first appeared in the *New York Times* in September 1943. Not until 1966 did an English-language dictionary reflect the shift in the meaning originated by Karl Abraham, when Webster's *Third New International Dictionary* defined "alcoholism" as "continuous and usually excessive use of alcoholic drinks; usually addiction."[24]

These linguistic developments reflected larger shifts in cultural meaning as the term "alcoholism" gained currency in a greater range of professional and popular writings. Because so many individuals and institutions disseminated new knowledge about alcoholism, the paradigm itself was inherently complex, and it was flexible enough to accommodate the agendas of various and sometimes conflicting groups. Psychiatrists, trained as they were to emphasize mental processes and disorders, brought very different ideas to bear on the problem than, say, physiologists. Public educators, clergymen, and social workers, not to mention members of Alcoholics Anonymous, were motivated by an even greater range of concerns. The engendering of alcoholism was a complex and sometimes contested process, reflecting the cross-fertilization of many disciplines. Yet despite such differences, individuals with a vested interest in alcoholism shared a number of common assumptions that lent the paradigm a certain coherence.

By the mid-twentieth century the meaning of "alcoholism" embodied the impact of psychoanalytic theory. Though the popular influence of psychological experts (and psychoanalysis in particular) reached a peak after World War II, from 1920 to 1940 increasing numbers of U.S. physicians pursued psychoanalytic training. These therapists believed that many maladies originated in patterns of psychosexual development and family relationships in early childhood. At first most psychoanalysts worked one-on-one with an educated, well-to-do clientele. Soon, however, they began to reshape public institutions, including schools, child guidance centers, and mental hygiene clinics. Believing that psychiatry and psychology would replace religion as the foundation of social order, they aimed to prevent mental illness in childhood, "creating through scientific child-rearing a personality adjusted to the demands of modern social life." For adults with mental disorders, the goal was to discover underlying causes of neuroses. Supported by an expanding clientele, the profession of psychiatry grew steadily, even during the Depression.[25]

At first many psychiatrists were reluctant to accept chronic drunkards as patients, for such individuals were notoriously resistant to their mode of therapy.[26] But during the late 1930s several psychiatrists gained recognition for their study of alcoholism, including Karl Menninger, director of the Menninger clinic in Topeka, Kansas, and Edward A. Strecker, a professor at the University of Pennsylvania who served as president of the American Psychiatric Association. In 1938 Menninger published *Man against Himself*, a widely read book focusing on suicide and self-destructive behavior. He devoted a chapter to "alcohol addiction," depicted as a form of "chronic suicide" in which a person was "impelled to ruin himself by self-poisoning." Menninger argued that alcohol addiction should be "thought of not as a disease, but as a suicidal *flight from* disease, a disastrous attempt at the self-cure of an unseen inner conflict, aggravated but not primarily caused . . . by external conflict."[27] That same year Strecker coauthored a book titled *Alcohol: One Man's Meat*. With former alcoholic and lay therapist Francis Chambers, Strecker argued that the sources of habitual drinking "often reach back into childhood, and, in general, have to do with defective early training and environment."[28] Both psychiatrists characterized compulsive drinking as a manifestation of inner emotional illness, a neurosis rooted deep in an individual's psyche.

Psychoanalysts also believed that alcoholics drank to escape from the confusion and pain of daily life. As Menninger argued, alcohol addicts sought "relief from deep, inner feelings of anxiety [and] insecurity." Another analyst explained that the typical alcoholic was "sick, vastly insecure and threatened from within." As a psychiatric concept, anxiety connoted a feeling of intense fear or dread, often lacking a specific cause or threat. Even lay experts—sober alcoholics who penned popular books on the subject—defined anxiety in essentially psychiatric terms. One such writer claimed that "the alcoholic suffers from fears of insecurity, suspense and impending danger; he suffers from a continual and exaggerated anxiety, constantly expecting some adverse thing to happen but not knowing what. . . . Anxiety is ever within him—unless he dissolves it in alcohol." Drinking offered a way to suppress tumultuous feelings of self-doubt. Strecker, in particular, emphasized the theme of escape. For him the main difference between the "normal, controlled social drinker" and the alcoholic lay in the latter's attempt to flee from an intolerable existence. While the moderate drinker drank to "minimize some of the irritations, smooth off some of the rough edges, and temporarily ease some of the burdens" of life, the alcoholic "cannot or will not face life, . . . and finds in alcohol a source of unreality and dangerous make-believe."[29]

During the 1940s the anxiety theory of drinking motivation began to acquire the status of common sense. Social science in particular reflected the popularization of anxiety theory. Sociologist Selden Bacon focused on the function of alcohol in "complex society." In his view modern society was characterized by social stratification, economic competitiveness, and personal alienation, factors that exacerbated anxiety. For Bacon the primary value of alcohol rested in its "socially integrating function," its ability to depress "inhibitions, anxieties, aggressions and tensions." Health administrator Joseph Hirsh offered a similar explanation for alcoholism: "The modern world is a world of acute tensions and violence, and it is from this kind of world that sick people come." Anthropologist Donald Horton agreed. But whereas Bacon differentiated between "complex" and "primitive" societies with respect to drinking, Horton argued that drinking to relieve anxiety was universal (even if the sources of that anxiety varied from culture to culture). As he wrote, "Alcohol appears to have the very important function throughout the world, in all kinds and levels of human social activity, of reducing the inevitable anxieties of human life."[30]

Such remarks about the angst-ridden state of modern society should not surprise readers familiar with recent scholarship in U.S. history. Indeed, it has become almost a cliché to assert that the 1940s and 1950s were a time of anxiety and self-absorption in American life. People living in the postwar era talked self-consciously about living in an "age of anxiety." It is ironic that after conquering the Depression at home and totalitarianism overseas—just as the nation seemed to be achieving its grandest economic and political goals—many Americans felt stifled by fear and disappointment. Underneath a cultural veneer promising material success and international supremacy lay thick layers of profound insecurity about the stability of U.S. democracy, the safety of the nation's cities, the vitality of intellectual life, and not least, the state of citizens' mental health. In many respects the 1940s were an "age of doubt," an era "colored by the atomic bomb and international communism, by rampant commercialism and materialism, and by a fragmentation of social and cultural life so severe that it seemed to deny people coherent personalities and stable existences." Alcoholism, then, was but one manifestation of the nation's troubled and rootless psyche.[31]

Intellectuals did not always agree on the sources of this anxiety. For psychiatrists anxiety was rooted in the self and in the tangle of family relationships in which the self was mired. For social scientists it emanated from broader social and economic forces. But no matter where they located the origins of their malaise, Americans increasingly turned inward, toward their inner selves, to cope with their profound sense of dis-ease.[32] Even Donald Horton, the anthropologist who articulated a "social philosophy of alcoholism," turned to psychological experts when addressing the practical matter of how to solve the problem. While the fundamental causes of alcoholism lay in "social engineering," Horton wrote, it was "the task of the psychiatrist and social psychologist" to analyze and relieve the anxiety experienced by alcoholics. "The reduction of excessive anxiety may be tackled as a problem of individual therapy, and that is the standard way of doing it," he explained. Horton's comment speaks volumes about the growing influence of psychiatry, the inward turn toward the troubled self, and the individualized quest for well-being that preoccupied so many citizens at the time.[33]

But if all Americans suffered from anxiety, how did experts account for alcoholism in a specific and relatively small segment of the population? Why did some "vastly insecure" individuals become compulsive drinkers? What personality traits, if any, did alcoholics share? Most writers disputed the notion that all alcoholics shared a single personality type. One psychologist, for instance, concluded that "there is no unitary grouping of personality traits or attitudes which truly characterizes any considerable number of the individuals addicted to the use of alcohol." E. M. Jellinek and Howard Haggard asserted that there was no single "inebriate personality" but, rather, a variety of traits represented by habitual drinkers.[34]

Yet certain features appeared to be common among alcoholics. First, alcoholic men were loners, incapable of forging sound friendships or community ties. According to experts of various stripes, excessive drinking prevented meaningful social interaction with others; indeed, the tendency to drink alone was a telling sign that drinking had progressed to the alcoholic stage. Jellinek expressed this view as follows: "A drinking behavior which has always and everywhere been regarded as the gravest form of inebriety is 'solitary drinking' . . . [which] proves that the drinker is using the beverage for a purpose for which it is culturally not intended. . . . Sooner or later nearly every alcoholic becomes a solitary drinker."[35] Psychiatrist Edward Strecker claimed that "at least ninety percent of all abnormal drinkers are predominantly of the introverted type." Yale sociologist Selden Bacon sketched a portrait of the alcoholic as an "unsocial dreamer," a far cry from someone who used liquor felicitously as a social lubricant. Whereas normal drinking facilitated sociability, pathological drinking was by definition antisocial. In drawing the line between moderation and alcoholism, experts emphasized the lonely descent of the alcoholic who drank his way "down the ladder in the social scheme of things." "Whether they are drinking with a friend, with 100 acquaintances, or alone, makes no difference," Bacon wrote. "There is no social purpose here; there is the complete opposite—individual in purpose, asocial in motive and antisocial in result."[36]

In defining alcoholism as a solitary perversion of normal drinking habits, experts implicitly condoned the use of alcohol in social situations. Certainly experts knew that it was not always easy to differentiate between moderate and problem drinkers. As a number of alcoholic men in the advertising business attested, a fine line divided executives who could handle their liquor and those whose three-martini lunches culminated in ever-worsening bouts of intoxication. But if antisocial behavior marked the alcoholic, then manly conviviality might help men maintain their status as healthy (or at least nonalcoholic) drinkers.

Though alcoholism experts themselves did not discuss drinking in terms of gift exchange, it is instructive to apply cultural theories of the gift to their formulations. As discussed in Chapter 1, prohibitionists' relentless attack on the saloon was, in large part, an attack on the culture of treating in which men used alcohol to forge social bonds among themselves (at the perceived expense of their families). But in contrast to temperance reformers, alcoholism experts did not attack the role of liquor in mediating social interactions among men. While the prohibitionists viewed drinking as a shameful waste of men's time and money, midcentury experts generally condoned social drinking as a tolerable use of resources, both emotional and material. By defining the solitary drinker as a pathological drinker, experts implied that drinks consumed within a culture of sociability were more acceptable than drinks consumed alone. For the alcoholic, liquor no longer functioned as a liquid binder of relationship; it was a perverse form of self-medication, an ill-advised tonic for psychic alienation. In his brooding isolation the modern alcoholic bore no resemblance to the gregarious saloon-goer of *John Barleycorn*, for whom rituals of reciprocity and camaraderie justified one's own self-indulgence. The alcoholic drank for the sheer effect of drinking. Unlike social drinkers in either mixed or same-sex company, the alcoholic's drinking was a kind of "therapeutic self-gift," a "*self*-indulgence to remedy negative behavioral or psychological states."[37]

So the question remained: what psychological states drove men to consume beyond the point where neither business etiquette nor neighborhood leisure finessed their self-gratification through drink? One factor, experts agreed, was immaturity. As Strecker explained, the alcoholic's flight from reality was a flight from adult responsibility, an "infantile form of regression" back to a "childlike state of mind." In his "careful study of the life histories" of alcoholics he found a "very frequent recurrence of a childhood environment which thwarted, and even blocked . . . the attainment of an adult emotional stature." Other writers agreed that "juvenile egocentricity" was a common trait and that alcoholics went on drinking sprees in the "same spirit as an undisciplined child goes into a tantrum." While he shunned psychoanalytic terminology, Selden Bacon classified alcoholics into three types: the unsocial dreamer, the aggressive individualist, and the immature man. Indeed, the last type could not properly be classified as a man at all, for he was really a "little boy masquerading as a man."[38]

As this last quotation especially suggests, immaturity was one way of signifying the alcoholic's failure to achieve a healthy masculine sex-role identity. For psychoanalysts steeped in Freudian theory, immaturity was not just an unwelcome personality trait; it was an emotional pathology, a "psychoneurotic predisposition." According to Strecker most neuroses stemmed from an "unfavorable home life," which, in turn, usually involved "parental over-indulgence" or "over-dominance." Such circumstances explained immaturity in men: a boy raised by overprotective or domineering parents was denied the chance to develop self-reliance and independence. Coddled or controlled by suffocating parents, such boys never learned to embrace the responsibilities required of mature men.[39] The diagnosis of immaturity represented one of several ways in which alcoholism was figured as a sign of compromised masculinity. The alcoholic was not a true man because at heart he was still a boy.

Furthermore, the same childhood patterns that bred immaturity were seen to engender effeminacy in boys. During the 1940s and 1950s a range of experts—including educators, doctors, journalists, and psychiatrists— argued that gender-appropriate behavior was not biologically determined; rather, it needed to be learned, just like a role in a high school play. Guided by the assumptions of functionalist sociology and psychoanalysis alike, experts promoted child care that would produce children with "correct" sex-role characteristics. One parenting manual summarized sex-role theory with the simple question and answer: "What kind of parents are best for children? Manly men and womanly women." Two parental role models, one masculine and one feminine, were required to instill healthy sex-role identification in children. But things did not always progress so smoothly. Boys could develop an identity crisis resulting from an abnormal attachment with the female/mother figure. The path to maturity required that a boy identify with a strong, masculine father figure, but in the presence of an overbearing mother the normal process of gender identification could go drastically awry. Such boys, according to one psychiatrist, "developed a feminine identification, a dynamic factor of determined force in leading to a feminine approach to life in these unfortunate individuals."[40]

Many writers, not just psychiatrists, lamented a full-blown crisis of masculinity in the 1940s. The most damned offenders in this affair were American mothers and wives, who received their most scornful indictment in Philip Wylie's best-selling *Generation of Vipers*, published in 1942. Wylie was infamous for his scathing attack on "Momism," which accused women of dominating their sons and husbands through their narcissistic, parasitic natures. According to Wylie, women sapped men of their masculinity in order to usurp power for themselves. The typical "Mom" craved all of her son's attention and love for herself—so much so that she smothered any chance of his developing a strong identity of his own. "Megaloid momworship has got completely out of hand," Wylie fumed. "Our land, subjectively mapped, would have more silver cords and apron strings crisscrossing it than railroads and telephone wires. Mom is everywhere and everything and damned near everybody. . . . Men live for her and die for her, dote upon her and whisper her name as they pass away." Behind this hatred and fear of women was a growing sense that men had somehow lost power. At the heart of Wylie's vituperation, historian Wini Breines has noted, lay "the unappealing image of a new feminized man who had lost his traditional manhood, a de-masculinized husband and father unable to hold his own in the face of restless and demanding women."[41]

While psychiatrists claimed to avoid the sensationalized rhetoric of Wylie's prose, the popular phenomenon of Momism influenced experts' research on alcoholism. Consider, for example, *Hope and Help for the Alcoholic*, a book written for a lay audience by psychiatrist Harold W. Lovell. As Lovell explained, most alcoholic men experienced intense "gender frustration." Because of their "silver-cord attachment" to their mothers, such men were "less aggressive, more feminine than they should be." The physical effects of alcoholism further accentuated men's effeminacy, causing "testicular atrophy," a "loss of body hair," and other bodily changes.[42] A decade earlier Wylie, too, had bemoaned the appearance of feminized men, with their high voices, fleshy breasts, and receding chins. The echoes of Wylie's prose in Lovell's account are unmistakable.

Yet the strongest link between Momism and alcoholism can be found in the work of Edward Strecker. If Strecker's 1938 book on alcoholism revealed the author's concern about parental overindulgence, his role as a military consultant during World War II further convinced him that women were turning the nation's men into a mass of "psychoneurotics." In 1946 Strecker published *Their Mothers' Sons*, a study based on thousands of war veterans discharged for combat fatigue and mental disorders. In essence the volume was a book-length version of Wylie's chapter on Momism, but it bore the imprimatur of scientific authority. Strecker even acknowledged his rhetorical debt to Wylie in his use of the word "Mom," which signified a "woman who has failed in the elementary mother function of weaning her offspring emotionally as well as physically." While Strecker stated that "Mr. Wylie's mom is described in too vindictive terms to satisfy a trained psychiatrist," his own book was hardly lacking in scornful criticism and hyperbole. Most of the book outlined the average Mom's modus operandi: her manipulative wiles and her self-serving martyrdom. The last section, titled "Are You A Mom?" featured a true-or-false diagnostic quiz to help readers recognize their own "momistic tendencies." Moreover, Strecker retained his interest in alcoholism and devoted a chapter to the subject. There he argued that alcoholics used liquor as a "mom surrogate," a dangerous substitute for mother's mollycoddling. "Alcohol is a mom that can be poured into a glass," he proclaimed. "To the heavy drinker, it provides all the protection, all the escape from life's hard knocks, and all the synthetic feeling of well-being that mom provides."[43] The mania over Momism dovetailed with psychiatrists' diagnosis of male alcoholics—so much so that they viewed alcoholism primarily as a flight from adult masculinity.

Most perplexing about this view, however, is its inversion of the cultural logic that figured heavy drinking as a sine qua non of manhood. Given the traditional view of drinking as a masculine affair—a view that held sway through the 1940s and beyond—how did experts envision excessive consumption as a sign of effeminacy? Here psychoanalysis played a major role. Armed with theories of unconscious motivation, analysts argued that alcoholics drank to compensate for effeminacy and the nagging insecurity it caused. Robert P. Knight of the Menninger clinic in Kansas explained that many young men felt torn between "passive, childish, feminine wishes" and the desire to conform to masculine norms. Drinking, he argued, allowed them to gratify "passive oral wishes" while adhering to the "distorted standards of masculinity of late adolescence." In other words, it provided "the illusion of being masculine through . . . trying to be a hard-drinking he-man who can 'hell around' with the boys." Raymond McCarthy, director of the Yale Plan alcoholism clinic, agreed, noting that "there is an ancient bit of folklore which suggests that a high capacity for liquor is a sign of masculinity. Some drinkers . . . attempt to prove their masculinity by drinking to capacity and beyond." Yet as psychiatrists pointed out, seeking "assertiveness and manliness" from the bottle was a futile way to resolve gender-role confusion.[44] Ironically, the alcoholic's attempt to "drink like a man" ultimately exposed the original neurosis that prompted it. If consumed to excess, booze exacerbated the gender insecurities men sought to overcome by drinking in the first place.

Psychiatrists' scrutiny of sex-role "failure" extended further into sexual matters. Indeed, the medical discourse is filled with remarks about the inability of alcoholic men to engage in normal heterosexual relations. The focus on the alcoholic's sexuality was part of a larger cultural development from the 1930s through the 1950s: the consolidation of a dominant sexual order based on a rigid binarism between homosexuality and heterosexuality. As numerous historians have argued, the homosexual/heterosexual binary, often taken for granted as a boundary between natural categories of behavior and identity, is in fact a social construction. Only in the early twentieth century did the concepts of heterosexuality and homosexuality emerge as "master categories of a sexual regime that defined the individual's sexual and personal identity and normatively regulated intimate desire and behavior."[45]

In his splendid history of New York's "gay male world" from 1890 to 1940, George Chauncey demonstrates that heterosexuality was *not* "a precondition of gender normativity in early twentieth-century working-class culture." As discussed earlier, the rough bachelor subculture of the 1910s was "based on a shared code of manliness and an ethic of male solidarity" symbolized by the customs of saloon conviviality, including treating. Through rituals of male solidarity and competition—rituals evoked so vividly in *John Barleycorn*—men "performed" and proved their manliness for one another, but their intense homosocial bonds, and even same-sex sexual encounters, did not call their masculinity into question. By midcentury, however, men "increasingly believed that their virility depended on their exclusive sexual interest in women," and they defined their identities as normal men by renouncing "any sentiments or behavior that might be marked as homosexual." The establishment of heterosexuality as a precondition of normal masculinity was reinforced by Freudian theory, in which successful psychosexual development centered on one's "object choice" in fulfilling the sexual libido. For Freudians this required an attachment to a member of the opposite sex; homosexual attraction signified arrested development. As psychoanalysis gained influence, Chauncey explains, "the homosexual man, defined solely by his capacity to find sexual satisfaction with another man, began to emerge as a distinct figure in medical discourse." By midcentury the terms "homosexual" and "heterosexual" circulated freely in popular discourses, and they became part of a system of normalizing, moralizing judgments about men (and women) of all classes.[46]

By the 1940s, therapists no longer equated heavy, habitual drinking with masculine virility and sexual prowess. In contrast, before the rise of Freudian theory, American psychiatrists were far less condemnatory of drunkenness and far less apt to interpret alcoholism in terms of sexual pathology. According to Elizabeth Lunbeck, early-twentieth-century experts maintained an abiding respect for saloon culture and the male prerogatives it endorsed. In the 1910s "psychiatrists realized that a touch of dissipation might figure among the qualities that made a man's reputation" *as* a man. These doctors, Lunbeck argues, were torn between the competing pulls of respectable and dissolute masculinity. Alarmed by the drunkard's extreme behavior and his flight from domestic responsibility, they nonetheless sympathized with his assertion of a vital, "glorious manhood unfettered by the nagging demands of women."[47] But by the 1940s the pathologization of both alcoholism and homosexuality had altered doctors' views of excessive homosocial drinking. Unlike earlier observers of manly saloon rituals, midcentury psychoanalysts were likely to find a latent homosexual hidden behind the facade of the "hard-drinking he-man." Again the words of Kansas psychiatrist Robert Knight are illuminating. Describing an alcoholic patient, Knight wrote, "He showed the typical behavior of alcoholics toward men friends in drinking and getting tenderly affectionate with them, swearing eternal friendship, becoming lovingly demonstrative toward them, thus acting out a strong and thinly disguised homosexual attraction."[48] What formerly signified rugged, normal masculinity—even to middle-class psychiatrists—was now interpreted as sexual pathology. Experts had put a new, psychoanalytical spin on Jack London's intimations of the romance of treating.

In study after study the specter of Momism and feminine identification hung over the diagnosis of homosexuality. According to psychiatrist Harold Lovell, excessive drinking caused men to regress or "step backward from the normal heterosexuality." Claiming that "there is a greater proportion of overt homosexuality among [alcoholics] than in the population as a whole," Lovell solidified the link between alcoholism and "abnormal" sexuality. Citing Karl Abraham's seminal article on alcoholism, Yale psychologist Jacob Levine asserted that "the alcoholic has a basic homosexual problem." Of the sixty-three male alcoholics he studied, Levine found that nearly 75 percent had a "strongly dominant and overprotective mother and a relatively weak, distant or absent father." But although only two men "were known to be overt homosexuals," Levine interpreted the other men's indifference to intercourse as a mark of their "repressed drive for relations with a partner of the same sex." "With such strong feminine identification," he wrote, "the development of a passive homosexual male is understandable."[49]

According to Karl Menninger, alcoholics "have secretly a great fear of women and of heterosexuality in general, apparently regarding it as fraught with much danger." In his view drinking served as a "substitute for heterosexual object love," with the bottle serving as a misplaced object of erotic desire. Jacob Levine's study quoted alcoholic men themselves on the subject of sexual apathy: "Sex is a pretty minor matter with me because I can get along without having any sex whatsoever," one man reported. "I never was interested in sex or in running around with women," declared another. While Levine interpreted such statements in terms of repressed homosexuality, other psychiatrists disagreed that alcoholics were latent homosexuals. Strecker conceded that a drunken man "may exhibit maudlin affection for his drinking companions" but thought it was presumptuous to "read homosexuality into weepy declarations of undying friendship."[50] Instead Strecker described the sexual dysfunction of alcoholics as "latent heterosexuality." As he vaguely defined it, "latent heterosexuality is part and parcel of emotional immaturity and reveals itself as a kind of trifling with sex; an incomplete sex life, . . . an unwillingness, or an inability to put down the foundations . . . needed in order to support a completed and mature structure of sex and its implications."[51]

What did Strecker mean by a "mature structure of sex?" In his 1938 book on alcoholism he offered a slightly less abstract description of mature sex in terms of adult responsibility: "In the phantasy of alcohol," he wrote, "there is little place for children and the home-building instinct." Though Strecker did not explicitly equate normal heterosexual desire with a man's acceptance of nuclear familial roles, his assumptions are evident enough. In order to be seen as sexually mature, a man needed to channel his lust within marriage, to embrace the role of the dutiful husband, father, and family breadwinner. As Barbara Ehrenreich has shown, psychiatrists at this time commonly invoked the theme of maturity to put forth a "scientific justification for the male breadwinner role." When discussing alcoholism Strecker, like so many experts of his day, assumed that marriage and parenthood comprised the only normal lifestyle for an adult male. Whether they depicted alcoholic men as latent homosexuals or disturbed heterosexuals, experts viewed habitual drinking as an escape from the demands of true manhood and the husband/provider role it entailed.[52]

Indeed, the discord between alcoholism and men's marital roles was a common theme in the literature. Throughout most of the decade it was usual for Americans to view the typical alcoholic as a loner estranged from family as well as community ties. In part this was due to the specific population of alcoholic men studied by researchers in the late 1930s and early 1940s. At that time most writers focused on skid-row alcoholics, homeless men who lived on the margins of society. Arrested for disorderly conduct or admitted to mental hospitals, these alcoholics were unlikely to be married or living in stable family units. For example, a 1946 study of homeless alcoholics reported that 56 percent of its sample had never been married, and of those who had, virtually all were divorced, separated, or widowed.[53] These studies lent scientific weight to the stereotype that alcoholics as a group were "undersocialized, poorly integrated individuals, comprising homeless derelicts, chronic offenders, and the mentally ill."[54]

Sociologists did, however, begin to study the relationship between alcoholism and marriage, which Selden Bacon defined as inherently incompatible. After surveying 1,200 Connecticut men arrested for public drunkenness, Bacon found that only 23 percent were married and living with their wives, compared with 72 percent of the "ordinary" adult male population. Alcoholic men were divorced twelve times as often and separated six times as often as nonalcoholic men. These figures did not surprise Bacon, nor were they likely to surprise most readers in 1945. The potentially devastating effect of liquor on marriage was hardly a new revelation. Bacon's interpretation, however, was innovative: alcoholism and marriage were incompatible not simply because drinking caused family disruption but because deep down, alcoholic men were not fit for the "intimate, reciprocating . . . and mature roles" entailed in married life. "The factors in personality leading to excessive drinking tend to preclude or debar marriage," Bacon claimed. From the start alcoholic men were "afraid of the close associational ties" of marriage. Those who did marry were doomed to failure because alcoholism enhanced "the very factors which are correlated with its onset," allowing "immaturity, . . . egoism, and self-pity even fuller play."[55]

The inability of alcoholics to perform the reciprocating and mature roles of marriage inhered in economic as well as interpersonal failure. Whether a skid-row bum or an affluent lush, the alcoholic man had a dubious reputation as a worker and wage earner. One clergyman speaking at the Yale Center on the subject of alcohol and pauperism in 1944 proclaimed that the "personality characteristics of the alcoholic will drive him to an unsound economic status fraught with peril both for his family and himself." Irregular in his work habits, the typical alcoholic moved "toward the status of the marginal employee more frequently than in the direction of advancement, promotion and further responsibility."[56] In a comparative study of alcoholics, former alcoholics, and nonalcoholic men, one psychologist found that the last category displayed the "greatest interest [in their vocation] as indicated by a successful career," while alcoholic men "showed little evidence of any personal life goal or ambition." The alcoholic man, in short, was a "bad financial risk"—to his employer and his family alike.[57]

Some experts elaborated on alcoholic men's inadequacy as family providers. Unlike advocates of Prohibition, the alcoholism movement did not view all drinking as an economic threat to all families or to society as a whole. Rather, the degree to which a man's drinking interfered with his breadwinning obligations helped experts differentiate between moderate and problem drinkers, a distinction that sometimes proved difficult to discern. Raymond McCarthy used an economic standard to distinguish between two categories of drinkers: "regular" and "alcoholic." The former drank frequently in social situations and even exhibited "occasional episodes of drunkenness." But while "his annual expenditure for alcohol may be a considerable item," it did not "jeopardize the economic welfare of his family or business." McCarthy's renowned colleague E. M. Jellinek concurred, defining the moderate drinker as one for whom "alcohol constitutes neither a necessity nor a considerable item in his budget." As he wrote, "Anybody who would spend money on alcoholic beverages in disproportion to his budget" would not qualify as a moderate drinker, "even if he were consuming very little."[58] Conversely, then, alcoholics could be recognized in part by the extent to which their drinking hindered family spending.

That experts incorporated economic standards into their definition of alcoholism is especially significant with respect to the gendering of the paradigm. While researchers disassociated themselves from dry rhetoric, they nonetheless shared ideas held by some prohibitionists, and the relationship between drinking and breadwinning could be quite subtle. Consider, for example, a comment by the Reverend A. J. Murphy following his "Alcohol and Pauperism" lecture at the Yale Summer School. During the question-and-answer session one female listener asked, "Isn't the moderate use of alcohol by a minimum wage earner a factor in bringing down the standard of living of the entire family?" While the clergyman had been quick to emphasize the "sad poverty" of alcoholic families, he was reluctant to impugn moderate drinkers in absolute terms. Rather, Murphy offered an "awfully cautious" response: every man's family should be assessed individually. "I think we'd have to know . . . whether the things that he has taken away from that family would be more conducive to its happiness than his drinking." Unlike temperance reformers, Murphy allowed men leeway to spend some of their money on drink. Yet he retained the assumption that a man's *primary* duty was to support his family. After repeal, experts granted men the right to drink, but not at the expense of a family's right to consume desired goods.[59] The ideology of male breadwinning thus continued to influence attitudes toward drinking and alcoholism.

The class biases inherent in these comments are also significant. In defining an excessive drinker in terms of the proportion of family income spent on drink, Jellinek gave affluent men more latitude than working-class men. According to his logic a wealthy man's alcoholism could not be measured by the relative deprivation of his wife and children, since his income was ample enough to cover all expenses. Likewise, in a society that condoned moderate drinking by any person who drank responsibly, working-class men were granted less of a right to enjoy alcohol simply because of their economic status. Neither Jellinek nor Murphy used financial matters as the *primary* diagnostic criteria for alcoholism; these remarks were made "off-the-cuff" during discussion sessions, and we should not exaggerate their importance. But their comments do reveal the extent to which scientific experts continued to assess men's drinking in terms of its social and economic effects on the family, in addition to physiological or psychological conditions.

In short, experts of the 1940s diagnosed the alcoholic man as a troubled, solitary, self-centered soul who drank to soothe or suppress anxiety, only to remove himself further from social and familial obligations. Despite the normalization of drink in post-repeal society, most Americans continued to view chronic or excessive drinking as detrimental to the benefits that restrained drinking was intended to promote: social enjoyment, professional status, and even family recreation. In scientific writings on alcoholism, experts incorporated shifting ideologies of masculinity to differentiate between normal and pathological drinkers, and their writings reveal both changes and continuities in dominant attitudes toward drinking.

Earlier in the twentieth century, psychiatrists and other social observers were concerned about inebriety, but many nonetheless countenanced saloon rituals of treating and conviviality. Like many men who frequented taverns in the decades before Prohibition, medical and psychological experts were torn between the competing lures of dissipated and respectable manhood. In the 1910s many of them viewed heavy drinking not as a sign of pathology but as a "ritual of masculine renewal" woven into the fabric of everyday life.[60] Prohibitionists, of course, tried vehemently to erase any such ambivalence. By equating the drinking customs of convivial manhood with sin and social dissolution, temperance crusaders enshrined the respectable breadwinner as the only acceptable masculine identity.

By midcentury the alcoholism movement had rejected the rhetoric of dry reformers, yet it continued to privilege the breadwinning ideal over the ethos of dissolute manhood. After repeal, alcoholism experts no longer condoned excessive drinking as a sign of fraternal sociability. To avoid the connotations of deviance and pathology inherent in the "alcoholic" label, a drinking man needed to demonstrate his sexual and economic commitment to women (and, by extension, his paternal commitment to children), preferably through marriage and parenthood. Moderate or social drinking was equated with normal, healthy, or mature masculinity. Business-oriented drinking could enhance manhood, not in the way that traditional saloon drinking did, but in its enhancement of career success, breadwinning, and thus domestic authority. Alcohol helped the social drinker straddle two ideals of manhood. While three-martini lunches allowed for manly social intercourse outside the home, they also bolstered men's dominance as family providers within it. Alcoholism, however, signified a man's *failure* to conform to prevailing norms. As an antisocial loner and a weak breadwinner, the alcoholic failed on both counts. The figure of the alcoholic man both reflected and exacerbated social concerns about men's conformity to gender norms. The construction of alcoholic identity became a primary means through which its creators expressed general anxieties about the inadequacies of American men.

But did the new model of alcoholic identity simply reflect the anxieties and biases of the professionals who created it? Was the alcoholism paradigm merely a manifestation of the increasing influence of Freudian thought among therapeutic experts themselves? To some extent it was. As members of the educated middle class—men whose reputations and livelihood depended on steady work and self-discipline as well as expertise—psychiatrists and sociologists could reassure themselves of their own normality by highlighting the social and psychological dysfunction of their alcoholic subjects. Though they recast the problem of drunkenness in a scientific rather than a moral idiom, they shared certain class-based values with dry reformers who preceded them. Qualities they ascribed to alcoholics—immaturity, egocentricity, and aggressiveness—were psychoanalytic labels to denote many of the cultural attributes of working-class manhood (which reformers had long interpreted as selfishness, brutishness, or immorality). While experts believed that alcoholism afflicted people of all classes, they rejected a model of excess that originated in working-class cultures of masculine fellowship. Perhaps by defining the alcoholic man as less manly than the moderate-drinking, responsible breadwinner, experts reaffirmed their own commitment to a domesticated, middle-class gendered order. Using scientific terms to reverse older assumptions about the virility of hard-drinking men, they reassured their patients, and perhaps themselves, that a sober commitment to marriage and breadwinning could enhance rather than inhibit one's manhood.

With respect to the popularization of the alcoholism model, however, many questions remain. Indeed, the above explanation for the gendered construction of alcoholism is as narrow as the social group of experts it addresses. Given the currents of gender anxiety that swirled around drinking problems in the 1940s, what broader social developments sparked those concerns in the first place, and why did the public at large begin to view alcoholism as a manifestation of gender crisis? How and why did alcoholism come to be perceived as a major social problem, not simply a medical diagnosis for a small segment of the population?

During the latter half of the 1940s the message of the alcoholism movement made its way from scholarly publications to popular culture, as magazines such as *Time*, *Newsweek*, and *Woman's Home Companion* depicted habitual drunkenness in terms of a medical model. Some articles appeared in the early years of the decade (a total of six in 1940 and seven in 1944), but the numbers multiplied in the years immediately following the end of World War II. Fifteen articles appeared in mass-circulation magazines in 1945, while the years 1946 to 1949 averaged twenty-five per year. The greatest number of articles, twenty-eight, occurred in 1949; that figure was not surpassed in any year from 1950 to 1970.[61] As one writer observed, the public's interest in alcoholism "renewed full-steam operation the year following V-E Day, the year that boasted an expenditure of $9,500,000,000 for alcoholic beverages, and . . . saw more ballyhoo for and against alcohol, more newspaper and magazine articles, books and films, than the previous ten years added together."[62] In part the abundance of articles in the later 1940s stemmed from effective public relations efforts by researchers and educators, especially Marty Mann. But rather than viewing these figures simply as evidence of the growing influence of the alcoholism movement, we might focus directly on the immediate postwar years and ask, What social conditions rendered Americans more responsive to a medicalized conception of problem drinking?

Most magazine articles summarized recent scientific research, while others offered "enlightening" stories of alcoholics' experiences. But arguably the most influential popular narratives about problem drinkers were Hollywood films. While the *Thin Man* films of the 1930s celebrated the nation's liberation from Prohibition, several motion pictures in the early postwar period registered concern about the negative effects of *overin*dulgence. In particular, two commercially successful films of the 1940s, *The Lost Weekend* and *The Best Years of Our Lives*, incorporated the emerging therapeutic language of alcoholism into cinematic dramas for a mass audience.

PROBLEM DRINKERS AND RETURNING VETERANS
IN POSTWAR POPULAR CULTURE

Drinking and drunkenness have been features of the American cinema since the early 1900s, but it was in 1945 that the first canonical "alcoholism film" was released: *The Lost Weekend*, which jolted movie audiences with its grim, heavy-handed depiction of a would-be novelist's besotted life. Based on Charles Jackson's best-selling novel of the same name, *The Lost Weekend* was the first U.S. film to depict its protagonist *as* an alcoholic, and it was the first to embody the essential tenets of the medical model. Winner of four Oscars, including those for best picture, best screenplay, best actor (Ray Milland), and best director (Billy Wilder), it was praised by critics as an "important," "courageous," and "shatteringly realistic and morbidly fascinating film," an "illustration of a drunkard's misery that ranks with the best and most disturbing character studies ever put on the screen."[63] Incorporating the fundamental ideas of the disease concept, the film played a major role in transforming public attitudes toward alcoholism.

The Lost Weekend tells the story of Don Birnam, a well-educated, well-bred, frustrated writer whose career has been stalled by an uncontrollable addiction to alcohol. The film begins as Don is packing for a weekend trip with his older brother, Wick, on whom he is financially dependent. Don has been sober for ten days, yet he dreads the prospect of spending the weekend without any access to drink. So instead of meeting Wick at the train, Don embarks on a five-day "bender" and drowns his profound self-doubts in a "lake of alcohol." Left with no money to fund his desperate pursuit of liquor, he pockets some cash intended for a cleaning lady, sells his typewriter, and ransacks his own apartment in search of hidden bottles. He even steals a stranger's purse at a nightclub, not to pay his tab so much as to see if he can get away with it. After his petty theft is discovered, he is thrown out of the nightclub and eventually passes out in the vestibule of his apartment building. He ends up in the alcoholic ward of a New York City hospital and experiences a nightmarish episode of delirium tremens in the apartment of Helen St. James (Jane Wyman), his love-stricken, long-suffering girlfriend who has been searching for him. In the end Don pawns Helen's cherished fur coat to buy a gun to kill himself, but Helen quells his suicidal intentions and persuades him to resume the novel he has abandoned for so long. Until he renews his commitment to his craft and overcomes his craving for drink, Don reels from his solitary ride on an alcoholic merry-go-round.[64]

In many ways the character of Don Birnam matched the experts' profile of the alcoholic—so much so that novelist Malcolm Lowry (an alcoholic himself) called Jackson's novel a purely clinical study.[65] In his perceptive reading of the novel (which applies in most respects to the film version) literary scholar John W. Crowley argues that *The Lost Weekend* served didactically to inform the public about the disease concept "by disclosing the inside story from the perspective of the 'alcoholic' himself." Before writing the novel Jackson had sought treatment for his own drinking, and he was familiar with psychoanalytic texts. Both novel and film focus relentlessly on the interior dimensions of Don's troubled psyche; both "remain largely in the mind of the alcoholic," as another critic has observed. Comparing Jackson's story to earlier twentieth-century "drunk narratives"—including Hemingway's *The Sun Also Rises* and London's *John Barleycorn*—Crowley argues convincingly that *The Lost Weekend* "inverts the gender assumptions of those novels in which alcohol is represented as the preservative of manliness and the alcoholic as the polar opposite of the homosexual." Just as the film's exposure of Don's "quiet desperation" subverts the modernist glorification of drinking culture, so too does it call into question the mature masculinity of the alcoholic subject.[66]

Though in classic psychoanalytic fashion the novel links Don's alcoholism to his latent homosexuality, the film codes Don's sex-role failure primarily through his inability to succeed as a long-term romantic partner to Helen. His self-absorption and "love affair" with the bottle prevent any kind of meaningful or reciprocal relationship with Helen; despite his love for her, Don cannot stop drinking and make a commitment that would lead to marriage. There are no scenes of sexual involvement between them; rather, alcohol has become the perverted object of Don's misplaced sexual desires. (In one scene, after Don searches maniacally for a hidden bottle of whiskey, the eerie, discordant music grows muted as he gazes into his full glass with a look of sexual ecstasy.) For her part Helen, with the apt surname *St.* James, remains faithful to Don, committed to "fight and fight and fight" until he recovers. Although Don cannot support her or fulfill her emotional needs, Helen maintains compassion for him; she regards him, after all, as a sick person in need of help and sympathy. Helen's steadfast loyalty helps Don regain his resolve to write and thus plays a role in his recovery. Throughout the story Don is portrayed as a pathetic figure. His failure to fulfill the responsibilities of mature manhood is neither excused nor condemned; rather, it is treated as a manifestation of disease in need of therapeutic intervention.

Yet to understand fully the historical significance of the film, we need to probe beyond the narrative itself and ponder why it struck such a chord among viewers. As Selden Bacon later assessed the influence of *The Lost Weekend*, the story "made it possible for the first time for large numbers of Americans to identify with the alcoholic."[67] On the surface such a grim picture might have disgusted viewers. As one film reviewer remarked, "It took a lot of courage . . . to bring Jackson's terrifying case study of an alcoholic to an escapist-minded movie audience."[68] But one opinion poll found that 90 percent of viewers enjoyed the film "very much" or "moderately well." Certainly the revised hopeful ending contributed to its appeal; 88 percent of respondents disagreed with the notion that the film portrayed alcoholism as "hopeless and incurable."[69] But in addition to a positive finale the film offered viewers a character whose class background and family connections rendered him more familiar, and hence more appealing, than the stereotypical saloon regular or skid-row drunk. Don's education and literary talent, his relationship with his morally upstanding brother, and his underlying love for the genteel, beautiful Helen signified that he was a man worth caring about. If he could only stop drinking, he could make a contribution to the world around him. In this respect the film invited broad ranks of self-identifying middle-class and affluent viewers to sympathize, and perhaps empathize, with Don's situation.

By the mid-1940s the cultural and psychological need for such narratives among middle- and upper-class Americans was greater than it had ever been. Whereas dry reformers enshrined temperance as a fundamental bourgeois value in the nineteenth century, after repeal the dominant middle class no longer used abstinence as a primary marker of class affiliation. As noted previously, the per capita consumption of alcohol had increased steadily from 1933 to 1946; logically, more drinking in the middle- and upper-middle classes led to an increase in habitual drunkenness among members of those classes.[70] This increase in consumption resulted not only from a sea change in cultural values but also from a shift in the social composition of the middle class itself. With the rise of the professional-managerial class in the early twentieth century, aspiring young men looked increasingly to specialized training and education rather than ownership of small businesses to secure a promising role in an increasingly bureaucratic, corporate workplace. In college and the business world, middle-class men came into greater contact with members of the established elite, men who had long blended alcohol into their recreational lifestyle. As colleges and universities attracted a more diverse student body in terms of class and ethnic background, many men assimilated themselves into patterns of social interaction that varied from the traditions they had learned at home. Young men began to serve drinks when entertaining friends and colleagues, and they continued this practice long after college. Drinking was also more common in smaller towns and rural areas as well as cities.[71] These trends began before repeal, but they accelerated after it was enacted, enlarging the sphere of America's cocktail culture beyond the urban avant-garde.

When *The Lost Weekend* aired, many viewers identified literally with Don Birnam (or with his concerned friends and relatives) and thus could take heart in the film's therapeutic message. While the film depicted alcoholism as a depressing illness, it nonetheless conferred a measure of respectability on the afflicted. As Bruce Holley Johnson argues about the disease concept in general, Don Birnam's story suggested that "if well educated, industrious members of the upwardly-mobile middle class could succumb to the ravages of habitual drunkenness, then perhaps problem drinking was not merely a matter of weak willpower and moral degeneracy."[72] As we may recall, sociologist Herbert Bloch noted in 1949 that experts were according a "belated respectability" to alcoholism; his words reflected not only the process of medicalization but also a rise in the typical alcoholic's class status. Don Birnam's masculine failure was the failure of a genteel man frustrated by his art and confused in his relationships with well-meaning friends and family. Through his character we see that the medicalization of alcoholism entailed an effort to eliminate the moral stigma of excessive drinking as a low-class condition.

The film's ability to register concerns about alcoholism rates was augmented by its appearance in 1945, a year that also witnessed a swell of anxiety about the impending return of war veterans. As World War II drew to a close, many experts began to forecast an increase in problem drinking when millions of soldiers returned from battle. In 1944, for example, the *Louisville Times* quoted Alcoholics Anonymous founder Bill Wilson: "Wartime strain is causing a wave of alcoholism and may reach flood proportions when post-war dislocations come. . . . Changing from the horror of war back to routine civilian life will prove too much for some of our returning service men and they will become chronic drunks."[73] As psychiatrists turned their attention to the rehabilitation of "psychoneurotic war veterans"—like those on whom Strecker based *Their Mothers' Sons*—they, too, predicted that alcoholism rates would escalate. By 1948 doctors at veterans' hospitals noted that thousands of "drunken vets" were staggering into their facilities "demanding the cure."[74]

Indeed, despite federal and corporate pronouncements that soldiers would drink in moderation, many servicemen drank heavily while overseas and returned to the home front with such habits fully entrenched. According to one public health administrator, "Some soldiers reacted to the horror of war by mental and physical collapse . . . and some became problem drinkers. Yet totally divorced from the thunder of bombs and shells were the strains—the loneliness, the boredom, the frustrations—all common enough to civilian life, which weighed especially heavily on men in the real echelons of combat theatres and in isolated posts. . . . Liquor was often their only escape."[75] Historians have confirmed the tangible link between returning soldiers and alcoholism. In his social history of childhood during World War II, for example, William Tuttle Jr. noted that "alcoholism was rampant among returning fathers." Tuttle analyzed a score of personal letters that described a parent's divorce in the years 1945 to 1950. In over one-half of those letters the writer attributed the breakup to the chronic drinking of one or both parents.[76]

While on one level *The Lost Weekend* addresses the literal problem of chronic drinking in the aftermath of war, it can also be interpreted metaphorically as a comment on the more general problem of the nation's readjustment to a postwar social order. In a brief yet provocative reading of the film, William Graebner suggests that alcoholism was one of several subjects through which postwar popular culture "showcased the ongoing disintegration of the idea of progress in the American mind." As he argues, "*The Lost Weekend* uses the subject of alcoholism to explore the postwar concern with commitment and purpose. . . . What we have here in civilian garb is the familiar saga of the returning veteran (and, perhaps, of the nation)—glad to be home from the war but curiously lacking in resolve and direction." When Helen tells Don that "other people have stopped [drinking]," Don replies that they are "people with a purpose, with something to do." Although Don does have something to do (a novel to write), he has not yet found meaning in his work—and so he continues to drink.[77] After the urgent, invigorating demands of war, many GIs and civilians felt listless in the face of the more mundane challenges of peacetime. After the victory celebrations ceased, an emotional pall of cynicism and passivity enveloped the nation as Americans groped for new sources of significance in their lives. Interpreting Don Birnam symbolically as a returning veteran in civilian garb—and, in turn, construing the returning veteran as a surrogate for the nation at large—Graebner suggests another reason why mass audiences may have identified, metaphorically, with the protagonist's stupor.

In 1945, however, the "familiar saga of the returning veteran" was just beginning to seem familiar to American movie audiences. If *The Lost Weekend* indirectly expressed concern about the debility of the nation's former warriors, it was soon followed by less oblique "reintegration dramas," movies that dealt explicitly with the social and psychological problems faced by demobilized veterans. Foremost among this cinematic genre, measured by its instant popularity, critical acclaim, and vast earnings at the box office, was *The Best Years of Our Lives* (1946). Produced by Samuel Goldwyn and directed by William Wyler, the film garnered numerous Academy Awards and became the second-highest-grossing film in the history of talking motion pictures at the time (surpassed only by *Gone With the Wind* in 1939).[78]

Recently historians have begun to analyze the enormous cultural significance of *Best Years*, in particular the film's role as a "powerful agent for representing . . . and for instantly and cathartically resolving the anticipated problems that prompted so much expert and lay concern." Just as *The Lost Weekend* mirrored the scientific discourse on alcoholism, so, too, did "the narrative elements of [*Best Years*] closely follow the expert discourse of 'the veterans problem.'" Indeed, doctors' remarks on the postwar escalation of alcoholism formed but a small part of a larger public discourse on the "readjustment" of de-enlisted men. With 16 million war veterans poised to return to the United States, sociologists, psychiatrists, and other writers produced a large body of advice literature designed to ease men's difficult transition into civilian life. The film contributed to this didactic literature and served "as an emotional reference point for its audience of millions . . . living out their own demobilization dramas." The movie weaves together a tripartite story about three discharged men who return to their hometown of Boone City on a military airplane. "The flight sequence introduces us to each man and suggests the problems he is likely to face as a civilian. Each has the problem of putting the traumas and dislocations of war behind him, of finding his way back into his family, and of re-establishing a relationship to a wife or girlfriend." Each man, representing a different social stratum, experiences a painful reintegration into work and domestic life, and each character, with the aid of concerned family members, exemplifies a personal lesson about the pitfalls and promises of postwar readjustment.[79]

In the few scholarly interpretations of *Best Years* written thus far, historians and film critics tend to focus on the representation of the physically disabled veteran.[80] The film's most affecting character is Homer Parrish, a young sailor who has lost both forearms in a naval battle. Fitted with prosthetic metal hooks in place of his hands, Homer is played by actor Harold Russell, himself a bilateral hand amputee. In a compelling essay David

Gerber argues that the disturbing figure of the disabled veteran personifies a host of anxious projections about the potential disempowerment and demasculinization of *all* returning servicemen. Of the three main characters, Homer faces the most difficult struggle "to salvage his self-respect and to create a new masculinity to fill the void created by the trauma" of his war injuries. For the other men, Al Stephenson (Fredric March) and Fred Derry (Dana Andrews), these wounds are largely psychic. Upon their return home both Al, a middle-aged, well-paid banker, and Fred, a younger air force pilot raised in a working-class home, fear that their wives will no longer care for them. But the maimed Homer has the greatest reason to fear sexual rejection. In large part the film's power derives from the story of Homer and his girl-next-door fiancée, Wilma (Cathy O'Donnell), a woman whose compassion and maternal solicitude help Homer to achieve some semblance of dignity and domestic security by the end of the movie. The sailor's emotional rehabilitation, slow and painful as it is, culminates in marriage to Wilma; in the film's final scene their wedding vows send "a powerful message of hope and reconciliation."[81]

Despite the film's (relatively) happy ending in which all three men form or maintain a marriage with a conventionally "good" woman, the movie also expressed negative messages about the social dangers posed by bitter, disillusioned men.[82] Moreover, this threatening subtext gave voice to the vexed issue of problem drinking. Unlike *The Lost Weekend*, *The Best Years of Our Lives* cannot be characterized specifically as an alcoholism film, but it features several important scenes involving one or more characters drinking. As we shall see, all three men use alcohol to manage their turbulent reactions to homecoming; drinking scenes chart the stages of the men's reintegration into civilian life. Of the three men, Al, the affluent banker, most clearly embodies anxiety about alcohol abuse. His character, like Homer's, is complex, and it deserves more sustained attention than it has previously received.

Best Years handles the subject of excessive drinking quite differently from *The Lost Weekend*, but it is precisely because of these differences that it provides a unique window into the cultural history of alcoholism. *Best Years* does not wear the subject of alcoholism soberly on its sleeve. Rather, Wyler treats the matter tangentially and semicomically; at no point does the problem of drinking itself loom larger than the social and emotional situations that prompt it. *The Lost Weekend*, in contrast, focuses relentlessly on the fact of Don's illness, yet it remains relatively silent on the actual causes of his addiction. As circumscribed by the film's narrative,

Don's alcoholism stems from a neurosis that exists a priori. *Best Years*, however, suggests more concrete reasons for men's problem drinking. As Fred remarks in the first scene, they are "nervous out of the service." Through Al's character especially, the film connects drinking to specific social developments in gender relations and in the workplace. As a result the film allows us to see how U.S. popular culture incorporated therapeutic ideas about alcoholism in order to exemplify and interpret other pressing issues at the time.

The subject of drinking first emerges when the veterans disembark in Boone City. After landing at the airport the three men share a taxi, which arrives first at the single-family residence in which Homer was raised. As the taxi approaches the house, Homer nearly panics with anxiety. He dreads his parents' reaction to his artificial limbs, and he fears rejection by Wilma and her family. As the cab comes to a halt, Homer suggests that they all go to Butch's Place, a local bar, and "have a couple of drinks" before going home. Fred and Al reply that Homer already *is* home, and they decline his invitation. But Fred and Al are equally nervous about returning to their respective families. When Al returns to his wife, Milly (Myrna Loy), and their two teenaged children, he barely recognizes them or the domestic routine they have fallen into during the war years. For Fred, a former soda jerk, home is a modest dwelling inhabited by his father, his stepmother, and—he assumes—his wife, Marie (Virginia Mayo), whom he married only two weeks before he left for war. But as Fred soon discovers, Marie has taken a job and an apartment of her own; her absence signifies the emotional distance between them.

In these initial scenes of homecoming, each man feels uncomfortable and out of place. If they had stopped off at the bar beforehand, they could have delayed their uneasy reunions and extended for one last time the all-male camaraderie they had enjoyed overseas. From the outset, then, the film posits drinking as a potential escape from the difficult task of domestic reintegration—a temptation that, for a brief moment, the men resist.

But it is not long before the men reconvene at Butch's, the bar with an aptly masculine name. That first night, after Wilma's father pressures him to waste no time finding a job, Homer grows increasingly upset and departs for the comforting atmosphere of the tavern, which his uncle owns. Indeed, Homer enjoys drinking and carousing at the bar; his participation in male drinking culture signifies the darker underside of his character.[83] Homer revels in his drinking prowess. After recalling the days when his uncle Butch denied him liquor on account of his youth, Homer proudly proclaims, "It's different now! I'm a veteran. Give me a whiskey straight." The navy has trained Homer well in the use of his hooks, so he has no problem holding a shot glass or opening a bottle of beer. The camera zooms in and lingers for a moment on Homer's hooks as he performs these actions, as if to underscore the fact that his disability does not restrict his participation in bar rituals.

While Homer drinks at the counter, Fred arrives. He has tried to locate Marie at her apartment, but she is nowhere to be found. Meanwhile Al reacquaints himself with his own family, but he has difficulty coping in a sober state. "Is there such a thing as a drink in this house?" he inquires of Milly. Irritated by the small quantity of liquor in the cabinet, Al suggests to his wife and daughter Peggy (Teresa Wright) that they "go out on the town" together. After visiting several nightclubs and cabarets, they stop "for one last drink at Butch's," where Al is reunited with Fred and Homer. As the men regale themselves, Milly and Peggy look on in knowing amusement. Later Milly and Peggy drive a drunken Fred back to Marie's apartment; but she is still not home, so they take him back to their place. On the way Al and Fred pass out in the backseat, an incident that prompts clever jokes from the mother and daughter in front. "They make a lovely couple, don't they?" quips Milly. "I think they'll be very happy together," Peggy replies, peering fondly in the rearview mirror.

In the above scenes the bar signifies escape from the resumed pressures of family responsibility and marital intimacy. In a nod to the rise in public mixed-sex drinking, Milly and Peggy do join the men at Butch's. (In fact the bar is where Peggy and Fred first kindle their romantic interest in each other, a relationship that triumphs just as surely as Fred's earlier marriage to the selfish Marie disintegrates.) Yet the two women are positioned as onlookers who view the men's debauchery with amused detachment. Mother and daughter, after all, do not get drunk. Moreover, the public space of the bar is positioned in opposition to the domestic realm. By going to Butch's Place, all three men avoid the intimate encounters that presumably await them. On her husband's first night home, all Milly can do is put her intoxicated spouse to bed, like a mother tending a small child. Peggy does the same for her new friend Fred.

Through Milly's and Peggy's lighthearted, good-natured response to the men's drinking, Wyler defuses the most disturbing implications of their intoxication. The jokes about the happy couple in the backseat dismiss any serious Freudian speculation that the men's drinking manifests a deep-rooted fear of heterosexuality or a latent homosexuality.

Rather, the women understand the men's sexual apprehension as a temporary problem that can be overcome through their own ministrations of tender loving care. It is as if the female characters have internalized the psychoanalytic view of drinking as a compensation for masculine insecurity. Milly and Peggy instinctively know that Fred and Al are fragile—that they need time to "get back to normal"—and the women are willing to help them reclaim the obligations and privileges of manhood.

Indeed, the need for women to facilitate the emotional adjustment of men was one of the film's central didactic messages. As Gerber argues, Milly, Peggy, and Wilma prove themselves "capable of devoting themselves to healing the wounds of war." All three women possess "the full repertory of emotions and beliefs that the experts deemed necessary to the reestablishment of the domesticity and the dominance of the recently demobilized men."[84] More generally, during the immediate postwar period women's behavior was seen as the linchpin of men's successful readjustment. Prescriptive literature enlisted women to bolster men's morale and urged families "to do more adjusting to the veteran than the veteran to the family." As the wives and girlfriends in *Best Years* smoothed the path of men's reintegration, they exemplified "the larger trend in popular psychology and sociology . . . which saw women as the causes and/or potential redeemers of a deteriorating society."[85]

Wyler's treatment of the men's homecoming thus dramatized a common theme in postwar mass culture: women should proceed delicately if they hoped to lure men back into domestic routine. In depicting Milly as a good sport about Al's drinking spree, the film recommended that women show patience toward such initial bouts of manly irresponsibility. If Milly had berated Al for drinking too much, the film implied, she would have given him one more reason to seek solace in the bottle. In Homer's case Wilma's compassion helps him overcome his helplessness and loss of manhood. At the end of the film the more aggressive, violent side of Homer's character is overshadowed by a tender passivity (which, for him, is tied to his disability).[86] Although Wyler does arouse concern about Homer's drinking—at one point Butch tells his nephew "to stay away" from the bar for awhile—by the end, alcohol no longer threatens his commitment to domestic culture. In the final wedding scene Wyler underscores the message of Homer's domestication. Before the ceremony Al imbibes freely of the champagne punch and asks Homer and Fred to drink with him. Tellingly, Fred and Homer refuse. Fred simply does not wish to drink, while Homer replies that he needs his full concentration to place Wilma's wedding band on her finger. At the wedding Fred also seals his happy fate with Peggy, and they, too, pledge to marry. Fred's and Homer's refusal to drink at the wedding symbolizes their decision to renounce dissolute manhood. Bolstered by the care of nurturing women, they commit themselves instead to domestic responsibility, with all of the risks that commitment entails.

Al, however, is another matter. Despite his promotion at the bank, his wife's easygoing charm, and his wealth and prestige, Al has trouble accepting his postwar fate. It is significant that drinking marks his continuing restlessness. After the initial encounter at Butch's, two more incidents depict Al as a problem drinker. One occurs in the wedding scene, in which Al continues to drink even after his friends abstain: "If I have to be a solitary drinker," so be it, Al replies, as he downs another glass of punch. Watching her husband refill his glass, Milly gently chides him: "Al, you promised you wouldn't." While Al is not the focus of the film's last scene, his drinking nonetheless reminds viewers of the movie's more ominous subtext. Al's admission that he may cross the line into solitary drinking, coupled with Milly's growing concern, suggest that he is beginning to abuse alcohol, not unlike *The Lost Weekend's* Don Birnam. As in scientific writings, the antisocial nature of Al's and Don's drinking marks it as even more threatening than Fred's and Homer's fraternal carousing.

The other problem drinking scene occurs at a Union Club banquet given by the owners of Al's bank. As husband and wife dress for dinner, Milly reminds Al that he will be asked to give an acceptance speech; on account of his war service, he is the evening's guest of honor. "I plan to handle that situation by getting well plastered," replies Al as he makes his way to the replenished cocktail cabinet. Before leaving, Al even consumes one of the mixed drinks Peggy has prepared for her own date. At the club he continues to drink, prompting Milly to track his consumption with tally marks on the tablecloth. After dinner the bank president praises Al as a man who "valiantly fought for the freedom" of his country, that "citadel of individual initiative, the land of unlimited opportunity for all." By this time Al is indeed plastered. He slurs his words, loses his train of thought, and vacillates between professing his devotion to the "Cornbelt Loan and Trust Company" and criticizing the bank's loan policies. But once again Wyler avoids a grim drinking scene. Despite Al's intoxication, the guests applaud his speech, and Milly gazes at Al with doe-eyed admiration.

Why is Al so uncomfortable being honored by his bank? By the time the banquet occurs, it has become clear that Al feels constrained, and even compromised, in his job. After Al hears of his job promotion to vice-president of small loans, he cynically remarks to Milly, "I've got to make money. Last year it was kill Japs, now it's make money. . . . They want me back for a nice fat job at the nice fat bank." Although he is well paid, Al dislikes his job. He disagrees with the bank's strict loan policies toward veterans, and he raises eyebrows when he approves a loan for a kind farmer who lacks collateral. Ironically, while the bank president proclaims the United States a "citadel of individual initiative," Al cannot exercise his own moral judgment when administering loans. To keep his "nice fat job," he must be obsequious to a boss and an institution he does not respect. Al's dissatisfaction is conveyed in subtle, indirect ways, through sarcastic comments and facial expressions and gestures that actor Fredric March employs to convey a feeling of angst and dis-ease. Through Al's character *Best Years* criticizes the callousness and hypocrisy of large corporations such as banks. Yet the film does not offer Al a way out of his bureaucratic job. Al may feel disempowered in his soulless career, but he maintains a charade of corporate loyalty. In the process, though, his psychic wounds fester.[87]

Al's drinking helps convey the message that the postwar workplace is full of pitfalls for men. Even the best jobs could prove dissatisfying and ultimately emasculating for the nation's men. Fred, too, faces hardship in the workplace. Uneducated and lacking skills applicable to civilian life, the former air force pilot resorts to selling perfume at a drugstore (and to being humiliated by the effeminate store manager in front of his female customers). Determined to find a more credible and more manly job, Fred eventually labors as a construction worker building prefabricated houses to shelter war veterans and their newly formed families. Between Al, Fred, and Homer, *Best Years* offered viewers a range of employment scenarios and class affiliations with which to identify. But in all cases, as Gerber notes, the film focused "not on the workings of public social processes and institutions but on individuals who are embedded in private dramas of blocked ambition."[88] By the final scene Fred and Homer not only acquiesce to a life of private stability; they also learn to accept the kinds of work available to them in the peacetime economy. (Homer's options, of course, are even more limited due to his war injury, but the film makes clear that he will receive federal disability compensation.) But Al, the only member of the managerial upper-middle class, must pay an emotional toll for maintaining his social status.

Certainly the businessman's narrative of disillusionment was not new to American culture in the mid-1940s. Sinclair Lewis's chronicle of George Babbitt had exposed the emotional pitfalls of the conformity of salaried men to the commercial breadwinning ethos in the early 1920s. Moreover, both *Babbitt* and *Best Years* harbored implicit critiques of what historian William Leach has called "the brokering style." The rise of consumer culture resulted in an expansion of sales, banking, trading, real estate, and advertising, fields in which competitive brokers are required to repress personal convictions and withhold judgment in the interest of forging profitable relationships.[89] While promising high salaries and social prestige for the successful, these careers also bred cynicism and anxiety. Far removed from the world of materially productive labor, many men felt psychologically bereft of real fulfillment. *Babbitt* illustrated one man's attempt to compensate for such angst through competitive consumer acquisition. *Best Years* demonstrated that drinking, too, could be used as an anodyne against the nagging, effeminizing effects of white-collar work. With the further expansion of such fields in the postwar era, the link between alcoholism and professional-managerial anguish grew stronger. Ironically, while standards of middle-class work and consumption had been used to attack masculine rituals of intemperance in the 1920s, Americans found that those same standards could generate a malaise of their own, one that often led to excessive drinking in the post–World War II age of anxiety.

Best Years was not the only postwar medium to comment on the potential abuse of alcohol by white-collar professionals and corporate managers. Many observers commented on businessmen's use of alcohol to smooth social interactions in and out of the workplace, to manage the task of self-presentation among clients and superiors. Often such writers were addictive drinkers themselves. One anonymous writer in *Printer's Ink* was one of those unlucky fellows for whom the three-martini lunch became a dangerous habit. Defining himself as a recovering alcoholic, he informed his audience about the experience of seeing "his boss and clients or employees having a hell of a good time over a few drinks" while lamenting that he could no longer "share in the fun." But far from criticizing his colleagues for drinking, the writer simply aimed to enlighten them about the special circumstances of recovering alcoholics.[90]

Several novels about alcoholics also reveal how corporate men used alcohol to cope with or mask ambivalent feelings about their careers. Writer Henry Beetle Hough's narrator claims to have used alcohol for "self-administered acts of creation." As he confesses, "Without liquor I was like a tightly-coiled spring from which any impact or even any stir of air could evoke shrill twanging sounds. With the mysterious power of alcohol I had tried . . . to make myself a man of charm, wit, and urbanity, a man of prowess in professional life, a man not troubled by nerves." Even more telling was the narrator of *September Remember*, written in 1945, who argued that corporate brokers drank to cope with self-hatred induced by the meaninglessness and banality of their work. Advertising executives, especially, "are always making excuses and telling you they have to drink because they work under such terrific pressure . . . getting all steamed up about selling some damn product, putting good minds to work on copy for soap or nail polish. No wonder those guys drink—not just to speed themselves up but to keep from puking at themselves."[91]

Academic experts and journalists also analyzed drinking among the professional middle class. Selden Bacon, for instance, argued that many men drank to cope with the stresses of work in a "complex, competitive, individualistic" society. In his view the traveling salesman epitomized the "highly competitive" role of the white-collar worker who "lived in a world of strangers." As Bacon observed, "Alcohol is obviously functional for achieving the relaxation of suspicion, of competitive tension, of the barriers usually present in our society."[92] Although the fictional Al Stephenson was not a salesman, Bacon no doubt would have found the character a fitting illustration of his point. Though he acts chummy and respectful toward the bank president, Al actually feels suspicious and at times even contemptuous; emotionally if not literally, Al and his boss are strangers. And for Al, getting well plastered dissolved that tension.

Consider, finally, the following comment on the place of alcohol in postwar U.S. business culture:

> If you're an average successful career climber, you begin to get large and responsible jobs, are entrusted with an expense account and company credit card, begin to attend business lunches and dinners and cocktail gatherings—and, very likely, conventions. From that time on you must practice the delicate and difficult art of handling alcohol in business situations. You may be able to escape the requirement, but you probably won't. Drinking has become an inextricable component of business as practiced in this half of the twentieth century.[93]

Though written in 1970, this passage describes a male-dominated, managerial work culture fairly well established by the immediate postwar decades, and it speaks to the ubiquity of alcohol in the lives and careers of salaried, white-collar men. To succeed as breadwinners in the competitive corporate world, men needed to manage, and sometimes mask, any feelings of disillusionment that accompanied their work. By the mid-1940s, men like Al Stephenson increasingly used alcohol as a tool of "emotion management," drinking to reclaim the very manhood leached away by bureaucratized, spiritless work.[94] Most important, it was on the eve of the nation's demobilization—a time when men's roles were in flux and the perceived masculinity of returning soldiers was threatened by the strictures of the postwar economy—that the literature of scientific experts was converted into a narrative form that resonated among the wider public.

Finally, Al's drinking may be seen as a sign of another kind of disappointment: the discontentment of a lackluster marriage. Indeed, the film's subtext includes the theme of faded romance, and it is expressed primarily through Fred and Marie Derry. Implicitly, *Best Years* blames Marie for the couple's breakup. Depicted as a shallow, gold-digging, promiscuous woman, Marie loses interest in Fred as soon as the glory of his military career, and the promise of high wages, fades. Dissatisfied with Fred's meager earnings, Marie resumes working, further emasculating her beleaguered husband. Marie thus acts as a foil to Milly, Peggy, and Wilma. She is the antithesis of the kind of woman Fred believes "ought to be put into mass production." Yet in a more subtle way Al and Milly, too, give voice to the matter of marital disenchantment. In one scene Al and Milly reveal that despite the appearance of a stable and happy marriage, they have had their share of problems. Turning to Al, Milly asks, "How many times have I said I hated you and believed it with all my heart? How many times have you said you were sick and tired of me, that we were all washed up? How many times have we had to fall in love all over again?" Certainly these lines touched a nerve in many viewers—married men and women who stayed together despite periods of strife or boredom. Thus while the film ultimately held the promise of romantic fulfillment in marriage, it also allowed audiences a moment to recognize the all-too-common reality of long-term partnerships. While Al's ambivalent feelings toward his wife do not seem directly to prompt his drinking (in most scenes he and Milly get along quite well), they nonetheless add to his sense of diminished expectations.

In different ways *The Lost Weekend* and *The Best Years of Our Lives* offered cautionary tales about the potential hazards of alcohol. Unlike temperance narratives, neither film sermonized on the evils of liquor, the depravity of saloon-keepers, or the unraveling of society's moral fabric. Rather, as documents of the post-repeal era, they targeted an audience for whom the line between moderate and excessive drinking—or between alcoholism and conventional business practice—was not always easy to discern. When did normal consumption shade into the realm of problem drinking? By the mid-twentieth century, Americans were looking to doctors, psychiatrists, and other experts for answers. But as these films suggest, they could also turn to popular culture for clues to this conundrum.

In the persona of Don Birnam *The Lost Weekend* offered an unambiguous personification of alcoholic identity: a restless, deeply troubled man who lacked the will to commit himself fully to work or family. In contrast *Best Years* did not instruct viewers in the prevailing medical wisdom; rather, it subtly incorporated the anxiety theory of drinking motivation into its plot. Because *Best Years* did not treat Al's drinking in a heavy-handed way, the audience was left to speculate on the potential threat liquor posed to the character, his family, and society at large. (The appearance of the film one year after *The Lost Weekend*, incidentally, may have predisposed viewers to pick up this subtext.) But while *Best Years* avoided the diagnostic vocabulary of experts, it situated alcoholism within a social context that implicitly explained its incidence among American men. Both films dramatized a vexed relationship between alcoholism and a perceived crisis of masculinity, a crisis that resonated especially among upwardly mobile men of blocked ambition.

To the extent that the alcoholism paradigm served as a therapeutic sanction against male deviance from dominant gender norms, both *The Lost Weekend* and *Best Years* reinforced experts' ideological assumptions about healthy masculinity. As Don Birnam himself stated, alcoholism and the inability to find fulfillment in work and marriage were two components of a vicious circle: one led to the other, and vice versa. Indeed, in *The Lost Weekend* alcoholism rendered marriage all but impossible. In *Best Years* Fred and Homer demonstrated that alcoholic excess was at odds with postwar visions of domestic happiness and material progress; ultimately, the film suggested, life with a woman like Peggy or Wilma would prove more satisfying—and more restorative—than a perpetual round of drinks with the boys.

In a subtle yet significant way, however, *Best Years* departed from and even inverted the logic of psychiatrists who viewed alcoholism as a sign of failure to achieve manly authority. Whereas experts such as Strecker and Jellinek stressed alcoholic men's inability to live up to the (hetero)sexual and financial obligations of mature manhood, in Al Stephenson *Best Years* dramatized the possibility that problem drinking could result when men tried too hard to conform to ideals of monogamous marriage and family breadwinning. Apparently the emotional price exacted by one's adherence to masculine norms could be, well, emasculating. Insofar as the film denied the need of social or political solutions to the plight of returning veterans—insofar as it presented every social problem as a "problem of personal morality" that could be solved only through individual or familial solutions—Al's drinking was a logical, if troubling, progression.[95] Because the film circumscribed any means by which Al might have challenged (or at least circumvented) the confining, conservative dictates of the dominant culture, he resorted to a solitary and perversely therapeutic course of action: drowning his discomfort in drink. Thus while psychoanalysts argued that sex-role confusion in early childhood predisposed men to alcoholism, *Best Years* suggested that work and family obligations in adulthood could also prompt men to seek solace in the bottle. Unlike saloon patrons at the turn of the century, Al did not drink in a space physically distanced from the realm of work and family. For him alcoholic escape was psychic, interiorized. Even in the absence of fellow men to drink with, Al used alcohol as a self-gift to dull the pain of his social conformity.

In its incorporation of therapeutic claims, *Best Years* not only enacted elements of the experts' discourse on alcoholism; it also prefigured a shift in Americans' thinking about the disease. Most scientific researchers in the late 1930s and early 1940s envisioned alcoholism as a disease of individual men. In the academic literature published before 1945, writers seldom discussed the onset or potential arrest of alcoholism in relation to men's marital relationships with women.[96] But the gender politics implicit in *Best Years* highlighted the supporting role played by actress Myrna Loy. As Milly, Loy played a character quite different from the bibulous Nora Charles of the early *Thin Man* films. Whereas Nora reveled with her husband, Nick, in the immediate aftermath of Prohibition, Milly worried about her husband, Al, in the immediate aftermath of World War II. By including alcoholism within a range of postwar social problems that could ostensibly be solved on the level of personal and family relations, the film registered the early stages of a shift in which Americans would increasingly envision alcoholism as a family disease.

In part, the fictional Milly had other women, especially repeal leaders such as Pauline Sabin, to thank for a social and legal climate that condoned drinking, but Milly foreshadowed a figure that was just beginning to emerge in American culture: the alcoholic's wife. If postwar women were exhorted generally to facilitate men's renewed authority at home, then it followed that they be urged to prevent or reverse any specific situation (such as chronic drinking) that threatened men's success therein. *The Lost Weekend*'s Helen, too, suggested that women could play a role in curing a man's chronic drinking: by remaining ever faithful, ever supportive, and ever strong in the face of her struggling partner. Gendered narratives of reconversion in the immediate postwar years thus signaled a new direction in the popular and scientific construction of alcoholism, one in which the nuclear family, and especially marriage, provided the context in which dramas of drink and sobriety would play themselves out. Family dramas of alcoholism would not emerge full-blown until the 1950s, but they had precedents in the popular culture of the mid-1940s.

Yet while profitable Hollywood films introduced the largest numbers of Americans to modern notions of alcoholism, they were not alone in reshaping the cultural landscape of drink. Indeed, the fashioning of alcoholic identity cannot be understood without addressing the segment of the alcoholism movement most responsible for its existence as a movement: Alcoholics Anonymous. More and more American men who recognized themselves in Don Birnam or Al Stephenson turned not to medical experts for therapy but to a largely male fellowship of recovering alcoholics. For while psychiatrists and researchers engendered scientific theories of alcoholism in the 1930s and 1940s, their potential subjects were living out their own personal crises of work and family life. Some of these men, moreover, formulated a compelling theory—and therapeutic fellowship—of their own. They are the subject of the next chapter.

3 ALCOHOLICS ANONYMOUS AND THE CULTURE OF SOBRIETY

THE SOCIAL FOUNDATIONS OF MUTUAL
HELP IN THE 1930S AND 1940S

In May 1935 a thirty-nine-year-old New York stock speculator named Bill Wilson visited Akron, Ohio, on business. Saddled with debt in the midst of the Great Depression, he traveled to the Midwest to negotiate a buyout of a local machine tool factory. Unfortunately his attempt was unsuccessful. When he learned of his failure, his first impulse was to reach for a drink. In fact, for nearly twenty years few occasions or experiences did *not* prompt Wilson to reach for a drink, and then another, until he reached a state of extreme intoxication. But this time he had been sober for four months, and he knew that even one drink could spell disaster. Afraid to swill away his newfound sobriety, he resisted the temptation to enter the hotel bar but reached instead for a telephone in hopes of finding a fellow "drunk" to talk to. After speaking to a minister, he eventually made contact with a local surgeon named Robert Holbrook Smith. Several weeks later, after days of intense conversation, Wilson reaffirmed his pledge of sobriety, and Dr. Bob (as he was known) took his last drink. Thrilled about the prospect of helping more drunks achieve sobriety, Wilson stayed in Akron with Dr. Bob and his wife, Anne, for several months before returning to New York City.

Within decades of its occurrence, this incident in Akron was assigned historic significance as the founding moment of Alcoholics Anonymous (AA). From the initial meeting between Bill and Dr. Bob grew a small network of men dedicated to helping themselves stay sober.[1] By 1939 over

100 individuals in the cofounders' home states of New York and Ohio claimed membership in AA, a not-for-profit association of locally based groups whose members meet on an egalitarian basis in the hope of recovering from their common affliction. From the beginning AA has called itself a fellowship, reflecting its origins in a voluntary act of mutual compassion and self-identification between two men. In retrospect Dr. Bob recalled his first encounter with Bill: Here "was a man who experienced many years of frightful drinking, who had had most all the drunkard's experience known to man. . . . *He was the first living human with whom I had ever talked, who knew what he was talking about in regard to alcoholism from actual experience. In other words, he talked my language.*"[2]

Bill Wilson's act of reaching out to another drunkard in order to maintain his own sobriety was the central dynamic behind the spread of AA, which is known today as the most influential self-help group in modern history. Recently some scholars have come to prefer the term "mutual-help" movement to reflect the importance of social interaction; the phrase "self-help," they believe, carries the inappropriate connotation of a person acting by him- or herself to bring about a desired personal change.[3] Both terms, however, position AA and similar therapeutic communities as alternatives (or at least adjuncts) to professional treatment. Though Wilson had sought the ministrations of New York physician William D. Silkworth (one of the few medical doctors at the time to devote his practice to alcoholics), he believed that conventional medical or psychiatric care was not enough to ensure long-term sobriety. Rather, he found that certain spiritual beliefs and attitudes could help people overcome their craving for alcohol, especially if they shared those beliefs with others. While scientific experts possessed important knowledge, both cofounders believed, only an alcoholic could "talk the same language" to another alcoholic.

In 1938 Wilson codified the beliefs and methods that he and Dr. Bob found helpful in ensuring their sobriety. These became the now-famous Twelve Steps, guidelines for spiritual commitment and interpersonal behavior that form the heart of the fellowship's philosophy.[4] Only two of the steps actually mention alcohol or alcoholics: the first, in which one admits that one is "powerless over alcohol" and that life has "become unmanageable," and the twelfth, in which one pledges to carry the AA message to other alcoholics. The steps in between encourage members to "surrender" to a higher power, to turn their will and their lives "over to the care of God" as they understand him. They also instruct followers to take a "searching and fearless moral inventory" of themselves, admit their shortcomings, and make amends to others they have harmed in the past. The social component of the program takes place in regularly scheduled meetings, which involve prayer and meditation, confessions of past drinking abuses, the celebration of milestones in abstinence, and support for those who have relapsed. Taken together, the fellowship's guiding principles (as inscribed in the Twelve Steps) and rituals (as performed in meetings) eschew the notion of individual willpower as a means to control addictive behavior. Instead they exhort members to admit, and even relish, their dependence on a higher power and other alcoholics in the quest for sobriety.[5]

In turning to one another for mutual support the cofounders and early members of AA responded to a lack of effective treatment options for problem drinkers. Indeed, in the mid-1930s alcoholics like Bill Wilson had few places to turn for help. The decline of the temperance movement spelled the end of evangelical reform clubs urging abstinence through moral suasion.[6] As a result of Prohibition, most hospitals and inebriate asylums that once catered to habitual drinkers remained shuttered during the 1920s. After repeal some institutions, such as the Towns Hospital in New York City where Wilson was hospitalized, attracted a generally well-to-do clientele. But for most inebriates, quality medical care was scarce. Poor people who became drunk in public were often jailed or committed to insane asylums. New treatment facilities associated with the alcoholism movement, such as the Yale Plan Clinic, did not proliferate until the mid-1940s.[7] In large part AA took on the long-standing task of reforming and treating drunkards, but it added a new, crucial twist to an old idea. While its founders agreed with earlier reformers that alcohol was an addictive substance, they believed that alcohol produced uniquely negative effects in one group of drinkers whom they labeled alcoholics. Like scientific experts, AA members defined this effect as "a loss of control over drinking, an irresistible craving that drove the alcoholic toward destruction."[8]

In 1941 AA began to attract members nationwide, thanks in large part to favorable press coverage in mass-circulation magazines, especially the *Saturday Evening Post*.[9] By 1945, the year *The Lost Weekend* premiered on-screen, the fellowship had gathered over 15,000 members, most of whom were white men of the middle and lower-middle classes. In 1950 Dr. Bob died, but Bill W. continued to expand the fellowship with local groups in forty-eight states and ten Canadian provinces. Exactly two decades after its founding in Akron, AA commemorated its twenty-year anniversary at a national convention in St. Louis, Missouri. There Wilson declared to an audience of over 5,000 members that the fellowship had officially come of age. At the time of the convention, in 1955, AA's membership was over 130,000, a figure that mushroomed to approximately 200,000 two years later.[10] As its influence spread throughout the country, AA became ever more influential in shaping the modern paradigm of alcoholism as a disease.

As mentioned in Chapter 2, the notion of alcoholism as a disease was a contested issue among experts, and this included the lay experts of AA as well. In fact Bill Wilson generally avoided the term "disease," preferring instead the words "illness" and "malady." He rejected a narrowly clinical definition of alcoholism as a disease entity and stressed that alcoholics suffered from a threefold physical, mental, and spiritual affliction. He and other AA founders distanced themselves from scientific debates about the nature of alcohol*ism* and focused on the practical matter of treating individual alcoholics. Yet AA has shaped the cultural understanding of the disease as a metaphor in profound ways. Following Susan Sontag's perceptive treatment of "illness as metaphor," historian Ernest Kurtz suggests that AA positions the alcoholic as one who experiences the "subjective condition of modernity" itself as a kind of "dis-ease." Taken on both literal and metaphorical levels, AA's understanding of the alcoholic's experience—and its own self-definition as a form of therapy—further broke down traditional, moralistic notions of habitual drunkenness that had prevailed during the decades surrounding the turn of the century.[11]

In recent decades scholars have investigated the significance of AA from historical, sociological, and even literary perspectives. Social scientists have studied the role of the fellowship as a social movement; folklore scholars have analyzed its oral narrative tradition; religious leaders have interpreted its spiritual workings; and addiction treatment professionals have assessed its therapeutic effectiveness.[12] In 1979 Ernest Kurtz published *Not God*, an account of AA's development from its founding through the 1970s. Widely regarded as the most important historical study of the fellowship, *Not God* offers a fine interpretation of AA's intellectual and spiritual significance, tracing the influence of such figures as Carl Jung, William James, John D. Rockefeller, and various religious leaders on Bill Wilson and the fellowship he inspired.

Yet many facets of AA's history remain unexplored. Given AA's prominence and perceived success in rehabilitating alcoholics, observers have long asked, How and why does the fellowship work for so many people? Often this question prompts musings about the spiritual principles, psychological attitudes, or social connections that the fellowship offers its members, such as "AA works because it lets people surrender to a Higher Power and thus free themselves from self-blame" or "AA succeeds because it replaces dependence upon alcohol with dependence upon the group."[13] Such explanations assume that certain beliefs or behaviors have a timeless, universal effectiveness in controlling a timeless, universal form of addiction. But from a historical perspective this approach assumes the very thing that needs to be explained: why and how this *particular* approach began to make sense and work for many self-defined alcoholics when it did. For the historian, in fact, the question of AA's success needs to be reformulated from a matter of therapeutic efficacy to one of cultural hegemony: How did AA, as an ideology and a social organization, gain the cultural authority not simply to cure or arrest alcoholism but to create and disseminate the very terms and categories through which Americans have come to understand the recovery process itself?

In other words, we need to interpret AA as a social formation that "invented" a new emotional vocabulary and set of rituals to address the problem of habitual drunkenness. As Joel Pfister and Nancy Schnog argue in their volume *Inventing the Psychological*, "therapeutic common sense" should be viewed not as a set of psychological insights into an eternal human nature but, rather, as a welter of "historically contingent, socially specific, and politically situated" assumptions that in turn shape prevailing concepts of selfhood. The modern paradigm of alcoholic identity, as defined by scientific and public relations experts, gained influence because it resonated among large segments of the population for underlying historical reasons. The rise of AA is a crucial part of that story, and it is important to examine how it addressed some of the felt psychological needs that accompanied broader social transformations at the time. As Pfister writes, "What still needs to be investigated historically is the degree to which and the ways in which modern 'therapeutic' discourses, while often presuming to fathom and repair universal 'human nature,' have in fact contributed ideologically" to normative constructions of race, class, and gender identity.[14]

This chapter focuses on the gendered dimensions of the "culture of sobriety" as it developed during AA's formative decades. A number of scholars have commented on the social composition of the fellowship and the role that gender played during its early years. Consider, for example, media critic Elayne Rapping's brief yet suggestive discussion:

> It is important to realize . . . that AA—so traditionally white, middle-class, and masculinist in its assumptions—was the perfect organization for the times precisely because it did focus primarily upon the segment of the population, white Christian males, whose traditional roles and perquisites were being most severely challenged and usurped. . . . AA was understandably concerned with preserving and bolstering male authority. . . . AA reproduced the basic structures of patriarchal family life, at a time when its economic foundations were shifting and failing for many men.[15]

The founding of AA took place in the midst of the Great Depression, and the connection between the social crisis of the era and the apparent interest of the fellowship in "bolstering male authority" deserves more sustained attention. As discussed in Chapter 1, many Americans expressed anxiety about the nation's economic decline in explicitly gendered terms, often interpreting the Depression as a crisis of gender roles, family stability, and domestic consumption. The figure of the forgotten man represented the loss of financial and familial authority once enjoyed by the employed breadwinner. In such a context the individual pathology of the alcoholic man further epitomized masculine debility. Indeed, drinking weakened the roles of both cofounders as breadwinners. After the stock market crash of 1929, prospective Wall Street employers (increasingly scarce to begin with) passed over Bill Wilson on account of his frequent drunkenness, while Dr. Bob lost surgical patients who feared his shaky hand. As his alcoholism progressed, Bill depleted his savings, defaulted on his mortgage, and even pilfered change from the purse of his wife, Lois—a far cry from the domestic-masculine ideal. As members of the professional-managerial class, both cofounders had enjoyed perquisites of manly authority in the 1920s, when their alcoholism was in its early stages, only to lose those privileges in the 1930s when the Depression, combined with their drinking, exacted a more formidable toll.

The changes in the personal lives of the early participants of AA played a major role in shaping the fellowship. In fact, Robin Room has suggested that AA is best understood as a "generational solution" to the problems faced by the "wet generations," middle-class men who came of age during the 1910s and early 1920s and who adopted heavy drinking as a revolt against Victorian moral standards.[16] Among the original members who contributed autobiographical sketches to AA's first book in 1939, the average age was around forty-five, which meant that most of them reached adulthood during or after World War I. While liquor once symbolized youthful rebellion and cosmopolitanism, however, by 1940 many members of these generations found themselves in trouble with their drinking, and some experienced illness, job loss, separation from family members, divorce, or financial ruin. Thus by this time alcohol was associated with despair rather than celebration. Because of its egalitarianism, its separation from institutionalized religion, and its rejection of sententious rhetoric, AA attracted men who repudiated moralistic temperance ideology yet needed to control their drinking. AA provided a way "to understand and transcend the personal anguish many had experienced by middle age as they lived out the cultural commitments of their youth." Moreover, AA allowed its members to deal with conflicts in gender roles and family life. AA, and the alcoholism concept more generally, "offered an account not only of their loss of control over drinking, but also of their failure to live up to expectations at work and at home." For men who came of age after the first generation of AA founders, the fellowship continued to offer a solution to drink-related problems that worsened over the course of the adult life cycle.[17]

Many questions remain about the cultural and ideological work of AA during the 1930s and 1940s. Does it make sense to characterize AA as a masculine fellowship during its early decades? If so, exactly how did the fellowship allow its male members to reconcile or cope with personal failure? Did it aim explicitly to bolster male authority, or did its literature and social rituals accomplish this end indirectly? Given the prevailing definition of alcoholism as emasculating, along with lingering perceptions of social drinking as manly, how did AA work to renew masculinity while simultaneously requiring complete abstinence? If it did function to restore a sense of manhood for alcoholics, how did that process contribute to AA's influence in society at large? In short, how was gender shaped and reformulated by AA during its early decades?

Manhood was seldom invoked explicitly by AA members, who referred to themselves first and foremost as alcoholics and not as men (much less failed men) per se. Over the course of U.S. history, women traditionally have been the problematic or "marked" sex, whereas the male gender "has often been rendered invisible by reason of its seeming naturalness." Following Elizabeth Lunbeck and other historians of gender, my approach aims "to tease the gendered man out of the universal Man" and to address the gendered thinking that informed AA members' ideas and experiences. We need not only to ask whether certain organizations or rituals are comprised *of* men but to investigate whether they are also *about* men, affirming or reconstructing maleness for their participants.[18]

Moreover, our understanding of the history of AA will benefit from a more supple, dynamic, and complex definition of gender. Many recent scholars reject defining gender as a unified collection of attributes or roles. For example, Gail Bederman persuasively argues that "attempting to define manhood as a coherent set of prescriptive ideals, traits, or sex roles obscures the complexities and contradictions of any historical moment." Gender, whether manhood or womanhood, is a historical, ideological process in which coexisting and even contradictory ideas function to explain what men (or women) are, how they ought to behave, and what sorts of powers and authorities they may claim (or not claim) based on their sex. The ideological process of gender "works through a complex political technology, composed of a variety of institutions, ideas, and daily practices." It is also important to consider AA as a site of gender formation, defined as the dynamic process by which *both* male and female genders are formed, renegotiated, and contested. The narratives and rituals of AA provide an especially promising opportunity to analyze this process.[19]

This theoretical approach is especially enlightening in relation to the history of drink and alcoholism. Gendered discourses of alcohol consumption have long embodied multiple, contradictory ideals of manhood. In the late nineteenth and early twentieth centuries the dominant construction of manhood for white, middle-class men embodied a balancing act between two elements: a preoccupation with virility and toughness, on one hand, and a softer ideal of domestic masculinity, on the other.[20] AA redefined masculine identity by relying on two different (and often opposing) models of manhood: one rooted in male camaraderie and brotherhood, and the other defined by marital connection and familial authority. Indeed, a large number of early AA members, including the two cofounders, were married, and many stayed married despite their alcoholism. Thus AA's implicit ideal of renewed masculinity, which we might call sober manhood, reflected the particular life situations of white, middle-aged, married men. In some respects AA functioned as an alcoholic fraternity, creating a new, drink-free, homosocial environment. Yet at other times it enveloped the domestic sphere, incorporating men's familial roles within the culture of sobriety. To understand fully AA's contribution to the engendering of alcoholism, we need to explore and account for this dualism.

The rest of this chapter analyzes the gendered dimensions of AA from 1935 through the early postwar years. It is neither an intellectual history, a study of the systems of thought and belief that influenced the fellowship, nor a social history, an account of the demographic patterns, organizational structures, and lived experiences of members.[21] Rather, it explores a significant piece of AA's *cultural history*, relying on the fellowship's published literature as well as accounts by outside observers or members who wrote independently. It treats AA as a discourse, a complex collection of ideas, terms, and beliefs that took shape within a particular set of material practices and social relations. Although the AA's early literature was produced by a relatively small number of self-identifying alcoholics, it shaped many other people's experiences in profound ways.[22]

Finally, a focus on AA highlights the issue of historical agency. The preceding chapter illustrated how the popular acceptance of alcoholism functioned metaphorically to express gendered anxieties about national vitality during and after World War II. But medical literature and popular films do not allow us to explore the relationship between cultural representation and lived experience, between the alcoholic as a narrative figure and the living individuals who suffered from chronic drunkenness. Along with psychiatrists and film producers, AA played a crucial role in the construction of alcoholism, a paradigm that was forged in the crucible of experts' encounters with excessive drinkers but that also influenced how those drinkers viewed themselves and their behavior. Yet unlike most professional discourses, AA provided a context in which excessive drinkers could define their *own* identities as alcoholics—sometimes alongside and sometimes in contrast to credentialed authorities. Significantly, the degree of agency granted to individual members, in the context of an essentially prescriptive Twelve Step program, has been a matter of some debate. But if popular and scientific writers used narratives of alcoholism to project social concerns about failed masculinity, AA members responded (if not always explicitly) to those narratives in deeply personal ways. AA thus provides a window into the process of gender formation in which individuals both internalized and resisted societal norms, reshaping American culture even as it shaped them.[23]

In the beginning AA was a "fellowship" in a literal sense: the term signified an association of individuals on equal terms, and usually the "fellows" were men. As they spread their message in the late 1930s, Bill Wilson and Bob Smith shared the common scientific view that alcoholism was largely a masculine affair. Anecdotal evidence and archival research support this claim. Basing his research on records in Akron, Ohio, one chronicler of the early history of AA, Wally P., listed the first names and last initials of thirteen people, including Dr. Bob, who achieved sobriety between 1935 and 1937.[24] With one exception, a woman named Jane S., all of the members had recognizable male names. Wally also uncovered the names of six people, all men, who founded the Baltimore group in 1940. Within sixteen months the group included fifty members, but only "several women." The history of the Philadelphia chapter adds a thread to this pattern. Jimmy B., who joined AA in New York but later moved to Pennsylvania, recalled that "in the Fall of 1940 . . . our fellowship . . . numbered about 75, including three girls." By 1941 the active membership in Philadelphia was around 125, with "about five active girls," or 4 percent of the total. Of thirty-seven members in the "central city group" of Minneapolis in 1943, only two were women. In 1951 AA was featured in *Fortune* magazine, which reported that 10 to 15 percent of the national active membership was female.[25]

The demographic composition of the fellowship was reflected in the gendered language used to describe it. Nonalcoholic journalists writing for local presses often referred to AA as a brotherhood or a fraternity. In a series of articles for the *Washington Star* during the summer of 1940, journalist Bob Erwin wrote that AA was "more of a club or brotherhood than anything else." Erwin also cited a member who claimed that AA helped him to become "interested in the welfare of [his] fellowmen from the standpoint of brotherly love." In 1942 a reporter in Dayton, Ohio, mentioned that both men and women participated in AA, yet he described the group in specifically gendered terms: "At the meeting of Alcoholics Anonymous we saw what miracles can still be wrought . . . when the fatherhood of God and the brotherhood of man become the guiding principles of life." A writer for the *San Francisco News* referred to members, even female members, as "brothers." Observing the time and money some members devoted to helping fellow "AA's," he noted that one man "in the same week helped a male brother with his room rent and took a female brother to a rather expensive show when boredom threatened." As the oxymoron "female brother" reveals, observers tended to define the fellowship in essentially masculine terms and even applied those terms to the few women in the group.[26]

Many of AA's early members, especially Bill Wilson, did not *overtly* exclude women, even if their implicit assumptions tended to privilege men. Sex ratios varied from group to group and from region to region. Evidence suggests that groups in New York City, for example, were more successful in attracting women to the fellowship. In the late 1950s one sociologist found that women made up almost 40 percent of some Manhattan groups.[27] Marty Mann's publicized status as the first woman to remain sober through the AA program—not to mention her subsequent leadership of the National Council for Education on Alcoholism—should caution us against underestimating the role of women in the early days of AA. During the 1940s Wilson supported Mann's efforts to increase the number of women in the fellowship, and he sometimes accompanied her at public speaking engagements designed for this purpose. Moreover, Wilson's overarching rhetorical strategy when disseminating "conference-approved" literature was to stress the democratic, egalitarian nature of AA and to insist that alcoholism could afflict *any* person, regardless of race, class, gender, or sexual orientation. "The only requirement for membership is an honest desire to stop drinking," wrote Wilson in his first major publication of 1939.[28] Officially AA was not the exclusive domain of men. In theory and often in practice AA offered support to male and female alcoholics during its formative years.

But the AA movement did not always deliver on the theoretically universal promise it held out to alcoholics of both sexes. By and large the general observation that AA appealed and catered primarily to men holds true, at least during the first several decades.[29] Even Wilson's midwestern cofounder was slow to welcome women drinkers. According to the anonymous authors of *Dr. Bob and the Good Old-timers*, an account of Robert Smith's life and role in AA, Dr. Bob was reluctant to confront "the most troublesome and, in some ways, the most unwelcome minority in AA's olden days—women! . . . Women alcoholics had to overcome a double standard that was even more rigid in the 1930s than it is today—the notion that nice women didn't drink to excess. This made it difficult for a woman to admit to the problem in the first place, to say nothing of being accepted in AA." In her biography of Sister Mary Ignatia, an Ohio nun who worked with Dr. Bob to rehabilitate alcoholics, historian Mary Darrah argues that "neither male AA members nor their wives readily accepted women alcoholics into their kinship. Even Dr. Bob had difficulty extending the AA message . . . to 'fallen' alcoholic women who were far more stigmatized for their drinking than the men." Alcoholic men were treated like members of the Smith family, sobered up, and provided with room and board. But "this was not as readily so with alcoholic women"; while Dr. Bob sometimes housed them in his basement, he was apparently uncomfortable in their presence.[30]

Dr. Bob's views were shared by many throughout Ohio and elsewhere in the 1930s and 1940s. By 1939 there were seventy AA participants in the Akron and Cleveland areas, and according to a report filed that year, "Members saw that the difficulty in working with women was primarily because of sexual problems. It was considered safer for the nonalcoholic wives to work with them." This report articulated a widely held view that "twelfth-step work" must occur on a same-sex basis, lest potential romantic interest between two alcoholics threaten the recovery process.[31] Moreover, Dr. Bob believed that women alcoholics had different therapeutic needs *because* of their sex. In his view female drinkers were so different from male drinkers that they benefited more from interaction with *non*-alcoholic women than with alcoholic men, a blatant contradiction to the central AA belief that alcoholics are best suited to help one another. Thus while many AA members welcomed women into the fellowship as a sign of the movement's inclusive or egalitarian spirit, male AA members allowed gender stereotypes to trump AA ideology and, in the process, made the recovery process more difficult for the (relatively) few women who did join.[32]

While a thorough study of female alcoholics lies beyond the scope of this book, the voices of early AA women are instructive if only because they underscore the masculinist orientation of the fellowship as a whole. By virtue of their culturally defined differences, women were more apt to notice the gendered dimensions of AA, which seemed so natural and unproblematic to male members. Consider, then, an anonymous letter published in AA's national newsletter, the *Grapevine*, in 1953. Writing from her home in Woodside, New York, the author claimed that "women are only tolerated in AA; they are the orphans of AA!" She lamented the "ridiculously small percentage of women members" who achieved sobriety and complained of the "hostility" she encountered "by other women, by men members, and by non-alcoholics." In fact, until she joined a separate women's discussion group, she found AA to be a "tremendous handicap." "The men, conditioned by their bar experiences," she wrote, "view the female alcoholic with suspicion and hostility. . . . Far too many [women] . . . have found our groups or our set-up, somewhere, somehow not appealing or attractive to them, and have never returned. The men, on the other hand, seem to fit in and find what they are looking for. . . . AA meetings as they stand now are geared for the male member, especially the closed meetings . . . [which] are rarely conducted by women speakers. Why, I don't know. There's no tradition that makes this a rule."[33] In expressing confusion about why the fellowship "somehow" seemed to be "geared for the male member," this writer spoke to the implicit ideas and behaviors of many AA participants. As she indicated, no official rules excluded women. But in actual practice, men shaped the organization to suit their own purposes—purposes that, as we shall see, had much to do with defining and restoring their own identities *as* men.

AA's masculinist roots are evident in its most important publication: *Alcoholics Anonymous: The Story of How More Than One Hundred Men Have Recovered from Alcoholism*. Also known as the Big Book, this volume is often regarded as the bible of AA. First published in 1939 (with later editions in 1946, 1955, and 1976), it has become the most widely read book on alcoholism in the twentieth century, selling more than 22 million copies to date. The first half of the book describes the workings of the AA program and is followed by brief autobiographical sketches by AA members. Anonymously Bill Wilson wrote the first eleven chapters (which have remained virtually the same since the first edition) and edited the autobiographical stories. Of the twenty-eight "personal stories" of sober alcoholics in the original publication, only one, titled "A Feminine Victory," was written by an alcoholic woman. The title of her story betrayed its distinctiveness (no man's story was dubbed a "masculine victory"), which was reinforced in the first sentence: "To my lot falls the rather doubtful distinction of being the only 'lady' alcoholic in our particular section." The gender identities of the other anonymous writers were announced more subtly in titles such as "A Business Man's Recovery," "On His Way," and "My Wife and I." In a typical ending one author concluded, "Today . . . I have a warm fellowship among men who understand my problems; I have tasks to do and am glad to do them, to see others who are alcoholics and to help them in any way I can to become sober men."[34] This writer's experience of warmth and community contradicted the sense of exclusion and "otherness" described by the female member above.

In 1946 AA printed a slightly revised version of the 1939 edition that, from the outset, invited male and female readers as potential members. As the foreword to the 1946 printing states, "We, of Alcoholics Anonymous, are many thousands of men and women who have recovered from a seemingly hopeless state of mind and body. To show other alcoholics PRECISELY HOW WE HAVE RECOVERED is the main purpose of this book." Although in this reprinting the Big Book mentioned "thousands of men and women" (as opposed to the reference to "more than one hundred men" in the original 1939 version), the book did not add a single autobiographical vignette by a woman. Indeed, the Big Book remained virtually the same from 1939 to 1955, when editors revised the second half substantially. At that time they changed the personal stories to include eleven women and twenty-six men—roughly 30 percent women. According to Ernest Kurtz, editors increased the women's stories in order to remedy the fact that the first edition had not furnished sufficient models with which female participants might identify.[35] By the mid-1950s, then, the fellowship had made efforts to be more inclusive of women, but the very need for such an attempt betrays the extent to which AA first took root in masculine soil.

Was this implicit definition of gender itself constituted by specific racial and class identities? Again, the matter of social inclusiveness is complex; it has been a contested issue since the early years of the fellowship. Officially there were no exclusionary rules based on race, ethnicity, or class status. In 1946 Bill Wilson wrote an impassioned article in the *Grapevine* titled "Who Is a Member of Alcoholics Anonymous?" Quoting the first edition of the Big Book, he reiterated that "we are not allied with any particular faith, sect or denomination nor do we oppose anyone." A year later the *Grapevine* offered another statement of the fellowship's democratic philosophy: "Rich and poor, educated and illiterate, men and women, of all ages, from all walks of life, they meet and talk openly, in all humility, about how each can build a finer, richer life the AA way." Many writers stressed the range of members' occupations and income levels. "There were business men, professional men, and factory workers," wrote one contributor to the Big Book. Others, publishing outside AA's own apparatus, made similar claims: "I found just what any newcomer will find—a group of men and women from all social, financial, intellectual and educational levels."[36] Sociologist Oscar W. Ritchie published one of the earliest academic studies of AA in 1948. Membership, he found, was "heterogeneous," composed of "white and black, Jew and Gentile, Catholic and Protestant, believer and nonbeliever, rich and poor. There are no rigid membership requirements which must be met."[37]

According to the limited evidence available, however, there was often a gap between rhetorical pronouncements and realities at the local level. In its first several decades AA generally attracted men who shared the racial and class backgrounds of the cofounders. As Bill Wilson indicated in his 1946 *Grapevine* article, the call for inclusiveness in AA was prompted by numerous informal cases of exclusion and discrimination nationwide. In 1957, reflecting on AA's twentieth anniversary, Wilson recalled that "in the beginning we could not sober up women. They were different, they said. . . . The derelict, the rich man, the socialite—all these once thought A.A. was not for them. So did certain people of other races and tongues and creeds."[38] Over the years Wilson received letters from members across the country stating that people had been rejected "because they slipped too much, because their morals were too bad, because they had mental difficulties . . . or because they did not come from the so-called better classes of society." Some observers, including scientific experts who based their research on AA participants, found that most members fit a sociological profile similar to that of Bill and Dr. Bob themselves. The foreword to the Big Book in 1946 indicated that most of AA's recovered alcoholics were "business or professional folk." Psychologist Charles Hewitt reported that the average AA member in Minneapolis was forty-four years old and "relatively superior" in intelligence, education, occupational skills, and social status. Another researcher traced the effectiveness of AA in an unnamed southwestern city from 1945 to 1962. Of 188 active members who had remained sober for more than one year, 182 were white, in a city with "a sizable Negro and Latin American (Mexican) population."[39]

The most flagrant acts of exclusion targeted African Americans. Following his praise of AA's heterogeneity, sociologist Oscar Ritchie noted that "one situation in which the principle of open membership seems to be involved centers around the admission of the Negro alcoholic." Ritchie corresponded with group secretaries from Alabama, Georgia, New Jersey, and Ohio and found a range of opinions and informal membership policies. "While Negroes do belong to AA," he concluded, "there are evidences of certain local group practices which tend to bar them or discourage their membership. . . . In some communities they are encouraged to form 'their own' groups; in others the matter has received no consideration; and in still others they are simply 'not eligible.'"[40] In some areas African Americans were denied formal membership but were granted special status to attend meetings as "visitors" or "observers." A common solution allowed African Americans to form their own groups, the first of which were started in 1945 in Washington, D.C., and St. Louis. By the late 1940s some areas, including Greenwich Village in New York City and Ann Arbor, Michigan, were hosting integrated meetings. In 1951 an article in the AA *Grapevine* announced that Chicago's AA membership of 5,000 included more than 300 African Americans, a fact noted with pride. Attitudes toward blacks in AA thus varied from region to region.[41]

On the "sensitive matter" of racial discrimination and segregation in AA, Ernest Kurtz offers a mixed assessment of the early decades. Given the status of race relations before the Civil Rights movement hammered away at racial segregation, AA was not unusual. Though Bill Wilson opposed "race prejudice" and wanted the AA umbrella to encompass as many alcoholics as possible, regardless of color, he was generally silent about racial issues. It was not his goal to transform "different customs and situations in different parts of this country." According to Kurtz, Wilson rationalized racially divided groups in terms of AA's spiritual principles: "Alcoholics Anonymous would never print 'whites only' or 'blacks only' in a listing of meetings, but if the community understood such from the listed meeting place, well that was reality. . . . Those excluded, given the AA understanding of its history and tradition, were perhaps by this very fact being invited by their Higher Power to form a needed new group." Ultimately, Kurtz argues, Wilson accepted the existence of prejudice as one example of the fellowship's—and indeed, of humankind's—"limitations," a weakness that might eventually be remedied but that did not spark in him a sense of urgency for concerted political action.[42]

Some people simply believed that alcoholism was less common among blacks than among whites. In 1943 Wilson expressed astonishment "at the apparent prevalence of alcoholism among the colored people" as reported to him by one physician. That same year a writer for *Sales Management* magazine claimed that while "all races and nationalities" were welcome in AA, "not all races . . . are equally susceptible to the peculiar combination that makes an alcoholic. The Negro, for instance, may be a hard drinker and he may even get drunk, but he . . . rarely faces the problem of being unable to stop drinking if he wants to do so."[43] These last comments suggest the extent to which the alcoholism paradigm itself was grounded in perceptions of racial as well as gender difference—perceptions that not only influenced popular representations of alcoholics but circumscribed treatment prerogatives as well.

My purpose is neither to excuse nor to criticize early members for their actions and attitudes toward various racial and ethnic groups, which must be considered in historical context. Prejudicial assumptions about non-white, non-middle-class Americans often coexisted with a genuine humanitarian impulse that extended to all citizens regardless of class or color. Rather, I would stress that the fellowship *originated* in the perceived needs of a particular segment of the population. Given the persistence of racial and class-based biases, we might question whether the egalitarian rhetoric of AA served the specific needs of white, downwardly mobile, middle-class men. The very notion that alcoholism transcended social categories helped to destigmatize and demoralize habitual drunkenness for educated, professional men who suffered blows to their class standing as well as gender identity. Although the founders and early members extended their therapeutic program to people unlike themselves, pronouncements that alcoholism was rare among blacks or that women had difficulty with the Twelve Steps reveal the extent to which AA revolved initially around the problems of white, middle-class men who had fallen on hard times.[44]

It is not surprising that the social backgrounds of most early AA members were consistent with representations of alcoholic identity in scientific writings and popular films of the 1940s. The active membership of AA was skewed to the middle classes, and especially "to those among the middle classes whose background or aspirations were above the median of even this modal population." Regular members usually "hit the rocks of alcoholism" for one of two related reasons: the frustration of attempts to move up the social ladder (recall *The Best Years of Our Lives* as a drama of aspiring men's blocked ambition) or the pain of downward mobility (a plight shared by AA's cofounders as well the fictional Don Birnam). While rich and poor members—and occasionally, people of color—were welcomed at meetings because they demonstrated the "universality" of the disease, they often felt uncomfortable and frequently abandoned the fellowship. As one "old-timer" recalled of the early decades, AA "turned out to be a middle-class, largely white phenomenon."[45] While AA leaders tried to minimize the fact that few members came from the farther ends of the socioeconomic spectrum, in fact "AA's ideology has remained inveterately bourgeois."[46]

The growth of AA also paralleled the expansion of public drinking cultures into suburban areas and small towns. Whereas temperance narratives of sin and redemption emphasized urban saloon culture, AA emerged as an alternative to drinking in a broad range of residential areas. After repeal, nightclubs and cabarets attracted clienteles beyond the cosmopolitan centers such as New York City, while the expansion of suburbs facilitated "suburban" drinking cultures in restaurants, bars, and private homes. And so, too, did AA expand to fill the needs of habitual drinkers in different locales. Indeed, AA's two original "hometowns" were a small midwestern city (Akron) and a large East Coast metropolis (New York); this initial diversity, moreover, was maintained as the fellowship expanded. As the original local groups mushroomed into constellations of neighborhood meeting sites, both urban and suburban residents were likely to find an alcoholic support network in their own backyards.

GENDERED RITUALS OF FELLOWSHIP

How, then, did AA perform therapeutic and cultural work for its members? How did excessive drinkers acquire the identity of sober manhood? If alcoholic men were characterized first and foremost as loners, one of the fellowship's primary tasks was to resocialize them into a new community. It is no surprise that experts who emphasized alcoholics' social maladjustment evaluated AA in terms of social rehabilitation. Psychologist Charles Hewitt noted that AA offered members companionship, recreation, and "friendship based on mutual respect." Sociologist Selden Bacon argued that AA was "peculiarly suited to bring the isolated alcoholic back into social circulation," enabling the individual "to participate step by step in social living." Combining the vocabularies of social science and medicine, Bacon described AA as a "social structure which provides for re-socializing the sick and isolated individual" through new personal contacts and reciprocal relationships.[47]

AA publications, too, commented on members' newfound sociability. One *Grapevine* article asserted that "alcoholics long for fellowship. As humiliations and misbehavior add up, they withdraw from society—from life itself. The cold fog of loneliness closes down. . . . Together the AAs learn to escape disaster, and shoulder to shoulder commence the common journey, sharing their own experiences, and working together to help someone worse off." In this way AA construed sociability as therapy; the shared journey of recovery was as important as the twelve steps along the way. Other writers equated the social element of AA with the camaraderie of the saloon, but without the alcohol. A journalist in Omaha, Nebraska, explained that "many drunks get started that way because they are gregarious, affable fellows. They want someone to talk to and go to a tavern for a drink and a chat with a bartender. Then they're off on a stem-winder. The [AA] get-togethers are a preventative substitute."[48] After alcoholism eroded the congeniality of social drinking, AA provided a much-needed alternative.

The collective experience of sobriety thus represented a new, therapeutic twist on the long-standing connection between drinking and sociability. In a melding of AA rituals and the popular discourse on alcoholism, novelist Charles Jackson spoke at an open AA meeting in Hartford, Connecticut, in 1945, the same year that *The Lost Weekend* premiered on-screen. Jackson explained that his role as a writer did not entail solving Don Birnam's problem; his task was merely to present it. But while the novel did not depict AA as a cure for the protagonist, Jackson did "have nice things to say about AA." As reported in the *Grapevine*, he told the audience that "AA would be good for Don Birnam . . . because AA gives the solitary drinker a social outlet. It would give Don friends who did not consider addiction a stigma. Don hid from the people he knew because he . . . knew others thought ill of him. He would not have to feel this way among AA members, who would be eager to give him true fellowship."[49] As this *Grapevine* article suggests, AA accepted the image of alcoholic solipsism, which Jackson himself had popularized, and offered itself as a means to counter social isolation. In this respect AA's self-endorsement dovetailed with the emerging paradigm of alcoholic pathology.

So important was the link between recovery and sociability, in fact, that AA members began to socialize outside regular meetings held in living rooms and church basements. By the 1940s AA members in many cities had established "clubhouses," communal spaces where they could spend leisure time with newfound friends. Although these establishments were not officially connected to AA (from the beginning Wilson and other leaders stipulated that AA, as a not-for-profit institution, could not own property in its name), members paid small dues to cover the rent for recreational spaces in converted apartment buildings, restaurants, and urban men's clubs. The first and most well-known social center was the 41st Street Clubhouse in New York City, founded in 1940. In a building previously used as a chapel and a men's club, AA members transformed the space into a "recreation hall" complete with a bowling alley, card and billiard room, library, gymnasium, and wood-paneled meeting room. Various leisure activities, including chamber music performances and informal dances, were held there. In other cities "Alano clubs," as they were often called, "contained nothing more than a few simple furnishings" and perhaps a kitchen for preparing sandwiches and coffee.[50]

While most *Grapevine* articles discussed the spiritual and psychological workings of the program, others covered social aspects to boost readers' morale. One issue in 1951 featured a photograph of AA members, most of whom were men, sitting and conversing at the Chicago Alano Club. The accompanying text described "Saturday night Coffee Klatches" where "members and their families gathered . . . to exorcise the Demon by playing cards, bingo and indulging in heavy conversation, with coffee and food added." Later that year another article depicted the New York clubhouse as a perfect place "to grab a cup of coffee and . . . have a little AA conversation."[51] All clubs, and all AA meetings, served coffee, which was known as the universal AA beverage. Using the abbreviation for the fellowship as an adjective—connoting a specific kind of conversation—the *Grapevine* represented AA itself as a form of sociability premised on abstinence. For many the combination of coffee and conversation was as important as the Twelve Steps in creating a culture of sobriety. One postwar sociologist characterized AA as "an unusually intimate primary group which sponsors . . . a new way of life—a new subculture. . . . The fellowship of the coffee bar, the bull sessions, the games, the parties, or the hours of private conversation over a cup of coffee somewhere. In countless ways, AA provides the rewards of satisfying social activities to replace the rewards previously sought in a drinking group, or . . . the bottle itself."[52]

The question of how these activities renewed men's fragile sense of masculinity is more complicated, however. Although the majority of AA members were men, other friends and family members, including wives and romantic partners, were welcome at AA clubhouses. Two *Grapevine* issues from 1951 offer contrasting evidence and suggest that AA men socialized both among themselves and in heterosocial groups. The February issue describes New York's 41st Street Clubhouse as a "hangout for guys and gals who like each other's company" and features two photographs of white, middle-aged men and women sitting on sofas and chairs, reading or conversing. The September issue, however, includes two photographs of the Chicago club, one of which shows men playing cards around a table. Together the images depict fifteen people, all white men of different ages. For many participants AA became a total social network providing opportunities for male camaraderie as well as an extension of their family lives. But the inclusion of women at some AA-related events (such as the popular New Year's Eve Party held annually in many cities) did not disqualify AA as a site for reconstructing manhood. In different ways both mixed-sex leisure and homosocial recreation could encourage AA men to restore a gendered sense of identity.

Because the renewal of masculinity was not the fellowship's explicit goal, the importance of manly camaraderie in AA must often be discerned through subtle clues. In 1944 a *Grapevine* submission described how AA Luncheons boosted morale. While AA members could not drink together, they derived "considerable benefit and pleasure from eating together . . . at convenient times and places throughout the week. The ritual of breaking bread at a common board never fails to produce that good fellowship sometimes attributed solely to the glass and the bottle." As the writer exclaimed, luncheon groups offered New York City members an "unsurpassed opportunity to make lasting friendships" and to "absorb invaluable pointers on the workings of the Program." But underneath the writer's enthusiasm lay a potentially disturbing concern, not about the therapeutic benefits of the luncheons, but about their feminine connotations. Indeed, daytime meals, easily associated with a dainty "ladies who lunch crowd," differed from the more robust, nighttime fellowship of "the glass and the bottle." Why else would the writer need to assure his reader that he would "find the conversation free from sentimentality and affectation, as the members explore . . . an infinite variety of topics with the gusto, assurance and fluency characteristic of their kind"?[53] By depicting the AA diners as full of "gusto," implying vigorous, hearty enjoyment, the writer offered a foil to emasculating images of effete consumption. The anxiety underlying his caution against "sentimentality and affectation" was, indeed, gender anxiety, and it offers telling insight into AA's creation of an alternative social culture in the absence of that traditional social lubricant, liquor. Apparently many AA members needed reassurance that sober manhood could be, well, manly.

Yet the primary basis of AA as an agent of resocialization lay not in new opportunities for leisure but, more fundamentally, in the Twelve Step program of recovery. In fact, some members criticized others for focusing too much on parties and social activities. One member from Cincinnati argued that "big events" like banquets and golf tournaments became "a hindrance rather than a help" because they distracted members from the serious work of rehabilitation. At the heart of the fellowship was the Twelfth Step, in which members carried the AA message to other alcoholics. As the Cincinnati member claimed, some men were "spending so much time arranging parties, running clubhouses, attending committee meetings that they [did not] have any time to go work with some poor, miserable and troublesome drunk."[54] Most members, in fact, agreed that the recreational advantages were secondary to the spiritual and psychological transformation effected by the AA program. The true meaning of fellowship reached beyond mere sociability and inhered in the mutual acts of compassion that Bill W. and Dr. Bob had pioneered. Ultimately the bond among members was deeper than conversation or common social interests; it resulted when one alcoholic profoundly influenced another's view of himself, his addiction, his relationships, and his place in the world.

The social and cultural meaning of Twelfth Step work can be interpreted in various ways. First and most obviously, AA drew on evangelical temperance reform and its missionary impulse. While AA's blend of an addiction model with discrete therapeutic steps was new in the history of drink, the idea of self-help had originated earlier, in the Reform Clubs and Washingtonian Societies of the mid-nineteenth century. In the 1840s ideas about self-transformation arising out of the Second Great Awakening provided key resources for drinking men in search of sobriety. A dry revival, sparked by six "reformed drunkards" in Baltimore, swept the nation and persuaded nearly 600,000 drinkers to sign an abstinence pledge as a means to social and moral purification. Like AA in the twentieth century, the Washingtonians offered hope to individuals too often dismissed as beyond help.[55] While AA rejected the moralistic rhetoric of nineteenth-century Protestant reform, it incorporated an essentially evangelical understanding of pietism. As Kurtz explains, "AA understood its message to be not the 'bad news' that salvation was necessary, but the 'good news' that salvation was available." What the Washingtonians saw as redemption, AA called recovery. Bill Wilson recognized the similarity between his own movement and the Washingtonians, who in his estimation had "almost discovered the answer to alcoholism." At first the Washingtonians focused solely on saving individual alcoholics; however, after they adopted other reform goals, such as abolition, they "lost their effectiveness in helping alcoholics." Wilson aimed to reconstruct his predecessors' original, single-minded goal of individual salvation. Although the founders characterized AA as a spiritual and not a denominationally religious institution, "even in secular and modern garb they firmly located Alcoholics Anonymous as a significant phenomenon in the history of religious ideas." While they departed from the attempt of evangelical groups to rescue sinners from Demon Rum, the teachings of AA were clearly based on traditional Protestant theology.[56]

AA had more recent religious roots as well. Bill Wilson had been the recipient of a religiously inspired Twelfth Step call even before he coined the phrase. Six months before Wilson traveled to Akron and met Dr. Bob, an old drinking buddy named Ebby T. encouraged him to join the Oxford Groups, a nondenominational evangelical movement based on a return to the ways of primitive Christianity. In November 1935 Ebby found sobriety through participation in the New York City Oxford Group, which promulgated the means to live a "Christian moral life." Curious about the organization that had influenced his friend, Wilson joined the group himself and was impressed by its principles of self-scrutiny, confession, restitution, and service to others. The notion of surrender to a higher power as a prerequisite for changing one's life also stemmed from Oxford Group teachings. At first the connection between the Oxford movement and AA was so strong that the AA groups in New York and Ohio remained part of the Oxford Group chapters, but within a few years AA had separated from its original sponsor. As Wilson later explained, "The Oxford Groups wanted to save the world, and I only wanted to save the drunks." Wilson was also troubled by the Oxford Group's insistence on moral absolutes, such as absolute purity and honesty, which he believed would intimidate potential recruits.[57]

Despite this connection to evangelical Christian tradition, however, AA members tended not to use religious rhetoric to describe Twelfth Step rituals. Advising readers about "working with others," the Big Book warned, "Don't start out as an evangelist or reformer." This advice echoed the founders' decision not to incorporate specific theological propositions into the program. Recounting his experience of writing the book, Wilson noted that some members "thought the book ought to be Christian in the doctrinal sense of the word, . . . using Biblical terms and expressions." Yet others espoused liberal or radical views toward religion; given the diverse beliefs among alcoholics, they rejected the "specifically religious approach" of Christian missionary work. As Wilson reasoned, "When it came to theology we could not possibly agree among ourselves, so how could we write a book that contained any such matter?" From this debate emerged the flexible wording of the Second and Third Steps: "Came to believe that a Power greater than ourselves could restore us to sanity" and "Made a decision to turn our will and our lives over to the care of God *as we understood Him.*" Here lay the fellowship's crucial distinction between religion and spirituality. The goal of AA when recruiting members was to "lure the alcoholic in" through psychological appeals; "once in, the prospect could take God or leave Him alone as he wished." According to Wilson the wording of the Twelve Steps "widened our gateway so that all who suffer might pass through, regardless of their belief or *lack of belief.* God was certainly there in our Steps, but He was now expressed in terms that anybody—*anybody at all*—could accept and try."[58] When describing their efforts to "carry the message," members were more likely to stress their connection with other people than with God's will. While they relied on a higher power to reform their own lives, they regarded Twelfth Step work *not* as an essentially religious calling but as a response to fellow human beings.

In this respect the insights of cultural anthropologists are especially illuminating. In his creative meditation on the symbolic meaning of gift exchange, literary and cultural critic Lewis Hyde interprets AA as a contemporary "gift economy." In his fascinating book *The Gift: Imagination and the Erotic Life of Property*, Hyde distinguishes between commodity exchange in a market economy and "the commerce of gifts" that occurs within small groups such as families, close-knit communities, brotherhoods, and tribes. Whereas commodities are subject to the "rational" laws of the market, bought and sold between parties for a specific "exchange value," gifts establish deeper relationships among the parties involved. "It is the cardinal difference between gift and commodity exchange that a gift establishes a feeling-bond between two people, while the sale of a commodity leaves no necessary connection," Hyde explains. Gift exchange is marked by obligation: obligations to give, to accept, and to reciprocate. Moreover, gifts are commonly circulated within "gift communities" where "their commerce leaves a series of interconnected relationships in its wake" and results in a "kind of decentralized cohesiveness." The bonds that gifts establish are not simply social; they may be spiritual and psychological as well. And gifts are not necessarily objects; they can also be "teachings," "interior gifts," or acts of emotional or psychological labor that affect the personal lives of those who receive them.[59]

As Hyde suggests, this last form of gift exchange—the circulation of "those infrequent lessons in living that alter, or even save, our lives"— describes the AA program. Indeed, the Twelfth Step exhorts AA members to become spiritual gift givers, agents who bestow the teachings of sobriety on fellow alcoholics. Such transformative gifts "carry an identity with them, and to accept the gift amounts to incorporating the new identity." Because the not-for-profit fellowship operates independently of the therapeutic marketplace, AA's teachings are free, a literal gift to members. Thus new members who become sober have received a gift of sobriety, but they have not yet passed along that gift to others, an essential characteristic of gift exchange communities. As in all gift exchanges, between the time one receives the gift and the time one passes it along, one feels a burden of gratitude. With gifts that are "agents of change," it is only when the gift has "worked" on the self that one can give it away to others. "Getting the program" in AA is a difficult personal labor, one that entails indebtedness. The Twelfth Step, then, is an "act of gratitude: recovered alcoholics help other alcoholics when called upon to do so. It is a step in which the gift is passed along, so it is right that it should be the final one." Systems of gift exchange thrive when recipients become givers and "the gifted become one with their gifts."[60]

Hyde's application of gift exchange theory to AA is stunningly apt. One of AA's most popular maxims is "Pass It On," a perfect example of "circular gift giving" in which "every gift calls for a return gift" but not a direct reciprocation. "When the gift moves in a circle no one ever receives it from the same person he gives it to. . . . [The gift's] motion is beyond the control of the personal ego, and so each bearer must be a part of the group and each donation is an act of social faith."[61] The gift of sobriety is indeed figured as a kind of spiritual rebirth, the acquisition of a new identity (literally marked by celebrating one year of abstinence with a "birthday party," complete with a cake). Hyde's interpretation moves beyond the commonly observed notion that AA provides a new social outlet for its members. It locates the source of social bonds in acts of personal commitment and collective faith. Bill Wilson stressed the importance of reciprocation from the outset; recalling his first meeting with Dr. Bob, he wrote, "Our talk was a completely *mutual* thing. . . . I knew that I needed this alcoholic as much as he needed me. *This was it.* And this mutual give-and-take is at the very heart of all of A.A's Twelfth Step work today."[62] As the fellowship grew from a single act of give-and-take, it created an interiorized gift economy based on psychic labor and group loyalty, forms of emotional currency with which members repay their debts of sobriety.

The language of gift exchange resonates throughout AA literature. In 1955, for example, one Indianapolis member writing under the pseudonym Father John Doe penned an unofficial companion volume to the more widely circulated Big Book. In no uncertain terms Father Doe described

AA as "a GIVE program." Paradoxically, he argued, "we keep only what we give away; for it is in the giving that we receive." Sobriety was merely "loaned" to the recovering alcoholic, so that he in turn "may give it to other alcoholics." Quite simply, the Twelfth Step was "gratitude in action." For readers who wondered how they might actually give to the fellowship, the author spared no details. He described almost every AA activity as a gift: giving talks at meetings, "lending an ear" to newcomers, donating change for refreshments, distributing the Big Book to others, and especially, sponsoring new members. In summary, he exclaimed, "Give whatever was given to you!"[63] The purpose of all this giving was not only benevolent; it was, ironically, selfish as well. The Twelfth Step was figured as essential to one's own sobriety; recovery *required* commitment to the group, which in turn thrived on members' continuing participation. Perhaps the most striking reference to gift exchange was offered by Ebby T., the man who inspired Wilson to join the Oxford Groups: "I did learn . . . to sum up my own character and confide all my faults to another person; to put right any wrongs I might have perpetrated; and, above all, to make a *present* of myself to other people."[64]

In some cases AA members expressed the theme of reciprocity in explicitly masculine language. In 1949, for instance, the Seattle group published a local newsletter containing a short poem titled "How is Your Twelfth Step Work Coming Along?"

> There is a destiny that makes us brothers,
> None goes his way alone; All that we send into the lives of others
> Comes back into our own.[65]

Such fraternal rhetoric was bolstered by the belief that Twelfth Step work literally had to take place among members of the same sex. As noted above, from the mid-1930s AA's founding members held fast to the notion that "man shouldn't sponsor woman and woman shouldn't sponsor man."[66] Sponsorship was the most intense form of bonding between members. The sponsor counseled his new recruit (also known as a "baby" or "pigeon") from the first days of detoxification and shepherded him through the program at all stages. The possibility of heterosexual attraction increased chances for emotional confusion and jealousy and thus was considered a "grave danger" for the already vulnerable alcoholic. This insistence on sex-segregated sponsorship, combined with AA's demographic composition, meant that most members experienced sponsorship as a bond between men. Familial language was frequently used; if not brotherhood, then father-son connections were invoked. Describing the path of resocialization, Selden Bacon explained that in "the first step toward the rebuilding of inter-personal relationships, the alcoholic learns to lean on his sponsor. This sort of father-son relationship is easy for him and is quite rewarding."[67]

The notion of Twelfth Step work as a male endeavor was reinforced in a number of Hollywood films. Characters inspired by AA first appeared on-screen in the early 1950s. From 1951 to 1962 at least six motion pictures featured AA (or AA-inspired) characters, including *Come Fill the Cup* (1951), *Come Back, Little Sheba* (1952), *I'll Cry Tomorrow* (1955), and *The Voice in the Mirror* (1958). "The hallmark of an AA-influenced movie," one scholar has noted, "seems to be the presence of a recovering alcoholic doing his (it is always a male) 'twelfth-step' work." The AA-oriented presentation of recovery was so far from typical Hollywood plot conventions that it can be read as a marker of direct AA influence. Even in plots revolving around female alcoholics, the sponsor was always a man. In *I'll Cry Tomorrow* (a film based on the autobiography of actress Lillian Roth), for example, the producers fit Twelfth Step work into conventional cinematic formulas by inventing a boy-meets-girl scenario, a convenient plot for the filmmakers but a historically inaccurate detail.[68] What is important, however, is the prevailing image of sponsorship as a masculine calling.

The Voice in the Mirror, for example, featured Jim (Richard Egan), a commercial artist whose alcoholic recovery centered on his role in a chain of "drunks helping drunks" reminiscent of AA. The film faithfully reflected the contemporaneous AA worldview, showing Jim recruiting down-and-out drunks from soup kitchens, hospitals, and police stations. In *Come Back, Little Sheba*, Doc Delaney (Burt Lancaster) is a middle-aged chiropractor about to celebrate his first year of sobriety in AA. The film opens with the scene of an AA meeting, which Doc attends every night with his own sponsor, Ed (Philip Ober). Doc and Ed make frequent Twelfth Step calls together, "carrying the AA message" to ensure their own sobriety. When Doc eventually suffers a relapse, his wife, Lola (Shirley Booth), frantically calls Ed, who arrives with another male AA member to take Doc to the hospital. The first cinematic treatment of "drunks helping drunks" was in *Come Fill the Cup*, starring James Cagney as Lew Marsh, a hard-boiled newspaper editor who loses his job due to heavy drinking. After he "hits bottom" with delirium tremens in a detoxification ward, he moves in with Charlie (James Gleason), an unmarried recovering alcoholic who teaches him how to abstain from drink "one day at a time." After benefiting from Charlie's wise counsel, Lew returns to work and devotes himself to sobering up fellow journalists. Although the plot includes a romantic love interest on Lew's part, his relationship with Paula (a former coeditor) founders on the shoals of his alcoholism; once Lew moves in with Charlie, the film centers on same-sex therapeutic relationships among alcoholic bachelors.[69] While *Come Fill the Cup* does not mention AA explicitly, its debt to the fellowship is obvious.

Considering the culture of sobriety as a form of gift exchange is especially apt when it is compared to the culture of drink. As discussed in Chapter 1, the definition of circular giving applies equally well to the ritual of treating in a bar or tavern. There each drinker must treat the others to a round of drinks; after consuming drinks purchased by others, one must pay a collective debt to the group rather than to any one individual. As people come and go, the treating continues; the group coheres as long as enough people keep paying the tab in sequence. The connection of liquor to sociability stems not only from its intoxicating effects but from its status as a gift, a tangible, consumable binder of relationship.[70] To the extent that AA functioned as an alternative social arena to the tavern, the non-hierarchical rituals of the Twelfth Step mirrored the ethic of mutuality embodied in treating customs. Neither treating nor "Twelfth Stepping" was figured as an exact, measured payment for gifts or services received; rather, both implied a continued state of obligation. Consider how easily the dynamics of drinking customs apply to AA: "Drinking in groups . . . became a symbol of egalitarianism. All men were equal before the bottle." In AA, of course, all men were equal before the task of *avoiding* the bottle, but in both cases, gift exchange positioned men within moral economies of reciprocity, loyalty, and solidarity.[71]

In some cases AA members figured the labor of sobriety as a literal effort to avoid the bottle—as much a "ritual of masculine renewal" as the custom of treating had been. While visiting local archives throughout the United States and Canada, AA historian Wally P. discovered a telling object displayed in the Vancouver Central Office: an original bottle of imported brandy that was transferred annually from alcoholic to alcoholic from 1946 to 1979. Quoting a local history of AA in British Columbia, Wally noted that "this bottle was bought by Fred's son back in 1946. Fred was an A.A. member. The son gave it to his dad so he could continue to help the drinking alcoholic. Fred decided to pass the bottle from one member to another on an honor system. Each member who held the bottle had the honor of passing it on to another who was active and felt that he could carry it for a year without opening it."[72] In an ironic reversal, AA members used an actual bottle to symbolize abstinence, the opposite of its usual cultural meaning. Given AA's view of alcoholism as a progressive illness, within AA "the bottle" not only signifies drunkenness but also self-destruction and, ultimately, death.[73] Yet in the hands of Vancouver's recovering alcoholics, an *unopened* bottle embodied sobriety, even life itself, and it made concrete the chain of gift exchange linking one sober member to another. Whereas alcohol consumption once enacted masculine affiliation and entitlement, now one's manly honor was proven by resisting consumption, by being "man" enough to leave the bottle alone. While social drinking could be a sign of manliness, excessive alcohol consumption, and especially dependence, was an emasculating mark of weakness. Receiving a sealed bottle of brandy allowed members to test their manhood while simultaneously testing their sobriety. Fittingly, the protagonist of *A Voice in the Mirror* keeps a bottle of liquor at home, showing that "temptation is to be faced up to rather than avoided."[74] In this way AA men redefined the cultural meaning of the bottle in their quest for sober manhood.

For some AA members the bottle had other symbolic definitions as well; it could be "battled" and "fought," not merely avoided. While many observers viewed AA men as spiritual missionaries or healing gift givers, others depicted them as valiant fighters, warriors against the formidable foes of drink and drunkenness. This metaphor was not embraced by all members or even by founders Wilson and Smith. In fact, the emphasis in the official literature on "surrendering" oneself to a higher power and "giving up" a willful struggle against one's affliction contrasted with martial metaphors. Nonetheless, a number of sources suggest that many recruits perceived their recovery efforts as a battle against the bottle even as they applied the spiritual principles of the Twelve Steps. Such a paradox suggests that AA's therapeutic program was rhetorically and ideologically flexible and allowed various metaphorical interpretations.

One article in the 1945 *Grapevine*, for example, described the recovering drinker's task as a daily battle of vigilance. Another member wrote an AA-inspired novel titled *The Bottle Fighters*. Consider how author George E. Willis described a fictionalized "local club" of AA: "They are good men, smart men, and they fight a terminal disease that many a doctor in private practice will not touch with a ten-foot pole. . . . They did it by sitting at tables, two by two, or sometimes by two sponsors and two pupils sitting together. They fight by mutual encouragement." According to Willis, AA members adhered to the program "for themselves, for the sake of their manhood, and not for the dubious privilege of passing their hymnals around among the saved."[75] Replacing images of temperance crusaders saving the fallen with the rhetoric of regeneration through discipline, Willis figured fellowship not as a feminizing sign of dependence but as a source of vitality and collective strength.

In another passage Willis used a militaristic vocabulary to describe AA's brand of comradeship. Near the end of the novel, after telling the story of two married couples from the perspective of an unnamed, first-person narrator (an AA Twelfth Stepper), Willis offered a philosophical digression. As the narrator speculated, one day historians would wonder "if the AA movement was not the first application of the exhortation of William James that we should find a moral equivalent for war." He continued, "likening a meeting of AA members to a company of soldiers gathered under the leadership of an elected captain, a company of soldiers with the morale of a crack combat outfit in the line." Invoking James's famous essay of 1910, Willis portrayed his "bottle fighters" as heirs to an enduring martial tradition of strenuous exertion, honor, and service. How else could one "explain the camaraderie of men who are fighting together for their lives and yet have no guns in their hands?"[76]

As a novelist and unwitting cultural critic, Willis offered a compelling interpretation of AA's gendered ideological work. Indeed, William James had been the central figure in a significant cultural effort to reconstruct manhood in the United States. The subject of manhood was indisputably important to the nation's preeminent psychologist and philosopher, who guided a coterie of New England intellectuals in creating an ideal of manliness rooted in "active, healthy, and gentlemanly" pursuits. At the heart of James's teachings was an effort to "teach men manhood," to instill in students a masculinist ethos of individual character, moral responsibility, and social commitment. In "The Moral Equivalent of War," written one year before his death, James critiqued the "irrationality and horror" of war yet heralded the values of military life. While shunning the "cruelty" and "callousness" of bloody battle, James held fast to the "military ideals of hardihood and discipline." Paradoxically, he urged pacifists to "make new energies and hardihoods continue the manliness to which the military mind so faithfully clings." In his view men would always be pugnacious, but they would do more good if they ceased fighting one another and battled the obstacles of civic progress instead. According to James, American men needed a "moral equivalent of war," a system of social organization that would inculcate virtues such as "intrepidity, contempt of softness, surrender of private interest, and obedience to command." "Such a conscription," would "preserve manliness" by producing citizens with "healthier sympathies and soberer ideas."[77]

Obviously sympathetic to James's vision, Willis found in AA a suitably Jamesian climate of service and cooperation, an honorable means "for awakening the higher ranges of men's spiritual energy." Willis posited the AA program as a means of preserving manhood: the collective fight against alcoholism not only saved men's lives, it also ensured that their lives would remain worth living. Indeed, the metaphor of AA group as battalion was a far cry from contemporaneous accounts of Twelve Step "luncheons" or clubhouse "bull sessions." Here the Twelfth Step caller was not merely a friend or counselor; he was a kind of experienced soldier, ready to boost the esprit de corps of his fellow infantrymen. When a recovering alcoholic "slipped," he was like a wounded warrior, and it was the duty of his fellow soldiers to secure a passage to safety. As the narrator explained, "When one man falls, it hurts the morale of all the men, any place it happens. I was happy that I was bringing new tools, new thoughts and new ideas to them." If alcoholic excess had imperiled one's manhood—as experts and producers of popular culture suggested—then the fellowship's martial camaraderie would restore it anew.

Although *The Bottle Fighters* was not published until 1963, earlier writers prefigured Willis's mobilizing rhetoric of collective duty. In 1943 a Chicago judge delivered an inspirational speech titled "Why We Were Chosen" in honor of his local chapter's fourth anniversary. The speech began, "God in His wisdom selected this group of men to be the purveyors of His Goodness." As the judge explained, God had turned to "the drunkard, the so-called weakling of the world . . . to spread the message of recovery." He then spoke to his audience as if they were addressed by God himself.

Well might He have said to us: To you has been given that which has been denied the most learned of your fellows. Not to scientists or statesmen, not to wives or mothers, not even to my priests or ministers have I given this gift of healing other alcoholics. . . . It must be used unselfishly; no demands upon our time can be too urgent; no case be too pitiful; no task too hard; no effort too great. . . . Personal criticism you must expect; lack of appreciation will be common. . . . You must be prepared for adversity, for what men call adversity is the ladder . . . toward spiritual perfection.[78]

Inspiring listeners to face "adversity" in mind and body, the judge offered a Jamesian call to arms; combining evangelical exhortation with martial imagery, he hailed the sober alcoholic as a steady Christian soldier for whom no task would "be too great." Later reprinted by groups throughout the country, this speech positioned AA men in contrast to both male authorities and the female "wives and mothers" of the Woman's Christian Temperance Union. Although in later years local chapters changed the first sentence of the passage to include both men and women, the original text entrusted the battle against drunkenness to an army of rank-and-file alcoholics, men whose healing power derived from experience, fortitude, and a gendered claim to public service.

The link between AA and war was not, however, merely rhetorical; it was rooted in history. When novelist George Willis likened an AA meeting "to a company of soldiers gathered under the leadership of an elected captain," his analogy rang true on several levels. For one thing, Bill Wilson was a veteran of World War I, and his years in the armed services were formative. In July 1918, six months after he married his fiancée, Lois Burnham, Wilson set sail on a battleship for France, one of 2 million Americans transferred overseas. According to Wilson's biographer Robert Thomsen, Bill "believed deeply in what the war was about"; some even said that he gloried in the war. If that was true, Thomsen writes, "it was not because he loved bloodshed but because of his staunch belief in the rightness of 'our cause' and because the army was offering him a new outlet for his energies." His heady experiences as a second lieutenant at war continued after he returned to the United States, where he enjoyed the respect and adulation accorded the nation's war heroes. As Wilson recalled his homecoming, at "twenty-two, and a veteran of foreign wars, I went home at last. I fancied myself a leader, for had not the men of my battery given me a special token of appreciation? My talent for leadership, I imagined, would place me at the head of vast enterprises which I would manage with utmost assurance." Ambitious to achieve wealth and power, Wilson aimed to re-create at home the "glorious campaign" he pursued at war. As Thomsen suggests, Wilson's alcoholism worsened as he was plagued with self-doubt about his ability to achieve this goal. Though he studied law and succeeded on Wall Street, he never recaptured the sense of glory he had felt during the war—until he founded AA. On a personal level, then, Wilson experienced AA as a "moral equivalent of war," a new outlet for his talent at stewardship and a fitting substitute for the "rough comradeship of active service" he had missed for nearly two decades.[79]

In fact Bill's exposure to the notion of a moral equivalent of war began even before he fought abroad, when he trained as a cadet at the military training camp in Plattsburgh, New York. In 1917, while attending college at Norwich University in Vermont, Bill enlisted in the Reserve Officers' Training Corps and was sent to the army base at Plattsburgh, which was hailed in 1915 as a practical application of James's theory. That year the *New Republic* argued that Plattsburgh men not only learned to fight against external enemies; they also received basic "training . . . in American citizenship." Plattsburgh's officers sought "to attach soldiering to citizenship . . . in such a way as to make the soldier really a civilian." Habits of mental and physical discipline would be useful not just in waging war but in assuring "the body politic the benefits of disinterested service." Apparently his short time at Plattsburgh made a lasting impression, for almost two decades later Wilson incorporated many of the principles he learned there, especially the ideal of a "moral economy" based on self-discipline and collective service, into the therapeutic community of AA.[80]

While the memory of the Great War informed Wilson's role as founder, however, the decade of AA's national expansion witnessed a war of its own. American society in the 1940s was dominated by World War II, and the demobilization of veterans in 1945 was as important to AA's growing hegemony as the psychic legacy of homecoming in 1918. Chapter 2 has already explored the crucial role of World War II in the representation of alcoholism in the mass media. AA also recognized the need for rehabilitation among alcoholic veterans and positioned itself as an alternative to life in the military. In 1945 the *Grapevine* featured an article titled "A Postwar Challenge," written by a World War I veteran who "began his own drinking career as a result of boredom with readjustment to civilian life." Many returning servicemen, he argued, faced "another unfinished battle" against another "dangerous enemy, John Barleycorn." Because veterans would miss "that rare sense of comradeship that often is the best part of life in the service," they would need even more help evading "the booby traps and mine fields old John places so skillfully in the path of the alcoholic." The following year a World War II veteran testified to AA's success. The normal problems of readjustment—finding "a home and a job and a chance to earn security"—were especially hard on "the demobilized AA" because he could no longer turn to liquor for solace. "We AAs who are also veterans need our group . . . as much or more than ever before. . . . It is only when we look at life with the sanity that AA teaches, that we can win out. . . . It has been no bed of roses. It has been damned hard. Five years ago

I had my last drink after ten years of drunkenness. With the help of God and AA that will still continue to be my last drink."[81]

Finally, some local groups allied AA with the military effort during World War II. Apparently AA was not exempt from the tendency to construe everyday tasks (whether working overtime at a factory, shopping for rationed groceries, or riding the bus to save gasoline) as valiant efforts on the home front "battlefield." In 1942 at least one local chapter defined itself as a civilian equivalent to the nation's fighting armies. A flyer titled "An AA's Pledge for National Defense and Self-Preservation" invited members to take a ten-part pledge to support the war effort. Underneath a patriotic image of the American flag, the text exhorted readers to keep fit "physically, mentally, spiritually—to be ready for any crisis"; to conduct one's business "with a clear eye, a cool head and a stout heart"; to "take an active interest in government . . . and public affairs"; and to "vote in every election." The flyer did not mention sobriety per se; rather, it implied that individual health—and the nation's very survival—depended on continued abstinence.[82]

Though it might seem like a typical example of home front propaganda, this flyer is an unusual document in the AA archives. In 1946 Bill Wilson inscribed a series of Twelve Traditions to complement the Twelve Steps. The steps were precepts for individual members, while the traditions guided the fellowship itself. Included were regulations that AA may never endorse any enterprise or political cause, that it "has no opinion on outside issues," and that its sole purpose is to "carry its message to the alcoholic who still suffers." Even before the Twelve Traditions were published, local groups tended not to ally themselves publicly with social causes or political actions. According to these nascent traditions, even World War II fell outside the fellowship's circumscribed domain of concern. But in this instance the magnitude and popularity of the war effort overwhelmed the group's isolationism. Given the all-encompassing presence of the war, it is not surprising that some members figured the AA program as a patriotic equivalent of active military service, and not merely a metaphorical alternative in the war's aftermath.

Through its rituals of fellowship, AA offered members a way to achieve sobriety apart from two traditionally masculine spheres of social life: the tavern and the trenches. When the fellowship took root in the 1930s and 1940s, most male members would have inhabited one or both of these social milieus during their lifetimes. For such men the Twelve Steps provided spiritual and psychological guidelines to reconstruct their lives, while social events created further opportunities for mutual support. Yet to understand the culture of sobriety in its full complexity, we also need to consider how sober alcoholics acquired and expressed their identities through oral and written narratives. As folklore scholar Edmund O'Reilly has argued, in AA "stories are the essential medium of currency, the means by which consolation and admonition, theory and counsel are exchanged."[83] The content of autobiographical recovery narratives reveals as much about the history of the fellowship as its social rituals.

GENDERED NARRATIVES OF ILLNESS AND RECOVERY

The centrality of autobiography—and especially of individual confession narratives—in AA is well known even to the fellowship's most casual observers. Many who have never attended an AA gathering know that meetings revolve around the telling of stories, personal monologues that invariably begin with the phrase, "My name is —, and I'm an alcoholic." These stories follow a set of established narrative conventions, including the recitation of past drinking abuses and the relative benefits of a sober lifestyle. Indeed, storytelling is the primary means through which AA members reconstruct their identities as recovering alcoholics. "Telling the story," Edmund O'Reilly writes, "enables the speaker to reconstruct a chaotic, absurd, or violent past as a meaningful, indeed a *necessary*, prelude to the structured, purposeful, and comparatively serene present." Autobiographical narratives are preeminent in the Big Book, which devotes over half of its pages to the personal stories of members. Bill Wilson's story, which encapsulates the early history of AA itself, is the paradigmatic tale of the fellowship. It comprises the first chapter of the Big Book and thus sets the stage for all the others.[84] In a sense the Big Book functions as a textual version of an AA meeting, inviting readers to formulate their own stories after hearing (or reading) those of others.

The personal stories in the Big Book provide the best extant evidence of early recovery narratives. Because speeches given by AA members were rarely transcribed or recorded at meetings, uncovering the history of AA's oral narrative tradition is a difficult task. While current observers have access to monologues delivered at present-day AA gatherings, we must rely on secondary accounts for glimpses into the form and content of spoken narratives in the past. Nonetheless, even fragmentary evidence allows us to understand these stories as gendered performances of identity and provides a framework for contextualizing the printed narratives of the Big Book.

Numerous contemporary observers commented on the nature of storytelling at meetings. Monologues touched on a variety of topics. Some focused on the Twelve Steps, some emphasized the disease concept of alcoholism, and others stressed the importance of regular attendance at meetings. But according to one Chicago sociologist who analyzed dozens of speeches in the early 1950s, the most common topic was a "personal story or confession of speaker."[85] Public health administrator Joseph Hirsh agreed. "AA's are the world's most constant confessors," he wrote. "About as modest as a burlesque queen, they're quick to tell anyone who'll listen—in a happy kind of catharsis—of the days when they ranged from bottle-nursers and tipplers to tosspots and just plain drunks." Speakers recounted the litany of excuses, deceptions, ruses, and other "guilty secrets" they once used to rationalize or hide their drinking. Another sociologist argued that "the whole process of relating past experiences and comparing notes" created a common "alcoholic culture" forged through a continual "process of half-humorous confession."[86]

According to several first-person accounts in the *Grapevine*, there was a gendered dimension to many storytelling sessions. One California member wrote to the newsletter about the "Saturday night bull sessions" at his local AA club. In one room, he explained, men and women played poker and bingo together. But in another anteroom nicknamed the "dry saloon," men gathered to trade vivid stories of their drinking days. Dubbed the "dry saloon boys," an exclusive membership of men regaled themselves with exaggerated, "sometimes gruesome tales" of past alcoholic exploits. "Since most of us did our drinking in other parts of the State, or outside the State, we are allowed to exaggerate, lie to our hearts' content. The only requirement is that once having related a particular drinking bout, we must remember to relate the same bout in the same way every time. . . . Spoons rattle in coffee cups while minds aren't on coffee at all," he reported. But despite his lighthearted tone, he noted a negative consequence to these manly tales of bravado. Often this narrative entertainment heightened nostalgia for drink, leading to a relapse among the "least stable" members. "Statistically," he wrote, "it's a fact that if you want to slip in my city, the place to condition yourself is the Saturday night bull session at the social club."[87]

A writer from Atlanta was even more critical of the speeches he heard at meetings. In his view many members told graphic stories of past abuses to prove their manhood to fellow members, a practice he found distasteful:

> That the measure of manhood to a drunk is how much liquor he can drink at any given time, or how much he did drink upon some historical occasion, is not surprising; but it is perhaps a little more difficult to see why this should be true of an AA member who has been away from the stuff for years. Nevertheless, this seems to be the criterion, in speech after speech I have heard at meetings. Of course the quantities of alcohol consumed can be interesting and often inspiring to listen to, but it sometimes shames me and I have to hang my head. . . . I question if I ever "drank like a man"; I always drank like a pig.[88]

Even while maintaining their sobriety, many members bolstered their self-image by invoking the cultural association between drinking and masculinity. If they could no longer drink heavily, at least they could *talk* about drinking heavily, and such talk might ensure manly self-esteem. In challenging what seems to have been a common strategy among male members, this writer hoped that the reader "who shyly avoids swapping stories for fear he will not look 'man' enough would take heart" in his letter. Like the California member cited above, he found that confessional narratives sometimes went too far, threatening members' dignity as well as their sobriety. In his view memories of "drinking like a pig," a gluttonous animal, comprised a lame foundation indeed for reconstructing manhood.

This Atlanta writer was interested in redefining his role as a man, but he rejected the swapping of "dry saloon tales" as a suitable means to that end. Like many members of AA, he was married and felt great remorse about the unhappiness his drinking caused his family. But he had never beaten his wife, lost his job, or spent weeks in a sanitarium, so how would it benefit him to hear stories of such gruesome events? For him the path to sober manhood entailed more than a dry version of manly conviviality. It needed to encompass, not to neglect, his marital role as a husband. Fortunately, however, the fellowship offered a more complex and multivalent model of gender identity than he found in so many spoken bull sessions. Indeed, the Big Book offered alternative stories of sober manhood—stories in which past drinking exploits or homosocial bonding were mere preludes to men's reclamation of familial authority. Apparently many members found both aspects of gender identity essential to the formation of sober manhood; taken together, spoken and written AA narratives fulfilled this double need.

The twofold task of re-creating manly camaraderie and reclaiming domestic masculinity was a pervasive, if sometimes implicit, theme in the Big Book. One narrative, titled "A Business Man's Recovery," told the story of a World War I veteran who "sowed his wild oats" in his youth but resolved to "settle down to be a good husband and live a normal happy life" upon marrying his beloved bride. Yet after six months of abstinence he resumed drinking, until he "met that band of life-savers, Alcoholics Anonymous" many years later. While his story subtly invoked the gendered rhetoric of AA as a manly therapeutic community, the author assessed his sobriety in terms of its effects on his marriage and his work. "It was plain to see that my wife was radiantly happy. All of the . . . worry, confusion, the hectic days and nights that my drinking had poured into our life together, vanished. There was peace. There was real love, . . . kindness and consideration. There was everything that goes into the fabric of a happy normal existence together." The spiritual magic of AA also permeated the workplace, where he was rewarded with a promotion. In this account the masculine fellowship of AA was not an end in itself but, rather, a means to achieving marital harmony and career success. "Come into my home and see what a happy one it is," he wrote. "Look into my office, it is a happy human beehive of activity."[89] The total corpus of AA narratives represented the turbulent past as a prelude to a relatively serene present, but some stories emphasized one temporal moment over another. Some, including the businessman cited above, remembered the camaraderie of drink as an obstacle to marriage and domestic commitment. If a member equated the sober present with a harmonious home life, he was likely to censure rather than celebrate the sociability of the past.

Many writers emphasized their roles as husbands and family providers. Far from regaling readers with tales of drinking bouts, one contributor to the Big Book stressed that he had been "an injured husband and an unappreciated father." When his wife left him temporarily, he was despondent over the separation. For him the ultimate reward of sobriety, and of continued Twelfth Step work, was domestic reconciliation. "Our home is a happy one," he concluded. "My children no longer hide when they see me coming. My business has improved. . . . In our town there are some 70 of us, ready and willing . . . to show the way to sobriety and sanity to men who are like what we used to be." Another chapter, titled "The Salesman," ended on a similar note. "I have been reunited with my wife, making good in businesses, and paying off debts as I am able."[90] In his novel *An Alcoholic to His Sons*, written on behalf of an anonymous AA member in New

England, author Henry Beetle Hough also stressed the havoc drinking wrought upon family life. When he drank, the narrator confessed, he was "penitent." "I loved Alice [his wife]. I loved my sons. I felt great pride in my family and my home. . . . I wanted to stop drinking . . . and make a good husband and father. I wanted to be clear-headed and to do the best work of which I was capable. . . . But it did not prevent me, at some given moment, from needing a drink." Ironically, Hough's narrator mused, drinking and the "cult of hard liquor" made men feel manly, but it ruined the personal lives of many individuals. Feeling guilty and humiliated in the face of his wife's disappointment was the opposite of robust masculinity.[91] For many married alcoholics sobriety was linked with the promise of renewed family life and the heightened self-confidence it entailed.

Other writers wove both models of masculine identity into their stories, associating each with a different stage of their drinking (or nondrinking) careers. In one typical Big Book narrative, the "Home Brewmeister" invoked the paradigm of dissolute manhood when describing his years of alcoholic excess. When he was not spending time in "beer joints" with friends, he entertained guests at parties that "waxed more liquid and hilarious as time went on." Soon he was a "top flight drunkard," with a lackluster career to show for it. After he was fired from his job as a salesman, he tried to find other employment, but he soon learned that "a person just can't find a job hanging in a dive or a barroom all day and all night." He also confessed to committing "other indiscretions of which [he saw] no particular point in relating. Anyone who is a rummy or is close to rummies knows what all those things amount to without having to be told about them." This confession immediately followed a remark about his "not so patient wife" and the difficulties she faced in coping with his drunkenness. Although married, he still behaved like a carousing bachelor; adultery, he implied, was a shameful part of his alcoholic past.[92]

Despite mounting debts and "other indiscretions," however, his wife stayed with him and eventually convinced him to consult a doctor about his alcoholism. In his life and his narrative, hospitalization and AA functioned as a crucial "turning point" that led him to substitute sobriety for intoxication and to exchange domestic respectability for his wanton ways. Contrast his earlier confessional rhetoric with the latter half of his vignette:

After being in the hospital for several days, a plan of living was outlined to me . . . that I find much joy and happiness in following. It is impossible to put on paper all the benefits I have derived . . . physical, mental, domestic, spiritual, and monetary. . . . From a domestic standpoint, we really have a home now. I am anxious to get home after dark. My wife is ever glad to see me come in. My youngster has adopted me. Our home is always full of friends and visitors (No home brew as an inducement). . . . I have reduced my reckless debts to almost nothing, and have had money to get along comfortably. . . . For all of these blessings, I thank Him.[93]

This writer figured the transition from alcoholism to sobriety as a move from dissolute to respectable manhood. He used the spiritual and therapeutic vocabulary of AA to understand the significant changes he made in his life—changes that went far beyond mere abstinence from alcohol. In addition to improved physical and mental health, the "blessings of sobriety" included "domestic" and "monetary" successes that benefited the family as a whole. From the hindsight of recovery the author recalled his drinking past with both nostalgia and regret, for the unbridled pleasures of "wine, women, and song" were also the lamentable failures of domestic masculinity.

The gendered prerogatives of manhood could be subtle, however. Consider the following passage from Bill Wilson's own story, in which he recounted the achievements of the nascent fellowship in 1939: "I have seen hundreds of families set their feet in the path that really goes somewhere; have seen the most impossible domestic situations righted; feuds and bitterness of all sorts wiped out. I have seen men come out of asylums and resume a vital place in the lives of their families and communities. Business and professional men have regained their standing." Surely, Wilson implied, wives and children benefited from the improved "domestic situations" of sober alcoholics, but he emphasized the "vital place" and restored "standing" of the men themselves. The renewal of men's breadwinning ability was especially important. Although Wilson embraced spiritual values over material aspirations once he achieved sobriety, he stressed the benefits of financial solvency and security for recovering alcoholics. AA could not guarantee men success at work, nor was it properly regarded as a job placement service. But as AA literature suggested, sobriety promised economic improvement, almost axiomatically. "When sober and working," Wilson claimed, "few alcoholics have any money trouble. Our earning power as individuals may actually be double the average. The material pay-off, as well as the spiritual pay-off, of AA's way of life is downright incredible."[94] As Wilson retold his own life story, his darkest alcoholic days were marked by the humiliation of financial dependence on his wife, Lois. After the stock market crash of 1929, Lois worked as a saleswoman and interior decorator at a department store; her earnings were the couple's sole support for many years. In keeping with dominant attitudes at the time, Wilson believed that a husband was supposed to support his wife; for him the baneful effects of alcoholism were intertwined with the shame of economic dependence. In promising good fortune as well as good health, AA's vision of sobriety invited men to reclaim the familial status and privileges that came with breadwinning.

Nonetheless, money was a vexed issue in the fellowship. As a not-for-profit organization AA was (and remains) an essentially anticommercial institution. As stipulated in the Sixth Tradition, AA groups promise never to "endorse, finance, or lend the AA name to any related facility or outside enterprise, lest problems of money, property, and prestige divert us from our primary purpose." If mercenary interests could threaten the integrity of the fellowship as a whole, so, too, could the quest for material gain threaten the moral and psychic well-being of individual members. Thus many AA members, including Wilson, emphasized spiritual commitment and serenity over worldly success. In *Sobriety and Beyond* Father John Doe classified three categories of attitudes among AA members: good, bad, and "half-and-half." Members in the first category regulated their entire lives according to spiritual values, relegating the pursuit of prosperity to "the Will of God." Individuals in the latter group had a "partly spiritual, partly material attitude" and sometimes sought material advancement over peace of mind. The worst attitude was "completely material," in which "every striving and longing and determination [was] for material advancement, material pleasure, material well-being."[95] Another writer, publishing under the pseudonym Jay Clancy, agreed that "money cannot buy what we want most of AA—serenity." Yet at the same time Clancy confessed to a "strange coincidence": the less he concentrated on making money, the more he made. His message was that benevolence toward other alcoholics—what he called "Alley charity"—could pay financial as well as moral dividends (although he did not explain how Twelfth Step work translated into actual profit).[96] He implied that the renunciation of materialism could result, paradoxically, in a financial windfall, one that was all the more deserved because it did not stem from mercenary striving.

Affluence and financial stability were not the same, however, and most

AA spokespersons emphasized the latter. In part Bill Wilson attributed his alcoholism to his earlier obsession with wealth and power. In his view the relentless pursuit of prosperity fueled the very anxieties that alcoholics sought to alleviate through drink. While some sober members boasted about the lucrative salaries they earned, most described a gradual process of finding employment and paying off debts. One AA novel featured a speaker who "described his drinking career up to the point where his wife was about to leave him and take the three children with her. At that time the house was mortgaged and he was unable to meet the payments, and all the furniture was hocked with a finance company." He contrasted such a dire predicament with his status after three months of sobriety: "I'm not worried about tomorrow. The boss that I formerly thought was such a tyrant has taken me back. I've even had a raise. The bank has extended me all the time that I need. . . . The furniture did not get taken away . . . [and] we are even able, occasionally, to afford a baby-sitter."[97]

The typical AA narrative told a story of modest gains, yet even modest stories revealed a deep dedication to the role of self-reliant breadwinner. Indeed, AA offered itself as an antidote to one of the alcoholic's greatest failures: economic dependence and insolvency. If the active alcoholic man was a bad financial risk to his employer and his family, the sober AA member was virtually a sure bet. While psychologists diagnosed "immature" alcoholics who shirked adult responsibility, the Big Book recounted "A Businessman's Recovery" that culminated in "more confidence, more trust," and "a key executive position" for its sober narrator. While *The Lost Weekend* depicted a besotted, indebted, frustrated novelist, *Come Fill the Cup* portrayed a recovering newspaper editor who profited from his renewed commitment to his career. By emphasizing breadwinning as a primary benefit of recovery, AA writers underscored their commitment to family life and domestic consumption. When they listed the material advantages of sobriety, they mentioned home mortgages, furniture, and the monthly bills of workaday life. Thus even as they engaged in rituals and rhetoric of male bonding, AA members often described the rewards of sobriety in familial terms. In different ways the masculine cultures of drink and sobriety lured men away from the domestic domain, but for those who were married (a majority, it seems), the demands and promises of marriage marked the successes of recovery as surely as they had once signaled the failures of alcoholism.

Moreover, recovery narratives helped to explain the occurrence of personal failure in the first place. By positing alcoholism as a physical, mental, and spiritual malady circumscribed within the self, and by construing alcoholism as the primary (if not only) variable leading to men's defeat in the workplace, AA ignored the broader social factors that weakened men's economic status during the 1930s and 1940s. In subsequent printings of the Big Book from 1939 to 1955, the personal stories remained virtually unchanged; throughout this period the story of alcoholic declension over-shadowed other structural factors affecting men's breadwinning ability (such as the skyrocketing unemployment rate during the Great Depression or the fierce competition for skilled jobs after World War II). By linking sobriety to individual success, these narratives facilitated the trend that historian William Graebner has termed "turning inward"—looking within the self and not to society at large to bring about a desired life change.[98] In this sense AA furthered the depoliticization of alcohol in U.S. society, a process engendered by lay Twelfth Step healers and professional experts alike.

The early members of AA created new conventions of fellowship, which in turn fostered a culture of reciprocity and loyalty among men. AA's ideal of sober manhood drew simultaneously on multiple, even opposing paradigms of masculine identity, normative ideals of gender that had long shaped cultural experiences of drink and alcoholism. On one hand, AA restored its members' wounded manhood by immersing them in a social and psychological sphere that replaced the manly camaraderie once forged in bars and battalions. But on the other hand, many perceived their participation in AA as a training ground for respectable manhood, rooted in the obligations of marriage and family life. If they viewed their quest for sobriety as a battle against the bottle and their fellow "brothers" as comrades-without-arms, they fought in part for the ability, and perhaps the will, to become better husbands and fathers. While they relished and protected the fraternal bonds they cemented in AA, many found that the sweetest fruits of fellowship ripened at home. Indeed, AA's implicit model of masculinity was supple and complex, and for men torn between the competing pulls of dissipated and dependable manhood, the fellowship allowed them to reconcile both at the same time.

AA's model of sober manhood was available to men across the class spectrum. The fellowship invited working-class, middle-class, and well-to-do men to replace their former drinking ways with the camaraderie of sobriety. But no matter the social standing of individual AA members (and many, as we have seen, had been part of the professional or salaried middle classes), AA's homosocial culture of sobriety maintained a symbolic link to the rough world of working-class masculinity. In the words of one female member from the 1950s, most AA men had been "conditioned by their bar experiences" to view fellow drinkers as comrades bound by treating rituals. As a fellowship for ex-drinkers, AA replaced the currency of liquor with spiritual and therapeutic gift exchange and thus reformulated working-class patterns of interaction into a program befitting the needs of middle-class members at midcentury. The material payoffs of sobriety manifested the fellowship's ability to translate traditional saloon culture into terms useful to a more "respectable" culture of accumulation and domestic consumption. By appropriating gendered conventions that had originated in working-class drinking establishments, AA allowed men to strengthen their claims to middle-class status.

And yet the fellowship's implicit project of reconstructing masculinity was more complex still. Men's personal narratives and other writings reveal an important part of the cultural work of gender reconfiguration—but only part. To understand fully AA's relationship to gender ideology and domestic life, we need to take literally Mariana Valverde's definition of gender formation as the historical process by which "the two genders are formed and reformed, renegotiated, contested." That is, we need to explore the relationships between AA men and the women with whom they shared their lives. For the majority of AA members, achieving sober manhood entailed marital and familial roles as well as individual character traits. After all, marriage involves two people. As we will discover in the next chapter, the roles and identities of husbands *and* wives were subjected to debate and renegotiation by members of the fellowship. The spouses of AA members not only played an active role in AA; they also spawned an auxiliary organization, called the Al-Anon Family Groups, in which women, too, grappled with vexing issues of gender identity in the context of an alcoholic marriage.

THE DILEMMA OF THE ALCOHOLIC MARRIAGE

DIAGNOSING THE ALCOHOLIC'S WIFE

As the alcoholism movement took hold in the 1940s, many Americans understood habitual drunkenness in relation to the institution of marriage. Sociologists and psychiatrists studying alcoholic men often mentioned their subjects' failure as marital partners. Popular films such as *The Lost Weekend* and *The Best Years of Our Lives* constructed models of male emotion in relation to men's monogamous relationships with women. The former implied that Don Birnam's recovery would benefit from his loyal girlfriend's continued encouragement, while the latter figured Al Stephenson's drinking in part as a response to the disappointments of middle-class marriage. The founders and early members of Alcoholics Anonymous (AA), too, tended to view sobriety in familial terms. As we have seen, AA members' roles as husbands and fathers profoundly shaped their experiences of drinking and recovery. Yet given the nature of marriage as a dual partnership, the alcoholic's wife soon became an object of scientific and therapeutic scrutiny herself. Mirroring the films' inclusion of wives (or wives-to-be) in supporting roles, AA publications made explicit references to members' spouses, and so, too, did scientific experts writing in professional (and sometimes popular) journals. In fact the alcoholism expert's role in establishing new terms of masculine authority coexisted with and even required gender prescriptions for women as well as men.[1] If the alcoholism movement of the mid-twentieth century had much to do with remaking sober men, it enlisted women, too, in that effort, giving shape to the pathological drinker's compliment, the modern figure of the alcoholic's wife.

Before the alcoholism movement emerged in the 1930s and 1940s, medical practitioners expressed ambivalent views toward the wives of inebriates. In contrast to the sympathetic (if also pathetic) portrayal of drunkards' wives in temperance literature, nineteenth-century physicians in inebriate asylums often saw family members as hostile interlopers who interfered with institutional treatment. While some nineteenth-century doctors credited wives for convincing their husbands to seek treatment or for cheerfully visiting their partners in asylums, others believed that wives hindered their patients' recovery. In 1881, for example, physician H. H. Kane noted that "very often the relatives, not understanding the meaning of certain symptoms, . . . will interpose and at once put an end to treatment, thus unwittingly and with well meaning doing the patient injury of the gravest kind." In an 1896 treatise titled *Inebriety*, another doctor was among the first to suggest that well-intentioned wives could play a hidden role, "however innocently, in the downfall of their husbands."[2] But because their ideas did not circulate far beyond the domain of inebriety specialists, such practitioners possessed little cultural authority in society at large. While they no doubt affected their own patients' families, their influence paled in comparison with mainstream narratives of the drunkard's wife.

By the 1910s experts in the emerging field of social work were also taking an interest in inebriates' wives. Early in the twentieth century college-educated social workers forged a new profession, applying specialized training and knowledge to casework in hospitals, clinics, and family service agencies. Their efforts contributed to a division of labor within the mental health professions, as psychiatrists, social workers, and nurses engendered a team approach to therapeutic care. In contrast to the male-dominated realm of psychiatry, social work was overwhelmingly a female profession. The field of social work extended yet revised the nineteenth-century tradition of benevolent reform in which middle-class women offered material assistance and moral guidance to their less fortunate sisters. While social workers in some ways threatened the higher authority of psychiatrists, they carved out a professional niche for themselves while supporting the interests and efforts of their male superiors. In this context social workers often investigated the role of family members in helping or hindering a patient's therapy.[3]

A case study written by E. E. Southard and Mary Jarrett of the Boston Psychopathic Hospital exemplifies how experts treated alcoholism in a marital context before repeal. In their monumental casebook *The Kingdom of Evils*, published in 1922, the authors told the story of Michael Piso, a "feeble-minded teamster ten years married to a good wife." Apparently Piso suffered from "alcoholic jealousy-psychosis," a condition that led him to abuse his spouse and predispose his family to poverty. His wife, identified only as Mrs. Piso, was "in point of fact an exceptionally good woman" and a pregnant mother of three when her husband entered the treatment facility. Although Southard and Jarrett eschewed sensationalized dry rhetoric, they portrayed Mrs. Piso as a victim of marital violence and "excessive sex demands." Fortunately, after a period of relapses, Michael Piso stopped drinking, and the family's situation improved. Although they remained poor, Michael Piso worked steadily; moreover, he was no longer deluded that his wife was sexually unfaithful. The authors noted approvingly that their patient was kinder and more financially generous toward his wife and children. But Mrs. Piso, too, was subject to the social worker's counsel. While Michael was the primary patient, the caseworker also advised Mrs. Piso about ways to amend her housekeeping and to "improve the moral situation between the spouses." Apparently "the wife was told 'to be nice' to her husband, to 'dress up' Saturdays . . . [when] taking her husband shopping." And "on the economic side she was discouraged from working to supplement the family income, so that Michael should not be dissuaded from trying to get a better paying job."[4] Thus while Mrs. Piso was never blamed for Michael's alcoholism, she was exhorted to conform to specific (and highly gendered) prescriptions to reinforce her husband's rehabilitation.

Early social workers such as Jarrett and her colleagues prefigured a later generation of family experts. Increasingly, social workers treated married alcoholic men and their wives as a unit, focusing on how one spouse's behavior affected the other. But before the post–World War II period, experts seldom regarded the wives of alcoholics as subjects of research and treatment in their own right. In the 1930s and 1940s psychiatrists and scientists such as Edward Strecker and E. M. Jellinek emphasized the causes and consequences of alcoholism in individual drinkers. By the mid-1940s, however, nonmedical family caseworkers had begun to stress the importance of treating the "alcoholic marriage" as an entity of its own. Although by this time many social workers were engaged directly in psychotherapy and made diagnoses, they continued to perform a range of general tasks: interviewing new patients and transcribing case histories, administering mental tests, following up on psychiatrists' recommendations, and conducting research. Moreover, they paid attention to the external environment of patients' lives; in the words of one social worker, they attended to "problems of 'outer' rather than 'inner' life."[5] Psychiatrists typically focused on patients' inner "neuroses," while social workers consulted with relatives—often wives and mothers—to alter patterns of familial interaction they deemed detrimental to constructive change.[6]

Social workers who specialized in alcoholism were no exception. According to Gladys M. Price, who directed the social service division at the Washingtonian Hospital (an alcoholism treatment facility in Boston) in the 1940s and 1950s, social workers coordinated the "intake process" designed to measure "the patient's motivation and readiness for treatment" and determine "to what lengths the family may go to cooperate or interfere with the treatment." In many cases the caseworker's first contact with alcoholic men came at the request of wives seeking help.[7] After an initial evaluation by a social worker, alcoholics often consulted with physicians (if they needed drug therapy) or psychiatrists (if psychotherapy was deemed essential). Wives, however, were "almost always assigned to a social worker."[8] Thus the gendered hierarchy within the therapeutic professions mirrored that of the married couple seeking treatment: male psychiatrists supervised treatment of the primary (male) patient, while female caseworkers counseled the supporting (female) spouse. Some social workers favored working one-on-one with spouses, while others combined individual counseling with group therapy.[9] Because social workers spent the most time observing alcoholics' wives, they published the largest share of scholarship on the subject. During this period some psychiatrists worked directly with alcoholics' wives, but caseworkers (and, eventually, academic sociologists) were the most prolific professional writers on the topic. Indirectly, however, psychiatrists wielded influence over many social workers, who had been utilizing psychoanalytic theory and methods for several decades.

Since alcoholism was generally perceived as a disease of men, the drinker's spouse in question was usually a woman. Among experts who studied the alcoholic marriage, few referred to the husbands of female alcoholics. One Connecticut psychologist offered approximate statistics on the marriage rates of male and female drinkers. Based on an estimate of 4 million male alcoholics in the United States, she hypothesized that "the likelihood of a woman marrying an alcoholic or a potential alcoholic" was one in ten, while the probability of a man marrying an alcoholic woman was only one in fifty. In 1962 social worker Margaret Bailey reviewed the existing professional literature on alcoholism and marriage and found "no research on the husbands of alcoholic women reported" in over forty articles published between 1941 and 1959. Among the smaller numbers of alcoholic women seeking treatment, she noted, an even smaller percentage were married, due to the fact that "the husbands of alcoholic women are generally less patient and accepting and more likely to terminate the marriage than are the wives of alcoholic men."[10] Thus with very few exceptions the paradigm of the alcoholic family centered on the alcoholic husband and his wife.

One of the earliest studies was published by Boston social worker Gladys Price in the *Quarterly Journal of Studies on Alcohol*. Based on data compiled from her work with nonalcoholic wives in 1943 and 1944, Price reported on a representative sample of twenty women referred to her department. Nineteen of the wives were white; only one was African American. Fifteen wives in her sample had between one and eight children, while five had none. Most of the women had been married between nine and twenty years, while one was a newlywed. Half of the women worked for pay (some only for financial reasons), while the others stayed home. But putting such differences aside, Price summarized the personality traits she discovered among the women and painted a "composite picture" of the typical alcoholic's wife. Price discovered a pattern in which a "basically insecure" woman had expected her husband to be a "strong, dependable, responsible person." But as her husband failed to manage his responsibilities, she felt increasingly unloved, resentful, and aggressive. In her disappointment the wife "strove to prove that [her husband] was inadequate in order to justify his seeming lack of love for her." Eventually she began to use his drinking as a way to "prove him and keep him inadequate," thus impeding his recovery.[11] In Price's view the alcoholic's wife had a subconscious need to select a passive, irresponsible partner—a man whose personality presumably predisposed him to alcohol abuse. The caseworker's goal was to illuminate this destructive pattern so as to facilitate a "permanent adjustment" in the wife's attitude.

From such observations of marital hostility emerged a classic depiction of the alcoholic's wife. Price was not the only expert to apply theories of unconscious motivation and underlying aggression to the treatment of troubled family members. As another writer described the alcoholic's spouse, "She knocks the props from under him at all turns, seemingly needing to keep him ineffectual so that she feels relatively strong and has external justification for her hostile impulses. Thus she keeps the lid on her own inadequacies and conflicts."[12] Some psychiatrists agreed that wives had a vested interest in maintaining their husbands' incompetence; as one asserted, the typical wife "unconsciously, because of her own needs, seems to encourage her husband's alcoholism."[13] This view was common among mental health experts by the 1950s, especially those schooled in psychoanalytic theory, which became increasingly popular during this period. In 1953 Texas caseworker Thelma Whalen wrote about the "striking similarities" she discovered while counseling women married to alcoholic men. Refuting claims that the alcoholic's wife was a helpless victim of circumstance, she contended that women contributed to their husbands' inebriety. "The wife of an alcoholic is not simply the object of mistreatment in a situation which she had no part in creating," Whalen wrote. "Her personality was just as responsible for the making of this marriage as her husband's was; and in the sordid sequence of marital misery which follows, she is not an innocent bystander. She is an active participant in the creation of the problems which ensue."[14] For all of these experts, then, alcoholism was a problem located squarely in the domestic sphere, entwined in the psychological dynamics between husbands and wives.

Thelma Whalen offered the most detailed account of the alcoholic spouse's psyche. Assuming that all wives chose husbands who would meet their underlying psychological needs, she classified alcoholics' wives into four personality types with alliterative names: Suffering Susan, Controlling Catherine, Wavering Winnifred, and Punitive Polly. Suffering Susan, whose dominant characteristic was her need to punish herself, selected a mate "who was obviously so troublesome that her need to be miserable would always be gratified." Wavering Winnifred was motivated by insecurity and self-doubt; Winnifred "always chooses a husband who, to her, is weak, who she thinks 'needs her' and would therefore be unlikely to leave her." Such a woman cannot form "relationships with adequate, self-sufficient individuals because . . . she doubts her ability to hold their interest." Controlling Catherine and Punitive Polly played a less passive role in perpetuating their husbands' alcoholism. Catherine selected a spouse whom she could dominate and control; marriage to "a more adequate man" would be too threatening for her. To overcome economic insecurity the controlling wife usually took a job herself and gripped the family purse strings with an iron hand. Even more destructive was Punitive Polly, whose "relationship to her husband resembles that of a boa constrictor to a rabbit." Rather than allow her husband gradually to relinquish his marital duties, as Suffering Susan had done, Polly instinctively performed them herself and emasculated him in the process. As Whalen explained, "Polly's husband always seems to her to be limited in some way in his essential masculinity. If he did not, she would have never married him." Polly spurned housework and child care, allowing her alcoholic spouse to indulge his "submissive and passive impulses" while she earned the family income. Polly treated her husband like a helpless child; their relationship was "similar to that of . . . a scolding but indulgent mother—and her very small boy."[15]

Psychiatric social workers perceived the wife's behavior as a sign of neurosis that existed *prior to* the onset of the partner's alcohol abuse.[16] All of Whalen's characterizations, for example, described the woman's decision to marry an ineffectual, alcoholic man as a sign of psychopathology in the woman herself. Implicit in Whalen's study is the assumption that normal women would seek strong, independent, self-sufficient husbands. In her view, proper husbands were responsible, dominant, and able to provide financially for their families; normal wives, in turn, had the good sense and psychological health to select them in the first place. But rather than emphasize the alcoholic's deviant behavior or his failure to conform to masculine norms, Whalen faulted wives for their misguided marital choices. According to Whalen's theory, alcoholic men were not only sick themselves, but they also suffered from the neuroses of their insecure or aggressive spouses.

Whalen's depiction of Punitive Polly is especially significant as a manifestation of postwar gender anxiety. In Chapter 2 we discovered that widespread cultural concerns about masculine debility and effeminacy were expressed in the psychiatric discourse on alcoholism. The popular phenomenon of Momism reverberated fears that a crisis of masculinity was preventing men from reaching mature manhood. Seeking to explain the childhood origins of alcoholism, psychiatrist Edward Strecker faulted mothers for stifling and effeminizing their sons, an unfortunate development that ostensibly led to chronic drinking in adulthood. Female experts on marriage, however, focused more on wives than mothers. Yet the implicit gender politics and the impulse to blame the woman remained the same. Indeed, Whalen's depiction of Punitive Polly matched Philip Wylie's caricature of Mom in substance if not in prose style. Polly was a power-hungry, domineering woman who preyed on her husband's weakness. She treated her spouse like Wylie's Mom treated her son, smothering him with a crippling combination of indulgence and aggression. In the throes of such a dysfunctional marriage, the alcoholic man found that "drinking was often the only way he [could] find to assert himself." But such behavior only kept him submissive in the face of his wife, who was "willing for him to have almost anything he wants—except his manhood."[17] In the context of gender prescriptions for manly men and womanly women, experts viewed alcoholic husbands as failed men and their wives as deficient women. For social workers like Thelma Whalen, family dramas of alcoholism played out when women, as well as men, failed to follow the proper psychological script.

Social workers' insistence that wives subconsciously invited their partners' drinking owed much to the rising influence of psychoanalytic thought in the mental health professions and society at large. Indeed, such logic was not limited to the field of alcoholism. In their respective histories of domestic violence in the United States, Linda Gordon and Elizabeth Pleck each document a shift in the conceptualization of physically abused women in the post–World War II period. Influenced by the ideas of Freudian psychiatrist Helene Deutsch (who published the two-volume *The Psychology of Women* in 1944 and 1945), experts on family and sexual violence argued that many women had latent masochistic wishes to suffer abuse at the hands of men. In the 1940s, for example, the first psychoanalytic articles on rape began to appear, and these noted the victim's unconscious desire to be raped. Similarly, the negative image of the nagging wife was used to rationalize and sometimes defend incidents of wife beating. According to Linda Gordon, Freudian thought offered social workers terms and categories with which to explain away the complaints of abused wives. "Blaming family problems on women was part of a change in family and gender ideology evident by the 1930s," Gordon writes. "As child neglect became . . . a sign of maternal inadequacy, so did marital violence become a sign of wifely dysfunction." In tackling a range of family problems social workers increasingly stressed the victim's complicity in causing domestic trouble. As Pleck summarizes, "In overthrowing Victorian attitudes toward sexuality, Freudian ideas also discarded a system of morality in which perpetrators of family violence were held responsible for having committed illegal and immoral acts." Although drinking was no longer illegal in the postwar period, we can see how social workers' depiction of wives rendered alcoholic men less responsible for the marital misery wrought by their consumption of liquor.[18]

While psychiatric social workers regarded the wife's behavior as a result of a preexisting neurosis, other experts relied on a different conceptual framework. Boston caseworker Sybil Baker, for instance, focused less on wives' neurotic predispositions and more on the social dynamics that ensued while a husband drank heavily. "Inebriety almost invariably affects others as well as the alcoholic," she wrote. "It produces innumerable emotional reactions so that the behavior of others close to him, the marital partner, for example, is altered or aggravated. . . . Therefore, the social case worker seldom sees the alcoholic as an isolated person but rather as an integral part of the world he lives in." Whereas Whalen's research was guided by psychoanalytic theory, Baker drew on her interdisciplinary training in sociology, community organization, and household management as well as psychology. Successful social work, in her view, borrowed insights from "all the professions for diagnosis and treatment, as its goal is well-rounded, satisfying and productive living."[19]

Social workers were not the only researchers to study the alcoholic marriage. In fact, the leading authority on the topic by the late 1950s was sociologist Joan K. Jackson. Initially Jackson interviewed alcoholics admitted to Seattle hospitals in an effort better to understand why medical treatment often failed. But she soon became more interested in the coping strategies of family members who shaped the "social milieu of active alcoholics."[20] Eschewing the psychoanalytic determinism that informed depictions of wives' marital hostility, Jackson viewed "the behavior of the wife . . . as a reaction to a cumulative crisis in which the wife experiences progressively more stress." While Whalen viewed women in terms of fixed personality traits, Jackson argued that they passed through a series of chronological stages *in response to* their husbands' recurrent drinking. Most previous writers had portrayed wives' behavior as dysfunctional because they viewed family dynamics in terms of what was best for the husband. But "when viewed in the context of the rest of the family," she argued, wives' behavior "might appear to be functional" instead. Jackson believed that wives aimed not to punish their spouses but to restore stability to their troubled families.[21] Describing seven stages of adjustment to alcoholism, she credited wives for "reorganizing" their households in the face of adversity. If Whalen's account sounded a shrill, anxious note in the postwar discourse on gender-role confusion, Jackson offered a more moderate, measured depiction of marital malaise.

Yet despite Jackson's sympathetic stance toward wives, the language of sex-role identification permeated her work as well. Though her analytical approach was more subtle than Whalen's, Jackson, too, provided a highly gendered account of women's behavior that reinforced the ideology of sexual difference inherent in psychiatric thought. Throughout her study Jackson interpreted the family's response to alcoholism in terms of how the wife perceived her own performance *as a woman* in a domestic setting.[22] As Jackson described the first stage of family adjustment, "Both husband and wife . . . try to play their conceptions of the ideal husband and wife roles . . . and create the illusion of a 'perfect' marriage." At this point the wife desperately wants her family to be normal. When her husband is sober, she defers to him "in his role as head of the household" and expects the children to obey their father. As her husband continues to drink, however, she resents him for not living up to her expectations. Yet rather than dwell on his behavior, the typical wife blames herself: "On her part, the wife begins to feel that she is a failure, that she has been unable to fulfill the major cultural obligations of a wife to meet her husband's needs. With her increasing isolation, her sense of worth derives almost entirely from her roles as wife and mother. Each failure to help her husband gnaws away at her sense of adequacy as a person." According to Jackson the husband's social deviance causes the wife to question her own gender-role performance. With alcoholism comes frustration, anger, and sometimes violence on the wife's part. Unable to maintain the calm, submissive demeanor of the ideal wife, she feels "intense shame at having deviated so far from what she conceives to be 'the behavior of a normal woman.'"[23] During these early stages, Jackson points out, the wife most resembles Whalen's Wavering Winnifred.

Over time, however, necessity requires that she act more like Controlling Catherine. Realizing that she cannot rely on her husband, the typical wife "begins to ease [him] out of his family roles . . . and assumes the husband and father roles" herself. In addition to her homemaking duties she must also perform the manly roles of breadwinner, decision maker, and discipliner of the children. As she "takes over control of the family with some degree of success," the alcoholic husband becomes "less and less necessary to the ongoing activity" of the household. Unlike Whalen, Jackson did not criticize women for taking over their husbands' duties but, rather, complimented them for bringing "some semblance of order and stability" to their homes. In her view such behavior allowed women to regain self-worth and to distance themselves from their husbands' destructive behavior.[24] But while Jackson rejected Whalen's rigid classification of women into four personality types, favoring instead a model of familial change over time, she borrowed Whalen's terminology and thus reinforced the same gendered assumptions.

While empathetic to the wives' situation, Jackson viewed the family's sex-role inversion as a temporary compromise in trying circumstances. Her support of conventional gender norms is most evident in her discussion of family rehabilitation. While admitting that divorce was unavoidable at times, she applauded marital reconciliation when the husband achieved sobriety. In the last stage of domestic adjustment—the "recovery and reorganization of the whole family"—the wife needed to readjust to life with a sober partner. On this matter Jackson and Whalen generally agreed. "Counseling with Polly," Whalen wrote, "is always directed toward helping her reduce her controls and achieve satisfaction from more womanly and motherly roles." Whalen thus steered patients toward conformity to feminine ideals. Jackson, too, accepted the idea that sober men would reclaim their familial authority. At first the wife "feels an unwillingness to let control slip from her hands." But at the same time "she realizes that reinstatement of her husband in his family roles is necessary to his sobriety."[25] Here Jackson supported the view that an alcoholic's recovery depended on his wife's behavior. Both authors also assumed that men, if sober, were entitled to resume their dominant status. Another social worker was even more emphatic on this point: "The overly managing wife may be encouraged . . . to relax control as her husband starts to take over responsibilities which are clearly his own, and she may learn . . . to enjoy the new family situation which results."[26]

Thus, whether they saw wives' familial dominance as a response to crisis or as a sign of neurosis, postwar alcoholism experts agreed on one thing: a healthy family required allegiance to traditional sex-role prescriptions.[27] If men were to recover from alcoholism, they would need to reclaim their masculine authority and resume their roles as breadwinners and household heads. But so, too, were women exhorted to resume their feminine roles, allowing their partners once again to wear the pants in the family. For many postwar experts a husband's chronic drunkenness was viewed as evidence of a diseased or dysfunctional family in which both spouses deviated from prevailing sex roles.

Moreover, therapeutic and sociological diagnoses of the alcoholic marriage invite us to consider gender formation as a dynamic historical process in which both genders are formed and reformed, contested and negotiated, in relation to each other.[28] Following Mariana Valverde's suggestion that historians pay more attention to the relationships between male and female gender constructions, we can see how alcoholism experts reinscribed assumptions about the rights and obligations accorded to both husbands and wives by virtue of their sex and marital status. Building as well on Valverde's theory of gender formation, historian Nancy F. Cott argues that "marriage has been a cardinal—arguably the cardinal—agent of gender formation and has institutionalized gender roles" over the course of U.S. history.[29] Postwar alcoholism discourses, with their implicit and explicit focus on marriage, eloquently exemplify this argument, reminding us that the cultural histories of masculinity and femininity have, to a great extent, been intertwined.

For the alcoholic's wife, then, the battle did not end with the husband's sobriety. Showing sensitivity to the wives' situation, Joan Jackson explained that it was difficult for them to adjust to a new status quo and trust their husbands again. If performing her partner's duties had come to seem natural, or at least necessary, to a wife, how could she relearn her proper role? Significantly, experts conceptualized the wife's readjustment in terms of the same therapeutic paradigm used for alcoholics themselves. If alcoholism was a family illness, then the whole family would need to convalesce. If wives suffered from their husband's alcoholism, then they, too, would need to recover. But *how*, specifically, could wives recover from their predicament? And what, exactly, did they need to recover from?

In their scholarly articles professional experts offered few answers to these questions. At least in their published writings social workers and sociologists spent more time describing the alcoholic family than offering concrete suggestions for therapy. When they did discuss therapeutic recommendations, social workers focused on helping women to understand and express their feelings in more constructive ways. Typically, Gladys Price stressed that wives "stop mothering" their alcoholic husbands so the men had more incentive to take responsibility for themselves. Another goal was to dampen the wife's feelings of anger and hostility toward her spouse so she could understand the emotional dynamics underlying the disease rather than harbor resentment or dwell on her own pain.[30] As discussed above, caseworkers also urged women to relinquish control of their husbands' rightful duties.

By the 1950s, however, several writers had begun to advocate more specific treatment methods. Some psychiatrists and social workers published studies of professional group therapy with alcoholics' wives, a practice that became increasingly popular after World War II.[31] Moreover, Joan Jackson had a telling suggestion for wives: Alcoholics Anonymous.

Toward the end of her article, Jackson opined that AA had much to offer alcoholics *and* their spouses. "If the husband becomes sober through Alcoholics Anonymous and the wife participates actively in the groups open to her," she wrote, "the thoughts of what is happening to her, to her husband and to her family will be verbalized and interpreted within the framework of the [AA] philosophy and the situation will probably be more tolerable and more easily worked out." Jackson was familiar with AA, for in addition to interviewing wives of hospitalized alcoholics, she based her study on women members of the AA Auxiliary in Seattle.[32] Some social workers also stressed the importance of working with "community organizations" such as AA. As one noted, many patients at alcoholism clinics also attended AA or Al-Anon meetings. In her view it was vital that clinic personnel "endorse and respect the AA movement" as a supplement to clinical therapy.[33]

To understand how women learned to play out the final acts in their marital dramas of alcoholism, we need to move from the pages of professional journals to the pages of newsletters, books, and other documents written by AA and Al-Anon members. Just as alcoholic men formed their own mutual help groups beginning in the 1930s, so, too, did their spouses band together in a common purpose. While researchers were busy interpreting their data, AA created an alternative realm in which alcoholic couples could address their concerns. From its beginning in 1935 AA encouraged members' spouses to participate informally in the fellowship's program of ritual disclosure, spiritual rebirth, and mutual support. AA's founders believed that family members could play a major role in perpetuating—or arresting—an alcoholic's drinking. In 1951 Lois Wilson, the wife of AA co-founder Bill Wilson, officially established the Al-Anon Family Groups, which encouraged wives to follow a Twelve Step program similar to the one used by alcoholics themselves. The founders of AA and Al-Anon believed that women could help their husbands by creating an emotional and spiritual climate conducive to a life of sobriety.

As important as professional experts were in regulating clinical practice, AA and Al-Anon were arguably more influential in shaping public opinion and experience.[34] During the 1950s these fellowships enjoyed remarkable growth: AA's membership doubled from 100,000 in 1951 to over 200,000 in 1957, while the number of spouses' groups nationwide increased from 87 in 1951 to 1,500 by 1963. We cannot fully understand the gender ideologies embedded in alcoholism treatment without addressing the wives of AA and Al-Anon. Indeed, their history offers a unique window into the norms and experiences that have defined marriage and family life in modern America, for alcoholic and nonalcoholic families alike.

THE WIVES OF AA AND AL-ANON
IN THE 1940S AND 1950S

In its first several decades AA was predominantly comprised of men; few women alcoholics joined the fellowship. But unlike some men's fraternal organizations, AA did not exclude members' female relatives from attending meetings, relaxing at AA clubhouses, or socializing with men at semiofficial gatherings. Certainly some meetings and events were attended exclusively by men, and few women were included when male members made "Twelve Step calls" to recruit fellow alcoholics. But as we have discovered, a large percentage of AA participants were married, and from the beginning they viewed their lives, their alcoholism, and their AA experience in a familial context. Although the fellowship functioned implicitly to prepare men for sober manhood (a process that relied on gendered rhetoric and rituals to revitalize abstinent men's masculine identity) female spouses formed a strong, if sometimes contested, relationship to AA on both a personal and an organizational level. In fact, AA's role in establishing new terms of manly authority paralleled and even necessitated tasks of gender formation for women as well as men. The role of nonalcoholic spouses in AA (and, later, in Al-Anon) even suggests the paradox that AA's fraternal brotherhood itself depended on the emotional labor of women, in ways that were sometimes hidden and sometimes overt. AA and Al-Anon wives were far from passive spectators or bystanders; they played active, supporting roles in their husbands' quest for sobriety. Moreover, throughout the 1940s and 1950s the wives of AA (as some called themselves) regarded the fellowship as a vehicle through which to effect positive psychological and spiritual change in their own lives.

Wives made their presence known from the very beginning. When Bill Wilson and Dr. Bob Smith first met at the Smiths' house in Akron, Ohio, in 1935, Dr. Bob's wife, Anne, provided hot coffee and good cheer while the men talked about their problems. Though Lois Wilson was not present at this initial meeting (she was at the Wilsons' home in New York), she soon visited Akron and developed a friendship with Anne and Dr.

Bob. Although the role Anne Smith played in developing the ideas underlying fellowship remains somewhat murky to historians, she was a serious and spiritual woman whose advocacy of the Oxford Group and whose quiet intellect undoubtedly influenced her husband and perhaps Bill Wilson as well. At the time and for years afterward, however, AA literature discussed the contributions of Anne and Lois in domestic terms, focusing on the behind-the-scenes encouragement and gracious hospitality they displayed toward alcoholic men in their lives.

As the Akron group garnered new members, it held meetings in the Smiths' home, in a decidedly domestic atmosphere, until more space was needed. In early 1936 Anne organized the Woman's Group for the alcoholics' wives, a new outlet for her deep spirituality and an antidote to the loneliness she had endured for years. Anne formed an especially close bond with Henrietta D., the wife of a local attorney who was the first alcoholic to join the cofounders. According to historian Mary C. Darrah, "Both women were the long-suffering partners of professional men gone astray, men whose drinking had imperiled their careers, families and reputations. Anne and Henrietta understood each other's deepest feelings. . . . With their meeting, the strength gained of sharing hope transformed their mental outlooks."[35] As AA expanded beyond the founders' home states of Ohio and New York, the spouses of new members were encouraged to attend meetings and to socialize with other AA families. By 1940 AA wives in several cities had begun to meet on their own, helping one another with the common problems they faced. Though spouses were not officially AA members, women formed quasi-independent groups in their own communities. With names like Non-AA, AA Auxiliary, AA Helpmates, and the Triple-A's, these groups affirmed their own identity within the larger social organization of AA during the 1940s.[36]

In a short time the wives' involvement acquired an almost legendary status within the fellowship. When writing and selecting images for the organization's first self-narrated history (titled *Alcoholics Anonymous Comes of Age*, published in honor of AA's twentieth anniversary in 1955), Bill Wilson featured a full-page photograph of the Smiths' three-story house accompanied by a smaller picture of the "actual coffee pot that Anne used to make the first AA coffee." The coffeepot and the house were concrete symbols of AA's historic initiation. "This is where it all started," explained the caption below the image of the coffeepot. As noted, these photographs commemorated not only the place "where Bill and Dr. Bob applied the first principles of recovery" for alcoholics but also the site "where Lois and Anne laid the groundwork of what would one day be called the Family Groups."[37] In a book devoted to chronicling the history and philosophy of the AA movement, it is telling that the caption accorded equal weight to the groundwork laid by both the cofounders *and* their wives.

Given the role of coffee as a semiofficial AA beverage served almost universally at meetings, the symbolic associations of Anne's coffeepot are especially significant. Both before and after Al-Anon was officially founded, spouses' groups performed tangible services for AA members: serving homemade cakes and cookies, planning potluck suppers and barbecues, decorating bulletin boards, and cleaning up after meetings, in addition to serving the ubiquitous caffeinated brew. One AA document described the Akron wives' group as a "non-alcoholic kitchen brigade" that "was allowed to wash dishes, make coffee, organize picnics, and things like that."[38] Another pamphlet printed by the Denver wives' auxiliary in 1951 explained that members "scrubbed the floors when needed, washed the windows, washed the cups and spoons, cleaned the ash trays, furnished the cream and sugar, and did any other chore that came within the scope of need."[39] Certainly many wives took such tasks for granted and found them an enjoyable way to socialize with others. In any case the gendered dimensions of these activities, which naturalized the wife's role as a supportive helpmate, dovetailed with the advice of professional experts for wives to resume and even relish their proper domestic orientation.

AA's alcoholic members had mixed reactions to the wives' participation and the formation of spouses' auxiliaries. Some men were suspicious of the women's motives; they worried that spouses were telling gruesome stories of past drinking exploits to the detriment of their (already fragile) reputations. As Bill W. recalled, many AAs in the 1940s "wondered what these Family Groups were all about. Were they gossip clubs, commiseration societies? Were they coffee and cake auxiliaries? Did they divert AA from its single purpose of sobriety?"[40] One Hawaii member who harbored such suspicions stationed himself outside a spouses' meeting and pretended to sleep on a couch. After listening in on the conversation, he reported back to his own group (although the results of his eavesdropping efforts remain unknown). In another telling anecdote an AA wife in Oregon reported that her fledgling group met in a space accessible only by passing through the main AA meeting room. Many spouses preferred to brave the outside fire escape rather than confront a roomful of skeptical or sneering AA members.[41] Some members did not mind the wives gathering on their own but disapproved of their presence at meetings. In their view the AA program was designed uniquely for chronic drinkers, and only an alcoholic could help a fellow alcoholic find sobriety through the Twelve Steps. With respect to their own therapeutic goals, they found the wives' presence a distraction at best and an obstacle at worst.

Other men bristled at the wives' involvement because it seemed threatening to AA's masculine social culture. As discussed in the preceding chapter, male AA members relied on gift exchange rituals and militaristic rhetoric to bolster their authority and identity *as* men. AA's implicit vision of sober manhood allowed members to strike a balance between robust fraternalism and masculine domesticity, but too much participation by wives could tilt the balance too far in a feminized direction. Consider the following passage from a 1956 novella based on the author's earlier experiences in AA. Describing the "Birthday Party" ritual designed to celebrate a member's first full year of sobriety, the narrator explained how one character, Paul, received a tiny, decorative cake "made by women members of the happy wives of the dried-out drunks. At first Paul hated these occasions. . . . [The displays] of maudlin sentiment seemed so childish to him. Surely, he thought, an alcoholic could be man enough to stay sober for a year without being rewarded with a cake or a fancy metal disc, gushed over and smothered in kisses by happy wives and other female members of the group."[42] In his view well-meaning wives infantilized and feminized their partners with sentimental displays of emotion. By his lights men who were "man enough to stay sober" deserved more restrained expressions of praise and respect.

Yet for every AA member who disapproved of the wives' auxiliaries, many others welcomed them. In 1952, soon after Lois Wilson and her fellow volunteers inaugurated the national Al-Anon Clearing House in New York City, AA delegates from around the country expressed their feelings about the Family Groups in their respective hometowns. Responding to a letter in which Lois inquired about the relationship between the local AA group and the spouses' auxiliary, a Kansas City delegate wrote, "Our Family Group is called the Woman's Auxiliary. . . . In the eight years they have been operating they have made themselves just about indispensable to our comfort and well-being. I have never heard of any trouble or complaints from members about anything they have ever done." A member from West Palm Beach, Florida, was even more specific, exclaiming that the spouses' group was "a wonderful group of gals— loving and unselfish—and through their amateur entertainments, suppers, dances, rummage sales, etc., they turned in almost $1,000 in their first year which they turned over to the Club or the Group to help defray expenses. We are indeed proud of them." Other correspondents admitted that a few AA men had "some honest differences of opinion with the [Family] Group" or harbored a "belligerent attitude" toward them. But according to a delegate from New Orleans, such men were in the minority. "I am sure an overwhelming majority of AA members feel as I do," he concluded, adding another voice to the chorus of positive responses Lois received.[43]

Countless AA members supported the spouses' groups, and not simply because they raised money or provided refreshments. More importantly, they believed, the wives' efforts facilitated the recovery process itself. Consider the following testimony from an Oregon delegate who responded with enthusiasm to Lois's query: "I have always been of the opinion that if it had not been for the present members of the Family Groups that just maybe there would have never been such a great number of we Alkies who were able to find a new way of life through a Power greater than ourselves."[44] Through interaction with his local Family Group, this Oregon representative found that the wives' support helped alcoholics maintain sobriety. Moreover, this writer was not alone. From the very beginning both Bill W. and Dr. Bob encouraged wives' participation in the fellowship and influenced their followers to do the same.

The Smiths and the Wilsons played different roles in shaping the development of Al-Anon, due in large part to the deaths of Anne and Dr. Bob. Although Anne Smith's kitchen would always symbolize the emotional and spiritual contributions of AA's "first wife," the Akron matron's death in 1949 at age sixty-eight meant that she would never witness the expansion of Al-Anon on a national level. Dr. Bob died the following year. Lois was only ten years younger than Anne, but she enjoyed relatively good health until she was in her mid-nineties; she worked on behalf of the fellowship almost until her death in 1988. In the 1940s, from Long Beach, California, to Amarillo, Texas, and from Denver, Colorado, to Richmond, Virginia, wives' groups formed across the country, sending encouraging letters to Bill and Lois reporting on their experiences. In 1951 Bill suggested to his wife that she assume separate leadership of the budding Family Group movement. At the time the Wilsons were living at Stepping Stones, their cherished home in Bedford Hills, New York. Responding with alacrity to her husband's suggestion, Lois, aided by a group of dedicated volunteers in the greater New York City area, founded the

Al-Anon Family Group Headquarters and Clearing House. Based on the correspondence records of AA's Alcoholic Foundation (similar to a board of trustees) Lois and her close friend Anne B. sent a letter to eighty-seven Family Groups in 1951 expressing the resolve to unify them under one organizational umbrella. Lois and Anne B. received forty-eight responses, and it was decided that the name Al-Anon be used by all the groups. AA's newsletter, the *Grapevine*, featured an article promoting the new "sister fellowship," and by July the number of registered groups had increased to 145. In all, thirty-nine states were represented in addition to eleven groups flourishing in Canada. By 1952 the number of Family Groups had risen to 250; by 1954 it had surpassed 500; and by 1963 more than 1,500 local groups had registered nationwide.[45]

Lois and other representatives from the Al-Anon headquarters in New York traveled across the country, sharing their enthusiasm wherever family groups were meeting. (By this time Al-Anon referred to local units as Family Groups rather than Wives' Groups, to indicate that mothers, husbands, siblings, and children were also welcome. Yet wives remained by far the largest category of participants.) Before Al-Anon began its own series of regional and national conferences, Lois played a role in AA's conference and convention schedule. At a regional conference held in Toronto, Canada, in 1951, for example, Lois chaired a panel and discussion session titled "Right Relationships (AA Wives)." Many AA members attended such conferences with their spouses, and family-oriented speeches and panels catered to their special concerns. The following year AA spokespersons reported that "more time was spent in reviewing and discussing the . . . status of the so-called 'family groups' than was devoted to any other item on the 1952 Conference agenda." AA delegates from more than thirty cities and towns spoke on the topic; the result was a vote by participants to "approve unanimously the work that Lois and Bill have done to encourage . . . the sound growth of the Family Group Movement."[46] In 1955 AA commemorated its twentieth anniversary at a national convention in St. Louis, where Bill W. declared that AA had officially come of age. The convention was a defining moment for the fellowship, attracting more than 5,000 members from all fifty states, Canada, and several foreign countries. Referring to the panel sessions sponsored by Al-Anon, Bill claimed that they were "among the biggest eye-openers" of the convention. Praising Lois during his keynote speech, he proudly proclaimed that "AA is for the whole family" and promised that adherence to AA philosophy could "do wonders for domestic relations."[47]

Over time the Al-Anon movement became more formalized. What began as a constellation of local wives' groups chatting around kitchen tables emerged into a national organization with its own referral, publishing, and public relations operations. In 1955 Al-Anon's founders published their first book, simply titled *The Al-Anon Family Groups*, which served as an equivalent to AA's Big Book. The volume had multiple authors, but it was conceived and written mostly by Lois, with assistance from her husband. Local groups continued to print their own pamphlets and newsletters, some of which were reproduced and circulated by the national headquarters in New York. In the mid-1950s Al-Anon leaders also facilitated journalists, radio producers, and television programmers in writing stories about the program. In 1955 reporter Jerome Ellison published a photo-illustrated feature titled "Help for the Alcoholic's Family" in the *Saturday Evening Post*, among the most widely read magazines in the country. In 1957 television's popular *Loretta Young Show*, along with corporate sponsor Procter and Gamble, produced a drama based on two married couples who found solutions to their problems through AA principles. Before the filming the show's producers consulted with Lois and other Al-Anon members for ideas. (A reel-to-reel film of the segment, titled "The Understanding Heart," was made available to Al-Anon; for several years local groups borrowed it for private screenings, until repeated use marred the quality of the film.)[48]

The Family Groups also became more ambitious and elaborate in their weekly programming. Their 1955 handbook, for example, suggested nine different themes for meetings. In Personal Story Meetings the leader designated two or three speakers to discuss how they came to believe that the AA program could help them as well as the alcoholics in their families. In a Twelve Step Meeting members focused on how they had applied a particular step to their own lives. The list also mentioned a Family-Adjustment Meeting, in which husband-and-wife teams demonstrated the "problems of home adjustments after the alcoholic joins AA." Other gatherings were less structured, but almost all included acts of "personal sharing," in which members related their own feelings, ideas, and experiences to the rest of the group.[49]

Despite its organizational growth, Al-Anon maintained strong values of personal interaction and compassion that prevented it from feeling bureaucratic to members. The main reason for this centered on the roles of AA's first wives, as well as the rhetorical strategies by which Al-Anon reenacted those roles in its internal "folklore." By the 1950s Al-Anon had been shaped in large part by the personalities and efforts of Anne Smith and Lois Wilson. Over time they realized that their experiences could help them address a need that existed in the wider culture, but they continued to stress their personal values and histories while expanding their organizational domain. Like AA, Al-Anon's organizational narrative has always entangled biography and history. In the Big Book, Bill W.'s alcoholic autobiography serves as the "origin myth" of AA itself;[50] likewise Al-Anon literature embodies the experiences and personalities of Anne and Lois as models for future members to understand and emulate.

Because Anne died before Lois, Anne's influence was felt primarily through her legacy and memory, which extended far beyond her hometown of Akron. Obituaries published in local and national publications praised Anne's deep "sympathetic understanding." Dr. Bob wrote that his wife had been "of inestimable value in her encouragement and moral support to me and to the movement." Bill W. also commemorated her character and involvement in AA, writing that "AA might never have been without Anne Smith. Her loyalty and devotion, her deep love, not only of Dr. Bob, but of all of us, these qualities secure for her the highest possible place in our affections and in the history of our AA society." Discussing Anne's personal legacy in terms of AA's institutional past and future, he expressed his hope that "succeeding generations of AAs may profit by her wise example and be inspired by her wonderful personality." Anne's personality, he recalled, featured many "outstanding qualities," such as "Love, Courage, Loyalty, Humor, Patience, Thoughtfulness, Humility, Unselfishness, Understanding, Spirituality."[51] The *Grapevine* expressed similar sentiments: "Anne was far more than a gracious lady. She was one of four people, chosen by a Higher Destiny, to perform a service to mankind. With Dr. Bob, Lois, and Bill, Anne stepped into history, not as a heroine but as one willing to accept God's will and ready to do what needed to be done."[52]

Lois Wilson shared many of these qualities. Like Anne, she remained by her husband's side through years of fear and disappointment, earning the reputation of a steadfast, loyal wife. As she wrote in her memoirs, before Bill founded AA, her "primary aim in life" was "helping Bill achieve sobriety"—a clear statement of a woman who prioritized her husband's needs as the cornerstone of her own existence. When Bill's alcoholism reached its nadir in the late 1920s, a despondent Lois poured out her heart in her diary, wondering, "Is it best to recognize life as it seems—a series of failures—and that my husband is a weak, spineless creature who is never going to get over his drinking?" Lois expressed her doubts but immediately sought to banish them by reconfirming the cherished ideals of "love and faith" enshrined in her wedding vows. Rather than dwell on Bill's failures or her own misery, Lois instead reflected on his "fine qualities" and "endearing personality" and agonized over the moral and physical effects of alcoholism on his well-being. "The problem is not about *my* life," she wrote, "for probably the suffering is doing me good, but about his—the frightful harm this resolving and breaking down . . . must be doing to him." Finally, Lois expressed her continued "faith in the ultimate success" of their twin struggle against the bottle. "I am going to appeal to the good in him and keep on everlastingly trying," she resolved. For his part Bill appreciated his wife's unwavering devotion. In 1930 he expressed thanks for "the love and devotion of my wife, whose whole life is given to the task of making me happy and successful in whatever I undertake. Her happiness is dependent on the outcome of her effort to help me."[53] At the time, of course, Lois's loyalty was not enough to cure Bill's alcoholism, but in retrospect Bill (like many alcoholic men) asserted that he might not have recovered if not for his wife's devotion. Because Lois lived much longer than Anne, she had more time directly to influence the AA and Al-Anon movements, humbly telling the story of her life and marriage as a way of inspiring others in need.

My purpose here is not to dwell on, and certainly not to judge, the personal qualities or decisions of these women. By all accounts they were warm, caring, unselfish people, and these qualities were manifested not only in their marriages but also in their dealings with friends, relatives, and the virtual strangers they encountered while working on behalf of the fellowship. Their historical significance, rather, lies in their role as public figures, in how their actions and personalities were commemorated and fashioned into a new cultural image of the alcoholic's wife. Through printed literature, public speeches, and public relations efforts (such as the television programs and magazine articles mentioned above), AA and Al-Anon leaders created a cultural alternative to the pitied drunkard's wife of temperance lore. Whereas pre-Prohibition narratives emphasized the abandonment of women by hard-drinking men and targeted social reform as the source of domestic salvation, AA and Al-Anon lore depicted wives who steadfastly supported their husbands and who turned to spirituality and mutual help to cope with the travails of alcoholism and recovery.[54] As moral and emotional exemplars, Anne and Lois asked not to be pitied or redeemed but to be respected for turning hardship into a source of personal strength and marital longevity. Although their experiences as wives of alcoholics reached back into the 1910s and 1920s, their public images were fashioned primarily during the late 1940s and 1950s, the same time that professional experts were forging their own ideas about the alcoholic marriage. Certainly AA's vision of marital cooperation differed from the psychoanalytic model of wives who subconsciously thrived on their husbands' pathological failures. But in terms of their social implications and impact on gender ideology in the postwar era, such varying depictions of alcoholic wifehood dovetailed in significant ways.

To understand the engendering of the alcoholic's wife in the mid-twentieth century, we need to explore in more depth the *ideological substance* of AA and Al-Anon literature. Beyond telling their own stories of marital distress and rejuvenation, Anne and Lois, like their husbands, emphasized the need for spouses to apply AA principles to their own lives. Beyond affirming support for their husbands' recovery, Al-Anon wives stressed how the fellowship fulfilled their *own* needs. Like Anne and Lois, many wives felt depressed and isolated during the years of their husbands' drinking. Long ashamed to socialize with friends or relatives for fear of embarrassing drunken episodes, spouses welcomed the chance to share feelings and advice with others. Moreover, they were intrigued by the Twelve Steps and eager to learn about the precepts that finally seemed to promise sobriety for alcoholics. AA's founding couples, followed by countless other members, created a therapeutic model of marital harmony that deserves close analysis.

REHABILITATING THE ALCOHOLIC MARRIAGE

From the earliest years of the fellowship's existence, Bill W. and Dr. Bob stressed the importance of wives' involvement and support of AA. When formulating the principles of the AA program, both co-founders drew on their experiences not simply as alcoholics but as *alcoholic husbands* married to women who had responded to their newfound sobriety in particular ways. In 1939, several years before AA developed a national reputation and more than a decade before the Family Groups became widespread, Bill W. infused his most important publication, the Big Book, with specific ideas about the role of wives. As discussed in the preceding chapter, the Big Book outlined AA's central precepts and demonstrated what alcoholics could hope to achieve by following them.

Although the Big Book was published anonymously, Bill actually wrote the first eleven chapters and edited the latter series of autobiographical sketches. Yet while the overall volume reflected Bill's assumption that men would comprise the primary readership, two chapters were addressed specifically to family members. The book's eighth chapter, titled "To Wives," as well as the next chapter, titled "The Family Afterward," moved from an implied audience of alcoholic men to one of nonalcoholic women. In devoting more than thirty pages to wives, Bill W. made clear his assumption that alcoholism and recovery were family affairs.

The "To Wives" chapter did not just shift the focus of the book to an explicitly female audience; it also signaled a shift in the work's (ostensible) authorial voice. It appeared to be narrated by several self-proclaimed "wives of Alcoholics Anonymous." At the start of the chapter the anonymous male narrator introduces his female counterparts and offers a rationale for the discussion that follows: "With few exceptions, our book thus far has spoken of men. But what we have said applies quite as much to women. . . . But for every man who drinks others are involved. . . . Among us are wives, relatives, and friends whose problem has been solved, as well as some who have not yet found a happy solution. We want the wives of Alcoholics Anonymous to address the wives of men who drink too much. What they say will apply to nearly everyone bound by ties of blood or affection to an alcoholic." After that introduction the authorial "we" shifts and addresses the female readership: "As wives of Alcoholics Anonymous, we would like you to feel that we understand as perhaps few can. We want to analyze the mistakes we have made. We want to leave you with the feeling that no situation is too difficult and no unhappiness too great to be overcome."[55] In this way the text invites readers to learn about and take heart in the fellowship's program.

Yet although "To Wives" claims to be narrated by women, Lois Wilson's memoirs reveal that Bill actually wrote the chapter. Apparently the authorship of chapters 8 and 9 was contested in 1938 when Bill W. was preparing the manuscript of the Big Book. A letter in the AA archives indicates that Bill's first inclination was to have Anne Smith write the chapter "portraying the wife of an alcoholic." According to one historian Anne declined the offer, possibly in deference to Bill's own wife. As Lois Wilson eventually revealed, she did indeed want to write it herself. Ultimately, however, Bill decided that the first eleven chapters should all be written in the same prose style. After Bill died, Lois admitted to feeling hurt by this, yet she deferred to her husband's editorial control.[56]

To a great extent, then, the Big Book reflected *male* AA members' (and especially Bill Wilson's) ideas about wives' roles more than it recorded women's voices.[57] Privately, however, Lois, Anne, and other wives in the early days of AA had already influenced Bill's ideas on the subject. Moreover, wives were quick to voice their own ideas and opinions, in letters to the AA *Grapevine*, in talks given at meetings, and eventually, in the pages of their own national newsletter, the *Family Forum*. In most cases the wives' writings sound remarkably similar to Bill's chapters in the Big Book. Indeed, given the overlapping beliefs and rituals of the two fellowships, it is not always easy to discern where the voices of male alcoholics end and those of female spouses begin. Sometimes Al-Anon members expressed resistance to the ideas of male AA members (including their own husbands), but in general they recorded their views within an ideological and organizational context that originated within and received continuing support from AA itself. At least insofar as we seek to understand the cultural history of marriage, such blurred boundaries between the values of husbands and wives should warn us not to separate women's history and men's history into mutually exclusive domains. It is important to tease out the differences between women's and men's consciousness and to assess the different social implications that marital arrangements have engendered for husbands and wives. But in order to do so, we must consider the gender formation of both sexes in relation to each other.

The Big Book offered female readers a systematic plan for coping with their husbands' alcoholism. The purpose was twofold: first, to enlist wives' support of their husbands' involvement in the AA program and, second, to persuade women that their *own* emotional, psychological, and spiritual well-being required adherence to AA principles. Indeed, the first goal (support of a husband's sobriety) was viewed as dependent on the second (the wife's personal immersion in the AA way of life).

Underlying AA's familial ideology was the assumption, shared by other experts, that the alcoholic's wife herself was sick. In 1948 the *Grapevine* published a letter from a Phoenix housewife titled "Your Wife May Be Sick, Too." The anonymous writer, who proudly identified herself as "an AA wife," wrote that "it seldom occurs to a new [sober] man that his wife is just as sick mentally, physically and emotionally as he is. His disease has a definite name and treatment. . . . The wife's maladjustment is a little more difficult to name and treat." Testing her skills of diagnosis, the writer stated that the alcoholic's wife is "a bundle of screaming nerves" and "definitely is a neurotic as a result of what she has been through over the years." Previously the *Grapevine* had published a letter arguing that the wife "is probably a pretty sick person, too, and helping her get rid of some of her complexes and neuroses will help her husband put his best foot forward faster." Other wives, viewing alcoholism in a metaphorical sense, argued that the disease afflicted all members of a family, not just the drinker himself. Along these lines one female writer claimed that "alcoholic thinking" affects everyone in a household: "The family is just as intoxicated as the victim," she wrote. "It takes longer to get the family sober—but sober we all must be."[58]

What did this writer mean when she suggested that wives, too, had been "intoxicated?" If other family members had not literally been drunk, what would it mean for them to get sober? Along these lines Bill Wilson offered an intriguing challenge to the AA spouse: "You can have more than alcoholic sobriety in your own family; you can have *emotional sobriety*, too. Even if the rest of the family . . . hasn't yet found stability, you can still have yours. And your own emotional sobriety often can hasten the happy day of change for them."[59] If literal sobriety is the goal for people who have overconsumed alcohol to dangerous extremes, the phrase "emotional sobriety" suggests a person who has "overindulged" in unsound, excessive emotions. If the literal alcoholic's illness stems from unhealthy, uncontrolled drinking, the metaphorical alcoholic's neurosis presumably stems from unhealthy, uncontrolled *feeling*. In large part the Twelve Step program centered on controlling and changing one's emotional responses to the environment and to other people. In essence what AA and Al-Anon offered wives was a program of emotion management that identified certain patterns of thought and feeling as unhealthy while extolling other emotions as salubrious for the self and family alike.

I borrow the term "emotion management" from sociologist Arlie Hochschild, who offers a compelling theory about how people create an observable display of feeling through bodily display and verbal communication.[60] In Hochschild's definition, emotion management (or "emotion work") "requires one to induce or suppress feeling in order to sustain the outward countenance that produces the proper state of mind in others." In a given historical and cultural context the private realm of marriage and family life is governed by "feeling rules," which prescribe the terms of emotional exchange. Feeling rules establish a system of entitlements and obligations that implicitly define what people expect to give and receive in their personal relationships. In this light the family is seen quietly to impose emotional obligations on its members. Social roles, including those of husband and wife, not only entail prescriptions for activities such as housework or money making; they also establish rules for what emotional responses people think they owe others, or deserve to receive themselves, in a given situation.

In published writings and personal correspondence AA wives described their emotional reactions while they lived with alcoholic men. In the narrative persona of an AA spouse, Bill Wilson wrote that "we wives found that . . . we were afflicted with pride, self-pity, vanity, and all the things which go to make up the self-centered person."[61] In the *Grapevine* one San Francisco wife confessed that she had "fairly swarmed with faults and deficiencies, prejudices, notions, neuroses, crooked thinking, cock-eyed emotions, rampaging interior conflicts . . . and doubt and suspicion."[62] Another woman believed that her "emotionalism" mixed with her husband's liquor to create "an explosive cocktail" that threw the entire family "into absolute chaos."[63] Perhaps the most profound description of feeling-as-affliction was offered by Lois Wilson. Speaking for all alcoholics' wives Lois described her reaction to Bill's drinking as a dangerous exercise in emotional intemperance:

> Either we tried running things with too high a hand, weighted ourselves down with . . . guilt for another's drinking, tried too hard to stop it, or we soothed deeply hurt feelings with luxurious baths of self-pity—none of it good. In our own way, though not as obviously, we were just as excessive as our compulsive drinkers were. . . . Indulgence in hot anger, violent reproach, neurotic frustration, our attempt to retreat as completely as possible to avoid embarrassment or shame, was exactly as uncontrolled as our partners' drinking. Whether we acknowledged it or not, ours was a disease too—a mental disorder we'd let ourselves fall into.[64]

After their husbands stopped drinking, and as a result of their own involvement in AA, these women viewed their previous emotions as impulsive and destructive in their own right.

Though Lois acknowledged her years of heartache and fear due to Bill's drinking, in retrospect she characterized her anger and resentment as excessive and self-indulgent. One of Lois's favorite stories concerned an incident in 1935 when she threw a shoe at her husband. Angry that Bill was leaving to spend the evening in a church basement in the company of other sobered-up drunks in the Oxford Group, she muttered, "Damn your old meetings," and flung her shoe across the room. But as she recalled in her memoirs, she regretted her display of bad temper almost as soon as the shoe went flying. At that moment she had an epiphany; that evening, and for years afterward, she puzzled over the meaning of her angry outburst and sought to banish her feelings of resentment. After all, she reasoned, Bill's attendance at spiritual meetings and his communication with other alcoholic men had done nothing less than save his life. In the end, however, Lois could not claim credit for Bill's sobriety. In hindsight her temper tantrum made her realize that she had been jealous of Bill's newfound friends for succeeding where she had failed. She also resented the time Bill devoted to his fellow ex-drunks, time that he could have been spending alone with her.[65] That Lois attached such personal and historical meaning to this incident invites us to explore its larger cultural significance. Why did Lois and other wives come to view their anger in this way?

Their responses, I believe, provide telling clues about how women conceptualized their roles as wives and how they viewed the social and emotional contract of marriage itself. AA leaders depicted the typical alcoholic home as a battleground in which the wife faced financial insecurity, emotional neglect, loneliness, and sometimes violence. "How could men who loved their wives and children be so unthinking, so callous, so cruel?" asked the Big Book. Lois, for her part, devoted many pages in her autobiography to her years of self-sacrifice and despair, professing her undying love for a man whose alcoholism prevented him from fulfilling the promises entailed by their marital bond. Like social workers and psychiatrists, Lois and other AA wives recognized the failure of alcoholic men as husbands. On one hand, they acknowledged that wives would feel resentful. But on the other hand, by characterizing wives' reactions as a mental disorder that they let themselves "fall into," Lois suggested that they had wittingly engaged in destructive behavior just like their husbands had continued to take chances with alcohol. Ultimately, Lois blamed herself for falling into an excessive, unhealthy reaction. These women measured their reactions against an implicit standard of behavior and found themselves deficient. Though their husbands had reneged on their own marital responsibilities, many AA wives faulted themselves for defying the emotional prescriptions that marital convention required of them.

What, then, were the emotional prescriptions, the feeling rules that AA endorsed for wives?[66] According to AA ideology the wife's first task lay in suppressing negative emotions. Though alcoholism had rendered her home a battleground, the AA wife would need to act more like a peacekeeper. As the Big Book counseled, "The first principle of success is that you should never be angry. Even though your husband becomes unbearable, and you have to leave him temporarily, you should, if you can, go without rancor. Patience and good temper are most necessary."[67] In an article about the AA auxiliary in Long Beach, California, a journalist described AA wives as "gallant women" who endured years of marital misery but who no longer permitted "their natural fear and worry to show through their shining shields of hope." With AA's help, he explained, wives learned to project an image of "courage and confidence."[68] *Coronet* magazine advised relatives of habitual drinkers to "show only confidence, no matter how many times [their] hopes had been shattered in the past." When the alcoholic became sullen or "just plain bad tempered," the article advised, readers should keep busy with their own affairs, "leaving the offender *gracefully* alone" until his mood improved.[69] Thus while a woman might naturally be fearful, worried, or angry due to her spouse's drinking or a potential relapse, it was her wifely duty to restrain those emotions and shield them from view.

Not just marital harmony but a husband's very sobriety depended on a woman's emotional restraint. For a man in the early stages of recovery, a wife's pessimism or "negative attitude" could spell disaster. According to the Big Book a wife must never nag or condemn her husband for his behavior.[70] If a wife wanted to see herself as a warrior of sorts, the proper enemy was not her husband but her husband's alcoholism. In 1945 a wife from Montpelier, Vermont, submitted "Credo for an AA Wife" to the *Grapevine* and encouraged wives to make the following pledge: "I believe that my husband is still the very human man I married and I will not expect him to do a complete about-face of character and personality, giving up all the little . . . faults that sometimes annoy me. . . . He will continue to gain . . . positive qualities that make a pleasing personality, . . . and I must never let my acceptance of this fact become humdrum . . . but offer frequent encouragement, stimulation and appreciation to arm him for his daily battle." Furthermore, she exhorted the AA wife to "maintain constant vigil" over her habits so as to "keep pace with the growth" of her recovering husband.[71] Depicting the alcoholic as an emotionally fragile person who could "go off the wagon" at the slightest provocation, this writer urged fellow wives to orient their thoughts and actions around the psychological needs of their husbands.

Perhaps it is not surprising that the Big Book also encouraged this attitude, explaining that if a man "gets the idea that [his wife is] a nag or a killjoy," he might even "use that as an excuse to drink some more." The AA wife needed to be constantly "on guard not to embarrass or harm [her] husband." The impulse to criticize or express resentment could develop into a "great thundercloud of dispute" and erupt into a "family dissension" of "deadly hazard to an alcoholic." It was the wife's task to "carry the burden of . . . keeping [conflict] under control." While the Big Book conceded that spouses could have "an honest difference of opinion," it nonetheless cautioned wives to "be careful not to disagree in a resentful or critical spirit." The AA spouse thus learned to differentiate between what she actually felt and what she should feel; between her inner, "natural" emotions and those she should reveal to others.[72] It is worth underscoring the prescriptive nature of these writings, especially the Big Book. As an anonymous advocate for other (usually male) alcoholics, Bill's exhortations here were obviously self-serving. Yet while Lois did not write these words, she greatly influenced Bill's ideas about wives' emotions. His prescription of the ideal wife—a model of "patience, tolerance, understanding, and love"—was apparently an accurate description of Lois herself; thus Lois, through her own actions and character, helped shape her husband's prescriptions (which eventually influenced millions of readers).

According to AA ideology a man's sobriety required a reformulated emotional contract between husband and wife. An alcoholic could face the arduous task of staying if his wife visibly affirmed and supported his efforts. A sober alcoholic would no longer "be so unthinking, so callous, so cruel" if his wife suppressed her resentment for past injustices. But while both husband and wife struggled to establish this new equilibrium, the work of emotion management was not evenly divided by gender. Indeed, the conditional nature of the above scenarios suggests that women bore the brunt of responsibility for ensuring marital success. The exhortations for wives to maintain constant vigil and carry the burden of defusing conflict suggest that it was primarily the *wife's* job to ensure an auspicious emotional climate at home. One 1948 contributor to the *Grapevine* blatantly inscribed such gender distinctions: "An AA wife makes her home as pleasant as possible. She gives her family the stability and security it has lacked perhaps for years. The financial security is the husband's responsibility—but the emotional security is the wife's."[73] The task of maintaining sobriety required great psychological effort; indeed many men found a payoff for their efforts in a more harmonious marital relationship. But the emotional labor of marital cooperation fell disproportionately to wives.

According to the language women used to describe their efforts, it was a demanding, laborious job indeed. Several scholars have noted that the emotional obligations of family life are tied to the gendered division of labor in the household; historically women have performed the work of "feeling management" more than men. Arlie Hochschild describes the private realm as a kind of emotional gift exchange in which women, lacking power, authority, and material resources, "make a resource out of feeling and offer it to men as a gift in return for the more material resources they lack." Especially among middle-class couples, she argues, women "tend to manage feeling more because in general they depend on men for money, and one of the various ways of repaying their debt is to do extra emotion work—especially emotion work that affirms, enhances, and celebrates the well-being and status of others."[74] This theoretical framework sheds light on the workings of AA and Al-Anon: as the recovering husband regained authority and his privileged role as breadwinner, the wife expanded her efforts to affirm, enhance, and celebrate her husband's new, sober status. In exchange for her partner's gift of sobriety (and the material and psychic benefits it afforded) the wife increasingly oriented herself around her husband's needs.

It is not surprising that the wife's emotion management also extended to her feelings about AA itself. AA publications admitted that wives often viewed AA in a negative light, especially at the beginning. Apparently many women resented the amount of time their husbands spent attending meetings, talking with fellow members, and visiting hospitals in order to help others—and themselves—stay sober. The Big Book addressed wives on this matter directly:

> You may become jealous of the attention he bestows on other people, especially alcoholics. You have been starving for his companionship, yet he spends long hours helping other men and their families. You feel he should now be yours. The fact is that he should work with other people to maintain his own sobriety. Sometimes he will be so interested that he becomes really neglectful. Your house is filled with strangers. You may not like some of them. He gets stirred up about their problems, but not at all about yours. It will do little good if you point that out and urge more attention for yourself. We find it a real mistake to dampen his enthusiasm for alcoholic work. You should join in his efforts as much as you possibly can.[75]

Ironically, while drink had once severed men's connection to hearth and home, now the recovery process threatened to distance men from their wives. But if wives indulged in self-pity or, even worse, "created a scene," they could threaten the recovery process. As one Al-Anon speaker warned listeners, "Some wives have taken that course. The consequences have not been pleasant. Their husbands, amazed and hurt to discover that their sobriety was not appreciated, have retreated to the bottle again."[76] These passages speak volumes about the exhortations of the fellowships to members to devote time and effort to the therapeutic program. AA's strategy was to welcome wives into the fold as well. While maintaining a division between alcoholic members (mostly men) and their spouses (mostly women), AA and Al-Anon made their programs into a family affair.

Some wives, however, resisted the AA program, and occasionally AA publications gave voice to their (often temporary) resentment. One anonymous wife urged fellow *Grapevine* readers to "guard against complacency" in their attitudes. Too many wives, she observed, complained that AA meetings were boring, the seats too hard, the people too dull. She countered that "the non-alcoholic wife's job . . . was to adjust [herself] happily and safely" to the changes that AA brought. In her view the best way to prevent apathy was to embrace other wives with "warmth, hope and comfort."[77] Lois Wilson, as we have seen, also went through a time when she resented Bill's work with other alcoholics. Another *Grapevine* contributor had even stronger negative feelings about AA. "When my husband first joined AA," she wrote, "it seemed as if he were being taken further away from me than ever. And by perfect strangers, too. . . . He was getting something out of his new associations—I was left out in the cold." Envious of the "sympathetic understanding" her husband gave to fellow inebriates, she asked bitterly, "Why shouldn't I, who had borne the brunt in the past, rate a little of that commodity?" Defining sympathetic understanding as a commodity, this writer referred to the faltering emotional economy of her alcoholic marriage; in her view sympathy and compassion were scarce resources better spent *within* marriage than squandered on a group of AA strangers.[78]

But like Lois, this wife eventually came to see AA in a positive light. Not only would it ensure her husband's sobriety; it would provide a better life for her as well. As she began to focus on her own character flaws rather than her husband's, she viewed AA as a means of personal and spiritual growth. "The sympathetic understanding, which I thought lacking . . . had been there all the time," she realized. Instead of seeking support from her husband alone, this woman turned to AA itself as a source of psychological well-being. As her *Grapevine* letter suggests, many wives turned to the AA and Al-Anon family to fulfill their emotional needs when the nuclear family fell short. As another contributor wrote, "Friendship within her own sex is as important to a woman as are the bonds between men."[79] Just as former drinkers turned to one another for mutual support and camaraderie, so, too, could their wives benefit from fellowship. When they began to see AA and Al-Anon as a gift to themselves as well, spouses no longer begrudged their husbands' commitment to AA's gift exchange system. Alcoholism had made life lonely for men *and* women; AA and Al-Anon helped both spouses overcome isolation, filling the emotional holes that remained in an alcoholic marriage.

For their participation in this system of marital gift exchange, wives received material as well as psychological benefits. Before sobriety one of the wife's greatest disappointments stemmed from a loss of family income and the reduction in social prestige that accompanied downward economic mobility. Like Anne Smith and Lois Wilson, many Al-Anon spouses were married to men whose occupations once placed them in the middle or upper-middle classes: managers, professionals, and semiprofessional workers. Most others were married to manual or service workers or to lower-paid managers or salesmen.[80] But no matter where they were on the socioeconomic spectrum, most wives experienced their husbands' alcoholism in the context of downward mobility and restricted consumption. As discussed in previous chapters, during the 1930s through the post–World War II period a male drinker's job insecurity, unemployment, career stagnation, or financial insolvency served as cultural markers of alcoholism, differentiating pathological drinkers from stable, sophisticated social drinkers. But AA literature reassured women that sobriety would revive men's breadwinning capabilities. According to the narrator of one fictional account published in 1950, AA wives "appear to be a happy group of women. The reasons for this are fairly obvious. They know that when their husbands go out at night, they'll be back sober, and at the end of each week or month the pay envelope is full and the paycheck intact."[81] Depending on their husbands' earning potential, then, many wives expected the basic accoutrements of a middle-class lifestyle; others at least anticipated modest financial security in the wake of recovery.

This material promise only underscored the undesirability of family life with an active alcoholic. Implicit in this ideology, of course, was the assumption that men would be the sole, or at least primary, breadwinners (a presumption by no means novel in the 1940s and 1950s). The notion that women would work to maintain the family's lifestyle was untenable.

In reality—as social workers and psychiatrists also discovered—countless alcoholics' wives did work for pay to supplement or replace lost income. For years Lois Wilson worked as a department store salesperson and interior decorator while Bill remained penniless. In a personal story she shared with her local Family Group, one anonymous wife told of returning to work when her husband, a "brilliant lawyer," "drank himself out of a fine firm." With money from her new job as well as savings from her own family, she was able to keep the children in private schools and reside at the same "good" address. But despite her ability to maintain this lifestyle, she resented her husband's financial failure. "I used to punish him by buying foolish things that we couldn't afford under the rosiest circumstances," she confessed. She also told the story of another woman who, "when her husband had a bad slip after they'd scrimped to get out of debt, went out and bought a piano—which not one member of the family could play!"[82] By punishing their husbands with concrete reminders of their failures as breadwinners, such wives literally and figuratively bought into an ideology of marriage that demanded their economic dependence on their husbands. Although they were not literally dependent, the specific *meaning* they ascribed to their purchases reflected their wish to be so.

Many AA and Al-Anon members reiterated concerns—voiced by professional experts—that women's continued breadwinning could hinder men's recovery. In a statement that could have been uttered by social worker Thelma Whalen, one AA husband (invited to speak at an Al-Anon meeting) explained that women "may begin to wear the pants in the family, especially if the husband is drinking up all the family funds." But faced with such circumstances, a wife "must be constantly aware that she is doing it and know this is only a temporary process . . . which she will drop as soon as her spouse begins to straighten up."[83] One locally printed pamphlet circulated in 1954 by the Tucson, Arizona, Family Group counseled women to stay out of the workplace even when faced with severe hardship. For mothers of young children the pamphlet advised, "Any amount of money you could make would not be worth [the] emotional health" of the little ones "already half-orphaned by their father's problem." According to this writer, the father's parental failure rendered the mother's conformity to female gender prescriptions all the more urgent. Rather than desert her children, such a woman was better off finding work "such as typing, sewing, telephone soliciting, or baby tending" that could be done at home.[84] These sentiments were reinforced in Al-Anon's first book, published in 1955. In most cases, the text asserted, there was a "usual bad warp in the marriage relation caused by the wife . . . having to assume the responsibilities of breadwinning."[85] Apparently, financial solvency was a worthwhile goal, but it required a *man's* earnings. To reinstate a proper balance of marital obligation, a wife needed to increase her unpaid emotional labor at home while relinquishing paid labor in the workplace.

These writings by alcoholics' wives mirrored dominant norms of family breadwinning and homemaking in postwar America. Of course, women married to jobless or underemployed alcoholic men were not the only females to work for pay outside the home. In fact, increasing numbers of women over age thirty-five, especially those whose children were in school or grown, were employed in both full- and part-time jobs during the 1950s and 1960s. But most middle-class wives expected to fit paid employment around their primary roles as housewives. Mothers of young children, in particular, were least likely to work for pay, and when they did, they usually did so for reasons of economic necessity. By the same token husbands and fathers overwhelmingly defined their familial responsibilities in terms of breadwinning. While newly married couples often shared the task of making money (with many young wives working to supplement their husbands' income or even to support them while they finished school), "after children, couples reverted to a more confining division of labor" and "reverted to customary spheres of influence and responsibility."[86] So while Al-Anon members, on one hand, applauded fellow wives for keeping their struggling families afloat, they tended, on the other hand, to view women's employment as a necessary evil. For downwardly mobile, middle-class wives whose gainful employment was not a mere supplement to a husband's primary income, the financial need to work could have negative connotations.

The issue of economic dependence also underlay one of the thorniest dilemmas of the alcoholic's wife: whether to separate from or divorce her husband. Whereas temperance rhetoric emphasized the wife's abandonment by her dissolute or degenerate husband, AA and Al-Anon literature seldom mentioned men deserting their wives. Rather, the fellowship became a forum in which wives discussed initiating a marital breakup. As Al-Anon acquired a national reputation in the 1950s, women from across the country wrote to the central headquarters for advice. Among the mailings sent out by volunteers was a form letter that focused specifically on this issue. At no time has Al-Anon advocated an official position on divorce. Indeed, the letter stated that the fellowship could not advise writers on "what would be best" in their particular situations; the choice to separate or divorce was a "personal decision" for each woman to make herself.[87] There are no records revealing the percentage of Al-Anon members who left their husbands—either temporarily or permanently—nor is it my purpose to reconstruct the full range of wives' experiences. In terms of ideology, however, it is clear that Al-Anon's founders and early members encouraged marital reconciliation whenever possible.

In some cases evidence suggests that members affirmed the decisions of other wives to leave their spouses. For example, one journalist, writing for a wide audience in the *Ladies Home Journal* in 1948, reported that AA could not help all alcoholics. Some chronic drinkers were "psychotics" or "mental defectives" whose drinking habits were far too entrenched to respond to AA methods. For women married to such men, being "trapped with an alcoholic husband" called for "nearly superhuman strength, love and patience." Based on conversations with AA family members, the writer concluded that there was hope for wives whose husbands achieved sobriety. But for others, he cautioned, divorce might be unavoidable. If the chance of sobriety "seems too slim you are probably not the woman who can be of real help to him," the article advised. "If this seems beyond your strength, or if after trying all that is possible you have failed, you should leave this alcoholic. It may be that he is not salvageable—not all alcoholics are. . . . And your staying with him, eventually becoming as bitter as he, as psychologically scarred, will be helpful to no one."[88] Note the writer's implication that divorce stemmed partly from the wife's failure to help her husband recover. Such an assertion departed from conventional Al-Anon wisdom; Al-Anon's founders believed that wives could facilitate recovery, but they did not blame or label them failures when they did not. They agreed with the journalist, however, that in some cases, marriage deteriorated to the point where a wife had no choice but to leave. Their open-ended form letter certainly suggests as much.

Nonetheless, Al-Anon's early members tended to view divorce as a last resort. Economic factors topped the list of reasons. According to Joan Jackson, who came to know dozens of Seattle Al-Anon wives during the course of her research, "in the early 1950s women with children were financially dependent on their husbands and did not have opportunities to leave." While husbands of women alcoholics tended to leave wives who were still imbibing, most women tried to cope with marriage to a habitual drinker. As she explained, welfare assistance was available only in extreme cases, and "the attitudes of women towards asking for welfare was that it was an admission of total defeat and unworthwhileness." Thus, she found, "women were much more likely to look for ways to make remaining in their family situations tolerable."[89] In a letter sent in 1953 to a Florida Al-Anon member, one of the relatively few men in the fellowship, Lois Wilson wrote that "a wife stays with her husband for many reasons. Of course the economic one can be a strong factor."[90]

Beyond economic considerations, dominant ideologies of marital love and commitment also influenced Al-Anon members to stay with their husbands. As discussed above, in the late 1920s and early 1930s Lois Wilson resolved to stay by Bill's side; leaving him would mean relinquishing her "lost ideals" of love and devotion. Lois's personal experience shaped her written and spoken contributions to Al-Anon lore, but as the fellowship expanded in the postwar era, she was certainly not alone. In their personal sharings some spouses stressed the fact that all marriages "have their stresses and strains; alcoholism is merely a rather pernicious and extremely difficult type of stress." Unlike in movies and "fairy stories," real couples do not "automatically 'live happily ever after,'" one member noted. Recalling the marital vow to stay together "in sickness and in health," she explained that the wife, "in asking herself the question, 'Do I love him?' comes to understand that his alcoholism is no reason for the dissolution of the marriage bond." The Bible, after all, held that "when a man and woman come together they become 'One flesh.' The intimate physical embrace is symbolical of their spiritual union." If the wife was unsure of her love, she might still "continue the relationship" out of concern for the welfare of her children or "sheer economic necessity." But those who still felt affection should remember that alcoholism is a disease; a drinking husband could still be a loving husband, with hope for recovery. Moreover, awareness of her husband's love could help a wife feel more secure. "To a woman, . . . the husband's love is the center of her security and the home is the be-all of her existence. . . . The average woman will do anything she can to protect her home and preserve it."[91] Believing that marriage was the center of a woman's existence, many wives viewed divorce as a worst-case scenario—even worse than staying in a troubled relationship.

One of the most influential individuals in Akron's AA circle was a nun named Sister Ignatia, who counseled alcoholics admitted to St. Thomas Hospital (where Dr. Bob worked tirelessly to spread the AA message). Ignatia also worked with Anne Smith to help wives, using "coercive but effective tactics to reconcile marriages" whenever possible. When told by a wife that she was filing for divorce, the nun pleaded with her to "give him one more chance." She also used reverse psychology, coaxing the wife to admit her own insecurity that her husband might want to leave her. Then she "hurried off to begin negotiating with the husband," with an eye toward "breaking the ice" that had frosted the marital relationship. Apparently, maintaining family unity and preserving marital harmony were second in importance only to sobriety. Sister Ignatia's methods worked hand in glove with Anne Smith's advice, reinforcing consistent guidelines to the newly united spouses. After Anne and Dr. Bob died, the nun continued her work with alcoholic families. In 1954 in a speech to the National Council of Catholic Women in Akron, Ignatia claimed that "the husband or wife who thinks legal separation or divorce from the alcoholic spouse is the answer . . . is making a very serious mistake. The family unit may be the last ray of hope for the floundering alcoholic."[92] While AA and Al-Anon were nondenominational organizations, doctrinaire religious ideas (such as Ignatia's Catholicism) played a powerful role in shaping people's views and experiences of marriage, both inside and outside the fellowships.

Certainly antidivorce sentiment among alcoholics' wives must be considered in a broader social context. In the late 1940s and 1950s Al-Anon members comprised a mere fraction of Americans who contributed to a reduction in the national divorce rate. From the nadir of the Depression in 1933 the U.S. divorce rate climbed slowly, peaking sharply in 1946 at approximately 18 divorces per 1,000 families before dropping to fewer than 10 divorces per 1,000 families during the entire decade of the 1950s. (The divorce rate did not surpass the 1946 figure again until the 1970s.) Social observers have long discussed the stability of marriage in the first two decades following World War II, a time when men and women married in greater numbers, at younger ages, and with fewer separations than in previous eras.[93] Social attitudes toward divorce were especially harsh during the 1950s. While some writers in the mass media expressed toleration for divorce, most articles on the subject depicted divorce as both a private failure and a public disgrace. One series published in four installments in the *Saturday Evening Post* in 1950 defined divorce as "the sordid story of America's broken homes" and stigmatized divorced women as emotionally immature and selfish in their quest for marital separation. (Divorced men, while hardly praised, were spared the author's most venomous criticism.)[94] Although by the late 1960s and 1970s divorced Americans would find more (if still limited) public support for their predicament, during the immediate postwar decades—the time when Al-Anon solidified its membership and ideology—the road to marital separation was emotionally and economically perilous, especially for women.[95]

Although marriage did not always live up to people's expectations, most postwar couples stayed together for better or for worse, compromising and accommodating themselves to less-than-ideal circumstances. Moreover, the popularization of psychology and the therapeutic worldview gave people a vocabulary with which to calm and manage their frustrations. Since material considerations made it nearly impossible for women to abandon their marriages, psychological adaptation became the modus operandi of countless discontented women. To maintain the benefits of postwar married life—security, stability, and social status—"women's adaptation took two forms: adapting to their husbands' needs and adapting their own goals and aspirations to fit the marriages they had created. Both husbands and wives recognized that marriage required more adjustments for women than for men." As historian Elaine Tyler May summarizes, "Women of the fifties, constrained by tremendous cultural and economic pressures to conform to domestic containment, gave up their independence and personal ambitions. Once they made the choice to embrace domesticity, they did their best to thrive within it and claimed that their sacrifices were ultimately worthwhile."[96]

Recently scholars have continued to probe beneath the saccharine image of the postwar "Leave It To Beaver" family.[97] Building on May's study, for example, Eva Moskowitz argues that marriage counselors voiced a "discourse of discontent" that betrayed women's unhappiness even as it proclaimed the virtue of traditional female roles. In magazine articles read by millions, marriage experts urged women to scrutinize their domestic relations and strive for self-fulfillment at home. But at the same time they admitted that many women were frustrated, lonely, or even miserable—a consequence, to be sure, of the inherent tension between self-fulfillment and the self-effacement their prescriptions required.[98] Paradoxically, while experts molded Americans into well-adjusted families, they conceded that family life remained fraught with problems.

This larger trend of psychological adaptation that underlay postwar marital stability was epitomized in the Al-Anon program. As the culture of sobriety began to acquire the status of common sense, more families accepted the idea that recovery from alcoholism demanded a profound emotional adjustment between husband and wife. Indeed, the very notion of personal adjustment invites further consideration. Experts and AA members discussed the nonalcoholic wife's task in terms of adjustment:

first, adjustment to a husband's progressive disease and, later, readjustment to the new status quo of sobriety. But it was not just families of alcoholics who perceived life as a matter of environmental adjustment; indeed, this concept applied to all Americans facing the challenges of reconstruction after World War II. The legislation known as the GI Bill was formally titled the Servicemen's Readjustment Act of 1944, as if to acknowledge that the social strains of "unemployment, housing shortages, racial conflict, and the dawn of the nuclear age all tested the mental and emotional stamina of soldiers and citizens fatigued by years of war." National and world events led to increased affluence and geopolitical supremacy during the 1950s, but these trends were accompanied by anxieties suggesting "irrationality and madness lurking just beneath the thin veneer of a civilized social order." As people struggled to cope with the stresses of everyday life, psychological authorities gained prominence. After 1945, Ellen Herman points out, "work associated with helping people adjust and cope constituted *the* popular reputation of psychological expertise during an era when the psychotherapeutic enterprise became, literally, a growth industry."[99]

The quest for psychological health was inextricably tied to family relationships in the wake of World War II. The therapeutic worldview that gained momentum during these years offered private solutions to social problems and aimed to help people feel better about their place in the world. Moreover, home was where personal adjustment was supposed to occur. The family environment was expected to generate individual well-being and self-satisfaction.[100] The emotional adjustment of men and women became an especially urgent issue as 16 million war veterans returned to the United States after a period of great social fragmentation. Authorities fretted about the problem of the returning veteran and how best to reintegrate him into society after years of sacrifice and disruption. Susan Hartmann argues that experts viewed the home and veterans' relationships with women as the linchpin of men's satisfactory adjustment. They enlisted women to ensure men's morale and urged families to "do more adjusting to the veteran than the veteran to the family." Articles exhorting women to privilege men's feelings and prerogatives before their own filled women's magazines. In assigning women the task of smoothing men's reintegration (even if it entailed self-abnegation), such writings exemplified a "larger trend in popular psychology and sociology . . . which saw women as the cause and/or potential redeemers of a deteriorating society."[101]

Given the social project of defining women's general obligations to men, it is clear that the alcohol establishment participated in a larger effort to establish the terms of social and emotional exchange within marriage. If the typical American family during the war years was bereft of masculine influence, the typical alcoholic family of the postwar years was similarly disadvantaged, not by the exigencies of war, but by the effects of disease. The gendered thinking that infused notions of marital duty and entitlement for normal couples also informed Americans' views of problem families. Given the threats the wartime social order posed to conventional family values, authorities developed allegedly therapeutic sanctions against deviance from sex-role prescriptions. Armed with a renewed conception of alcoholism as a disease, scientific experts and mutual-help communities viewed deviation from cultural norms as a cause of bodily and mental illness. Moreover, they proposed adherence to the normative gender system as a therapeutic solution to or cure for the problem of alcoholism.

Exploring the gendered history of alcoholism further illuminates the ambiguities and internal contradictions inherent in postwar domesticity. Of course the stereotype of the white, middle-class consumer family was a prescription for, not a description of, how most Americans actually lived. Despite the image of the happy family, an undercurrent of anxiety ran through postwar domestic culture. And what situation embodied familial discontent more than alcoholism? Experts documented the domestic failure of both spouses in an alcoholic marriage. AA invited members to look unflinchingly into the familial abyss, admitting that life with an alcoholic was no glib episode on a television sitcom. Yet underlying AA's philosophy, and perhaps its appeal, lay the possibility that the pathology of the alcoholic marriage was not so unusual after all. As one *Grapevine* contributor, advising sober readers not to expect "domestic bliss" immediately, suggested, "Sometimes [sobriety] requires that husband and wife get to know each other all over again. . . . Fewer cases of post-drinking domestic upsets would occur if husbands and wives could realize that the need for continuing readjustment is very natural. As a matter of fact, domestic bliss is rarely something that comes automatically, with or without a drinking problem. More often it [must] be compromised for and guarded vigilantly at all times, in so-called 'normal' families. So why doesn't the same hold true for us? We're almost as screwy as normal people!"[102] With humor and irony this writer reassured readers that so-called normal families were as prone to domestic discord as alcoholic ones.

In so doing he spoke to the psychic toll that marital conventions exacted of all Americans who conformed to them. In large part the cultural construction of the recovering alcoholic family—comprised of sober husbands and supportive wives—gained public acceptance because it reflected and reshaped familiar values in society at large.

Historians have virtually ignored the cultural history of the alcoholic's wife. Many scholars have explored the history, philosophy, and sociology of AA; but few have paid sustained attention to its "sister" fellowship, and none has investigated the contributions of female caseworkers and sociologists in creating a new vision of alcoholism as a family disease. How can we assess the significance of this topic with respect to women's history, family history, and the cultural history of drinking and addiction in the United States?

In many respects the history of Al-Anon supports existing scholarship about gender ideology and women's lives in the 1950s. Although Elaine Tyler May does not specifically mention alcoholism in her now-classic study of postwar family life, the ideological construction of the alcoholic family exemplifies her thesis that the "familial consensus of the Cold War era" served as a strategy of domestic containment, an attempt by ordinary Americans to shelter themselves from the threats of life in a modern, nuclear world. Yet normative family values in the 1940s and 1950s required conformity to strict gender assumptions that were fraught with potential frustrations and internal tensions. The alcoholic's wife faced these frustrations and tensions as much as anyone, and exploring her therapeutic response to domestic chaos sheds more light on the paradoxes inherent in postwar familial ideology.

The development of Al-Anon represents a complex, fascinating, neglected chapter in U.S. women's history. As a mutual-help organization created by and for women, it underscores the agency of ordinary women in constructing new visions of family pathology and well-being. On one hand, evidence suggests that Al-Anon helped married women to accept a repressive gendered social order. In a culture that strongly discouraged divorce and maintained formidable barriers to women's economic independence, Al-Anon could placate women who remained in less-than-desirable marriages. Such an analysis, offered from a feminist perspective, envisions Al-Anon as part of a therapeutic culture that recast women's political, social, and economic subordination simply as a matter of psychological and spiritual suffering.[103] Indeed, Al-Anon literature presented the emotional and material economy of marriage in ways that encouraged women to contain their anger and disappointment within an inegalitarian family system. Moreover, this interpretation would inspire skepticism of the collaboration between AA's largely male membership and Al-Anon's generally female population. Given AA's long-standing role in promoting wives' participation, alcoholic men influenced wives' values and actions in ways that shored up their own masculine dominance and authority. The marital ties between individual AA and Al-Anon members, not to mention the philosophical and institutional links between the two organizations, make it difficult to locate precise boundaries between men's and women's agency. But in any case, both parts of the mutual-help movement played a role in perpetuating sexual inequality in marriage and, by extension, in society at large.

On the other hand, such an analysis, compelling in some ways, is surely too simplistic. For one thing, it is important to recognize that Al-Anon members did not blindly or uncritically accept the ideas of experts or the prescriptions endorsed by the fellowship's literature. Although this chapter has not emphasized the range of experiences encountered by alcoholics' spouses, it is clear that Al-Anon in the 1950s was not monolithic. It was a diverse constellation of local auxiliaries, and the extent to which individual groups or members embraced, ignored, or resisted the fellowship's program of emotion management certainly varied. Although the prescriptive content and laudatory tone of Al-Anon's textual evidence sheds little light on such resistance, we can assume that despite allegiance to a common set of principles, many members expressed ideas that were alternative or even subversive by the standards of the time. The inherent possibilities for resistance and negotiation—a feature of all gender constructs—should caution us against overgeneralizing about the effects of any ideological norm.

Moreover, the conservative implications of these fellowships should not be overstated, as Al-Anon members solved problems in their lives as *they* perceived them. While hardly radical in its approach to domestic unhappiness—especially when compared with the feminist movement that had yet to come—the emergence of Al-Anon as separate from AA did suggest a budding gender consciousness and offered at least the possibility for women to challenge male authority. As psychologist Janice Haaken notes in her brief historical analysis of Al-Anon, "Women meeting separately to discuss their problems with men must have suggested to AA members the possibility of feminine resistance to male domination."

Although wives learned to contain their anger and resentment in ways consistent with AA philosophy, Al-Anon meetings did allow women to voice alternative viewpoints and "find subversive pleasure in feeling superior to the men they married." To channel such personal revelations into a political effort leading to social and structural change would require the support of the women's movement, which had yet to emerge.[104] But it is misguided simply to dismiss these women for not being social activists, for failing to repoliticize the problem of alcohol and the family, or for not applying feminist principles to their lives when they had few rhetorical and conceptual tools with which to do so. Rather, these women should be assessed on their own terms. While Al-Anon members generally acted within and contributed to the conservative gender ideology of the postwar era, they believed at the time that AA and Al-Anon offered something new and bold, a way to transform their lives in a powerful and empowering way. The mutual-help movement, on its way to becoming a central component of American therapeutic culture, held out the promise of a happier life for some very disenchanted women. Rather than view adherents to the therapeutic ethos merely as dupes or victims of false consciousness, we should ask why and how, at certain historical moments, psychological and spiritual change is perceived and experienced as socially empowering (and preferable to the political and legal reforms previously enacted to address family problems caused by alcoholism).

Postwar depictions of the alcoholic family highlight the implications of the larger shift in attitudes toward habitual drunkenness in the mid-twentieth century. Before the enactment and repeal of Prohibition, temperance reformers blamed drinkers, drink manufacturers, and drink sellers for harming family and society alike. But the dissemination of the disease concept of alcoholism absolved the drinker of much of the social harm he inflicted on others and encouraged society to offer him its ever-expanding therapeutic resources. In addition to engendering a more tolerant attitude toward drinking in U.S. society, the decriminalization of the liquor traffic bore social and economic implications for the alcohol industry and the addiction treatment professions.[105] Yet new ideas about alcoholism also affected attitudes toward nonalcoholic spouses and influenced the treatment they received. As professional and lay experts viewed alcoholic men as deserving benevolent treatment rather than social opprobrium, their wives, too, became objects of therapeutic scrutiny and practice. No longer simply pitied or used as a symbol to initiate political reforms, the postwar alcoholic's wife was enlisted in a private effort to enhance her spouse's recovery.

The modern model of alcoholic identity—a complex blend of psychoanalytic, physiological, sociological, and spiritual ideas—thus included male *and* female gender prescriptions. Moreover, new ideas about problem drinking entailed the formation of new social identities that were not, in the literal sense, alcoholic at all. To explore the *metaphorical* meaning of alcoholism in the twentieth century requires a foray into the cultural history of marriage. Marriage always reinforces or reshapes the gendered public order; it "operates as a systematic public sanction, enforcing privileges along with obligations."[106] While historians have recently stressed the role of marriage in the creation of public policy, law, and citizenship, the private *emotional economy* of marriage has also functioned as a site of gender formation and cultural regulation.[107] Because alcoholism so thoroughly destabilized the delicate balance of rights and responsibilities within postwar couples, it illuminates gendered norms in fine detail. Although alcoholic beverages became a widely accepted feature of the American recreational landscape in the post–World War II era, the addictive potential of alcohol meant that for some individuals, drinking was not merely part of a placid suburban lifestyle but, rather, a destructive force that could shatter the very foundations of familial stability. Given the nation's deep investment in marriage as a bedrock of tranquility and social order, it is apt that the deleterious effects of alcoholism would increasingly be measured in familial, and especially marital, terms.

The alcoholic marriage registered a range of cultural anxieties that permeated postwar U.S. society. But how did the problem drinker and his troubled wife appear against the cultural backdrop of normative drinking during this period? Beyond the realm of scientific research and Twelve Step programs, popular culture and imaginative literature also reflected relationships among drinking, domestic ideology, and social change. As the immediate postwar period gave way to the 1950s, the cultural meanings of alcohol consumption took on new accents; so, too, did the metaphorical significance of alcoholism.

5

DRINK AND DOMESTICITY IN POSTWAR AMERICA

THE ALCOHOLIC CULTURE OF THE POSTWAR SUBURBS

In the 1950s, as Alcoholics Anonymous (AA) and Al-Anon garnered more members struggling with habitual drunkenness, most drinkers in the United States enjoyed a relationship with intoxicating beverages that seemed more casual and less problematic than full-blown alcoholism. Taking their place alongside narratives of illness and recovery were more common references to the era's ubiquitous cocktail culture: magazine advertisements for champagne and whiskey, staid bartending manuals for home entertainers, fictional depictions of advertising executives imbibing after work, and movie scenes of men and women mingling in cocktail lounges. Two decades after repeal, drinking had become ever more domesticated, a taken-for-granted feature of recreational life among the middle classes. "Every aspect of drinking was becoming standardized," notes William Grimes, an astute observer of drinking customs. As the immediate postwar years gave way to the 1950s, social drinking acquired an aura of cool sophistication bordering on blandness, even banality. Mixed drinks were increasingly popular, especially "solid, conservative, establishment drinks, reflecting straight-down-the-middle taste." Streamlined, straightforward drinks such as martinis and Manhattans became the order of the day, a trend that Grimes suggests developed in sync with the general social and political climate of the period: "The fate of the cocktail after World War II can be read as a cold war allegory. The sanitized, commercialized version of middle-class life that defined the 1950s can be seen in the nation's drinking habits as well. The wayward creativity of the cocktail was tamed, a victim of social and political circumstances deeply hostile to eccentricity. . . . The man in the gray flannel suit drank a dry martini, a gin and tonic, a Scotch and soda—safe choices that put you in solidly with the right people."[1] In contrast to the distress suffered by alcoholic families, recreational drinking was perceived as an accepted, safe part of the postwar social landscape for urban and suburban citizens alike.

If saloon rituals loomed large in the days before Prohibition, the cocktail hour assumed prominence during the postwar era. Contemporary descriptions of this legendary institution abounded. One authority on U.S. drinking customs was a physician named Georgio Lolli, who forged close ties to E. M. Jellinek and the Yale Center for Studies on Alcohol. As he noted in *Social Drinking*, published in 1960, the term "cocktail hour" referred to "huge or small gatherings" in homes, bars, or hotel lobbies that were "prompted by the need for companionship or by social, business, or professional duties." In addition Lolli included all other drinking experiences "which occur after the daily activities have ended and before the evening meal is eaten." The standard time for the cocktail hour was around 5:30 or 6:00 P.M. While most early evening drinking occurred in groups, solitary imbibing could also be classified as cocktail hour drinking, including "the daily ritual of the exhausted salesman who gulps down two martinis before boarding the commuters' train" as well as "the slow highball sipping of his equally exhausted wife, waiting for him in the loneliness of their suburban cottage."[2]

In a clinical prose style that betrayed his profession, Lolli explained that many drinkers used alcohol "more for its effects on body and mind than for gustatory pleasure." Countless devotees of the cocktail hour could be characterized as "effect-seekers" looking temporarily to "escape from reality and from self-control . . . when the day's work is over." Lolli offered a scientific explanation for both the timing and the popularity of the cocktail hour. Several hours after lunch, people are "in a state of semistarvation frequently accompanied by fatigue and very low blood-sugar concentrations." Such physical depletion, moreover, is matched by the "mental-emotional fatigue" resulting from exposure to "unceasing outside stimulations" during the workday. Hastily consumed breakfasts and pressure-filled lunch breaks "give little relief to the individual who for seven or eight uninterrupted hours is exposed to the stresses and strains of the American way of life." Understandably, then, the cocktail hour dissolved tensions and anxiety for both "the skilled worker" and "the professional or businessman" in search of "quick relief."[3]

Historian and critic Bernard DeVoto offered a more lyrical account of cocktail rituals. In his breezy, opinionated paean succinctly titled *The Hour*, DeVoto celebrated the effects of social drinking on men and women who "made their spirits whole again" during that magical "appointed time" between daylight and dinner. "May 6:00 never find you alone," DeVoto cautioned. But if a man was not fortunate enough to be at home or at the home of a friend or acquaintance, he was best advised to find a local lounge or club. "When evening quickens in the street comes a pause in the day's occupation that is known as the cocktail hour. It marks the lifeward turn. The heart wakens from coma and its dyspnea ends." A properly made drink, individually mixed and devoid of sugar or grenadine, "softened" a man hardened by the strains of the day. As for alcohol's "effects on body and mind," DeVoto offered a colorful description: "The rat stops gnawing in the wood, the dungeon walls withdraw, the weight is lifted. Nerve ends that stuck through your skin like bristles when you blotted the last line or shut the office door behind you have withdrawn into their sheaths. Your pulse steadies and the sun has found your heart." For DeVoto a well-mixed martini was practically divine; the effects of alcohol were not merely somatic or social but spiritual as well. In his estimation the cocktail hour did nothing less than purify the soul, day after day. "The water of life was given to us to make us see for a while that we are more nearly men and women, more nearly kind and gentle and generous, pleasanter and stronger, than without its vision there is any evidence we are. It is the healer, the weaver of forgiveness and reconciliation, the justifier of us to ourselves and one another."[4]

As DeVoto's reverent prose suggests, many postwar drinkers virtually worshiped the cocktail as a source of daily renewal and redemption. Yet for such connoisseurs of drink, some libations were more divine than others. In line with the standardization of drink described by William Grimes, DeVoto satirized the use of sweet mixers and liqueurs by hosts and hostesses. If he condoned drinking in domestic settings, DeVoto shuddered at what might be called the feminization of cocktails, a trend influenced by cookbook writers indulging readers' sweet tooths with ingredients such as cherry brandy, crème de menthe, and raspberry syrup. "Cream and eggs have their place but that place is not an alcoholic drink," he opined, "and it is no more right to foul up honest liquor with them than to poison it with spinach juice."[5] If Lolli's observations are any indication, more and more Americans heeded this advice. By 1960, Lolli reported, the three standard cocktails dominating the U.S. drinking scene were martinis, Manhattans, and old-fashioneds. The martini, especially, elicited the physician's powers of observation and description: "Martinis have a strong appeal. The graceful, long-stemmed and glittering glass; the cool and colorless transparency of the fluid sketching the curves of a pitted olive or the floating irregularities of a lemon peel convey the impression of a powerful stillness, apt to affect with elegant explosiveness a person's body and mind. A martini is the epitome of sophisticated simplicity."[6] Popular reverence for the martini dated back at least as far as the early 1930s, when the *Thin Man* films equated the potables with urbane sophistication. But the martini was particularly suited to the culture of postwar America. As writer Joseph Lanza suggests, during the 1950s and early 1960s, "Martinis in particular soothed the 'Organization Man' as he contemplated the technological paradox that produced the atom bomb yet raised standards of living. Like the Protestant work ethic, Martinis were clean, severe, and bracing; like a Roman Catholic mass, they offered short-term ethereal rapture fraught with symbolism."[7]

Certainly Lolli and DeVoto were sparked by different motivations to write about cocktail culture. *The Hour*, with its humorous, pen-and-ink cartoon illustrations and its knowing, even smug tone, reassured drinking sophisticates of their superior taste while serving as a witty how-to manual for the uninitiated. Lolli fashioned himself a different kind of adviser. Influenced by his contact with alcoholic patients at the Yale Plan Clinic and elsewhere, Lolli aimed to help less compulsive drinkers enjoy liquor "without being hurt by it." *Social Drinking* outlined the differences between safe and dangerous drinking; it celebrated those styles and cultures of drink that increased human pleasure, while it cautioned readers against harmful excess. (While DeVoto did not emphasize restraint—indeed, his ideal drinker was a daily consumer of several strong cocktails—he did at one point advise readers not to "overdrink.") Ever mindful of the potentially damaging effects of liquor, Lolli combined sociological observation with scientific evidence. Yet both writers accepted social drinking as inevitable and even desirable, if properly pursued. "Whether or not we approve of this pacifying use of alcohol," Lolli argued, "we cannot deny that the anxieties of our age may broaden its indications for relaxation or even for sheer pleasure."[8]

Other writers who were well aware of the problems faced by alcoholics waxed poetic on the subject of drinking among nonalcoholics. New England author Henry Beetle Hough, who wrote a personal narrative on behalf of a sober male friend who wished to remain anonymous, discussed the social rituals of postwar Americans in positive terms. "At a party, a drink all round loosens tongues and enhances the feeling of friendship and wit. This is a normal, wholesome influence of alcohol." It would be a "grievous loss," he added, to deny those whose "inhibitions are slackened by the grace of a highball or cocktail." What concerned Hough was not drinking itself but the "cult of hard liquor" that he found to be pervasive in the mid-1950s. The "effeminate cocktails of yesterday" were scorned, replaced by dry Martinis and scotch on the rocks. In his view fruit juices and seltzer water were sensible ways to limit quantities of alcohol while still allowing imbibers to enjoy a mild intoxication. Offering what resembled a drinking aesthetic, he argued that "the real sophistication lies in moderation, artistry, the realization of grace in drinking."[9]

The image of the Organization Man dutifully drinking a "safe choice" such as the dry martini raises the issue of social conformity during the postwar era. Ever since William H. Whyte and other sociologists penned their now-classic studies of white, middle- and upper-middle-class communities, historians have emphasized the conformist atmosphere of the corporate bureaucracies and suburban enclaves that mushroomed during the 1950s. Whyte's best-selling *Organization Man*, published in 1956, argued that the "dominant members" of U.S. society held fast to a "social ethic" that valued "belongingness" as the ultimate need of the individual. After observing patterns of work, leisure, worship, and child-rearing in the postwar suburb of Park Forest, Illinois (a midwestern equivalent of Levittown), Whyte decried the extent to which Americans aimed to be accepted by others. With sociologists David Riesman and John Seeley, among others, Whyte argued that the new social ethic encouraged group identification at the expense of individuality. With privacy difficult to attain, peer groups dictated personal behavior. In evaluating the psychological impact of large-scale social change on personality (and especially the white, middle-class, masculine personality), these writers popularized the notion that American society was a "lonely crowd" of like-minded, "other-directed" conformists.[10]

Sociologists were joined by journalists, novelists, and other writers in a chorus of criticism against the soulless, consumerist lives of suburbanites. As one contemptuous critic noted, suburbia was a place where everyone "buys the right car, keeps his lawn like his neighbor, eats crunchy breakfast cereal, and votes Republican."[11] He might have added, "and drinks the same drinks." By 1947, nearly two decades after Prohibitionists engaged in a rearguard effort to maintain patterns of abstinence (or near-abstinence) among the middle class, experts documented that 65 percent of the adult population drank alcoholic beverages, including 75 percent of the men and 56 percent of the women surveyed. Moreover, they found that the percentage of drinkers increased from lower to higher economic levels and that citizens with advanced schooling drank more, and more often, than those with less than a high school education.[12] Given the trend toward conformity among educated, socially aspiring suburbanites, the popularity of drinking among this sector of the population seemed to rise all the more during the 1950s.

Although the authors of postwar community studies did not emphasize drinking, their works do offer indirect evidence about the role of alcohol consumption in patterns of sociability. In a chapter titled "The Web of Friendship," for example, Whyte described "social groupings" among suburban neighbors. The chapter includes two maps depicting the Park Forest suburb, with small squares representing individual houses. The drawings indicate various parties and social gatherings, ranging from bridge club meetings to potluck suppers, hosted by residents in 1953 and 1956, respectively. Each type of gathering is marked with a small symbol. Many of the categories explicitly involved drinking, including cocktail parties and pre-dance cocktails (symbolized by a miniature martini-glass icon), as well as eggnog soirees during the holiday season. Other events, including New Year's Eve parties, Saturday-night parties, and Fishhouse punch parties, most likely involved drinking as well.[13]

John Seeley and his coauthors, reporting on a Toronto suburb they labeled Crestwood Heights, were more explicit about the role of alcohol in the "complex network of human relationships" they discovered. Seeley offered a detailed account of social clubs and voluntary organizations comprised of middle- and upper-middle-class Crestwooders. Through membership in social clubs, especially golf clubs perched high on the status hierarchy, Crestwooders not only proclaimed their ability to "belong" to prestigious institutions; they also achieved a "form of psychological shelter, almost equivalent in potency to the protection afforded by the office or the home." But mere membership was not enough to achieve status within a club community; that accomplishment required adherence to the "pattern of activities" that prevailed therein. Apparently, drinking figured prominently in those activities. In the days before clubs had liquor permits, men kept flasks of scotch in their lockers and imbibed after an afternoon on the golf course. Quoting the wife of a member at a "high, but not the highest, status" club, Seeley recounted their drinking rituals:

Most of the men either liked to drink or thought it was expected of them and drank because it was good for business. All those who could not fit into this pattern moved their lockers to remote parts of the room where their strangeness was not so apparent. This resulted in a centrally located neighborly group of good fellows who called themselves the Scotch Block. Each man kept a bottle in his locker and at the end of a game the required amount was dispensed among the group. Spongers were not tolerated. Each man must have noticed how much he drank, himself, and how much each of the others drank because it seemed to end in a fair exchange. Those who could not pull their weight moved their lockers with the other "Strangers."[14]

According to Seeley's informant, supplying and drinking established quantities of straight whiskey was required of men who sought membership in this clique of "neighborly good fellows." Despite the fact that their class status, race, and cultural background allowed them to join the country club in the first place, men who did not drink the "required amount" were literally labeled "Strangers" and relegated to the margins of club social life. Certainly other criteria besides drinking habits (such as a man's occupation, personality, and "ability to tell jokes") influenced who was accepted into the Scotch Block. If a newcomer was considered "objectionable," he was "gradually frozen out" of the Scotch Block locker area. As Seeley explained, this atmosphere of social insecurity and conformity created a "tense situation" for men seeking companionship and sound business connections. "It is perhaps significant that liquor plays so important a part in creating intimacy," the author noted.[15] Using rituals of pooling and consuming liquor, the Scotch Block institutionalized an altered, upscale version of time-honored treating customs in a competitive atmosphere of postwar status-seeking. Not unlike the working-class saloon-goer of Jack London's day, affluent male club members placed liquor at the center of ritualized sociability.

Women members of the golf club also drank, but different rituals applied. For the most part women did not keep liquor in their lockers; instead their husbands sent them drinks via the club's "servants." After their usual locker-room quota of two drinks, the women waited for their husbands in the lounge for up to two hours. Apparently many women became annoyed by this and either stopped frequenting the club or began bringing their own liquor bottles; others "docilely sat" while the men cavorted among themselves. When they gathered in single-sex groups, club women did not enjoy the prerogative of supplying or serving alcoholic beverages; they did not control the terms or the timing of sociability. Unless they irreverently treated themselves, they waited for men to bestow drinks upon them. At parties and celebrations attended by married couples, women's drinking was apparently less restricted, or at least less formally regulated. Scotch Block members organized their own private parties, complete with orchestras, favors, corsages, and "drinks for the women." The men drank, too, fueling their talents for "songs, dancing, mimicry, and clowning." At heterosocial parties, women's drinking also was viewed as a gift bestowed by the men. During these "noisy, hilarious, and exhausting parties," the men gave speeches "extolling the beauty, desirability, and good sportsmanship of the wives."[16] Women enjoyed daytime golf games and elaborate evening parties at the behest of men whose incomes and social status afforded such leisure. Drinking was thus a major part of sociability and leisure among middle- and upper-middle-class married couples.

Dry journalists were even more scornful of social pressure to drink. One writer for *Christian Century* lamented that "in many homes the serving of alcoholic drinks has become the fundamental symbol of hospitality. Not to accept the proffered drink is to violate the unwritten code of conviviality." Just as drinkers were obliged to treat frequently if they were to count among the regulars in the neighborhood tavern, so, too, did postwar men and women face pressure to adhere to the "code of conviviality" on the cocktail party circuit. To violate that code, the writer continued, was to "run the risk of being considered offensive and labeled a *persona non grata*." Given his staunch antialcohol position, this observer was especially irritated by the use of "crowd psychology" as an "instrument of social coercion to consume liquor." Perhaps in response to the proliferating numbers of how-to hospitality manuals and drink manifestos, the author ironically titled his article "How to Refuse a Cocktail."[17] Couching his social critique in terms designed to influence individual behavior, he aimed to embolden like-minded readers with a spirited defense against social drinking.

Americans learned about implicit drinking rules not only through contact with friends and acquaintances but also through the mass media. Indeed the beer, wine, and liquor industries continued to fill newspapers and magazines with advertisements that contained subtle (and often not-so-subtle) pronouncements about the correct ways to consume their products and the advantages such consumption conferred. Alcoholic beverage ads in the 1950s were numerous and diverse, and their sheer variety speaks to the many different and sometimes overlapping drinking cultures that coalesced during the decade. Although it is not my purpose to analyze beer and liquor advertisements comprehensively, a brief survey of several suggestive ads reveals the extent to which postwar Americans integrated drinking into their daily lives at work, at play, and especially at home.

Continuing a tradition already prominent by the mid-1930s, many ads promoted the gift exchange of packaged liquor. Especially at Christmas, men of the professional-managerial classes gave and received gifts to cement social and business relationships. One 1958 ad for Martin's whiskey depicted a businessman sitting in his office behind a desk strewn with liquor bottles, wrapped presents, and holiday gift tags. The manicured fingernails of his secretary can be seen in the bottom corner, crossing off names on a Christmas gift list with a fine quill pen. "When the grand gesture is expected of you," the copy suggested, Martin's would be the perfect choice.[18] But like the masculine rituals of reciprocity in both urban taverns and suburban country clubs, the exchange of bottled liquor was also used to finesse one's own alcoholic indulgence. As one advertisement for Harwood's whiskey proclaimed in 1950, "It's better to give AND to receive!" Presumably, male readers of *Fortune* and other magazines would identify with illustrations of well-dressed men exchanging bottles adorned with gift cards inscribed "For Him." But the ad appealed to the reader's desire to drink as well as to give "Canada's finest whiskey."[19] As such ads implied, purchasing prestigious whiskey labels—for oneself as well as others— could reaffirm a man's place on the social hierarchy.

The growing number of ads for packaged liquor in the 1950s reflected the increase in home consumption after repeal. While advertisers continued to define distilled spirits as masculine beverages, they implied that hard liquor was appropriate to serve in domestic settings. Unlike temperance narratives depicting home and watering-hole as antithetical, these ads implied that given the proper presentation and decorum, the two could be synonymous. Consider, for example, an ad for Kentucky's Old Fitzgerald Whiskey, heralded as "Your Key to Holiday Hospitality." On one hand, the text betrayed long-standing assumptions about whiskey as a manly drink: "In Kentucky, where a man is judged by the whiskey he keeps, OLD FITZ is *first* for sending . . . *first* for serving." But the ad copy was displayed under a picture of an elegant buffet table, complete with hors d'oeuvres and a holiday punch bowl. Specifically, the ad promoted Old Fitz as an ingredient in eggnog. "Like our whiskey, our eggnog is a family affair—an old fashioned recipe bringing you . . . traditional flavor."[20] As suggested by the company's recipe, which was featured in the ad, cream, eggs, sugar, and cinnamon could tame whiskey into a wholesome drink the entire family would enjoy. Although the illustration did not depict human figures, it implied that women and possibly even children should drink eggnog to enhance holiday merriment.

Even cocktail connoisseurs who deplored concoctions such as eggnog heralded the home as an ideal setting for social drinking. As discussed earlier, home consumption at special events and parties was common among Victorian Americans during the nineteenth century; moreover, domestic drinking increased in popularity during Prohibition. This trend continued through the post–World War II era as well. For example, while praising the modern bar as a "glory of American culture"—an "upholder of the tavern's great tradition" and the "welcoming shelter and refuge and sanctuary" for all who enter—DeVoto nonetheless argued that the home was a superior watering-hole. Bars were a necessary convenience "for the fleeting hour," he observed, but "the Americans are a home-loving people and the best place for the devotions proper to their autochthonous liquors is the home." Like advertisers, he emphasized the role of women as hostesses, refuting "the widespread notion that women cannot make martinis." While men might more commonly drink them, women were capable of mixing them; indeed, he asserted, "the art of the martini is not a sex-linked character."[21] DeVoto's purpose, it seems, was to make the domestic realm conducive to manly drinking styles. In his view heterosocial leisure did not require the feminization of drink; rather, women could facilitate and participate in traditionally masculine forms of consumption.

Other liquor ads reinforced heterosocial drinking patterns; many depicted men and women mingling together in cocktail party settings. One ad in the December 1959 issue of the *New Yorker* featured a scene of fashionably dressed couples reflected on the surface of a large dinner bell. The bell referred to the product, Bell's Royal VAT Scotch Whiskey, as well as to the annual custom of "ringing in the New Year." The women in the picture were not, however, depicted in the act of drinking. Many ads portrayed liquor being served in a domestic context yet reinforced subtle differences between masculine and feminine drinks and drinking styles. In general, ads that included female figures depicted women as comfortable, even happy, in the presence of alcoholic beverages; they also portrayed women serving drinks as a mark of savvy hospitality. While whiskey ads often had masculine overtones, beverages with more feminine connotations, such as champagne and flavored liqueurs, often signified heterosocial or women's drinking. For example, an ad for Marie Brizard imported French liqueurs depicted a framed portrait of an elderly French matron behind a table swathed with a damask tablecloth. Bottles of crème de menthe and apricot liqueur, also adorned with the Marie Brizard name and portrait, evoked images of European luxury and a tradition of refined feminine hospitality.[22]

By the 1950s, advertisements signifying beer as a "family drink" were also common. Over the course of the decade the Miller Brewing Company ran ads heralding its High Life Milwaukee beer as an essential part of home hospitality. The ads focused on the wide appeal of beer and its role as a "choice companion for the fine foods" served by hostesses in the know. One Miller ad that appeared in the *New Yorker* in 1959 showed two young women and a man, dressed in festive attire, eating from buffet plates next to a cooler filled with bottled beer. The characters' youth and good looks, the simple yet stylish decor of the living room, and the focus on beer as a mealtime accompaniment all worked to portray it as a thoroughly domesticated beverage. The ad also appealed to the status consciousness of its readers: "Above all . . . The champagne of bottle beer gives you pride in your own good taste." It is significant that neither woman was shown drinking or even holding a glass of the featured beer, while the man, sitting cross-legged on the floor, had a bottle and a glass at his side. But the ad did suggest that beer was suitable for women's consumption and that female as well as male guests would enjoy its "good taste."[23]

Ads for intoxicating drinks thus appealed to people's social insecurities and their desire to impress others. Such goals were by no means novel among middle- and upper-middle-class Americans, but they intensified amidst the economic prosperity and consumer boom of the postwar period. After years of recession and war the nation's economy expanded enormously during the 1950s with a steady growth rate of 4.7 percent. Between 1950 and 1959, average spending power rose by 16 percent (while the increase from 1939 to 1959 was a whopping 62 percent). Padded with enticing advertisements, nationally circulated magazines such as *Life* ushered in a new era of material plenty. The year 1954, for example, witnessed the construction of 1.5 million new homes, the sale of 1.4 million power lawn mowers, and the introduction of sleek, low-priced automobiles adorned with fins. The nation's total income increased twice as fast as the population, and the biggest gains were experienced by working- and middle-class families. By the late 1940s, as Americans caught up with the consumption they had put off for over a decade, they launched "one of history's great shopping sprees."[24] Citizens had saved around $100 billion in war bonds and bank accounts and were eager to spend it on a cornucopia of household and luxury goods. The largest purchasing categories were geared toward suburban home and family life: cars, appliances, televisions, and of course, houses. Not only did advertisers and sellers aim to whip up a consumer frenzy; so, too, did the nation's highest elected officials. Cold War politicians, including Vice-President Richard Nixon, insisted that U.S. global superiority stemmed not only from military might but also from secure, abundant family life. According to historian Elaine Tyler May, just as housewives had been urged to battle on the consumer front during wartime, "women who marched off to the nation's shopping centers to equip their new homes joined the ranks of American cold warriors." The acquisition of commodities helped to forge an ideology of "domestic containment," which defined the nuclear family as a protective fortress against Cold War fears of communism and atomic destruction. The arena of competition between the United States and its global enemies was not only "the arms race or the space race; it was the consumer race—centered on the home."[25]

The beer and liquor industries hoped that Americans would spend much of their disposable income on drink, and they appealed not only to the consumer race underlying postwar foreign policy but also to the domestic consumer race of competitive acquisition, otherwise known as "keeping up with the Joneses." Serving the right brand of whiskey or champagne would impress one's friends and associates as much as a prestigious automobile or stylish home furnishings would. But as a mood-altering substance alcohol was more than a material commodity; it promised to facilitate the emotion work of managing the impression one made, a concern inherent in status seeking and professional social climbing. By relaxing people's inhibitions and smoothing off the rough edges of tense social interactions, drinking would finesse and solidify relationships between friends and neighbors, employers and employees.

Although most ads appealed to the sociability of the prospective drinker, others emphasized that alcohol could soften tensions and quell anxieties within the home. References to edgy men returning from work or to housewives sipping cocktails "in the loneliness of their suburban cottages" spoke to the role of alcohol in smoothing interactions between husbands and wives as they muddled through the day. While discourses on alcoholism portrayed drinking as a cause of, or at least a contributor to, domestic discontent, some advertisers suggested that alcohol could enhance marital relations that were already strained. Consider, for example, a rather astonishing ad for Paul Masson California Champagne printed in the *New Yorker* in December 1959. The full-page ad featured a photograph of two ceramic egg cups painted to represent human faces, a woman's and a man's. As the egg cup figurines topped with soft-boiled eggs faced each other with dour expressions, the ad's headline philosophized, "The critical period in matrimony is breakfast-time." Surrounding a small image of a champagne bottle, the ad copy presumed that the reader was stuck in a lackluster romance and offered its product as a tonic to marital disenchantment. "You know the feeling," coaxed the ad. "The married breakfast is an uneasy time, no matter how much in love the participants. You try to escape it by leaving the house before breakfast or sleeping through till lunch. Stop all that. Face up with Champagne. You break out a bottle of our effervescent stuff—midweek, say, when it feels like the bloom is off the marriage."[26] Accepting marital strife as routine and inevitable, the ad depicted breakfast as a tense, "uneasy" exercise worthy of escape. Such dissatisfaction, the advertiser claimed, could be assuaged not through couples therapy (and certainly not through divorce) but through a morning glass of sparkling wine. Positing breakfast as a counterpart to evening drink rituals—as a domestic cocktail party for two—the ad implied that champagne would recharge readers' emotional batteries and embolden them to "face up" to their less-than-perfect spouses. As a classic document of the postwar discourse of domestic discontent, this ad proffered alcohol as a pacifying antidote to familial boredom or tension.[27] Champagne, specifically, was just the ticket, light and bubbly enough to appeal to dispirited men and women first thing in the morning.

Thus while Twelve Step fellowships and alcoholism experts established a new paradigm of the alcoholic family, the beverage industries and other drink advocates increasingly depicted social drinking as a family affair. It was conceivable that the normal middle-class or affluent husband drank in various settings and for various purposes; so, too, did the normal wife (although the specific settings and styles often differed by sex). Frequent or extreme drunkenness, however, was not condoned. As mentioned above, pro-drink observers from physicians to intellectuals cautioned Americans not to consume *too much*. John Seeley noted that many members of golfing clubs refused to drink excessively during the week, expecting that their "moderate drinking would create the impression that . . .

nothing [would] interfere with the excellence" of their work the next day.[28] William Whyte remarked in passing that the postwar suburbs shielded residents from such social undesirables as "embittered spinsters" and "crazy drunkards," outcasts who flouted dominant conventions of marriage or personal comportment.[29] Most of all, advertisers created a symbolic promotional world in which alcohol was enjoyed but not abused and was never deleterious to social or domestic order.

Of course, the boundary between acceptable domestic drinking and alcoholism was not always clear, and the line was especially blurry when the drinker was a woman. In many social circles, if a suburban housewife took a daily drink to spice up her routine (or to overlook her husband's flaws), such behavior would have seemed unremarkable. Yet some alcoholism experts realized that for some women, domestic pressures and dissatisfactions could cause excessive or pathological drinking. During the 1950s most social workers and therapists counseled women alcoholics to adjust to their appropriate feminine roles as wives and mothers as part of the treatment process. Just as male alcoholics were urged to resume traditional masculine prerogatives of breadwinning and familial authority, so, too, were alcoholic women exhorted to follow gendered prescriptions of responsible maternal and domestic behavior. Yet a small fraction of social workers took the opposite tack and instead advised their patients to develop interests and occupations outside the home and even to yield the care of their children to others, at least temporarily. Although these therapists did not advocate any social or systemic responses to the difficulties such women faced, their approach was unusual in that it recognized that domesticity itself could be a major source of discontent leading to alcoholism.[30] In the promotional world of cocktail culture, however, neither emotional despair nor alcoholic excess figured into the rosy picture of postwar domestic drinking.

While advertisers used images of women symbolically to represent the domestication of drink, others assigned women the literal task of ensuring moderate consumption. Church leaders, especially, aimed to prevent excess while condoning social drinking among parishioners. In 1956, for example, clergymen in Greenwich, Connecticut, convened a conference called "Alcoholism and Alcohol Education," which "set forth a moral theology concerning alcoholism and the use of alcoholic beverages" in a context of "new standards in the perplexing field of social drinking." Affiliated with the National Council's Department of Christian Social Relations, the conference participants established guidelines for local churches to enforce, including a Program for Women to advance alcohol education. Women, the ministers argued, could influence society "with singular effectiveness" through "three distinctive family roles which they exercise—as mothers, as wives, and as hostesses." As mothers they would help children counter peer pressure to drink; as wives they would learn how men's occupational stress could lead to habitual drinking; and as hostesses they would abide by a "good hostess code." Such a code required women always to serve food with alcoholic drinks, always to serve non-alcoholic as well as intoxicating drinks, never to pressure guests to drink, and never to "delegate to cocktails the hostess' responsibility to create an atmosphere and relationships conducive to wholesome recreation." Here the authors of the code assigned to women the task of ensuring social conviviality among party guests, rather than relying on alcohol itself. Unlike evangelical temperance crusaders, these postwar religious leaders accepted drinking among men and women, yet they still enlisted women to contain the worst potential social effects of alcohol.[31]

The concerns of the clergymen about drinking among children underscored the fact that American youth, too, were part of the nation's postwar alcoholic culture. With drinking a fixture of daily life at home, many boys did not have to wait until they were deemed old enough to enter the neighborhood tavern with their fathers or other male elders (as writer Pete Hamill had done in working-class Brooklyn in the 1940s). Although children were not the explicit targets of beer or liquor advertising, ads suggested that adults could drink responsibly in the presence of young family members. Moderate drinking, in other words, was not something parents needed to hide from children and youth. By the time young men and women were old enough to enter college, the majority of them were drinking alcoholic beverages. The first major sociological study of drinking among American youth in college, published in 1953, found that 79 to 92 percent of males and 40 to 89 percent of females drank alcohol with some degree of frequency. (The percentages varied among private and public colleges of different types.)[32] The sociologists also discovered a correlation between family income and consumption rates. Students (and especially female students) from families in the highest income brackets imbibed more than those from modest backgrounds. Although some abstained for religious or moral reasons, because of familial or peer pressure, or because they did not like the taste, more youth did drink "because of enjoyment of taste," "to comply with custom," "to be gay," or "to relieve fatigue or tension." Sixteen percent of male drinkers admitted drinking "to get drunk," while only 1 percent of female drinkers stated drunkenness as an explicit goal. Thus while most students believed that their institutions officially condemned (or merely tolerated) student drinking, as a peer group they often behaved otherwise.[33]

Other researchers studied drinking patterns among high school students throughout the nation. In 1951 68 percent of high school boys and girls in Utah reported that they never drank, while 30 percent identified themselves as occasional drinkers. In other states many parents apparently had more liberal attitudes toward their children's consumption. In 1954 researchers in Nassau County, Long Island, found that 68 percent of fourteen-year-olds had parental permission to drink at home, while 29 percent enjoyed consent to "drink away from home sometimes." For eighteen-year olds those figures were 95 and 84 percent, respectively. A similar study of teenagers in Racine, Wisconsin, reported similar results. Like the experts on college drinking, high school researchers found that drinking was more prevalent among children from families of higher economic and educational levels. Most studies found that peer pressure was only one of several factors influencing a teenager's drinking behavior. As one author summarized, "The overwhelming majority of students agree that people don't need alcoholic beverages for good social relations and reject the statements that drinking at a party makes people get along better." Rather, they found that the most significant influence stemmed from "enduring patterns of conduct learned from persons with whom the child has close ties of intimacy and identification," especially the family. "Almost all of the students reported that they were introduced to alcoholic beverages by parents, relatives, or friends. Very few began alone or in the company of strangers."[34] Although peer group behavior and family attitudes sometimes conflicted, the researchers' findings reflected the domestication of drink in U.S. society more generally.

Other writers were more alarmed by potential peer pressure among school-aged children. As mentioned above, many religious leaders used their cultural authority to steer youth away from social drinking, or at least to inculcate values of moderation and responsibility. In 1947, for instance, the National Council of the Young Men's Christian Association published a pamphlet for teenaged boys and girls titled *It's Up to You*. The pamphlet tells the story of eighteen-year-old Charley, a "healthy young American who makes pretty good grades in school and throws a mean forward-pass." Although raised by abstinent parents, Charley took his first drink in response to social pressure at a party; indeed, he was "afraid *not* to take the drink." Moreover, Charley was portrayed as vulnerable to harsh judgments about his gender identity if he did not imbibe: "If he didn't, maybe Phyllis [a potential girlfriend] or the crowd would consider him a panty-waist or a wet blanket, at least not quite a he-man." Charley did not want the "dipsy-doodle effect" of alcohol, but "he hadn't figured out that he could still be a he-man and not drink." Depicting peer pressure as an affront to Charley's individuality and freedom to make his own choices, the author also countered the long-standing association between drinking and virility. "An abstainer *can* be a regular fellow," proclaimed a caption beneath a cartoon sketch of three young men laughing together at a party. Two of the men sipped drinks while the third graciously refused a glass offered by a cocktail waiter. Without condemning all forms of drinking as morally suspect, suggesting that drinkers and nondrinkers could socialize harmoniously, the pamphlet taught readers how to restrict their drinking while maintaining self-esteem and personal integrity.[35]

Thus while advertisers and liquor manufacturers exploited readers' feelings of insecurity and social patterns of belongingness to sell their products, other observers were more alarmed by the increasing prevalence of social drinking. But whether they aimed to increase or minimize alcohol consumption, postwar Americans generally viewed drinking as a matter of individual choice and alcoholism as a matter of individual or familial concern. As was the case in earlier post-repeal decades, the ideological distinction between moderation and alcoholism allowed for the further domestication of drink in the postwar period. By the late 1940s and 1950s, cocktail rituals were woven into the fabric of the dominant culture, both absorbing and reflecting anxieties that accompanied such trends as consumerism, status seeking, social conformity, and the bureaucratization of the corporate workplace. In a range of documents and discourses advertisers, cookbook writers, religious leaders, sociologists, and many others engendered and reflected on the alcoholic culture of the post-repeal, post–World War II era. Here the phrase "alcoholic culture" refers to the diverse ways in which men and women used alcoholic drinks—and drinking rituals—to establish, renew, or alter social bonds, both inside and outside the domestic domain. In this sense the word "alcoholic" is used as an adjective referring to intoxicating beverages, to signify the ubiquity of drink in American society. Whether sipping beer at a neighbor's backyard barbecue, downing martinis at an urban club, or refusing cocktails at a college party, Americans shaped a complex alcoholic culture.

But the phrase "alcoholic culture" had another meaning as well, one in which alcoholism, understood as pathology, came to represent a host of other anxieties and problems permeating mid-twentieth-century social and cultural life. Previously we explored how professional experts and lay therapeutic communities interpreted the problem of habitual drinking in ways that encompassed and even accounted for broader shifts in gender identity, marital expectations, class affiliation, and work experience. Members of the alcoholism and alcohol studies movements were aware of the broad social uses of alcohol, but they focused on identifying and treating Americans who drank alcoholically themselves (or who lived with alcoholic family members). But other cultural producers, including fiction writers and filmmakers, crafted narratives designed for general audiences that wrestled with the worst implications of the nation's alcoholic culture (defined in the first sense). To understand how alcoholism came to signify other darker, potentially damaging aspects of postwar social life, we turn now to several films and literary narratives of the 1950s and 1960s that subtly engendered this second meaning of "alcoholic culture."

ALCOHOL AND FAMILY TROUBLE IN POSTWAR FICTION AND POPULAR CULTURE

If *The Lost Weekend* marked the initial popular influence of the alcoholism movement in the mid-1940s, during the 1950s the alcoholism film matured into a distinct minigenre. *The Lost Weekend* ushered in what film historians have called the classic period of alcoholism films featuring a major character suffering from inebriety. Between 1945 and 1962 at least thirty-four Hollywood movies depicted alcoholism as a disease requiring therapeutic treatment. Most of these films, in turn, were part of a broader genre: the realistic "social problem" film, which didactically dramatized and informed audiences about serious issues such as juvenile delinquency, racial prejudice, poverty, or labor union corruption. In films of this genre (which emerged during the Depression and proliferated during the 1950s), a social condition, personal problem, or deviant stigma is turned into a dramatic device allowing the filmmaker to make moral, political, and ideological statements about the social causes of and potential solutions to the problem at hand.[36]

Moreover, during the postwar period many social problem films reflected larger cultural struggles over family structures and sex roles. As film scholar Jackie Byars argues, films dealing with serious social issues often situated those problems squarely in the domestic realm. By dramatizing national public concerns as they affected individuals and relationships within a particular family, such movies of the 1950s presented social problems essentially as family problems that could be "solved only by a return to traditional family values and structures."[37] Alcoholism films were no exception. Just as professional and lay experts envisioned alcoholism as a family disease in the 1950s, so, too, did Hollywood screenwriters and directors increasingly depict it as a family problem. Although *The Lost Weekend* prefigured later domestic melodramas in its focus on Don Birnam's troubled bond with his girlfriend Helen, it characterized alcoholism as an individual illness and only hinted at the conflict between (potential) marital commitment and inebriety. In several later films, however, the plots and characters portrayed a "complex interactional world" in which alcoholism infused all aspects of marital relationships. In such films "alcoholism creates all the emotional experiences that any intimate relationship could ever hope to contain: sexuality, eroticism, tabooed acts, bad faith, double-binds, violence, divided selves, twisted love, old dreams, absent father figures, dead children, alcoholic spouses, sick husbands, and sick wives."[38]

The 1952 film *Come Back, Little Sheba* best reveals how popular films engendered complex metaphorical meanings of alcoholism.[39] Directed by Daniel Mann and produced by Hal B. Wallis, the film adapted William Inge's play of the same name, which showed on Broadway to commercial and critical success in 1950. This heartrending movie garnered several Oscars and won special praise for its performances by Burt Lancaster and Shirley Booth, who played a husband and wife trapped in a stagnant, unfulfilling marriage.[40] *Come Back, Little Sheba* was also the first film to include explicit references to AA. The alcoholic in *Sheba* is Doc Delaney, a middle-aged chiropractor who has recently stopped drinking thanks to his involvement in AA. Endorsing the ideology of the fellowship, the film depicts a meeting where AA slogans, prayers, and rituals are celebrated. Moreover, the film concentrates equally on Doc's slovenly wife, Lola. While Lola herself is not an alcoholic, her angst-ridden life revolves around her husband's alcoholism. When Doc has a "slip" after his first full year of sobriety, his renewed drinking threatens Lola's fragile sense of security as thoroughly as it does his own. The pairing of husband and wife thus renders alcoholism a doubly gendered production, and the story relies on the characterization of Lola to define the effects of Doc's disease on the family.[41]

From the start the film makes clear that Doc is a recovering alcoholic and that Lola is pleased about her husband's abstinence. Near the beginning of the film Doc and Lola attend a meeting where Doc celebrates his first AA "birthday" marking a full year of sobriety. This is a special occasion, but otherwise the couple's daily routine is drab and monotonous, with minimal conversation at breakfast before Doc leaves for work and Lola, dressed in a shabby robe and slippers, idles at home. Because the Delaneys need extra money, Lola rents a room in the house to an attractive female art student named Marie Buckholder. A subplot revolves around Marie, who dates a sexually aggressive college athlete named Turk even while she is about to become engaged to Bruce, a clean-cut, well-paid university graduate who lives in another town. Both Lola and Doc become intrigued by Marie and Turk's dalliances; at different times they spy on the young couple kissing and flirting on the living room couch. Marie's presence not only stirs latent sexual feelings in Doc and Lola; the boarder also prompts them to reflect on their own troubled past. Before they married, Lola got pregnant and had a baby who died at birth, leaving her unable to have any more children. Offended and outraged by his daughter's promiscuous behavior, Lola's father refused to speak to her ever again. Due to social convention Lola and Doc married as soon as they discovered the pregnancy; in the film the couple reflects on their loss, struggling to accept the legacy of their painful past. (The title of the film refers to Lola's pet dog, Sheba, who has run away, symbolizing Lola's broken dreams and especially her lost child). Marie is the age their child would have been. Doc grows increasingly troubled by Marie's promiscuity and, the film implies, sexually aroused by her as well. Both protective and jealous of Marie's involvement with Turk, Doc takes to the bottle in an alcoholic rage. With a whiskey bottle in hand, Doc leaves home and then returns in a drunken stupor, violently threatening Lola with a knife before she escapes his grip and calls for help. After he is taken away by caring AA friends, Doc sobers up and returns home a week later. At the end Doc asks Lola for her forgiveness and affirms his love and commitment to her. Lola serves Doc's breakfast for the first time in years, content to have her husband back. Perhaps realizing that she cannot change the past, Lola tells Doc that "little Sheba is never coming back, and I'm not gonna call for her anymore." Lola tells Doc that she will never leave him, that he is "all [she] ever had." Doc tells his wife that he is glad to be home, and they smile at each other as the film ends.

On one level we may interpret *Sheba* as a dramatic illustration of a postwar alcoholic marriage, similar in ideological content to therapeutic narratives. As we have seen, experts commonly viewed alcoholism as a manifestation of failed gender-role performance. In keeping with the cultural definition of alcoholic manhood after repeal, Doc Delaney is a weakened, ineffectual patriarch. He has a lackluster career, few friends, and little money. Alcoholism signifies his failure as a provider and bread-winner. Because of his rushed, early marriage to Lola, Doc had to drop out of a prestigious medical school and attend a second-rate chiropractic college. He squandered his family inheritance on booze, and his drinking prevented him from returning to medical school. Before his relapse Doc reflects on the damage his drinking has wrought: "We need to forget the past, and live for the present. We could have had a nice house, friends, comforts. But we don't have any of that now. . . . I can't give up just because I made a few mistakes. I gotta keep going." At one point Doc philosophizes to Lola, "Alcoholics are mostly disappointed men." But drinking, the film implies, never allowed Doc to escape his past. Rather, it compounded his misery.

Doc's gendered failure is further signified through his wife's own weak-nesses: her slovenly clothing, her lax attitude toward housekeeping, and the lonely isolation of her life in a small midwestern town. Lola has lost her figure and former beauty; she often sleeps until noon and rarely combs her hair. Indeed, she takes on the visual characteristics of a female alco-holic, even though she never drinks.[42] Moreover, the couple's marital failure is signified by their lack of a child. In the context of postwar pronatalism, which celebrated child-rearing as the most important task of married couples and especially of women, the childlessness of the De-laneys is especially striking. At one point Lola's neighbor, an active house-wife and mother of four children, disparages Lola as a lazy, "good for nothing" wife. She urges her to "get busy" attending to domestic tasks. At the film's end Lola's renewed interest in domesticity and Doc's renewed commitment to sober manhood signal their conformity to normative gen-der roles—at least on the surface. Marital stability and Doc's recovery require that Doc rebuild his career as a chiropractor and that Lola im-prove her appearance and keep up with household chores. In so doing, the film suggests, the Delaneys might find a measure of domestic tranquility despite their troubled past.

Sociologists and film critics have emphasized the role of alcoholism and AA in this film. One interpretation, for example, locates *Sheba* within the context of postwar Freudian family melodramas and argues that Doc's recovery is identified with impotence and sexual abstinence in his marriage. This psychoanalytic reading of the film mirrors the diagnoses of Freudian therapists during the postwar era: Doc's alcoholism stems from inherent personality defects and failed sex-role identification that doom him to a life of tragedy and self-destruction. Others challenge this interpretation, stressing the symbolic interaction between Doc and Lola and their "shared biographical history." Film scholar Norman Denzin reads the film "not as a study of an alcoholic personality, but as a study of an alcoholic marriage, and of lost intimacy in the marriage." Lola's recurring, obsessive dreams about her lost dog are equivalent to Doc's alcoholism: both are used to kill the pain of past sexual transgressions. Rather than relying on psychoanalytic theory, this latter analysis reinforces the sociological view of alcoholism as a family disease inherent in the spousal relationship.[43] Both interpretations illuminate important aspects of the film, and their emphasis on alcoholism as a theme is certainly warranted.

As Denzin points out, however, contemporary film reviewers at the time of the movie's release did not stress the role of alcoholism or AA in the film. *Time* did not mention AA and merely noted that Doc "is a chiropractor and a reformed drunk." *Newsweek* simply observed that "Doc has managed, however precariously, to stay on the wagon for a year with the help of Alcoholics Anonymous." In Denzin's view, postwar reviewers sidestepped the vexing issue of the causes of alcoholism and failed to see that Doc's daily struggle with sobriety "created the underlying currents of discontent and malaise that defined the marriage for the two partners." Thus, he contends, reviewers missed one of the film's central messages: when dreams are shattered for middle-class Americans, alcoholism is not far behind.[44] Yet Denzin, I would argue, dwells too lightly on the issues reviewers *did* emphasize in the 1950s. Indeed, their relatively dismissive attitude toward alcoholism suggests that they interpreted Doc's illness as a metaphor for a broader set of social concerns. Bernard Kalb, writing for the *Saturday Review*, identified the film's main theme as "the heartbreak of little people, the frustration of their wholly conventional lives." *Time* called the film "a minor, but moving tragedy on a major theme: the lives of quiet desperation that men lead." The *New York Times* book reviewer focused on "the commonplace, middle-class home of the middle-aged couple . . . [and their] two pathetically cramped and wasted lives."[45] In retrospect it is clear that these critics read "through" the immediate problem of alcoholism, linking it to more widespread experiences of disillusionment and discontent in postwar society.

Come Back, Little Sheba, then, did not merely dramatize contemporary visions of alcoholism as a family disease; it was also a meditation on the damaging effects of social convention and conformity within the middle class more generally. Sexual taboos, in particular, haunt Doc and Lola. As Denzin notes, alcoholism functions as the ultimate price the Delaneys must pay for their episode of premarital sex. Although they dated for a year without even kissing, Lola recalls, one spring night they gave in to their lustful appetites despite rigid norms prohibiting such behavior. In the present Marie's flirtatious behavior and her fascination with male bodies and sexuality (evident in her drawings of Turk's muscular torso required for her portraiture class) remind the audience of the continuing power of dominant sexual mores. On one hand, Marie is figured as a clean, respectable girl attracted to the respectable, and respectful, Bruce (whom she eventually marries). Yet on the other hand, her simultaneous attraction to Turk's forceful, unrestrained sexuality marks her as a potential bad girl capable of making the same mistake Lola made twenty years before.[46] At one point in the film, Lola asks her husband, "Do you think we did wrong, Doc?" Doc's response is resigned: "You can't defy convention, I guess, or the laws of God." Although they were once in love, since the tragedy of Lola's stillborn child—a cruel punishment for their transgression—their marriage has become an empty shell, an arrangement which superficially conforms to social expectations, yet festers within. Doc's alcoholism is a form of self-deception, an attempt to escape from an emotional straitjacket long imposed by others.

Starting with *The Lost Weekend*, alcoholism films functioned metaphorically to represent larger social and psychic traumas that Americans faced as they adjusted to life after World War II. In 1945 the cinematic portrayal of alcoholic men not only referred to the literal problem of immoderate drinking among returning veterans; it also symbolized the confusion and lack of resolve permeating a society in search of stability and order. By the early 1950s, alcoholism films were depicting the problems inherent in postwar domestic arrangements that had solidified in response to the very social disruptions unleashed during the war years. As middle-class Americans turned to marriage and nuclear family roles to buffer themselves from a threatening external world, many discovered that conventional marriage failed to live up to its promises. When film critics emphasized the frustration and disillusionment of Doc and Lola's wholly conventional lives, they indicted what they perceived to be the blandness and repressive coercion of social norms. Alcoholism served as a cultural marker of domestic containment and the dissatisfactions it engendered.

Moreover, the film commented implicitly on the promises, both filled and unfulfilled, of therapeutic culture. Unlike Inge's original play, the film emphasized AA as a program of recovery and added the scene depicting Doc's "birthday" meeting. Only AA is posited as a successful form of therapy, and the film's modestly happy ending confirmed the assumption that a sober husband is better than an alcoholic one. Denzin argues that Doc's true recovery also requires that the couple reexamine their past: "Only after the past has been openly addressed can Lola and Doc have a free, open, cleansed intimate relationship based on mutual love and respect."[47] But this is a more optimistic reading of the ending than the film itself suggests, and it is certainly more optimistic than what many reviewers offered in 1952. Doc and Lola are better off if Doc remains sober, but their renewed commitment results as much from resignation as from tender feelings. The labor of emotion management, of regulating sexual desire and extinguishing the pain of past experiences, remains. In contrast to advertisements and other cultural messages celebrating drinking as a tonic to marital dissatisfaction, Doc realizes that drinking will not make their marriage more palatable. But will sobriety? Perhaps it will make it more bearable, but not necessarily blissful. It is interesting that the film ends with Doc and Lola sitting at the breakfast table, the same location that champagne advertisers would soon characterize as symbolic of daily boredom and repressed anger. Though the film ends on a relatively positive note, Doc and Lola will still muddle through each day of their commonplace, middle-class lives, beholden to gendered conventions of domestic containment.

Narratives outside the strictly defined genre of alcoholism films also voiced concerns about problem drinking. In the 1950s a number of writers treated the topic of habitual drinking without using the scientific terms of the alcoholism movement or the word "alcoholism" to signify the issue at hand. Rather, they relied on characterization and plot development to suggest the potential of alcohol to deceive and even destroy men and women as they coped with the pressures of daily life. Among the most prominent was the writer John Cheever, whose short stories exposed the uses and abuses of drink among middle- and upper-middle-class Americans. Publishing story after story in the *New Yorker* and other magazines from the 1940s through the 1970s, Cheever, with a concise economy of style employed only by accomplished authors of short fiction, captured the social settings and the emotions of postwar suburbanites. In 1958 he published a collection titled *The Housebreaker of Shady Hill and Other Stories*, a coherent sequence of tales in which he examined upscale suburban America most trenchantly.

Many of Cheever's stories offer glimpses of family life that might have developed if returning veterans (and their wives) had not reined in their social drinking. Setting his stories in the prosperous suburbs of New York City and Connecticut or summer vacation communities in New England, Cheever wrote primarily about affluent men, women, and children blessed with ample leisure time and material comforts. Rather than representing more modest citizens of small-town "middle America" (as portrayed in *Come Back, Little Sheba* and *The Best Years of Our Lives*), Cheever's stories depict social realms more frequently invoked in glossy advertisements: a world of country clubs, cocktail parties, white-steepled churches, and expensive outdoor sports—a world to which many readers of mass-circulation magazines presumably aspired. But despite this difference in the characters' class affiliation, as in so many other postwar alcoholism narratives Cheever's fictional milieu is decidedly domestic, defined by both the pleasures and the problems of family and suburban community life. Because Cheever wove themes of drinking and alcoholism more subtly into his narratives than did writers such as Charles Jackson or William Inge, his stories (and in one case, a film based on his story) offer a different yet complementary view into postwar alcoholic culture. Furthermore, when contrasted with Jack London's *John Barleycorn*, his stories illuminate with special clarity several strands of cultural change that developed over the course of the century.

"The Sorrows of Gin," first published in 1953 and reprinted in *The Housebreaker of Shady Hill*, reveals one of Cheever's most explicit efforts to suggest the damaging effects of drinking on familial relationships. The story takes place in the home of Mr. and Mrs. Lawton, residents of a wealthy commuter suburb called Shady Hill and the parents of Amy, a fourth-grader in a private day school. Despite the Lawtons' wealth, their life is as bland as Doc and Lola Delaney's. Mrs. Lawton's main concern centers on hiring and maintaining adequate domestic help, while Mr. Lawton's commuter train "seemed to have the gloss and the monotony of the rest of his life." The Lawtons pay little attention to their daughter's inner feelings. Rather than engage her in meaningful dialogue, they tend to bark commands at her (such as "Feed the cat," "Do your homework," or "Put your bicycle away"). The parents channel their conversational energies toward a set of like-minded friends and neighbors with whom they socialize almost every night.[48]

As the story begins, the Lawtons are about to leave Amy with Rosemary, the family cook, while they attend a dinner party at the home of the Parminters. That evening Rosemary talks to Amy about her parents' drinking: "Of course, the drinking that goes on here is all sociable, and what your parents do is none of my business, is it?" Rosemary is especially concerned because her sister, who also worked as a domestic servant, "drank too much" and died in a state of "*non compos mentis.*" Wielding as much influence on Amy as the Lawtons themselves, Rosemary urges Amy to empty her father's gin bottle secretly. Though wary of upsetting her stern father, Amy obliges Rosemary, whom her parents blame for "stealing" their liquor. Mr. Lawton yells at his wife for hiring a string of booze-pilfering laundresses, cooks, and painters: "Everybody is drinking my liquor," he shouts, "and I am God-damned sick and tired of it." The next night the Lawtons hire an elderly woman named Mrs. Henlein to baby-sit Amy while they attend another party. Again Amy empties her father's gin bottle, while Mrs. Henlein worries about being driven home by a "drunken gentleman" when the Lawtons return. Sure enough, Mr. Lawton discovers the empty bottle and accuses the baby-sitter of drinking a full quart of gin. The old woman defends her integrity and calls her employer a "son of a bitch." "You think you can get away with insulting me, but you're very, very, very much mistaken," she screams, threatening to call the police. Lying in bed, Amy is awakened by the loud voices and realizes that she is to blame for the wrong accusation and the chaos that has ensued. Amy resolves to run away from her troubled home, and in the morning she buys a one-way train ticket to New York City. Concerned about the girl's intentions, the station master calls the family, and Mr. Lawton comes to the station to retrieve his daughter. "Oh, why should she want to run away?" he thinks as he approaches her on the platform. The story ends ironically with a query: "How could he teach her that home sweet home was the best place of all?"

Cheever tells the story from the perspective of a knowing adult observing the scene from Amy's point of view. While the domestic employees mention the couple's drinking, through Amy's eyes the narrator offers the most pointed observations about "her father's cocktail things" and the effects of alcohol on the parents. After Mr. Lawton discovers the empty gin bottle, his anger subsides when he replenishes the decanter and has a couple of drinks. Cheever relates the incident as follows:

> Marcia Lawton held her empty glass toward her husband, who filled it from the shaker. Then she went upstairs. Mr. Lawton remained in the room, and studying her father closely, Amy saw that his tense look had begun to soften. He did not seem so unhappy anymore, and as she passed him on the way to the kitchen, he smiled at her tenderly and patted her on the top of the head. . . . [After a while] Amy noticed that the transformation that had begun with a softening of his features was even more advanced. At last, he seemed happy. Amy wondered if he was drunk, although his walk was not unsteady. If anything, it was more steady.[49]

At one point the girl compares her parents' behavior to circus clowns who pretend to fall down drunk. Though Amy once saw her father walk into a wall and break the glasses he was carrying, her parents were "never indecorous" and even "seemed to get more decorous and formal the more they drank." Occasionally one of their friends would fall, missing a chair and thumping down on the floor. In such cases the adults pretended as if nothing had happened; "they seemed like actors in a school play." By relating these impressions as if viewed through a child's eyes, the narrator exposes the adults' habits like an unwitting anthropologist. Those impressions, moreover, are infused with strong judgment. As Amy lay in bed, "she perceived vaguely the pitiful corruption of the adult world; how crude and frail it was, like a piece of worn burlap, patched with stupidities and mistakes, useless and ugly, and yet they never saw its worthlessness, and when you pointed it out to them, they were indignant."[50]

In "The Sorrows of Gin" alcohol functions on several levels as a tool of self-identification, deception, and self-deception. The righteous Mrs. Henlein defends her honor and dignity by proclaiming her abstinence. Though employed as a domestic caregiver, she asserts her superiority over the wealthy Mr. Lawton by proclaiming her ancestry of "Dutch nobility" and by claiming not to have "drunk enough to fill an eyeglass for twenty-five years." She exposes Mr. Lawton as a phony, a drunken gentleman who seems classy yet acts in unseemly, even immoral ways. In using cocktails to soften the frayed edges of their "crude and frail" relationships, the Lawtons represent the underside of suburban domesticity. Just as the Lawtons do not recognize their neglect of Amy, neither do they possess the insight to recognize that their daughter is suffering psychological damage due to their drinking and self-denial. Amy senses that her parents drink to transform themselves, like "actors in a school play," but she is unable to communicate with her parents except through quiet acts of sabotage. Because children learn values from their parents, Amy, too, becomes trapped in a drama of dishonesty and blame, which allows the family to maintain a false posture of domestic tranquility.[51]

Cheever further explored connections among drinking, denial, and familial disintegration in "The Swimmer," a highly symbolic story first published in *The New Yorker* in 1964. It became one of the author's most famous tales, not only in its textual form, but also through its screen adaptation in 1968. With a more fantastic and meandering plot than "The Sorrows of Gin," "The Swimmer" tells the story of Neddie Merrill, a middle-aged man who lives amidst the sprawling manicured lawns of suburban Connecticut. The tale begins with Neddie about to dive into the backyard pool of some old friends and neighbors, the Westerhazys. As he gazes at the pool's cool green water, almost in a trance, Neddie realizes that he can "swim" home by traversing the private property of friends and neighbors, taking a dip in each pool along the way. Strong and agile despite his fading youth, Neddie loves to swim, and he can think of no better way to spend a fine summer day. Neddie muses that the string of swimming pools symbolically forms a river, which he names in honor of his wife, Lucinda. Undeterred by the fact that the neighbors might object to his trespassing or by the worry that they would deem his behavior bizarre, Neddie makes his way from pool to pool. As the story unfolds, it becomes clear that Neddie has been out of touch with the acquaintances he encounters. Some are pleased to see him, while others treat him coldly. But the scene at each house is usually the same, as affluent men and women mingle on patios and pool decks, sipping cocktails in small gatherings or large, festive parties: "Oh, how bonny and lush were the banks of the Lucinda River! Prosperous men and women gathered by the sapphire colored waters while caterer's men in white coats passed them cold gin."[52]

"The Swimmer" combines a fanciful, allegorical plot with realistically observed details of social life. Many of these details, moreover, revolve around drinking. In the first line of the story the narrator explains, "It was one of those midsummer Sundays when everyone sits around saying, 'I *drank* too much last night.'" At each house Neddie is offered a drink by the host, hostess, or bartender. Once, when the owners are not home,

Neddie helps himself to a poolside cocktail: "After swimming the pool he got himself a glass and poured a drink. It was his fourth or fifth drink and he had swum nearly half the length of the Lucinda River. He felt tired, clean, and pleased at that moment to be alone; pleased with everything." On a symbolic level the refreshing waters of suburban swimming pools mirror the alcoholic refreshments Neddie imbibes along the way. At first both swimming and drinking are figured as rites of bracing invigoration, even purification. But as he makes his way from pool to pool, Neddie's limbs grow limp and lax; his energy is sapped from fatigue and liquor. At one point he decides he needs another drink: "Whiskey would warm him, pick him up, carry him through the last of his journey, refresh his feeling that it was original and valorous to swim across the county." But he soon loses the strength and concentration to dive; rather, he uses the steps and swims a "hobbled sidestroke" rather than the forceful crawl he is so proud of. Drunk and chilled from his swimming adventure, Neddie feels ill and bloated at the end of his journey. What began as an optimistic if outlandish adventure ends up seeming like a pathetic prank Neddie has played on himself.[53]

As the reader gradually discovers, Neddie's depleted physical condition also represents his disintegrating mental state. Indeed, Cheever's protagonist suffers from serious delusions about his life. At one house the owners tell him that they are sorry to hear about his misfortunes. "My misfortunes?" Ned asks. "I don't know what you mean?" Puzzled, his acquaintances remind him that he has sold his house and that something bad has happened with his two daughters. Neddie's "gift for concealing painful facts let him forget" that his wife had left him, he had lost his job, and his children "were in trouble."[54] Even Neddie's ultimate goal—returning home to his family—proves to be a fantasy. When he finally arrives in a pouring rainstorm, he finds that the house has been boarded up. After pounding on the door, he looks through the windows and realizes that the place is empty. Neddie's entire adventure is based on false illusions that he is still enjoying a life of wealth and domestic happiness. A chilling allegory of self-deception, "The Swimmer" reflects the profound psychic investment that many postwar Americans made in suburban family life and domestic consumption, even when their actual experiences fell short of those idealized visions. But the final image of an abandoned house suggests that the Merrill family's domestic life had been empty all along.

The film adaptation, produced and directed by Frank Perry and based on a screenplay by his wife, Eleanor Perry, emphasized the connections among alcohol, sociability, and self-deception even more prominently. The first scene zooms in on a full martini glass as Neddie, played by Burt Lancaster sixteen years after he starred in *Sheba*, emerges from the Westerhazys' pool. It is a visual equivalent of Georgio Lolli's description of the martini as a "graceful, long-stemmed and glittering . . . epitome of sophisticated simplicity." The film also features more dialogue in which the characters comment self-consciously on their drinking preferences and habits. Everywhere, it seems, men and women are drinking in ample quantities. The entire film betrays an atmosphere of excess and indulgence—even decadence—and cocktails play a central role in signifying those qualities. Husbands and wives, friends and neighbors, engage in conversation—cocktail party talk—that seems as shallow as Neddie's own self-awareness. At house after house Neddie uses alcohol to fuel his illusion that he still belongs in his old social circle. Smiling or tittering behind their highballs, Neddie's surprised (and often reluctant) hosts do little to convince Neddie of his painful reality. Honesty and forthrightness are scarce commodities in this social realm.[55]

The film also develops the theme of marital infidelity in more depth. In Cheever's version Neddie stops at the house of Shirley Adams, a former mistress, near the end of his journey. After being snubbed at a previous house, Neddie looks forward to seeing Shirley, hoping to rekindle the sexual affair he ended "last week, last month, last year. He couldn't remember." Sex with Shirley would be "the supreme elixir, the pain killer, the brightly colored pill that would put the spring back into his step, the joy of life in his heart."[56] Yet this, too, proves a wishful fantasy, for Neddie has forgotten that Shirley now despises him. Cheever's treatment of Ned and Shirley is brief and suggestive. He indicates that Shirley felt wounded after Ned broke off their relationship and that Ned had later asked Shirley to lend him money. In the story Shirley brusquely tells him that she has found another mate, and Neddie begins to cry as he makes his way home. The film, however, dwells on Shirley's bitterness toward Neddie and brings the subplot to a more dramatic, tragic conclusion. As she and her former lover drink cocktails, Shirley retaliates for the pain Neddie has caused her. Pretending not to know about Neddie's separation, she taunts him, asking, "Has the ideal all-American family found happiness on the hill?" She criticizes Neddie for turning to her for sexual fulfillment while remaining loyal to his snobbish wife. In a vengeful rage she tells Neddie that she never had feelings for him and that she was just pretending to love him. Neddie is devastated; his fragile ego crumbles. Both characters are trapped in a game of mutual exploitation and deception, trying to cure boredom and pain with the twin elixirs of sex and alcohol. Neddie's delusions shield him from self-loathing, but Shirley is not so fortunate. Neddie's reappearance has so unsettled her that she eventually runs back into her house. From outside Neddie hears a gunshot and then silence. The viewer assumes that Shirley has killed herself.

Cheever's stories were more restrained and subtle than the film version of "The Swimmer," but both genres illustrated the role of alcohol in smoothing the jagged emotional edges of middle- and upper-class suburban life.[57] Furthermore, fiction provided an indirect outlet for the author to express ideas rooted in his own life experience. During the 1950s Cheever lived in Ossining, New York (a suburb of Westchester County), with his wife and children. As one journalist noted in 1969, Cheever's stories were "magically animated" by the author's "great command over the artifacts of suburban life—the railroad stations and trains, the liquor, the dogs and swimming pools, the tape recorders and television sets."[58] During the peak of his short-story writing in the 1950s and 1960s, Cheever himself was a very heavy drinker. According to his daughter, Susan Cheever (who published a family memoir, *Home before Dark*, in 1984), he was proud of his ability to imbibe large quantities of hard liquor. "In those days," Susan recalled, "drinking was a manly indulgence, a confirmation of power and courage and masculine endurance. All great writers drank. My father's friendships were all drinking friendships." Her father's focus on liquor was so intense that he judged people by how much they drank and by the strength of the drinks they served him. "For him, hospitality meant offering each guest in his house a drink the moment they stepped through the door and then mixing whatever they asked for in proportions that would have knocked out an elephant." Cheever and his guests chatted in a "happy gaze, convinced that they had been unusually witty and charming."[59] Like the characters he fashioned, Cheever was captivated by the social effects of alcohol. Over time he perfected a drinking style that combined the generosity and gregariousness of manly indulgence with postwar rituals of domestic hospitality.

As he became a progressively more compulsive drinker, Cheever acquired a more "psychological" understanding of alcoholism specific to his own historical moment. His journal entries from the late 1950s and early 1960s are filled with references to feelings of depression. Cheever began to drink more frequently on his own from a profound sense of urgent need. Like the character Al Stephenson in *Best Years of Our Lives*, he referred to himself as a "solitary drunkard." Echoing E. M. Jellinek and other alcohol researchers, he claimed, "I must think of alcoholism as a progressive disease. It has been for a week or longer that I have, on almost every day, drunk too much. . . . I waste more days. I suffer deeper pangs of guilt. . . . Drink, its implements, environments, and effects all seem disgusting. I don't seem able to drink temperately and yet I don't seem able to stop."[60]

Years after he wrote most of the "suburban stories," the author talked with journalists and writers about the connections between fiction and his personal life. Alcoholism and drug addiction, he asserted, were metaphors for confinement and a loss of personal freedom. His stories were meditations on the "confinement of an improvised society." As one interviewer noted in 1980, drinking (as well as smoking) were important symbols for Cheever because "they are metaphors for all our pleasures and the choice we have about whether our pleasures will become addictions."[61] Excessive or compulsive consumption is viewed as a form of psychic escape from social strictures and domestic unhappiness, a continual (yet never satisfied) search for pleasure amidst disappointment. Unlike urban saloon-goers in Jack London's day, Cheever's characters do not physically remove themselves from the domestic scenes that confine them but, rather, use drink to pacify themselves internally. Susan Cheever reflected on her father's internal struggle "to escape the trappings and traps he had so carefully constructed for himself, to free himself from marriage and the legal and emotional constraints of the conventional upper-middle-class life, to leave behind the torpid stability of the suburbs and the responsibilities of a house and family, and most of all to escape the pressure to continually surpass himself as a writer."[62]

Just as Jack London fashioned a text that reflected the author's personal experience at a specific time in history, Cheever's attitudes attested to broad shifts in the cultural understanding of alcoholism. *John Barleycorn*, we may recall, advocated Prohibition as men's ultimate savior from the bottle. While London demonstrated a keen awareness of alcohol's psychological hold on the drinker, his narrative—penned before the rise of therapeutic alcoholism discourses—reinforced legal reform as the best way to protect the family from manly excess. True to the zeitgeist of his era, more than a half-century later Cheever ultimately experienced alcoholism in therapeutic terms. In 1975 he had a heart attack that prompted him to seek medical treatment for alcoholism. At his wife's urging he entered a rehabilitation facility, joined AA, and abstained until his death in 1982. In retrospect he characterized his drinking in medicalized, therapeutic terms. "I thoroughly enjoyed drinking," Cheever recalled. "I thought it was terrific, until it got out of hand. My drinking . . . simply got worse and worse. I got more and more dependent on it. I have what is known as an addictive disposition."[63] Though Cheever shunned strictly Freudian interpretations of motivations for drinking, he developed a deeply psychological conception of alcoholism in keeping with the paradigm endorsed by so many professional and lay experts. Just as Neddie Merrill's journey brought him from an imagined state of vigor to the depths of debility, Cheever mapped his own trajectory from a sophisticated devotee of cocktail culture to a sufferer from disease. As his daughter noted, Cheever struggled for decades to curtail his drinking. For more than twenty years his journals chronicled "his change from a dashing, hard-drinking writer, in a world where many of his friends polished off two martinis before lunch, to a dilapidated, compulsive, suicidal alcoholic, in a world where a lot of people drink only white wine and mineral water."[64]

Cheever's short stories not only revealed the author's inchoate attitudes toward alcoholism as pathology; they also reflected the shifting relationship between drinking and family life in the American cultural imagination. While earlier temperance reformers envisioned chronic drunkenness as a sign of a threatened family, both "The Sorrows of Gin" and "The Swimmer" coded drinking as an escape from a threatening family. As in *Come Back, Little Sheba*, in Cheever's fictional world the family is threatening not in a physical or material way but because it cannot ultimately fill the deep psychological and emotional needs of its members. The Lawtons do not know how to relate to one another, and so they turn to gin. For years Neddie Merrill vacillated between idolizing his socially prominent wife and satisfying his lust in an extramarital affair, turning to liquor to blot out the confusing blend of boredom and guilt that ensued.

Cheever, too, experienced his family as confining and threatening to his inner emotional life, and he engaged in heterosexual and, eventually, homosexual affairs while remaining committed to his wife, Mary. In particular Cheever's confessions about homosexual desire, recorded in his journals, illustrate a shift in the social construction of manly sociability and its relationship to both drinking and homoeroticism. In London's day saloon-going men experienced the romance of conviviality without fear of being labeled sexually deviant. In the post–World War II period, however, anticommunist and Cold War ideologues invoked the specter of the sick homosexual in their campaign to rid the nation of alleged internal enemies and threats to national security. In this context Cheever experienced heightened frustration over his own homosexual feelings, especially given his simultaneous commitment to his wife and to a heterosexual family lifestyle. While Cheever did not literally repress his urges to have affairs with other women and men, he experienced the psychology of repression and the guilt that resulted. In the social realm of *John Barleycorn* there was a murkier boundary between drunken conviviality and homoeroticism, in part because the diagnostic construct of "the homosexual" had not yet rendered intense all-male bonding suspect.[65] In London's novel the saloon regular's drinking signified escape from the physical confines of the home. For Cheever, however, the family represented a more psychological, interiorized form of repression that led him, increasingly, to seek solace in the bottle. In the post-Freudian, postwar era Cheever viewed drinking as a means to dull psychic pain unleashed by uncontrollable, deviant sexual desires. Significantly, Cheever shared with both Charles Jackson and William Inge an identity as a tortured, closeted homosexual. Although Cheever did not embrace psychoanalytic theory to the extent that Jackson did, all three alcoholic writers would have viewed their addictions in relation to the psychic turmoil caused by their homosexual desires and "dubious" manhood.[66]

Like the fellow AA members whom he finally embraced, however, Cheever also understood that addictive drinking—when allowed to run its course—threatened other family members in turn. Just as the alcoholic could not really escape his family, neither could family members live with an alcoholic without suffering emotional damage. On a certain level Cheever seems to have understood this decades before he quit drinking. By relating "The Sorrows of Gin" from the young daughter's point of view, Cheever indicated an awareness of the psychological effects of alcohol on children. In interviews he was candid about his stormy marriage and how alcoholism rendered it even worse for the wear. Ultimately Cheever's guilt and responsibility toward his family played a major role in spurring his recovery. Five years after he joined AA, Cheever wrote that he still missed drinking but that sobriety "did bring his wife back to him"; what more could he ever ask for?[67] In fiction and his personal life Cheever represented a world in which drinking and intense family relationships were enmeshed and inseparable, a world defined by inner dramas of emotional conflict that erupted and re-erupted again and again.

Finally, Cheever's fictional vignettes reflected the shift in the typical problem drinker's class affiliation over the course of the century. As character sketches of prosperous suburbanites, Cheever's stories revealed the extent to which the emotional problems of middle- and upper-class Americans increasingly set the terms of popular discourses about drinking and alcoholism. As he suggested, class identity was signified not primarily through one's work or occupation but through the realm of genteel recreation and consumption. Presumably, the adult male protagonists in both stories worked in managerial positions but found little intellectual or personal fulfillment in their jobs. Rather, the characters in this fictional milieu used conspicuous leisure, hospitality, and material acquisition to claim social status and prestige, yet such worldly pleasures ultimately proved banal and unsatisfying. Implicitly, then, Cheever connected habitual drunkenness to the perpetual restlessness of men and women who sought excitement and meaning in consumption yet found the object of their quest to be elusive.

DRINKING, CONSUMERISM, AND THE CULTURAL SIGNIFICANCE OF ALCOHOLISM

The ideas and actions of AA members and scientific experts shaped an alcoholic culture in which alcoholism symbolically represented a range of issues and problems in U.S. society. But as we have seen, this alcoholic culture did not include only people who suffered directly from compulsive drinking. In the post-repeal era alcoholic beverages were practically ubiquitous. From sleek bottles of beer and refined glasses of sherry to dry martinis and slim highballs, potent potables circulated among men and women in all manner of social settings and situations. Catalyzed by the unique circumstances of the Great Depression and World War II, the beverage industries and wet advocates, aided by countless advertisers, filmmakers, entrepreneurs, and writers, successfully normalized social drinking. By the 1950s the paradoxical nature of alcoholic culture—one that alternatively celebrated and denigrated the effects of alcohol—signified a larger set of cultural predicaments endemic to the Cold War era.

Some postwar commentators even defined drinking as the quintessential feature of leisure in the United States. One perceptive observer of twentieth-century drinking patterns was sociologist Herbert Bloch, who testified to a profound and distorted relationship "between excessive drinking and the peculiar American ideology concerning recreation." In Bloch's view the increasing commercialization of leisure had caused changes in citizens' recreational behavior. Commodified forms of entertainment led to heightened expectations of "speed, change, and sensationalism" in the leisure realm. The average American was obsessed with "having a good time." With intensity and zeal he or she pursued a "frenzied bent toward leisure-time activity," as if rushing to have as much fun as possible in the shortest span of time. The rise of social drinking, he believed, was part of this transformation, evidenced in the high consumption levels of hard liquor and the desire among many to keep up with fellow drinkers. Unlike most Europeans, he contended, "Americans at a drinking bout are much more apt to consume as much alcoholic fluid as can be expeditiously managed within the shortest time possible. The whole undertaking is approached in the spirit of attaining that pleasant state of aftermath in the peculiar American folkway of enjoining the latecomer to 'catch up.'" Bloch also lamented a contemporary shift toward passive forms of entertainment, in which Americans paid to be entertained rather than participate actively in entertainment itself. Likewise, he suggested, they relied increasingly on alcohol to inject exuberance into their lives, using commodified pleasures and substances to achieve an ever-elusive sense of immediate gratification. As long as recreational life remained shallow and frenetic, he implied, alcohol consumption rates would remain high.

Bloch's emphasis on the dulling social effects of commercialized leisure is especially significant. As he summarized, "The attitudes . . . of repression of spontaneous expression, of passivism and an acceptance of the priority of commercial values as earmarks of recreational merit, have ground themselves deeply into the American temperament." This vision of repressed emotional expression prefigured Cheever's descriptions of banal cocktail party talk and married couples unable to articulate their innermost feelings. The focus on "passivism" should remind readers of the simultaneous characterization of alcoholic men as ineffectual and flaccid. Finally, Bloch's argument about the centrality of "commercial values" among pleasure-seekers was echoed specifically in alcoholism discourses.[68] Indeed, just as Bloch defined drinking as a hallmark of contemporary culture, so, too, did some commentators define alcoholism as the paradigmatic illness of the age due to its strong connections to consumerism, acquisitiveness, and the values of the marketplace.

Although physicians and reformers had believed in the addictive qualities of intoxicants for more than a century, the concept of addiction as a disease of modern society emerged in the mid-twentieth century. To uncover the symbolic connection between alcoholism and materialism, we may turn briefly to a text that subtly employed the modern definition of alcoholism as part of a wider social critique. In January 1952 economist John Kenneth Galbraith published an article in *Harper's* magazine that criticized the excesses of daily life in prosperous postwar America. Galbraith aimed his assault at the advertising industry, which had just closed the books on its most stunning fiscal year yet. In 1951 annual advertising sales in the United States ballooned to an unprecedented $6.5 billion, the bankroll behind an "unseemly economics of opulence" that greatly troubled Galbraith. In his article Galbraith denounced advertisers for kindling public demand for "tobacco, liquor, [and] chocolates . . . in a land which is already suffering from nicotine poisoning and alcoholism, [and] which is nutritionally gorged with sugar."[69] As others extolled the virtues of postwar abundance, one of the country's leading economists painted a picture of consumer capitalism out of control; in his pessimistic view Americans were getting too much of some not very good things.

Galbraith's remarks updated a long-standing tradition of anticommercial moralism that censured unbridled materialism and conspicuous display. Indeed, his article formed part of the broader critique of affluence and domestic life developed by Whyte, Seeley, and other observers of postwar society.[70] On one level Galbraith criticized U.S. consumption in its economic sense—when "consumption" is defined to mean "the purchasing and using up of goods and services." But embedded within his critique of consumption on a national level lay concerns about consumption by individuals; his comments implicitly linked patterns of commerce to the bodily ingestion of advertised products. According to Galbraith, the "unseemly economics of opulence" were not merely distasteful; they could be downright dangerous to the individual and the social body alike. In an era that increasingly sanctioned compulsive spending, intense periodic leisure, and self-fulfillment through the purchase of goods and services, it is perhaps no surprise that Americans often came to see themselves as *victims* of their desires and appetites. Though the dominant ethos of modern consumerism celebrated the consumption of commodities (including alcoholic beverages) as the key to personal well-being, excessive drinking was figured not as a means to a therapeutic end but as a threat to emotional and physical health.

To the extent that postwar Americans defined alcoholism as the compulsive *over*consumption of a substance that in more restrained doses was deemed harmless or even salubrious, it is fitting that alcoholism metaphorically represented consumer culture run amok. The soulless lives of

John Cheever's fictional characters unfolded in a world of affluence, a realm in which money could never buy spiritual wholeness, psychic satisfaction, or true peace of mind. But while the leisured, country club lifestyle so devastatingly rendered by Cheever was by no means typical of middle-class communities during the 1950s, millions of relatively modest citizens clung to the promises held out to them by consumer capitalism as it responded to the pent-up demand of a population that had sacrificed material goods during recession and war.

To many contemporary observers, postwar Americans were a "people of plenty," to use a phrase coined by Yale historian David Potter in a book that explored the influence of economic abundance "upon the life and attitudes of the American people." To a large extent Potter's *People of Plenty* extolled the virtues of material amplitude and represented a scholarly contribution to the postwar faith in the continual expansion of the economic pie. But while Potter celebrated the historical impact of the nation's physical bounty, arguing that abundance had allowed the United States to boast "a greater measure of social equality and social mobility than any highly developed society in human history," the author was not entirely positive about the (relative) affluence he observed. For one thing, he noted that abundance perpetuated a myth of classlessness, which in turn made real differentials of power, status, and wealth seem all the more galling to those who could not achieve what their land of opportunity had promised them. Moreover, like Galbraith he argued that advertising had pernicious effects on Americans across the social spectrum. Potter lamented the fact that the total amount spent for advertising in 1951 was significantly more than what was spent on primary and secondary public education. In his view, "to fix the attention but not to engage the mind" was a precise statement of the advertiser's formula. In stimulating desire for goods only an abundant economy could produce, advertising exploited "materialistic drives and emulative anxieties," sanctioning a worldview that privileged sheer consumption and materialism over "socially responsible" values. As exemplified in *People of Plenty*, an undercurrent of doubt and anxiety ran beneath even positive endorsements of materialism and consumerism in the 1950s.[71]

In this context alcoholism was increasingly perceived as a form of mindless, anxiety-fueled consumption. Consider a series of speeches delivered by AA trustee Bernard B. Smith to the fellowship's General Service Conferences from 1951 to 1956. Smith was a self-defined nonalcoholic and New York attorney who served as chairman of the national board of trustees. Although Smith had not used the Twelve Steps to quit drinking, he found them inspiring on a personal and metaphorical level. The AA "way of life," he argued, had been conceived to "meet a serious and growing challenge" faced by *all* of his contemporaries, "nonalcoholic as well as alcoholic." That challenge, he explained, faced "a generation that would deny the spiritual basis for human existence and accept in its place a currently socially accepted basis that is mechanistic and materialistic." The drinking alcoholic had "no monopoly on unhappiness or on the feeling that life lacks purpose and fulfillment." But in his addiction to the bottle, the alcoholic epitomized the extent to which most Americans had become enslaved "to the false ideals of a materialistic society."[72]

By the mid-1950s members of the alcoholism movement had added threads to the fabric of social criticism that condemned rampant consumerism. Indeed, AA's brand of therapeutic culture sprang from the longings and needs of middle-class men who had not found fulfillment in a modern, materialistic society. But where alcohol failed to fill their empty lives, the culture of sobriety would succeed. As Bernard Smith continued, "As a nonalcoholic and as a student of those great social movements from which we derive the best of our heritage today, I regard . . . Alcoholics Anonymous as the outstanding spiritual phenomenon of our century. I see in the concept of living which is embodied in AA a glorious hope for all of mankind. For the members of this fellowship are truly witnesses of the living truth that man can live the life of the spirit and still function effectively in a materialistic world."[73] The "life of the spirit" rather than a life drinking spirits: ultimately therapeutic culture promised to cure Americans of alcoholism, defined metaphorically as a paradigmatic illness in a consumption-oriented age. This AA spokesperson viewed drinking as both a symptom and a symbol of commercial values run amok in the 1950s. If we take Smith's comments at face value, we see that advertisers were successful in linking liquor to the good life as defined by the dominant culture. But like all consumers who turn repeatedly to things and substances for fulfillment, the addicted drinker could never be satisfied and would return to the bottle for more.

Others affiliated with AA made similar connections between the consumption of goods and the consumption of alcohol. Writing under the pseudonym Father John Doe, one writer penned a tome that, while not endorsed as official AA literature, fashioned itself a companion to the Big Book. Drawing on his years of experience in the fellowship, Doe classified AA members into three categories based on their attitudes on a continuum from "materialistic" to "spiritual." Mincing no words in evaluating these categories, Doe explained that "good AAs" possessed a "completely spiritual attitude" toward the program and life in general. For them "material prosperity is secondary and dependent upon the will of God." The second category, "indifferent AAs," had a "partly spiritual, partly material attitude." Because such members sometimes sought material advancements, they would never know the full meaning of serenity that the "good AAs" enjoyed. Finally, among "bad AAs," "every striving and longing . . . [is] for material advancement, material pleasure, material well being."[74]

AA's foremost historian, Ernest Kurtz, has discussed the link between the fellowship and the consumer society in which it flourished. "The active alcoholic was attempting to attain the spiritual, the unlimited, by means of the material. He was trying to achieve a *quality* of living by the mere adding up of quantities of or experiences with alcohol." Recall here Herbert Bloch's observations about the speeded-up nature of social life and the continual attempt to acquire commodified experiences that might prove one's self-worth. Yet the insatiable craving for "more" and "again," Kurtz reminds us, signified an addiction to addiction itself: the more one drank in the search for pleasure, the less fulfilled one felt.[75] When AA spokespersons argued that the alcoholic represented an extreme version of any individual slavishly devoted to "the false ideals of a materialistic society," they clearly viewed excessive drinking as inextricable from the broader psychological and moral consequences of a lifestyle based on material acquisition. This is not to suggest that alcoholism as an actual condition occurred primarily among Americans of a particular social class or consumer-oriented group. Bernard Smith's point was that the spirit or zeitgeist of consumer society affected Americans in almost every social category, and that alcoholism could debilitate any person who did not contain impulses of competitive, accumulative striving.

On a larger organizational level AA fashioned itself into an anticommercial, antimaterialistic fellowship. Along with the Twelve Steps, which guided individuals in the quest for sobriety, AA developed a set of Twelve Traditions that anchored the fellowship's nonprofit status in the swelling sea that was the modern therapeutic marketplace. The Sixth Tradition stated that "an AA group ought never endorse, finance, or lend the AA name to any relative facility or outside enterprise, lest problems of money, property, and prestige divert us from our primary purpose." On a related note the Eleventh Tradition forbade groups to seek promotional forms of advertising or public relations. Indeed, the central tenet of anonymity itself had much to do with AA's staunch anticommercialism, preventing individuals from seeking personal fame or material gain from their affiliation. To this day AA and Al-Anon remain not-for-profit organizations.

The metaphorical and cultural significance of alcoholism in postwar America was thus inextricably tied to patterns of domesticity and consumption. Cocktail culture, which included the celebration of social drinking in advertising, the mass media, and recreational spaces, promoted an ethic of consuming behavior that could, for some individuals, lead to addiction. To recover from the malaise of addiction, one needed to go against the grain of consumer society, to master new forms of self-restraint. Indeed, the therapeutic response to alcoholism, epitomized by AA, offered an implicit critique of modern consumer culture in the 1940s and 1950s.

Certainly, alcohol was not the only addictive substance to generate a public health response during this period; indeed, Galbraith's references to cigarettes and sugar betrayed simultaneous concerns about smoking and overeating as dangerous forms of bodily ingestion. But the particular uses and abuses of drink combined with the experiences of certain social groups to render alcoholism the primary, even paradigmatic illness of overindulgence by the 1950s. It was the problems of white, middle-class, middle-aged, male *alcoholics* that sparked the most influential mutual-help movement in the twentieth century. The passionate and collective (if not coherent or coordinated) efforts of alcoholism experts convinced the general public that alcoholism was among the most pressing public health problems of the day.

CONCLUSION

Over the course of U.S. history alcohol has been a symbolic and culturally contested substance, linked to historical constructions of class, gender, and ethnicity. During the nineteenth and early twentieth centuries advocates of temperance culture aimed to regulate social order, and to shore up their own power and authority, by regulating the consumption of intoxicating beverages alternatively through moral suasion and legal coercion. The temperance crusade culminated in the passage of the Eighteenth Amendment and the Volstead Act, instituting national Prohibition for thirteen years. To a great extent the unique circumstances of Prohibition defined the decade of the 1920s, as speakeasy patrons and bootlegging outlaws defied the legislation in pursuit of pleasure and profits. If temperance reform had helped to define the nature of white, native-born, middle-class hegemony in U.S. society, then Prohibition, ironically, marked a transition between one era and the next. Viewed in retrospect as a flawed, culturally backward attempt to legislate private morality, Prohibition carried the seeds of its own eventual failure. The 1910s and 1920s witnessed the rise of a "modern era" characterized by the expansion of corporate bureaucracy, the growth of cities and suburbs, increasing racial and ethnic pluralism, the expanding influence of mass culture, and a move toward a more consumerist family life.[1] During a time of heady and rapid change the political and ideological coalition that engendered Prohibition disintegrated under the pressure of repeal advocates. In the post-repeal era alcohol acquired a new set of symbolic meanings as it melded into the dominant culture's recreational life.

It makes sense to define the post-repeal era roughly as the period between the mid-1930s and the mid-1960s. During this time several successive generations of men and women redefined their relationship to drink and its attendant problems. First, a cohort of men who came of age by the early years of Prohibition—men like Bill Wilson and Dr. Bob Smith—struggled to overcome habitual drunkenness without resorting to the moral strictures of their Victorian forebears. These men were members of the wet generations of middle-class youth, but by the time they reached middle age, heavy drinking had wrought havoc on both work and home life. In large part the emergence of Alcoholics Anonymous (AA) around 1940 can be seen as a reaction of the initial wet generations to the predicament in which they found themselves.[2] By the late 1940s and 1950s AA had attracted another generation of men, those likely to have fought in World War II rather than World War I. With the development of Al-Anon, several generations of women, too, developed a new language and a set of rituals to cope with problems of alcoholism. Given the influence of the alcoholism paradigm at midcentury—a paradigm that AA's founders helped to engender—these generations were more likely to envision excessive drinking as an illness and to seek therapeutic guidance toward rehabilitation.

As we have seen, the therapeutic vision of self-control extended beyond the avoidance of threatening substances; it also entailed adherence to a complex, gendered system of emotion management. Married men who aspired to sober manhood would need to balance masculine companionship with a heightened commitment to familial roles. The sober husband would control his desire for booze on a daily basis, but he would also restrain his more aggressive and selfish tendencies when relating to others. The alcoholic's wife, too, was exhorted to exhibit affective restraint. So as not to encourage a relapse of addictive behavior, she would need to ensure her own emotional sobriety and subordinate many of her own desires and goals to those of her spouse.

Ultimately, the cultural significance of alcoholism expanded beyond the immediate concerns of midcentury health practitioners and AA members. By the 1960s excessive or addicted consumers of other substances, such as food, narcotics, and caffeine, had begun to appropriate AA's Twelve Steps and formed therapeutic communities of their own. By the 1980s a diverse network of self-help groups, professional therapists, book publishers, entrepreneurs, and television producers had given rise to a vast recovery movement that applied a therapeutic model of addiction to almost every kind of excessive behavior, including gambling, sex, and shopping. Critics of contemporary therapeutic culture argue that the self-help movement's solipsistic rhetoric of disease and addiction encourages participants to disregard the social, economic, and political sources of personal problems, thus depoliticizing and redefining suffering as illness or familial dysfunction rather than as a product of social oppression.[3] Certainly, the recovery movement's more recent developments have transformed the worldview that originated during the formative decades of AA and Al-Anon. (For example, AA's initial focus on men has been replaced by an overwhelming emphasis on women's addictions as well as female "codependency"—the contemporary term for excessive emotional investment in another person's addictive behavior. Also, commercially minded therapists and businesses have appropriated and commodified the original Twelve Step program, inverting the fellowship's not-for-profit worldview). Yet the *historical* origins of this contemporary critique are rooted firmly in post-repeal alcoholic culture, recalling the "inward turn" from social reform and political action toward the interior realms of the somatic and psychological. Though ideas about the addictive properties of alcohol were not new, midcentury experts shifted the locus of addiction from the evil substance to the diseased person, a view that still informs the recovery movement today.[4]

Of course alcoholism still occupies an important place in the recovery movement at the turn of the twenty-first century. AA and the Al-Anon Family Groups attract countless new members each year, and each fellowship maintains a thriving national headquarters that coordinates an array of recruitment, publication, and public relations services. But while AA retains its status as the prototype of modern self-help groups, alcoholism has long shared bookstore shelf space, television programming time, conference planning resources, and research funding with a host of other addictive "pathologies." Furthermore, historians have shown that since the 1970s, public attitudes toward alcoholism have become more diffuse. Although many people still regard heavy drinking as the mark of a "real man," and while the nation spends huge sums annually on consumer purchases of beverage alcohol, alcohol consumption has leveled off in recent decades. A *Time* magazine survey taken in 1985 revealed that among Americans aged eighteen years or older, one-third remarked that they were drinking less than before, while only 6 percent said that they were drinking more. Wine makers and beer brewers reported slower sales throughout the 1980s and began distributing low-alcohol or nonalcoholic beers, wine coolers, and sparkling ciders in response to this decline. Furthermore, the three-martini lunch no longer dominates afternoon business culture, as employers take a dimmer view of drinking, especially during work hours.[5] In a changing social context—a recreational realm where, as Susan Cheever observed, more people were drinking "only white wine and mineral water"—alcoholism came to be regarded as a less-than-urgent issue, or at least no more pressing than many other public health problems. As a result alcoholism no longer carries the same metaphorical significance it had during the 1940s and 1950s.[6]

The historical decline of postwar alcoholic culture began before the 1980s, however. Just as the alcoholism movement emerged as a response to the cultural needs of a specific generation, so, too, did its weakening result from a subsequent shift in generational experience. During the 1940s and 1950s the problems of men and women reaching middle age defined the cultural ideals of the sober husband and the supportive wife. The social dislocation of the returning veteran, the brooding boredom of the Cheeveresque suburbanite, and the domestic containment of the 1950s housewife all served as cultural reference points in the engendering of alcoholism. But by 1970 the sons and daughters of those legendary alcoholic spouses had come of age, and *their* actions and attitudes displaced those of their parents as hallmarks of a new era.

The generation of 1960s youth grew up in an alcoholic culture—some in a literal sense and most in a figurative sense. But as they made their way into young adulthood, alcoholic drinking lost much of its symbolic resonance and cultural prominence. This may have been due in part to the emergence of the counterculture during the 1960s. First influenced by a group of writers and poets known as the Beats, many American youth rejected the materialism, domesticity, and social conformity of their parents' generation. Writers such as Jack Kerouac, Allen Ginsberg, and William Burroughs celebrated freedom of movement, spontaneity, and experimentation with mind-altering substances. Historian David Farber explains that throughout the 1960s young people learned "that a state of intoxication and psychic exploration were requisites to a higher wisdom of the body and soul. . . . The consumption and distribution of illegal and experimental drugs, more than any other single factor, was responsible for the creation and development of America's many countercultural enclaves." Although drinking rates did not decline (in fact, they increased over the course of the decade), marijuana and eventually LSD became drugs of choice among many pleasure-seeking youth. Marijuana, for example, appealed to people's longing for community and escapism from social barriers, as smokers passed around joints in a circle of shared experience. Before they ventured into the realm of illicit drugs, countercultural men and women were conditioned by the mainstream acceptance of drinking, cigarette smoking, and prescription drugs such as amphetamines and tranquilizers. But as Farber notes, "Tobacco and alcohol were old highs." If repeal advocates of the 1930s blurred the boundaries between forbidden vices and permissible pleasures, the drug culture of the 1960s collapsed them even further. By the early 1970s drug use had spread far beyond fringe hippie enclaves, as popular rock bands encouraged millions of suburban teenagers to adopt the clothing styles and drug habits of the counterculture.[7] Although we can only speculate about the relationship between an increase in recreational drug use and a dulling of public concern over alcoholism itself, some kind of correlation seems likely.

To the extent that rigid sexual norms fueled America's alcoholic culture, changing attitudes toward sexuality weakened the ideological link between heavy drinking and sexual repression. As we have seen, psychiatrists, playwrights, and other writers often depicted alcoholism as a symptom of sexual neurosis or repression (either homosexual or heterosexual). While the dominant culture of the 1950s celebrated self-indulgence through commodity consumption, there were still strong limitations on sexual expression and experimentation among single and married men and women. But by the late 1960s adults as well as youth were rethinking the boundaries of permissible conduct. Though more than two-thirds of the public believed that premarital sex was morally wrong in 1969, members of the countercultural free-love movement observed an ethic of open sexuality that gradually permeated larger sectors of U.S. society. Less than two decades after *Come Back, Little Sheba* reinforced proscriptions against premarital intercourse, mass-circulation magazines such as *Cosmopolitan* encouraged single, pink-collar working women to seek sexual delight outside (or at least prior to) committed monogamous relationships. As more Americans sought instant gratification and sensual pleasure in various realms—including sex and drugs—they ushered in an age of "consumption without limits," or at least fewer limits than the previous era had experienced.[8] So while per capita alcohol consumption levels actually increased from the 1950s through the 1970s, the cultural *meanings* of drinking and alcoholism were bound to change with the rise of a more permissive sexual ethos.

Furthermore, the demographic and ideological foundation of the postwar domestic consensus began to weaken. As early as 1960 the average age at marriage rose after decades of decline. The national marriage rate began to decrease, as did the birthrate. After years of stability the divorce rate started to rise gradually in the early 1960s, accelerated during the late 1960s, and soared to unprecedented heights by the early 1970s.[9] Of course, marriage has remained popular as the favored arrangement for familial reproduction. But the rise of feminism and the women's movement by the late 1960s encouraged many women to perceive and experience marriage anew. In 1963 Betty Friedan gave voice to the "problem that had no name," exposing how middle-class, suburban housewives subordinated their individual desires and goals to the needs of home, husband, and children. Three years after *The Feminine Mystique* became a national best-seller, Friedan was elected president of the newly formed National Organization for Women (NOW), which articulated a vision of marriage quite different from the one enshrined by Al-Anon's founders. NOW's founding members declared a revolt against postwar domesticity: "We reject the current assumptions that a man must carry the sole burden of supporting himself, his wife and family . . . or that marriage, home and family are primarily a woman's world and responsibility. . . . True partnership between the sexes demands a different concept of marriage, an equitable sharing of the responsibilities of home and of the economic burdens of their support."[10] Although most American wives did not identify themselves as members of either liberal or radical feminist groups, they behaved in ways that altered traditional marital arrangements. More often they worked for pay outside the home, they voluntarily bore fewer children, and they increasingly viewed divorce as a means to sever an unfulfilling partnership.[11]

Within the Al-Anon fellowship, members began to apply aspects of the emerging feminist critique. Throughout the 1960s and 1970s Al-Anon's primary focus remained the same: to help women cope with the challenges of living with an alcoholic spouse. To a great extent Al-Anon literature continued to support marriages based on traditional gender roles and to minimize the legitimacy of women's anger. Yet as psychologist Janice Haaken notes, "Women began to discuss their sexual frustrations with their husbands and their desire to go beyond shoring up their husbands' precariously held masculinity."[12] Al-Anon literature encouraged members to assert more autonomy in their marriages. In 1971, for example, the fellowship published a new book that emphasized each spouse's rights and roles "as an individual." The worst excesses of patriarchal marriage, the book implied, should not be tolerated: "Al-Anon teaches us the unique value of our own persons and lives. Just as no other human being should be subject to our control, so we, too, must feel free to reject tyrannical domination."[13] By the early 1970s the wife's need for personal control loomed as large as the need to exhibit patience and understanding toward the alcoholic spouse. Adopting a more assertive and pragmatic tone, Al-Anon publications of the late 1960s and 1970s implied that accepting a husband's illness no longer entailed a complete sacrifice of self. Though members were still exhorted to contain their anger and practice emotional detachment, they also learned how to communicate their own needs and feelings to their recovering husbands. "The tone of this practical advice," Haaken observes, "is empathic and supportive of the dignity and rights of individual women."[14]

Over time, then, the gendered framework that undergirded postwar alcoholic culture took on new dimensions, and by the late 1960s the distinctive mix of social, economic, and psychological concerns that gave rise to sober husbands and supportive wives no longer held fast. Although the conventional roles of male breadwinners and female caretakers have hardly been subject to a thorough reinvention, contemporary therapeutic culture betrays many signs of change since the 1940s and 1950s. Relatively new offshoots in the recovery movement, such as codependency support groups and Adult Children of Alcoholics, have appropriated many principles and social rituals of feminism even as they have turned them to decidedly conservative ends.[15] Americans from various racial, ethnic, religious, and class backgrounds have applied therapeutic principles in new ways. While today's mutual-help movements retain their roots in the mid-twentieth-century model of alcoholic family pathology, they have developed in response to a different set of generational needs and experiences.

Yet prevalent norms of emotion management are still inflected by gender ideology. Neither the diversification of recreational drug use nor the sexual revolution nor the gains of the feminist movement nor the shifting valences of therapeutic culture have liberated women from the traditional demands of affective labor. Since the decline of post-repeal alcoholic culture, addiction experts have reshaped the rhetoric of female caregiving, but countless women are still pulled between the perceived needs of family members and of self. And while more married couples pursue breadwinning as a shared task, the expectation that men will bear the primary burden of material support continues to structure family life in countless households across the class spectrum. The pressures of providership and the stresses of work continue to limit men's affective resources, even as women, too, increasingly find themselves strained by the dual and often conflicting tasks of paid work and domestic labor. The cultural history of emotional pathology—of "love on the rocks" between male alcoholics and their wives—suggests that rigid prescriptions of familial duty limit both men's and women's freedom to establish an effective, equitable, and enjoyable balance between work and leisure, between friends and family, between financial responsibilities and labors of love. Perhaps our knowledge of this history can point us toward such an equilibrium, minus the worst excesses of consumption and self-indulgence.

NOTES

ABBREVIATIONS

AA   Alcoholics Anonymous
AA   *Alcoholics Anonymous: The Story of How More Than One Hundred Men
        Have Recovered from Alcoholism.* New York: Works Publishing, 1939.
AACOA   *Alcoholics Anonymous Comes of Age, by a Co-Founder.* New York:
        Harper and Brothers, 1957.
QJSA   *Quarterly Journal of Studies on Alcohol*

INTRODUCTION

1. Ella Boole, *Give Prohibition Its Chance* (New York: Fleming H. Revell, 1929), 14. On the WCTU's platform of "home protection," see Ruth Bordin, *Women and Temperance: The Quest for Power and Liberty, 1873–1900* (Philadelphia: Temple University Press, 1981); Barbara Epstein, *The Politics of Domesticity: Women, Evangelism, and Temperance in Nineteenth-Century America* (Middletown, Conn.: Wesleyan University Press, 1981); Kenneth D. Rose, *American Women and the Repeal of Prohibition* (New York: New York University Press, 1996), 34–62; and Catherine Gilbert Murdock, *Domesticating Drink: Women, Men, and Alcohol in America, 1870–1940* (Baltimore: Johns Hopkins University Press, 1998).

2. The development of female reform ideology and organization in the nineteenth and early twentieth centuries has long been a central topic in U.S. women's history. Some of the most important studies include Bordin, *Women and Temperance*; Epstein, *Politics of Domesticity*; Lori D. Ginzberg, *Women and the Work of Benevolence: Morality, Politics, and Class in the Nineteenth-Century United States* (New Haven: Yale University Press, 1990); Mary P. Ryan, *Cradle of the Middle Class: The Family in Oneida County, New York, 1790–1865* (Cambridge: Cambridge University Press, 1981); and Nancy Hewitt, *Women's Activism and Social Change: Rochester, New York, 1822–1872* (Ithaca: Cornell University Press, 1984).

3. In 1785 physician Benjamin Rush defined inebriety as a disease and outlined the debilitating effects of drinking on the mind and body. Yet Rush's disease model paired signs of physical decay with symptoms of moral debility. Nineteenth- and early-twentieth-century inebriate asylums treated drunkards as victims of disease,

yet many doctors viewed drinking as a moral issue and supported Prohibition as the best way to prevent drunkenness. Given the hegemony of temperance reformers in shaping ideas about alcohol in the culture at large, such early attempts at medicalization were limited.

4. Bruce Holley Johnson, "The Alcoholism Movement in America: A Study in Cultural Innovation" (Ph.D. diss., University of Illinois, 1973), 233–34; Mark Edward Lender and James Kirby Martin, *Drinking in America: A History* (New York: Free Press, 1987), 39, 186–88.

5. Bruce Holley Johnson, "Alcoholism Movement in America," 233–34; Lender and Martin, *Drinking in America*, 189; Jack S. Blocker Jr., *American Temperance Movements: Cycles of Reform* (Boston: Twayne, 1989), 144–54. Some historians argue that the term "alcoholism movement" does not account for differences among researchers and therapists in the 1930s and 1940s. They contend that the modern alcoholism movement is a movement only in retrospect; in reality it consisted of multiple movements pursuing different agendas with often conflicting institutional and scientific interests. Yet for my purposes the term remains useful. Out of such divergent initiatives emerged a relatively coherent set of collective and cumulative effects—at least in terms of *public* attitudes toward alcohol-related problems. I am less interested in the differences among public health advocates and scientists because I do not believe they had a major impact on the broader cultural history explored in this study.

6. Thelma Whalen, "Wives of Alcoholics: Four Types Observed in a Family Service Agency," *QJSA* 14, no. 4 (December 1953): 632–40.

7. Evidence for these claims is cited in Chapter 2.

8. I use the term "lay therapists" to stress that the AA founders' claims to therapeutic expertise stemmed not from professional scientific or religious training but from their own personal experience. While AA members may not have referred to themselves as lay therapists or lay experts, the concept aptly describes their place and function within the alcoholism movement.

9. Elizabeth Lunbeck, *The Psychiatric Persuasion: Knowledge, Gender, and Power in Modern America* (Princeton: Princeton University Press, 1994), 1–6, 46–48. My understanding and use of gender as a category of historical interpretation derives from many theoretical sources, including Joan W. Scott, "Gender: A Useful Category of Analysis," in *Gender and the Politics of History* (New York: Columbia University Press, 1989); Joan W. Scott, "Deconstructing Equality-versus-Difference; Or, the Uses of Poststructuralist Theory for Feminism," *Feminist Studies* 14 (spring 1988): 33–50; and Teresa de Lauretis, "The Technology of Gender," in *Alice Doesn't: Feminism, Semiotics, Cinema* (Bloomington: Indiana University Press, 1984). Historian Gail Bederman offers a useful definition of gender as a historical, ideological process in her *Manliness and Civilization: A Cultural History of Gender and Race in the United States, 1880–1917* (Chicago: University of Chicago Press, 1995), 5–8. The concept of "gender formation," defined by Mariana Valverde as the dynamic process by which "the two genders are formed and reformed, renegotiated and contested," has proven especially compelling to me. See Valverde, "Comment," in "Dialogue: Gender History/

Women's History: Is Feminist Scholarship Losing Its Critical Edge?," *Journal of Women's History* 5 (spring 1993): 123.

10. Two comprehensive and detailed sociological studies of the alcoholism movement are unpublished dissertations: Bruce Holley Johnson, "Alcoholism Movement in America," and more recently, Ron Roizen, "The American Discovery of Alcoholism, 1933–1939" (Ph.D. diss. University of California, Berkeley, 1991). Neither study devotes any sustained attention to gender.

11. On alcoholism in U.S. film, see Norman K. Denzin, *Hollywood Shot by Shot: Alcoholism in American Cinema* (New York: Aldine de Gruyter, 1991), and Robin Room, "Alcoholism and Alcoholics Anonymous in U.S. Films, 1945–1962: The Party Ends for the 'Wet Generations,'" *Journal of Studies on Alcohol* 50, no. 4 (1989): 368–81. The topic of alcoholism and drink in U.S. literary history has begun to attract serious scholarly attention. For a perceptive study of the relationship between alcoholism and literary modernism, see John W. Crowley, *The White Logic: Alcoholism and Gender in American Modernist Fiction* (Amherst: University of Massachusetts Press, 1994). See also Tom Dardis, *The Thirsty Muse: Alcohol and the American Writer* (New York: Ticknor and Fields, 1989); Thomas Gilmore, *Equivocal Spirits: Alcoholism and Drinking in Twentieth-Century Literature* (Chapel Hill: University of North Carolina Press, 1987); and Ann Douglas, *Terrible Honesty: Mongrel Manhattan in the 1920s* (New York: Farrar, Straus and Giroux, 1995), 23–26, 416–19, 475–78. For a critical analysis of AA recovery narratives from the perspective of contemporary folklore studies, see Edmund B. O'Reilly, *Sobering Tales: Narratives of Alcoholism and Recovery* (Amherst: University of Massachusetts Press, 1997).

12. Stephanie Coontz, *The Social Origins of Private Life: A History of American Families, 1600–1900* (London: Verso, 1988), 1–2, 7–18. A leading historian of family life, Coontz views the family as both a social structure and an ideological construct "through which people express their ideals about how biological and social reproduction ought to be coordinated" (12). As such the family legitimizes certain socially constructed human relationships and roles as "natural." This view of the family as a changeable social and ideological unit is shaped by the work of feminist anthropologists, including Sylvia Yanagisako, "Family and Household: The Analysis of Domestic Groups," *American Review of Anthropology* 8 (1979): 186–98, and Jane Collier, Michelle Z. Rosaldo, and Sylvia Yanagisako, "Is There a Family? New Anthropological Views," in *Rethinking the Family: Some Feminist Questions*, ed. Barrie Thorne and Marilyn Yalom (New York: Longman, 1982), 25–39.

13. Coontz, *Social Origins of Private Life*, 345–56; John Demos, *Past, Present, and Personal: The Family and the Life Course in American History* (New York: Oxford University Press, 1986), 36–38. This argument about the transformation of family life in the early twentieth century is sweeping, but it is supported by many studies of specific historical developments. For example, on the rise of "companionate marriage," see Elaine Tyler May, *Great Expectations: Marriage and Divorce in Post-Victorian America* (Chicago: University of Chicago Press, 1980). On the changing social value of children and the rise of the emotionally "precious" child,

see Viviana Zelizer, *Pricing the Priceless Child: The Changing Social Value of Children* (New York: Basic Books, 1985). On the new cult of domestic intimacy as seen in the sentimentalization of Mother's Day, see Stephanie Coontz in *The Way We Never Were: American Families and the Nostalgia Trap* (New York: Basic Books, 1992), 151–55.

14. On postwar familial ideology, see Elaine Tyler May, *Homeward Bound: American Families in the Cold War Era* (New York: Basic Books, 1988); Wendy Kozol, *Life's America: Family and Nation in Postwar Photojournalism* (Philadelphia: Temple University Press, 1994); and Coontz, *Way We Never Were*.

15. Joanne Meyerowitz, ed., *Not June Cleaver: Women and Gender in Postwar America, 1945–1960* (Philadelphia: Temple University Press, 1994). Meyerowitz's essay "Beyond the Feminine Mystique: A Reassessment of Postwar Mass Culture" and the other articles in this excellent collection consider a range of topics in social and cultural history, including women's experiences in the workforce and labor unions, political activism, sexual deviance, and racialized constructions of gender roles.

16. Coontz, *Social Origins of Private Life*, 363.

17. Recently Wini Breines and Ruth Rosen explored the sexual confusions and generational conflicts that haunted those "daughters of the fifties" who found little happiness in domesticity. Elaine Tyler May (who has been criticized for oversimplifying matters) wisely points out that the dominant postwar vision of family life, even at its most luxurious, could be rife with conflict. As she writes, "Postwar domestic consumerism required conformity to strict gender assumptions that were fraught with potential tensions and frustrations." See May, *Homeward Bound*, 181; Wini Breines, *Young, White, and Miserable: Growing Up Female in the Fifties* (Boston: Beacon Press, 1992); Ruth Rosen, "The Female Generation Gap: Daughters of the Fifties and the Origins of Contemporary American Feminism," in *U.S. History as Women's History: New Feminist Essays*, ed. Linda K. Kerber, Alice Kessler-Harris and Kathryn Kish Sklar (Chapel Hill: University of North Carolina Press, 1995), 313–34; and Eva S. Moskowitz, "'It's Good to Blow Your Top': Women's Magazines and a Discourse of Discontent, 1945–1965," *Journal of Women's History* 8 (fall 1996): 66–98.

18. Collier, Rosaldo, and Yanagisako, "Is There a Family?," 34.

19. Ibid.

20. On maternalism as an ideology and form of women's civic action, see Theda Skocpol, *Protecting Soldiers and Mothers: The Political Origins of Social Policy in the United States* (Cambridge, Mass.: Harvard University Press, 1992), 318–19; Sonya Michel and Seth Koven, "Womanly Duties: Maternalist Politics and the Origins of Welfare States in France, Germany, Great Britain, and the United States, 1880–1920," *American Historical Review* 95 (October 1990): 1076–1108; and Katherine A. Lynch, "The Family and the History of Public Life," *Journal of Interdisciplinary History* 24, no. 4 (spring 1994): 665–84.

21. Madelon Powers, *Faces along the Bar: Lore and Order in the Workingman's Saloon, 1870–1920* (Chicago: University of Chicago Press, 1998), 55–62.

22. Issues of racial identity and racial exclusion have become controversial subjects in the history of AA. This matter is discussed further in Chapter 3.

23. On the rise of a therapeutic culture, see Philip Rieff, *The Triumph of the Therapeutic* (New York: Harper and Row, 1966); Christopher Lasch, *The Culture of Narcissism* (New York: Norton, 1978); Donald Meyer, *The Positive Thinkers* (New York: Doubleday, 1965); T. J. Jackson Lears, "From Salvation to Self-Realization: Advertising and the Therapeutic Roots of the Consumer Culture, 1880–1930," in *The Culture of Consumption: Critical Essays in American History, 1880–1980*, ed. Richard Wightman Fox and T. J. Jackson Lears (New York: Pantheon, 1983), 3–38; and Eva S. Moskowitz, *In Therapy We Trust: America's Obsession with Self-Fulfillment* (Baltimore: Johns Hopkins University Press, 2001). On the rise of the professional-managerial class, see Barbara Ehrenreich and John Ehrenreich, "The Professional-Managerial Class," in *Between Labor and Capital*, ed. Pat Walker (Boston: South End Press, 1970), and Richard Ohmann, *Selling Culture: Magazines, Markets, and Class at the Turn of the Century* (New York: Verso, 1996).

24. Joel Pfister, "On Conceptualizing the Cultural History of Emotional and Psychological Life in America," in *Inventing the Psychological: Toward a Cultural History of Emotional Life in America*, ed. Joel Pfister and Nancy Schnog (New Haven: Yale University Press, 1997), 17–59 (quote on 35–36).

25. Nancy F. Cott, *Public Vows: A History of Marriage and the Nation* (Cambridge, Mass.: Harvard University Press, 2000), 182.

26. Valverde, "Comment," 123.

27. In *On Drugs* (Minneapolis: University of Minnesota Press, 1995), 14–15, cultural critic David Lenson argues that "sobriety," literally defined, "is an empty concept, a null set defined only by what surrounds it, by its various negations." In this sense "sobriety" denotes a state of consciousness in opposition to one affected by mind-altering substances. AA imbued the concept with a different meaning, not only in terms of literal abstinence from drink, but also to connote a spiritual attitude toward one's place in the world. This is in contrast to the "dry drunk," who abstains from alcohol yet remains resentful, angry, and unhappy.

28. On women's drinking and alcoholism, see Sarah Stage, *Female Complaints: Lydia Pinkham and the Business of Women's Medicine* (New York: Norton, 1979); Mark Edward Lender, "A Special Stigma: Women and Alcoholism in the Late Nineteenth and Early Twentieth Centuries," in *Alcohol Interventions: Historical and Sociocultural Approaches*, ed. David L. Strug, S. Priyadarsini, and Merton M. Hyman (New York: Hayworth Press, 1986); Murdock, *Domesticating Drink*; and esp. Michelle Lee McClellan, "Lady Lushes: Women Alcoholics and American Society, 1880–1960" (Ph.D. diss. Stanford University, 1999).

29. AA is often referred to as a self-help movement, a term that positions it as an adjunct or alternative to professional treatment. On the sociology of self-help groups, see Hans Toch, *The Social Psychology of Social Movements* (Indianapolis: Bobbs-Merrill, 1965); Alfred H. Katz and Eugene I. Bender, *The Strength in Us: Self-Help Groups in the Modern World* (New York: Franklin Watts, 1976); and Alfred J. Katz, *Self-Help in America: A Social Movement Perspective* (Boston:

Twayne, 1993). Recently some scholars have come to prefer the term "mutual-help movement" to denote the importance of group interaction; the term "self-help," they believe, carries the misleading connotation of an individual acting alone to bring about a desired life change. See Klaus Makela et al., *Alcoholics Anonymous as a Mutual-Help Movement: A Study in Eight Societies* (Madison: University of Wisconsin Press, 1996), 8–13.

CHAPTER ONE

1. Jack London, *John Barleycorn* (New York: Century, 1913), 128, 339.
2. Madelon Powers, *Faces along the Bar: Lore and Order in the Workingman's Saloon, 1870–1920* (Chicago: University of Chicago Press, 1998), 234–36; George Chauncey, *Gay New York: Gender, Urban Culture, and the Making of the Gay Male World, 1890–1940* (New York: Basic Books, 1994), 75–86.
3. Elizabeth Lunbeck, *The Psychiatric Persuasion: Knowledge, Gender, and Power in Modern America* (Princeton: Princeton University Press, 1994), 229–31, 244–45.
4. John W. Crowley, *The White Logic: Alcoholism and Gender in American Modernist Fiction* (Amherst: University of Massachusetts Press, 1994), 28–41. On the significance of alcohol in American literature, see also Ann Douglas, *Terrible Honesty: Mongrel Manhattan in the 1920s* (New York: Farrar, Straus and Giroux, 1995), and Thomas B. Gilmore, *Equivocal Spirits: Alcoholism and Drinking in Twentieth-Century Literature* (Chapel Hill: University of North Carolina Press, 1987).
5. Crowley, *White Logic*, 20–23.
6. London, *John Barleycorn*, 39–43, 48–49, 74, 203.
7. Crowley, *White Logic*, 28.
8. Powers, *Faces along the Bar*, 26–36; Roy Rosenzweig, *Eight Hours for What We Will: Workers and Leisure in an Industrial City, 1870–1920* (New York: Cambridge University Press, 1983), 35–64, 240–49; Perry Duis, *The Saloon: Public Drinking in Chicago and Boston, 1880–1920* (Urbana: University of Illinois Press, 1983).
9. On the social functions of the saloon, see Powers, *Faces along the Bar*; Rosenzweig, *Eight Hours for What We Will*, 35–64; Duis, *Saloon*, 196; and Jon M. Kingsdale, "The 'Poor Man's Club': Social Functions of the Urban Working-Class Saloon," *American Quarterly* 24 (October 1975): 472–89.
10. James W. Johnson, *To Drink or Not to Drink* (n.p., 1930); Rosenzweig, *Eight Hours for What We Will*, 53.
11. Powers offers the most thorough account of working-class saloon culture on its own terms. She argues that historians have too often interpreted drinking history as "a mere adjunct of temperance history" and offers an important corrective to previous scholarship; see Powers, *Faces along the Bar*, 2. My brief account here complements her study but considers the cultural histories of drink and temperance together.
12. For a fascinating discussion of treating as gift exchange, see Lewis Hyde, *The Gift: Imagination and the Erotic Life of Property* (New York: Vintage, 1979), xi–xvii, 56–69.

13. Rosenzweig, *Eight Hours for What We Will*, 58–59; Powers, *Faces along the Bar*, 93–118.

14. W. J. Rorabaugh, *The Alcoholic Republic: An American Tradition* (New York: Oxford University Press, 1979), 151. On treating as a "norm of equality and solidarity," see also Richard Stivers, *A Hair of the Dog: Irish Drinking and American Stereotype* (University Park: Pennsylvania State University Press, 1976), 86–87.

15. London, *John Barleycorn*, 84–96; italics in original.

16. Crowley, *White Logic*, 30–31.

17. London, *John Barleycorn*, 183.

18. Rosenzweig, *Eight Hours for What We Will*, 60–61; Powers, *Faces along the Bar*, 22–25, 116.

19. London, *John Barleycorn*, 181–85.

20. Chauncey, *Gay New York*, 76–86.

21. Ibid., 80–81. For other discussions of masculine conviviality among working-class men, see Elliott J. Gorn, *The Manly Art: Bare-Knuckle Prize-Fighting in America* (Ithaca, N.Y.: Cornell University Press, 1986), 129–45; Leonard Ellis, "Men among Men: An Exploration of All-Male Relationships in Victorian America" (Ph.D. diss., Columbia University, 1982), 1–60; David Montgomery, *The Fall of the House of Labor: The Workplace, the State, and American Labor Activism, 1865–1920* (Cambridge: Cambridge University Press, 1987), 87–92; and Powers, *Faces along the Bar*, 89–91.

22. Travis Hoke, "The Corner Saloon," *American Mercury*, March 1931, 311–15, cited in Catherine Gilbert Murdock, *Domesticating Drink: Women, Men, and Alcohol in America, 1870–1940* (Baltimore: Johns Hopkins University Press, 1998), 14–15; Rosenzweig, *Eight Hours for What We Will*, 63.

23. Thorstein Veblen, *Theory of the Leisure Class: An Economic Study of Institutions* (New York: Macmillan, 1899; reprint, New York: Modern Library, 1934), 70.

24. Powers, *Faces along the Bar*, 89; George Ade, *The Old-Time Saloon* (New York: Long and Smith, 1931), 56–58.

25. Lunbeck, *Psychiatric Persuasion*, 245.

26. London, *John Barleycorn*, 43.

27. Murdock, *Domesticating Drink*, 137–38; Ellis, "Men among Men," 329–57; London, *John Barleycorn*, 243; Rosenzweig, *Eight Hours for What We Will*, 51; Mark Edward Lender and James Kirby Martin, *Drinking in America: A History* (New York: Free Press, 1987), 99–102.

28. Duis, *Saloon*, 143–51, 184–88.

29. Powers, *Faces along the Bar*, 76. With the exception of Murdock, *Domesticating Drink*, there is little scholarship on elite drinking patterns during the turn of the century.

30. John Hammond Moore, "The Cocktail: Our Contribution to Humanity's Salvation," *Virginia Quarterly Review* 56 (1980): 336–44.

31. Lender and Martin, *Drinking in America*, 102; Murdock, *Domesticating Drink*, 10–17; E. Anthony Rotundo, *American Manhood: Transformations in Masculinity from the Revolution to the Modern Era* (New York: Basic Books, 1993), 180, 200–205.

32. Jack S. Blocker Jr., *American Temperance Movements: Cycles of Reform* (Boston: Twayne, 1989), 70–71; Lender and Martin, *Drinking in America*, 102, 108.

33. In his classic essay Harry Gene Levine argues that the concept of addiction was central to temperance ideology; see his "The Discovery of Addiction: Changing Conceptions of Habitual Drunkenness in America," *Journal of Studies on Alcohol* 39, no. 1 (January 1978): 143–74.

34. General studies of the Volstead Act and Prohibition can be found in Lender and Martin, *Drinking in America*, 124–68; Joseph R. Gusfield, *Symbolic Crusade* (Urbana: University of Illinois Press, 1963); and John J. Rumbarger, *Profits, Power, and Prohibition: Alcohol Reform and the Industrialization of America, 1800–1930* (Albany: State University of New York Press, 1989).

35. London, *John Barleycorn*, 298–302.

36. On the turbulent relationship between London and his wife, including the effects of alcoholism on their marriage, see Clarice Stasz, *American Dreamers: Charmian and Jack London* (New York: St. Martin's Press, 1988), 227–46, 295.

37. Rotundo, *American Manhood*, 180.

38. London, *John Barleycorn*, 336–37.

39. Anna Gordon, quoted in Ella Boole, *Give Prohibition Its Chance* (New York: Fleming H. Revell, 1929), 90–91.

40. Kenneth D. Rose, *American Women and the Repeal of Prohibition* (New York: New York University Press, 1996), 11–14, 21–36, 73–74, 136–44.

41. On female reform ideology and organization in the nineteenth and early twentieth centuries, see Barbara Epstein, *The Politics of Domesticity: Women, Evangelism, and Temperance in Nineteenth-Century America* (Middletown, Conn.: Wesleyan University Press, 1981); Ruth Bordin, *Women and Temperance: The Quest for Power and Liberty, 1873–1900* (Philadelphia: Temple University Press, 1981); Lori D. Ginzberg, *Women and the Work of Benevolence: Morality, Politics, and Class in the Nineteenth-Century United States* (New Haven: Yale University Press, 1990); Rose, *American Women and the Repeal of Prohibition*, 34–62; and Murdock, *Domesticating Drink*, 28–52.

42. Robert C. Binkley, *Responsible Drinking: A Discreet Inquiry and a Modest Proposal* (New York: Vanguard, 1930), 134.

43. Mother Eliza A. Stewart, *Memories of the Crusade* (Chicago: H. J. Smith, 1890), 39–40.

44. *The Shadow of the Bottle* (Washington, D.C.: Review and Herald Publishing, 1925), 61–65.

45. For an analysis of other domestic temperance plots, see Karen Sanchez-Eppler, "Temperance in the Bed of a Child: Incest and Social Order in Nineteenth-Century America," *American Quarterly* 7 (March 1995): 1–33.

46. Elizabeth Pleck, *Domestic Tyranny: The Making of Social Policy against Family Violence from Colonial Times to the Present* (New York: Oxford University Press, 1987), 49–66.

47. Ibid., 100–101.

48. Harry Gene Levine, "Temperance and Women in the Nineteenth-Century United States," in *Alcohol and Drug Problems in Women*, ed. Oriana J. Kalant

(New York: Plenum, 1980), 62; Epstein, *Politics of Domesticity*, 100–107; Bordin, *Women and Temperance*, 162.

49. Frances Willard, *Glimpses of Fifty Years: The Autobiography of an American Woman* (Chicago: H. J. Smith, 1889), 597–611 (emphasis in original).

50. Margaret Marsh originated the term "masculine domesticity" in "Suburban Men and Masculine Domesticity, 1870–1915," *American Quarterly* 40 (June 1988): 165–86, and "From Separation to Togetherness: The Social Construction of Domestic Space in American Suburbs, 1840–1915," *Journal of American History* 76 (September 1989): 506–27. See also Clyde Griffen, "Reconstructing Masculinity from the Evangelical Revival to the Waning of Progressivism: A Speculative Synthesis," in *Meanings for Manhood: Constructions of Masculinity in Victorian America*, ed. Mark C. Carnes and Clyde Griffen (Chicago: University of Chicago Press, 1990), 183–201, and Robert Griswold, *Fatherhood in America: A History* (New York: Basic Books, 1993), 89–90, 116–17.

51. Powers, *Faces along the Bar*, 45–47, 172–73.

52. Griswold, *Fatherhood in America*, 1–67; Rotundo, *American Manhood*, 168–93.

53. Griswold, *Fatherhood in America*, 116–18; Lunbeck, *Psychiatric Persuasion*, 229–31.

54. Warren Susman, *Culture as History: The Transformation of American Society in the Twentieth Century* (New York: Pantheon, 1984); T. J. Jackson Lears, "From Salvation to Self-Realization: Advertising and the Therapeutic Roots of the Consumer Culture, 1880–1930," in *The Culture of Consumption: Critical Essays in American History, 1880–1980*, ed. Richard Wightman Fox and T. J. Jackson Lears (New York: Pantheon, 1983); Daniel Horowitz, *The Morality of Spending: Attitudes toward the Consumer Society in America* (Baltimore: Johns Hopkins University Press, 1985).

55. Horowitz, *Morality of Spending*, xxiii; William Leach, *Land of Desire: Merchants, Power, and the Rise of a New American Culture* (New York: Pantheon, 1993); Susan Strasser, *Satisfaction Guaranteed: The Making of an American Mass Market* (New York: Pantheon, 1989); Roland Marchand, *Advertising the American Dream: Making Way for Modernity* (Berkeley: University of California Press, 1985).

56. Griswold, *Fatherhood in America*, 115–18; Susan Porter Benson, "Living on the Margin: Working-Class Marriages and Family Survival Strategies in the United States, 1919–1941," in *The Sex of Things: Gender and Consumption in Historical Perspective*, ed. Victoria de Grazia (Berkeley: University of California Press, 1996), 212–43.

57. Madelon Powers stresses this point throughout *Faces along the Bar*.

58. Michael E. Parrish, *Anxious Decades: America in Prosperity and Depression, 1920–1942* (New York: Norton, 1992), 235, 413; Robert S. McElvaine, *The Great Depression* (New York: Times Books, 1984).

59. Lender and Martin, *Drinking in America*, 167–68; William Grimes, *Straight Up or On the Rocks: A Cultural History of American Drink* (New York: Simon and Schuster, 1993), 106; John Burnham, *Bad Habits: Drinking, Smoking, Taking Drugs, Gambling, Sexual Misbehavior, and Swearing in American History* (New York: New York University Press, 1993), 29–30. It should be noted that five southern states as well as Kansas, Oklahoma, and North Dakota remained dry;

see Frederick Lewis Allen, *Since Yesterday: The Nineteen Thirties in America* (New York: Harper and Brothers, 1939), 114.

60. McElvaine, *Great Depression*, 125.

61. Charles H. Lipsett, *The Effect of Repeal on Industrial Recovery* (New York: Atlas, 1935), 1–13, 24, 54–70.

62. Burnham, *Bad Habits*, 10–22, 64–76.

63. Murdock, *Domesticating Drink*, 48–69. On women's consumption of patent medicines, see Sarah Stage, *Female Complaints: Lydia Pinkham and the Business of Women's Medicine* (New York: Norton, 1979).

64. Murdock, *Domesticating Drink*, 156–58.

65. Ibid., 50–62.

66. David Nasaw, *Going Out: The Rise and Fall of Public Amusements* (New York: Basic Books, 1993); Kathy Peiss, *Cheap Amusements: Working Women and Leisure in Turn-of-the-Century New York* (Philadelphia: Temple University Press, 1986); Lewis Erenberg, *Steppin' Out: New York Nightlife and the Transformation of American Culture, 1890–1930* (Westport, Conn.: Greenwood Press, 1981); John F. Kasson, *Amusing the Million: Coney Island at the Turn of the Century* (New York: Hill and Wang, 1978); Murdock, *Domesticating Drink*, 210–14.

67. Paul Aaron and David Musto, "Temperance and Prohibition in America: A Historical Overview," in *Alcohol and Public Policy: Beyond the Shadow of Prohibition*, ed. Mark H. Moore and Dean R. Gerstein (Washington, D.C., National Academy Press, 1981), 158–60.

68. Ida Tarbell, "Ladies at the Bar," *Liberty*, July 26, 1930, 6–10.

69. Murdock, *Domesticating Drink*, 89–110; Joseph Lanza, *The Cocktail: The Influence of Spirits on the American Psyche* (New York: Picador, 1995).

70. Murdock, *Domesticating Drink*, 115–52. For another account of mixed-sex cocktail parties in the 1920s, see Moore, "Cocktail."

71. David Kyvig, *Repealing National Prohibition* (Chicago: University of Chicago Press, 1979) and "Women against Prohibition," *American Quarterly* 28 (winter 1976): 465–82; Rose, *American Women and the Repeal of Prohibition*, 67–147; Murdock, *Domesticating Drink*, 268–71, 281–322.

72. Frederick Lewis Allen, *Only Yesterday: An Informal History of the 1920's* (New York: Harper and Row, 1931), 92. The historical literature on the rise of a "modern" society and culture in the 1920s is vast; for a recent synthesis, see Lynn Dumenil, *The Modern Temper: American Culture and Society in the 1920s* (New York: Hill and Wang, 1995).

73. Rose, *American Women and the Repeal of Prohibition*, 109–13, figs. 14–17.

74. Ellen Wiley Todd, *The "New Woman" Revised: Painting and Gender Politics on Fourteenth Street* (Berkeley: University of California Press, 1993), xxvi–xxviii, 31–36.

75. Blocker, *American Temperance Movements*, 122–23; Murdock, *Domesticating Drink*, 114–33.

76. Murdock, *Domesticating Drink*, 169–170.

77. Recently scholars have disagreed on this latter point. While building on John Burnham's argument about the "normalization" of social drinking, Rose and Mur-

dock depart from the senior historian's view that repeal enacted a "complete inversion in values" toward a society that endorsed "action without restraint, not only the restraints of explicit law but even informal social restraints" (Burnham, *Bad Habits*, 49). They view repealers not as champions of untrammeled indulgence but as social conservatives who disdained extreme behavior on both sides of the wet/dry controversy. Rose refutes Burnham's contention that WONPR women supported the "cause" of drinking and "advocated" consumption per se. Murdock also discusses moderate drinking as an alternative to both dry extremism and unrestrained consumption. See Burnham, *Bad Habits*, 39–49; Rose, *American Women and the Repeal of Prohibition*, 139; Murdock, *Domesticating Drink*, 134–56, 169–70; and Aaron and Musto, "Temperance and Prohibition in America," 171.

78. On FDR's passion for cocktails, see Murdock, *Domesticating Drink*, 88, 156, 169, and Lanza, *Cocktail*, 38–39.

79. *An Alcoholic to His Sons*, as told to Henry Beetle Hough (New York: Simon and Schuster, 1954), 42.

80. Frederick Lewis Allen, *Since Yesterday*, 114–15.

81. This is not to suggest that liquor advertising was uncontroversial after repeal. Before World War II critics pressured radio networks to refuse advertising for hard liquor while accepting ads for beer and wine. Religious periodicals often criticized the pervasiveness of social drinking in U.S. society. But these critical voices were overpowered by publications such as *Life* and *Time*, whose annual profits from liquor ads ranged from $1 million to $4 million by 1945. See Burnham, *Bad Habits*, 63–70.

82. Benson Y. Landis, "Some Economic Aspects of Inebriety," in *Alcohol, Science, and Society: Twenty-nine Lectures with Discussions as Given at the Yale Summer School of Alcohol Studies* (New Haven: Quarterly Journal of Studies on Alcohol, 1945), 215–16.

83. Burnham, *Bad Habits*, 63–64.

84. *Life*, November 21, 1938, 63.

85. On advertisements as reflections of class aspirations, see Marchand, *Advertising the American Dream*, 197–200.

86. Lewis Erenberg, "From New York to Middletown: Repeal and the Legitimization of Nightlife in the Great Depression," *American Quarterly* 38 (winter 1986): 761–78.

87. Ibid., 37–38; Robin Room, "The Movies and the Wettening of America: The Media as Amplifiers of Cultural Change," *British Journal of Addiction* 83 (1988): 11–18. On movie censorship, see Robert Sklar, *Movie-Made America: A Social History of American Movies* (New York: Random House, 1975), 173–76, and John D'Emilio and Estelle B. Freedman, *Intimate Matters: A History of Sexuality in America* (New York: Harper and Row, 1988), 281–82.

88. *The Thin Man*, produced by Hunt Stromberg (Metro Goldwyn Mayer, 1934).

89. Lanza, *Cocktail*, 53–54.

90. *Murder at the Vanities*, produced by E. Lloyd Sheldon (Paramount, 1934).

91. See Lanza's discussion of films of the Depression era for further examples, in *Cocktail*, 53–63.

92. Margaret McFadden makes this point most persuasively in "Anything Goes: Gender and Knowledge in the Comic Popular Culture of the 1930s" (Ph.D. diss., Yale University, 1996). See also Holly Allen, "Fallen Women and Forgotten Men: Gendered Concepts of Community, Home, and Nation, 1932–1945" (Ph.D. diss., Yale University, 1996), and Barbara Melosh, *Engendering Culture: Manhood and Womanhood in New Deal Public Art and Theater* (Washington, D.C.: Smithsonian Institution Press, 1991).

93. On the gendered and familial dimensions of New Deal policies during the Depression, see Alan Dawley, *Struggles for Justice: Social Responsibility and the Liberal State* (Cambridge, Mass.: Harvard University Press, 1991), 370–95, and Lois Scharf, *To Work and to Wed: Female Employment, Feminism, and the Great Depression* (Westport, Conn.: Greenwood Press, 1980).

94. This quote is attributed to Harry Hopkins, director of the Works Progress Administration, cited in Griswold, *Fatherhood in America*, 155.

95. Ibid., 146–51; Mirra Komaravsky, *The Unemployed Man and His Family: The Effect of Unemployment upon the Status of the Man in Fifty-nine Families* (New York: Dryden Press, 1940).

96. Melosh, *Engendering Culture*, 33–81.

97. Burnham, *Bad Habits*, 70.

98. Jay L. Rubin, "The Wet War: American Liquor Control, 1941–1945," in *Alcohol, Reform, and Society: The Liquor Issue in Social Context*, ed. Jack S. Blocker (Westport, Conn.: Greenwood Press, 1979), 235–58; Burnham, *Bad Habits*, 70–72.

99. George Barton Cutten, *We Are at War*, speech delivered at the Northern Baptist Convention, Cleveland, Ohio, May 27, 1942 (Philadelphia: n.p., 1942).

100. Ibid., 6.

101. Ibid., 8.

102. Rubin, "Wet War," 237.

103. Ibid., 235–41; Burnham, *Bad Habits*, 70–71.

104. Alvin Grisedieck, "Beer and Brewing in a Nation at War," *QJSA* 3, no. 2 (September 1942): 293–301.

105. Rubin, "Wet War," 243; Burnham, *Bad Habits*, 71–74.

106. Rubin, "Wet War," 246–51.

107. "Alcoholism No Problem When Soldiers Have a Good Time," *Science News Letter*, August 1, 1942, 71; Burnham, *Bad Habits*, 71–74.

108. *Life*, September 4, 1944, 101.

109. Robert B. Westbrook, "Fighting for the American Family," in *The Power of Culture: Critical Essays in American History*, ed. Richard W. Fox and T. J. Jackson Lears (Chicago: University of Chicago Press, 1993), 195–221. See also Westbrook's article "I Want a Girl, Just Like the Girl That Married Harry James: American Women and the Problem of Political Obligation in World War II," *American Quarterly* 42 (December 1990): 587–614.

110. *Life*, April 5, 1943, 97.

111. Burnham, *Bad Habits*, 71.

112. Catherine Gilbert Murdock's *Domesticating Drink* is a fine, innovative study of the relationship between alcohol and gender in the early twentieth century, but it

overstates the extent to which mixed-sex drinking replaced traditional male drinking patterns. In order fully to understand postwar attitudes toward alcoholism and family life (a topic that falls outside the scope of Murdock's book), we need to address the *limits* of heterosocial drinking after repeal.

113. Herbert A. Bloch, "Alcohol and American Recreational Life," *American Scholar* 18, no. 1 (January 1949): 60–61.

114. Raymond G. McCarthy and Edgar M. Douglas, *Alcohol and Social Responsibility: A New Educational Approach* (New York: Thomas Y. Crowell, 1949), 60–61. The study quoted was John W. Riley and Charles F. Marden, "The Social Pattern of Alcoholic Drinking," *QJSA* 8, no. 2 (September 1947): 265–73.

115. Pete Hamill, *A Drinking Life* (Boston: Little, Brown, 1994), 16.

116. Ibid., 82, 146–47.

117. Warren Susman, "The Culture of the Thirties," in Susman, *Culture as History*.

118. Arthur J. Todd, *The Chicago Recreation Survey 1937* (Chicago: Chicago Recreation Committee, 1938), 143–55.

119. John Dollard, "Drinking Mores of the Social Classes," in *Alcohol, Science, and Society*, 95–104.

120. *Fortune*, October 1938, 40, 47; November 1938, 35; October 1935, 122; *Time*, December 20, 1937, 45.

121. "Alcoholics Anonymous and the Advertising Man," *Printer's Ink*, September 14, 1945, 98.

122. Eliot Taintor [Ruth Fitch Mason and Gregory Mason], *September Remember* (New York: Prentice Hall, 1945), 145–49.

123. *An Alcoholic to His Sons*, 73–75, 80–81.

124. Dollard, "Drinking Mores of the Social Classes," 99–100.

125. On the history of Christmas gift exchange, see William B. Waits, *The Modern Christmas in America: A Cultural History of Gift Giving* (New York: New York University Press, 1993).

126. John Morton Blum, *V Was for Victory: Politics and Culture during World War II* (San Diego: Harcourt, Brace, Jovanovich, 1976), 53–64.

127. Ibid.

CHAPTER TWO

1. Francis Sill Wickware, "Liquor: Current Studies in Medicine and Psychiatry Are Bringing Enlightenment to the 30,000 Year-Old Problem of Drinking," *Life*, May 27, 1946, 66–77.

2. Mark Edward Lender and James Kirby Martin, *Drinking in America: A History* (New York: Free Press, 1987), 205–6.

3. Wendy Kozol, *Life's America: Family and Nation in Postwar Photojournalism* (Philadelphia: Temple University Press, 1994), 11–14.

4. Wickware, "Liquor," 66.

5. Both of these drinking paradigms arose in the context of specific historical circumstances. What counts as moderate or excessive, or healthy or pathological

drinking in a given society or time period is socially defined. Words such as "moderate" or "abusive," used to denote the quantity or nature of bodily consumption, are relative terms; they vary over time and across boundaries of class, religion, ethnicity, etc.

6. See, for example, J. Maurice Trimmer, "The Menace of Moderation," *Christian Century*, August 28, 1946, 1037–38.

7. Herbert A. Bloch, "Alcohol and American Recreational Life," *American Scholar* 18, no. 1 (January 1949): 54–66 (emphasis added).

8. Lender and Martin, *Drinking in America*, 182–91; Jack S. Blocker Jr., *American Temperance Movements: Cycles of Reform* (Boston: Twayne, 1989), 144–54.

9. Harry Gene Levine, "The Discovery of Addiction: Changing Conceptions of Habitual Drunkenness in America," *Journal of Studies on Alcohol* 39, no. 1 (January 1978): 143–74.

10. On inebriate homes and asylums of the nineteenth and early twentieth centuries, see Sarah W. Tracy, "The Foxborough Experiment: Medicalizing Inebriety at the Massachusetts Hospital for Dipsomaniacs and Inebriates, 1833–1919" (Ph.D., diss., University of Pennsylvania, 1992); Jim Baumohl and Robin Room, "Inebriety, Doctors, and the State: Alcoholism Treatment Institutions before 1940," in *Recent Developments in Alcoholism*, ed. Mark Galanter, vol. 5 (New York: Plenum, 1987); and William L. White's useful summary in *Slaying the Dragon: The History of Addiction Treatment and Recovery in America* (Bloomington, Ill.: Chestnut Health Systems, 1998), 21–51.

11. White, *Slaying the Dragon*, 198.

12. Bruce Holley Johnson, "The Alcoholism Movement in America: A Study in Cultural Innovation" (Ph.D. diss., University of Illinois, 1973). Some scholars contend that the term "alcoholism movement" does not account for internal divisions within the alcoholism movement, which was not monolithic. In an article titled "Paradigm Sidetracked: Explaining Early Resistance to the Alcoholism Paradigm at Yale's Laboratory of Applied Physiology, 1940–1944" (published on the World Wide Web, 1994), Ron Roizen notes that the term "alcohol studies," favored by researchers at the Yale Center, implicitly questioned the validity of the disease concept of alcoholism. Leading scientific authorities, including E. M. Jellinek, privately doubted the empirical soundness of the disease paradigm.

Nevertheless, researchers condoned the social ramifications of the disease concept as promoted by public health advocates (especially its detachment from temperance politics and its sympathetic attitude toward the afflicted). Internal conflicts did not cause any cracks in the *public* face of the campaign during the 1940s and 1950s. William White suggests there were multiple alcoholism movements with varying commercial, therapeutic, and educational agendas. "If anything resembling a single 'alcoholism movement' arose," he writes, "it could be found only in the collective and cumulative effects of these divergent initiatives. So we will speak of a 'modern alcoholism movement' with an understanding of the divergent and sometimes conflicting interests collected under this linguistic umbrella." This is the connotation I also assign to the term. See White, *Slaying the Dragon*, 180.

13. Robin Room, "Governing Images of Alcohol and Drug Problems: The Structure, Sources, and Sequels of Conceptualizations of Intractable Problems" (Ph.D. diss., University of California, Berkeley, 1978); "Sociological Aspects of the Disease Concept of Alcoholism," in *Research Advances in Alcohol and Drug Problems*, ed. Robert J. Gibbens and Reginald G. Smart, vol. 7 (New York: Plenum, 1983), 47–91; Ron Roizen, "The American Discovery of Alcoholism, 1933–1939" (Ph.D. diss., University of California, Berkeley, 1991).

14. Classic studies on the rise of the therapeutic ethos include Christopher Lasch, *The Culture of Narcissism* (New York: Norton, 1978); Philip Rieff, *The Triumph of the Therapeutic* (New York: Harper and Row, 1966); Donald Meyer, *The Positive Thinkers* (New York: Doubleday, 1965); and T. J. Jackson Lears, "From Salvation to Self-Realization: Advertising and the Therapeutic Roots of the Consumer Culture, 1880–1930," in *The Culture of Consumption: Critical Essays in American History, 1880–1980*, ed. Richard Wightman Fox and T. J. Jackson Lears (New York: Pantheon, 1983), 3–38. For an excellent recent history, see Eva S. Moskowitz, *In Therapy We Trust: America's Obsession with Self-Fulfillment* (Baltimore: Johns Hopkins University Press, 2001).

15. "Mrs. Drunkard," *Newsweek*, March 8, 1948, 22–23.

16. Howard W. Haggard, "The Physiology of Alcohol," *Yale Review* 35, no. 2 (December 1945): 297–99.

17. "Alcoholism Seven Times More Prevalent among Men," *Science News Letter*, January 13, 1945, 22.

18. On the gendered nature of the modern alcoholism paradigm, see also Michelle Lee McClellan, "Lady Lushes: Women Alcoholics and American Society, 1880–1960" (Ph.D. diss., Stanford University, 1999), 131–84.

19. "Mrs. Drunkard," 22–23.

20. McClellan, "Lady Lushes," 131–44.

21. Ibid.

22. The topic of women and alcoholism in this period is thoroughly covered in ibid.

23. Blocker, *American Temperance Movements*, 144–47; William J. Filstead, Jean J. Rossi, and Mark Keller, eds., *Alcohol and Alcohol Problems: New Thinking and New Directions* (Cambridge, Mass: Ballinger, 1976), 5–6. Significantly, the first edition of *Alcoholics Anonymous*, also known as the fellowship's *Big Book*, was also published during this period, in 1939. The focus of the present discussion, however, is limited to academic and medical literature; AA publications are discussed in Chapter 3.

24. Bruce Holley Johnson, "Alcoholism Movement in America," 70–72, 387, 471–76.

25. Nathan G. Hale, *The Rise and Crisis of Psychoanalysis in the United States: Freud and the Americans, 1917–1985* (New York: Oxford University Press, 1995), 25–166.

26. Bruce Holley Johnson, "Alcoholism Movement in America," 222–25; White, *Slaying the Dragon*, 98–99. William White notes that alcoholics were generally considered unsuitable for psychoanalysis and were "on the bottom of the list of

desired candidates" for therapy. He distinguishes between the intellectual impact of Freudian ideas about addiction (which laid a solid foundation for the rise of the disease concept) and the use of psychoanalysis as a viable form of treatment.

27. Karl Menninger, *Man against Himself* (New York: Harcourt, Brace and World, 1938), 141, 147.

28. Edward A. Strecker and Francis T. Chambers Jr., *Alcohol: One Man's Meat* (New York: Macmillan, 1938), xv.

29. Menninger, *Man against Himself*, 159; Leslie Osborn, "New Attitudes toward Alcoholism," *QJSA* 12, no. 1 (March 1951): 58–60; Thomas Fullam [pseud.], *Here's to Sobriety: A Plain Approach to Understanding the Compulsive Drinker and His Problems* (New York: Abelard Press, 1950), 172; Strecker and Chambers, *Alcohol*, 37–38.

30. Selden D. Bacon, "Alcohol and Complex Society," in *Alcohol, Science, and Society: Twenty-nine Lectures with Discussions as Given at the Yale Summer School of Alcohol Studies* (New Haven: Quarterly Journal of Studies on Alcohol, 1945), 190–94; Joseph Hirsh, quoted in "Problem Drinking," *Time*, January 31, 1949, 54; Donald Horton, "The Functions of Alcohol in Primitive Societies," in *Alcohol, Science, and Society*, 158.

31. Warren Susman, "Did Success Spoil the United States? Dual Representations in Postwar America," in *Recasting America: Culture and Politics in the Age of Cold War*, ed. Lary May (Chicago: University of Chicago Press, 1989), 19–33, and *Culture as History: The Transformation of American Society in the Twentieth Century* (New York: Pantheon, 1984), 284–85; William Graebner, *The Age of Doubt: American Thought and Culture in the 1940s* (Boston: Twayne, 1991), 101–6; Wini Breines, *Young, White, and Miserable: Growing Up Female in the Fifties* (Boston: Beacon Press, 1992), 1–10.

32. I borrow the apt phrase "turning inward" from Graebner, *Age of Doubt*, 102.

33. On the newfound prominence of psychological experts and therapeutic authority in the 1940s, see Hale, *Rise and Crisis of Psychoanalysis*, 185–300; Ellen Herman, *The Romance of American Psychology: Political Culture in the Age of Experts* (Berkeley: University of California Press, 1995); and Moskowitz, *In Therapy We Trust*, 100–148.

34. Carney Landis, "Theories of the Alcoholic Personality," in *Alcohol, Science, and Society*, 130; Howard W. Haggard and E. M. Jellinek, *Alcohol Explored* (New York: Doubleday, 1942), 174–75.

35. E. M. Jellinek, "Phases in Drinking History of Alcoholics," *QJSA* 7, no. 1 (June 1947): 1–88.

36. Selden D. Bacon, "Excessive Drinking and the Institution of the Family," in *Alcohol, Science, and Society*, 229; Ralph M. Henderson, "Profile of the Alcoholic," *Proceedings of the First Annual Alberta Conference on Alcohol Studies* (Alberta, Canada: Alcoholism Foundation of Alberta, 1954), 38; Strecker and Chambers, *Alcohol*, 42.

37. David Glen Mick, "Self-Gifts," in *Gift Giving: A Research Anthology*, ed. Cele Otnes and Richard F. Beltramini (Bowling Green, Ohio: Bowling Green University Press, 1996), 99–116. Mick differentiates among several types of self-gifts:

rationalized self-indulgence after times of delayed gratification, holiday-based self-gifts, and "the darker side of self-indulgence," including shoplifting and addictive behaviors.

38. Strecker and Chambers, *Alcohol*, 20, 29; Edward A. Strecker, "Chronic Alcoholism: A Psychological Survey," *QJSA* 1, no. 2 (September 1941): 12–17; Haggard, "Physiology of Alcohol," 301; Harold W. Lovell, *Hope and Help for the Alcoholic* (New York: Doubleday, 1951), 70–74; Bacon, "Excessive Drinking and the Family," 227, 231.

39. Strecker and Chambers, *Alcohol*, 82, 106.

40. J. H. Wall, "A Study of Alcoholism in Men," *American Journal of Psychiatry* 92 (1936): 1391. The child-rearing book cited is David Goodman, *A Parent's Guide to the Emotional Needs of Children* (New York: Hawthorne Books, 1959), 246. See also Barbara Ehrenreich and Deirdre English, *"For Her Own Good": 150 Years of the Experts' Advice to Women* (London: Pluto Press, 1979), 235–50, and Robert Griswold, *Fatherhood in America: A History* (New York: Basic Books, 1993), 206–10.

41. Philip Wylie, *Generation of Vipers* (New York: Holt, Rinehart and Winston, 1942), 184–204; Breines, *Young, White, and Miserable*, 28, 44; Ehrenreich and English, *"For Her Own Good,"* 235–50. Historians have granted Wylie the dubious distinction of instigating the phenomenon of Momism, a trend in the cultural representation of female dominance and masculine weakness. Although some critics dismiss Wylie's book as an extreme diatribe, the author's attitude toward women struck a nerve among producers of popular culture, and it set the stage for other depictions of manly failure in the postwar era.

42. Lovell, *Hope and Help for the Alcoholic*, 75–76, 199–200.

43. Edward A. Strecker, *Their Mothers' Sons: The Psychiatrist Examines an American Problem* (Philadelphia: Lippincott, 1946), 13–14, 122–27, 205–10.

44. R. P. Knight, "The Psychoanalytic Treatment in a Sanatorium of Chronic Addiction to Alcohol," *Journal of the American Medical Association* 111 (October 15, 1938): 1444; Raymond G. McCarthy, *A Manual of Facts and Fancies about Alcohol* (New Haven: Yale Plan Clinic, 1950), 53; Lovell, *Hope and Help for the Alcoholic*, 76.

45. George Chauncey, *Gay New York: Gender, Urban Culture, and the Making of the Gay Male World, 1890–1940* (New York: Basic Books, 1994), 12–29; Steven Seidman, *Romantic Longings: Love in America, 1830–1980* (New York: Routledge, 1991), 189; Jonathan Ned Katz, *The Invention of Heterosexuality* (New York: Plume, 1996), 34–43; 181–91.

46. Chauncey, *Gay New York*, 65, 76–86, 95–97, 100–118; Jonathan Ned Katz, *Invention of Heterosexuality*, 55–82.

47. Elizabeth Lunbeck, *The Psychiatric Persuasion: Knowledge, Gender, and Power in Modern America* (Princeton: Princeton University Press, 1994), 244–54.

48. R. P. Knight, "The Psychodynamics of Chronic Alcoholism," *Journal of Nervous and Mental Diseases* 86 (November 1937): 544–45.

49. Jacob Levine, "The Sexual Adjustment of Alcoholics: A Clinical Study of a Selected Sample," *QJSA* 16, no. 4 (December 1955): 675–80. American Freudians borrowed from Karl Abraham's seminal article "The Psychological Relations

between Sexuality and Alcoholism," first published in 1908 and reprinted in the *International Journal of Psycho-Analysis* 7 (January 1926). As Abraham wrote, "When drinking, men fall on each other's necks and kiss one another: they feel that they are united by peculiarly intimate ties and this moves them to tears and to intimate modes of address." Thus, he concluded, "every drinking bout is tinged with homosexuality" (4). On the relationship between alcoholism and homosexuality, see also John W. Crowley, *The White Logic: Alcoholism and Gender in American Modernist Fiction* (Amherst: University of Massachusetts Press, 1994), 148–55.

50. Strecker and Chambers, *Alcohol*, 111.
51. Menninger, *Man against Himself*, 157–59; Jacob Levine, "Sexual Adjustment of Alcoholics," 678; Strecker, "Chronic Alcoholism," 17.
52. Barbara Ehrenreich, *The Hearts of Men: American Dreams and the Flight from Commitment* (New York: Anchor Books, 1983), 14–28.
53. Robert Straus, "Alcohol and the Homeless Man," *QJSA* 7, no. 3 (December 1946): 360–404.
54. Margaret B. Bailey, "Alcoholism and Marriage: A Review of Research and Professional Literature," *QJSA* 22, no. 1 (March 1961): 81–82.
55. Bacon, "Excessive Drinking and the Family," 229.
56. A. J. Murphy, "Alcohol and Pauperism," in *Alcohol, Science, and Society*, 242.
57. Carney Landis, "Theories of the Alcoholic Personality," 132. On alcoholics' career failure and financial irresponsibility, see also Fullam, *Here's to Sobriety*, 173.
58. McCarthy, *Manual of Facts and Fancies*, 58; Haggard and Jellinek, *Alcohol Explored*, 11–12; E. M. Jellinek "Effects of Alcohol on Psychological Functions," in *Alcohol, Science, and Society*, 92.
59. A. J. Murphy, "Alcohol and Pauperism," 246; Jellinek, "Effects of Alcohol," 92.
60. Lunbeck, *Psychiatric Persuasion*, 245.
61. These figures are based on Bruce Johnson's survey of the *Reader's Guide to Periodical Literature* from 1935 to 1970. In contrast, according to another survey of magazine articles, from 1900 to 1919 more than 85 percent of popular articles on the subject of drunkenness treated the problem in terms of moral values, "weakness of character," or the greed of saloonkeepers and liquor manufacturers. See Bruce Holley Johnson, "Alcoholism Movement in America," 133–34.
62. Joseph Hirsh, *The Problem Drinker* (New York: Duell, Sloan and Pearce, 1949), 160.
63. *The Lost Weekend*, produced by Charles Brackett (Paramount, 1945); Philip T. Hartung, "Review of *The Lost Weekend*," *Commonweal*, December 7, 1945, 205–6; John C. McCarten, "Review of *The Lost Weekend*," *New Yorker*, December 1, 1945, 112, cited in Norman K. Denzin, *Hollywood Shot by Shot: Alcoholism in American Cinema* (New York: Aldine de Gruyter, 1991), 3, 53. As defined by Denzin, "alcoholism film" refers to a movie "in which the inebriety, alcoholism, and excessive drinking of one or more of the major characters is presented as a problem which the character, his or her friends, family, and employers, and other members of society self-consciously struggle to resolve" (3).

64. As John Crowley notes, the film's ending differs from that of Charles Jackson's original narrative. Although the screenplay is generally faithful to the novel, the film's optimistic "Hollywood ending"—written by Jackson himself at the request of director Billy Wilder—reveals the pressure the producers felt to provide an upbeat ending to an otherwise grim story. "Whereas the novel closes darkly, with Birnam ready for another bender, the movie ends happily as Don suddenly gives up the booze and starts to work on the novel that his drunkenness has blocked for years" (Crowley, *White Logic*, 190).
65. Malcolm Lowry's novel *Under the Volcano* (New York: Reynal and Hitchcock, 1947) itself is a classic work in the literature on alcoholism.
66. Crowley, *White Logic*, 143–55.
67. Selden Bacon, preface to *The Lost Weekend*, Time Reading Program Special Edition (New York: Time, 1963), xv, cited in Crowley, *White Logic*, 191.
68. Review of *The Lost Weekend*, *Newsweek*, December 10, 1945, 112–15, cited in Denzin, *Hollywood Shot by Shot*, 53.
69. Daniel Brower, "An Opinion Poll on Reactions to *The Lost Weekend*," *QJSA* 1, no. 1 (March 1946): 596–98.
70. Blocker, *American Temperance Movements*, 142–43.
71. On the relationship between alcohol and the "new middle class," see Bruce Holley Johnson, "Alcoholism Movement in America," 167–83.
72. Ibid., 183.
73. "Drinking Increasing during World War II," *Louisville Times*, March 9, 1944.
74. See, for example, a relevant article in the *New York Times*, March 20, 1945, and "The Alcoholic Veteran," *Newsweek*, February 23, 1948, 44–45.
75. Hirsh, *Problem Drinker*, 97–100.
76. William M. Tuttle Jr., *"Daddy's Gone to War": The Second World War in the Lives of America's Children* (New York: Oxford University Press, 1993), 218–19.
77. Graebner, *Age of Doubt*, 41–45.
78. *The Best Years of Our Lives*, produced by Samuel Goldwyn (Metro Goldwyn Mayer, 1946); David A. Gerber, "Heroes and Misfits: The Troubled Social Reintegration of Disabled Veterans in *The Best Years of Our Lives*," *American Quarterly* 46 (December 1994): 571.
79. Gerber, "Heroes and Misfits," 545–46, 555.
80. Ibid.; Kaja Silverman, *Male Subjectivity at the Margins* (New York: Routledge, 1992), 65–90.
81. Gerber, "Heroes and Misfits," 546. Silverman, *Male Subjectivity*, 87, reads the film's ending differently, employing psychoanalytic film theory to argue that Homer and Wilma's union further dramatizes male castration "rather than affirming the cultural order." While it is true that the film forces viewers to dwell on the "severely denaturalized spectacle" of Homer's metal hook against Wilma's flesh—an image hardly consistent with traditional wedding sentiment—I agree with Gerber that the film ultimately affirms marriage as an institution that might contain (if not completely eradicate) viewers' anxieties about male disempowerment.
82. Gerber, "Heroes and Misfits," 551–52.

83. Ibid., 561.

84. Ibid., 265–66.

85. Susan M. Hartmann, "Prescriptions for Penelope: Literature on Women's Obligations to Returning World War II Veterans," *Women's Studies* 5 (1978): 223–39.

86. Gerber, "Heroes and Misfits," 566–67.

87. The screenplay of *Best Years* was based loosely on a novel written by MacKinlay Kantor titled *Glory for Me* (1945). The novel, however, offered a more biting social criticism that film producer Samuel Goldwyn refused to translate onto the screen. In the book version Al leaves the bank for a career in landscape gardening, a trade he finds more personally rewarding. He also experiences an ideological conversion from Republican conservatism to New Deal liberalism. See Gerber, "Heroes and Misfits," 545–54.

88. Gerber, "Heroes and Misfits," 554.

89. William Leach, *Land of Desire: Merchants, Power, and the Rise of a New American Culture* (New York: Pantheon, 1993), 10–11.

90. "Alcoholics Anonymous and the Advertising Man," *Printer's Ink*, September 14, 1945, 98.

91. *An Alcoholic to His Sons*, as told to Henry Beetle Hough (New York: Simon and Schuster, 1954), 63; Eliot Taintor [Ruth Fitch Mason and Gregory Mason], *September Remember* (New York: Prentice Hall, 1945), 148.

92. Bacon, "Alcohol and Complex Society," 89–90.

93. Max Gunther, "Alcohol and Your Job: Do They Mix?," *True*, July 1970, 54, cited in Bruce Holley Johnson, "Alcoholism Movement in America," 182.

94. I borrow the term "emotion management" from sociologist Arlie Hochschild, who offers a compelling theory about how people create a show of feeling through bodily display and verbal communication. In her definition emotion management "requires one to induce or suppress feeling in order to sustain the outward countenance that produces the proper state of mind in others." See *The Managed Heart: Commercialization of Human Feeling* (Berkeley: University of California Press, 1983), 1–75 (quote on 7).

95. In one of the few critical film reviews at the time, *Partisan Review* contributor Robert Warshow argued that *Best Years* was premised on fundamental "falsehood" that denied "the reality of politics, if politics means the existence of real incompatibilities of interest and real *social* problems not susceptible of individual solution." The 1947 review, titled "Anatomy of a Falsehood," is reprinted in Warshow, *The Immediate Experience: Movies, Comics, Theater, and Other Aspects of Popular Culture* (Garden City, N.Y.: 1962), 155–61 (quote on 158).

96. Margaret B. Bailey, "Alcoholism and Marriage," 81–84.

CHAPTER THREE

1. Throughout this chapter I often refer to Wilson and Smith as Bill W. and Dr. Bob, which reflects the way they presented themselves to the public and within the AA movement. Although the cofounders' identities have long been disclosed,

most other early AA members maintained their anonymity, a practice central to the group's philosophy. Out of respect for their anonymity, I refer to other AA members by pseudonyms or by their first names and last initials only.

2. *AA*, 192 (emphasis in original).

3. Jack S. Blocker Jr., *American Temperance Movements: Cycles of Reform* (Boston: Twayne, 1989); Klaus Makela et al., *Alcoholics Anonymous as a Mutual-Help Movement: A Study in Eight Societies* (Madison: University of Wisconsin Press, 1996), 8–13; Alfred H. Katz and Eugene I. Bender, *The Strength in Us: Self-Help Groups in the Modern World* (New York: Franklin Watts, 1976); Edward Sagarin, *Odd Man In: Societies of Deviants in America* (Chicago: Quadrangle Books, 1969); Hans Toch, *The Social Psychology of Social Movements* (Indianapolis: Bobbs-Merrill, 1965).

4. As early as 1948 sociologists regarded the Twelve Steps as the "ideology of the movement." Oscar W. Ritchie, for example, described the steps as a "unifying force which gives direction to [AA's] growth and development. They furnish A.A. with its philosophy and set of values." See Ritchie, "A Sociohistorical Survey of Alcoholics Anonymous," *QJSA* 9, no. 1 (1948): 119–56 (quote on 120).

5. AA's foremost historian, Ernest Kurtz, discusses the central notion of dependence in AA ideology in *Not God: A History of Alcoholics Anonymous* (Center City, Minn.: Hazelden, 1979), esp. 204–19. The Twelve Steps are printed in almost all AA books and pamphlets and have been analyzed in many other sources, including Paul Antze, "Symbolic Action in Alcoholics Anonymous," in *Constructive Drinking: Perspectives on Drink From Anthropology*, ed. Mary Douglas (Cambridge: Cambridge University Press, 1987), 149–81, and Norman K. Denzin, *The Recovering Alcoholic* (Newbury Park, Calif.: Sage, 1987).

6. Such tactics would not have appealed to Wilson, Smith, and others of their generation in the first place, given their rejection of evangelical temperance ideology decades earlier.

7. On the limits of medical treatment for inebriates before and after Prohibition, see Blocker, *American Temperance Movements*, 139–44; Jim Baumohl and Robin Room, "Inebriety, Doctors, and the State: Alcoholism Treatment Institutions before 1940," in *Recent Developments in Alcoholism*, ed. Marc Galanter, vol. 5 (New York: Plenum, 1987), 135–74; and Sarah W. Tracy, "Therapeutic and Civic Ideals in the Rehabilitation of Inebriates: The Evolution of State Hospital Care for Habitual Drunkards in Massachusetts, 1890–1920" (paper delivered at the conference "Historical Perspectives on Alcohol and Drug Use in American Society," College of Physicians and Surgeons, May 1997), in author's possession.

8. Blocker, *American Temperance Movements*, 132.

9. Jack Alexander, "Alcoholics Anonymous: Freed Slaves of Drink, Now They Free Others," *Saturday Evening Post*, March 1, 1941, 9–11. See also Genevieve Parkhurst, "Laymen and Alcoholics," *Harper's*, September 1941, 422–29.

10. These approximate membership figures are from Makela et al., *Alcoholics Anonymous as a Mutual-Help Movement*, 22–23, and *AACOA*, vii–ix. *AACOA*, written in large part by Bill Wilson as the fellowship's first institutional history, includes many of the speeches delivered at the 1955 St. Louis convention.

11. Susan Sontag, *Illness as Metaphor* (New York: Farrar, Straus and Giroux, 1978); Kurtz, *Not God*, 199–204.

12. For a comprehensive bibliography of over 2,500 documents related to the fellowship, see Charlie Bishop Jr. and Bill Pittman, *To Be Continued . . . The Alcoholics Anonymous World Bibliography* (Wheeling, W.Va.: Bishop of Books, 1994).

13. Although it is not my aim to assess debates about the success rate of AA as a treatment method, it is worth mentioning that the fellowship has had detractors as well as supporters. In 1969, for example, Edward Sagarin argued that because AA did not publish records about members' rates of recidivism, many of its claims were of "doubtful validity" (*Odd Man In*, 45). He speculated that AA had a success rate of only 50 percent, a statistic that other critics would find even too generous. Yet despite such criticisms, AA has enjoyed tremendous influence and is seen by many as the best solution to problem drinking. Even recent critics, such as Stanton Peele in *The Diseasing of America: Addiction Treatment out of Control* (Lexington, Mass.: Lexington Books, 1989) and Wendy Kaminer in *"I'm Dysfunctional, You're Dysfunctional": The Recovery Movement and Other Self-Help Fashions* (New York: Vintage, 1993) acknowledge the widespread acceptance of AA. For a summary of the criticism aimed at AA since its inception, see William L. White, *Slaying the Dragon: The History of Addiction Treatment and Recovery in America* (Bloomington, Ill.: Chestnut Health Systems, 1998), 156–58.

14. Joel Pfister and Nancy Schnog, eds., *Inventing the Psychological: Toward a Cultural History of Emotional Life in America* (New Haven: Yale University Press, 1997), 3–14, 42.

15. Elayne Rapping, *The Culture of Recovery: Making Sense of the Self-Help Movement in Women's Lives* (Boston: Beacon Press, 1996), 73.

16. Robin Room, "Alcoholism and Alcoholics Anonymous in U.S. Films, 1945–1962: The Party Ends for the 'Wet Generations,'" *Journal of Studies on Alcohol* 50, no. 4 (1989): 368–81. For another approach to generational rebellion among hard-drinking writers, see Ann Douglas, *Terrible Honesty: Mongrel Manhattan in the 1920s* (New York: Farrar, Straus and Giroux, 1995).

17. Room, "Alcoholism and Alcoholics Anonymous in U.S. Films," 368–81.

18. Elizabeth Lunbeck, *The Psychiatric Persuasion: Knowledge, Gender, and Power in Modern America* (Princeton: Princeton University Press, 1994), 229–31; Nancy F. Cott, "On Men's History and Women's History," in *Meanings for Manhood: Constructions of Masculinity in Victorian America*, ed. Mark C. Carnes and Clyde Griffen (Chicago: University of Chicago Press, 1990), 206.

19. Gail Bederman, *Manliness and Civilization: A Cultural History of Gender and Race in the United States, 1880–1917* (Chicago: University of Chicago Press, 1995), 5–8; Mariana Valverde, "Comment," in "Dialogue: Gender History/Women's History: Is Feminist Scholarship Losing Its Critical Edge?," *Journal of Women's History* 5 (spring 1993): 123; Joan W. Scott, "Gender: A Useful Category of Analysis," in *Gender and the Politics of History* (New York: Columbia University Press, 1989), and "Deconstructing Equality-versus-Difference; Or, the Uses of Poststructuralist Theory for Feminism," *Feminist Studies* 14 (spring 1988): 33–50;

Teresa de Lauretis, *Technologies of Gender: Essays on Theory, Film, and Fiction* (Bloomington: University of Indiana Press, 1987), 1–30.

20. Clyde Griffen, "Reconstructing Masculinity from the Evangelical Revival to the Waning of Progressivism: A Speculative Synthesis," in Carnes and Griffen, *Meanings for Manhood*, 201–3.

21. The fellowship manifested striking diversity in terms of the demographic composition, organizational procedures, and social experiences of local groups. Even if one aimed to reconstruct AA's social history based on archival research, this would be a challenging project indeed. AA's reliance on word-of-mouth attraction at the grassroots level, its emphasis on spoken narratives, and its commitment to anonymity mean that demographic information and transcriptions of meetings are scarce. Moreover, unfettered access to AA's national archives in New York City would be necessary for a thorough social history—a scholarly privilege that I did not enjoy during the course of my research.

22. While central texts such as *AA* (also known as the Big Book) and *AACOA* were written primarily by Bill Wilson and a small group of other early members, other sources, including the newsletter the *Grapevine*, represented a wider array of alcoholics' voices. However, the views of habitual drinkers *outside* AA in the mid-twentieth century remain to be explored.

23. On how gendered discourses allow for "human agency and the possibility of intentional change," see Bederman, *Manliness and Civilization*, 24.

24. Wally P. is an independent historian who has documented many aspects of the fellowship's early history; see his *But, for the Grace of God... How Intergroups and Central Offices Carried the Message of Alcoholics Anonymous in the 1940s* (Wheeling, W.Va.: Bishop of Books, 1995).

25. Ibid., 47–49, 154–56; Charles C. Hewitt, "A Personality Study of Alcohol Addiction," *QJSA* 4, no. 3 (December 1943): 368–86; "Alcoholics Anonymous: A Uniquely American Phenomenon," *Fortune*, February 1951, 99–100, 138, 141–42, 144.

26. The *Washington Star* articles are reprinted in Charles E. Schamel, *The Washington Group: Foundations, 1936–1941* (Washington, D.C.: Washington Intergroup Association, 1995), 93–103. References to AA as a fraternity or brotherhood can be found in Press Clippings Scrapbooks, AA Archives, New York, N.Y., including an article from the *St. Louis Star Times* in 1940 (vol. 1939–42, p. 6b) and a clipping from an unnamed paper in Dayton, Ohio, in 1942 (vol. 1939–42, p. 19f). The 1941 *San Francisco News* article, by Arthur Caylor, is cited in Wally P., *But, for the Grace of God*, 172.

27. New York sociologist Irving Peter Gellman wrote that "the female A.A. is highly regarded and pursues many activities in the organization"; see his *The Sober Alcoholic: An Organizational Analysis of Alcoholics Anonymous* (New Haven: College and University Press, 1964), 77–79. Yet Gellman's study was published during a time when AA was starting to become more gender inclusive nationwide; also, New York City's size and diversity make it an exceptional case to begin with.

28. *AA*, viii. One of Bill Wilson's recent biographers writes that "Bill certainly had his

male chauvinist side, yet he worked to open the AA franchise to women virtually from AA's inception, and he encouraged women to hold executive positions in AA" (Francis Hartigan, *Bill W.: A Biography of Alcoholics Anonymous Cofounder Bill Wilson* [New York: St. Martin's Press, 2000], 8).

29. Michelle Lee McClellan, "Lady Lushes: Women Alcoholics and American Society, 1880–1960" (Ph.D. diss., Stanford University, 1999), 243–46.

30. *Dr. Bob and the Good Old-timers: A Biography, with Recollections of Early AA in the Midwest* (New York: AA World Services, 1980), 241–43; Mary C. Darrah, *Sister Ignatia: Angel of Alcoholics Anonymous* (Chicago: Loyola University Press, 1992), 122–23.

31. *Dr. Bob and the Good Old-timers*, 135–36. The heterosexual bias of this assumption is obvious; Dr. Bob and like-minded members did not seem to consider the possibility of sexual attraction between men or between women. The ideology and rituals of "twelfth-step" interaction are discussed in more detail below.

32. For a thorough account of the experiences of women in the early decades of AA, see McClellan, "Lady Lushes," 247–90.

33. "Are Women the Orphans of AA?," *Grapevine*, April 1953.

34. *AA*, vi, 217, 264.

35. Kurtz, *Not God*, 132.

36. "Who Is a Member of Alcoholics Anonymous," *Grapevine*, August 1946, reprinted in *The Language of the Heart: Bill W.'s Grapevine Writings* (New York: AA Grapevine, 1988), 37; "Do You Yearn For Fellowship?," *Grapevine*, October 1947; Thomas Fullam [pseud.], *Here's to Sobriety: A Plain Approach to Understanding the Compulsive Drinker and His Problems* (New York: Abelard Press, 1950), 190–99.

37. Ritchie, "Sociohistorical Survey of Alcoholics Anonymous," 132–35.

38. *AACOA*, 199.

39. *AA*, vii; Charles C. Hewitt, "Personality Study of Alcohol Addiction," 383–86; Bill C., "The Growth and Effectiveness of Alcoholics Anonymous in a Southwestern City, 1945–1962," *QJSA* 26, no. 2 (June 1965): 279–84.

40. Ritchie, "Sociohistorical Survey of Alcoholics Anonymous," 135; Schamel, *Washington Group*, 65–66.

41. White, *Slaying the Dragon*, 160–61.

42. Kurtz, *Not God*, 148–49, 304–5.

43. Letter from Bill Wilson to Dr. Conrad S., 18 July 1938, quoted in Kurtz, *Not God*, 304; undated article in *Sales Management* magazine, Press Clippings Scrapbooks, vol. 1943, AA Archives, 27.

44. White, *Slaying the Dragon*, 159, makes a similar argument: "When critics say that AA's program was designed primarily on the experience of white men, they are correct. But that fact, in and of itself, does not mean that AA's program did not work for women and people of color who later entered AA."

45. Kurtz, *Not God*, 132–33.

46. Matthew J. Raphael, *Bill W. and Mr. Wilson: The Legend and Life of A.A.'s Cofounder* (Amherst: University of Massachusetts Press, 2000), 154.

47. Charles C. Hewitt, "Personality Study of Alcohol Addiction," 383–86; Selden D. Bacon, "A Sociologist Looks at A.A.," *Proceedings of the First Annual Alberta*

Conference on Alcohol Studies (Edmonton: Alcoholism Foundation of Alberta, 1954), 71–72.

48. "Do You Yearn for Fellowship?"; Press Clippings Scrapbooks, vol. 1943, AA Archives.

49. "Charles Jackson Speaks at Hartford AA," *Grapevine*, June 1945.

50. *Grapevine*, January 1945; undated memorandum, "AA Clubs" file, AA Archives; *Language of the Heart*, 46–50.

51. *Grapevine*, September, February 1951.

52. Milton A. Maxwell, "Alcoholics Anonymous: An Interpretation," in *Society, Culture, and Drinking Patterns*, ed. David J. Pittman and Charles R. Snyder (New York: John Wiley and Sons, 1962), 577–85.

53. "A.A. Luncheons Build Morale," *Grapevine*, July 1944.

54. "A.A. Meetings Seem More Social Than A.A.," *Grapevine*, July 1948.

55. Blocker, *American Temperance Movements*, 40–47; Mark Edward Lender and James Kirby Martin, *Drinking in America: A History* (New York: Free Press, 1987), 74–79; Milton A. Maxwell, "The Washingtonian Movement," *QJSA* 11, no. 3 (September 1950): 410–51; Ian Tyrrell, *Sobering Up: From Temperance to Prohibition in Antebellum America, 1800–1860* (Westport, Conn.: Greenwood Press, 1979); Leonard U. Blumberg (with William Pittman), *Beware the First Drink! The Washington Temperance Movement and Alcoholics Anonymous* (Seattle: Glen Abbey, 1991); Katherine A. Chavigny, "Reforming Drunkards in Nineteenth-Century America: A Religious Therapeutic Tradition" (paper delivered at the conference "Historical Perspectives on Alcohol and Drug Use in American Society," College of Physicians and Surgeons, May 1997), in author's possession.

56. Kurtz, *Not God*, 197–98; Antze, "Symbolic Action in Alcoholics Anonymous," 149–81; Raphael, *Bill W. and Mr. Wilson*, 67–73.

57. Blocker, *American Temperance Movements*, 139–40; *AACOA*, 39, 64–68.

58. *AA*, 101; *AACOA*, 161–67 (emphases in original).

59. Lewis Hyde, *The Gift: Imagination and the Erotic Life of Property* (New York: Vintage, 1979), xi–xvii, 56–69.

60. Ibid., 45–73. Edmund B. O'Reilly, *Sobering Tales: Narratives of Alcoholism and Recovery* (Amherst: University of Massachusetts Press, 1997), 27–28, briefly discusses AA in relation to gift exchange.

61. Hyde, *Gift*, 11–24.

62. *AACOA*, 70 (emphasis in original).

63. Father John Doe [pseud.], *Sobriety and Beyond* (Indianapolis: SMT Publishing, 1955), 313–39.

64. Joseph Kessell, *The Road Back: A Report on Alcoholics Anonymous*, trans. Frances Partridge (New York: Knopf, 1962), 98 (emphasis added).

65. Quoted in Wally P., *But, for the Grace of God*, 188.

66. Doe, *Sobriety and Beyond*, 346.

67. Bacon, "Sociologist Looks at A.A.," 71.

68. Room, "Alcoholism and Alcoholics Anonymous in U.S. Films," 368–70.

69. *The Voice in the Mirror*, produced by Gordon Kay (Universal-International, 1958); *Come Back, Little Sheba*, produced by Hal B. Wallis (Paramount, 1952); *Come Fill*

the Cup, produced by Henry Blanke (Warner, 1951). On these and other alcoholism films from 1945 to 1962, see Room, "Alcoholism and Alcoholics Anonymous in U.S. Films," 368–83. The bonds forged among "drunks helping drunks" are portrayed in these films as platonic and therapeutic, with few hints of homosexual attraction. In *The Voice in the Mirror* and *Come Back, Little Sheba*, the male alcoholics are married; in the latter the unhappily wed Doc Delaney longs for sexual contact with an attractive female student who takes room and board in his home. *Come Fill the Cup* presents Lew and Charlie's residence as a "bachelor apartment"; Lew's undying attraction to Paula marks him as "safely" heterosexual and shows that AA relationships pose no threat to his masculinity. If any character depicts the psychiatric persona of the effeminate alcoholic, it is Boyd, the son of Lew's wealthy publisher-boss and Paula's new husband. A struggling musician stifled by his overbearing mother, Boyd is passive and demasculinized, but Lew's attempt to help him recover is not coded in homoerotic terms. In documents produced by and about AA at this time, the possibility of same-sex attractions among members was seldom suggested.

70. Hyde, *Gift*, 8–9.
71. W. J. Rorabaugh, *The Alcoholic Republic: An American Tradition* (New York: Oxford University Press, 1979).
72. Wally P., *But, for the Grace of God*, 198.
73. Antze, "Symbolic Action in Alcoholics Anonymous," 149–81.
74. Room, "Alcoholism and Alcoholics Anonymous in U.S. Films," 372.
75. George E. Willis, *The Bottle Fighters* (New York: Random House, 1963), 289. Unlike many AA writers, Willis published under his real name.
76. Ibid., 280–81.
77. William James, "The Moral Equivalent of War," in *Essays on Faith and Morals* (New York: Longmans, Green, 1943), 323–25 (originally published in 1910 in *McClure's Magazine* and *Popular Science Monthly*); Kim Townsend, *Manhood at Harvard: William James and Others* (New York: Norton, 1996) 11–29, 159–73, 195; George Frederickson, *The Inner Civil War: Northern Intellectuals and the Crisis of the Union* (New York: Harper and Row, 1965); E. Anthony Rotundo, *American Manhood: Transformations in Masculinity from the Revolution to the Modern Era* (New York: Basic Books, 1993), 232–44; Bederman, *Manliness and Civilization*, 184–96.
78. Wally P., *But, for the Grace of God*, 178–80.
79. Robert Thomsen, *Bill W.* (New York: Harper and Row, 1975), 114–47; *AA*, 10–11; Kessel, *Road Back*, 88.
80. Wilson briefly mentioned his time at Plattsburgh in his autobiographical contribution to the Big Book: "War fever ran high in the New England town to which we new, young officers from Plattsburgh were assigned" (*AA*, 10). See also "The Plattsburgh Idea," *New Republic*, October 9, 1915, 247–49, and Thomsen, *Bill W.*, 101–2.
81. *Grapevine*, September 1945, April 1946.
82. Undated flyer in Press Clippings Scrapbooks, vol. 1939–42, AA Archives. The location and date of the flyer is not available, but it appears midway in the

chronologically organized scrapbook on pages covering February and March 1942.

83. O'Reilly, *Sobering Tales*, 103–96; see also Edmund B. O'Reilly, "Bill's Story: Form and Meaning in A.A. Recovery Narratives," in *The Serpent in the Cup: Temperance in American Literature*, ed. David S. Reynolds and Debra J. Rosenthal (Amherst: University of Massachusetts Press, 1997), 180.

84. O'Reilly, *Sobering Tales*, 107.

85. Mary Martha Murphy, "Values Stressed by Two Social Class Levels at Meetings of Alcoholics Anonymous," *QJSA* 14, no. 4 (December 1953): 576–85.

86. Joseph Hirsh, *The Problem Drinker* (New York: Duell, Sloan and Pearce, 1949), 124; Robert Freed Bales, "The Therapeutic Role of Alcoholics Anonymous as Seen by a Sociologist," *QJSA* 5 (1944): 267–78.

87. Undated *Grapevine* article in "Clubs" correspondence file, AA Archives. I estimate that the article appeared sometime in the late 1940s or early 1950s.

88. "We Too Are Alcoholics," *Grapevine*, February 1956.

89. *AA*, 249–51.

90. *AA*, 295, 323.

91. *An Alcoholic to His Sons*, as told to Henry Beetle Hough (New York: Simon and Schuster, 1954), 54, 61, 221, 238–39.

92. *AA*, 274–79. The author of this story was Clarence Snyder, founder of the third AA group in Cleveland and a rival for AA leadership with Bill W. and Dr. Bob.

93. *AA*, 280–81.

94. *AA*, 25; *AACOA*, 111.

95. Doe, *Sobriety and Beyond*, 112–13.

96. Jay R. Clancy [pseud.], *Clancy Got Well* (Des Moines, Iowa: McGreevey, 1951), 81–82, 145–46.

97. Hugh Reilly [pseud.] *Easy Does It: The Story of Mac* (New York: P. J. Kenedy, 1950), 145–46.

98. William Graebner, *The Age of Doubt: American Thought and Culture in the 1940s* (Boston: Twayne, 1991), 102.

CHAPTER FOUR

1. I use the term "experts" loosely here to refer to social workers and academic researchers as well as the lay experts of AA and Al-Anon. While AA members did not think of themselves as experts, they relied on their own personal experiences and convictions to help others cope with their common affliction.

2. Cited in William L. White, *Slaying the Dragon: The History of Addiction Treatment and Recovery in America* (Bloomington, Ill.: Chestnut Health Systems, 1998), 40.

3. On the division of labor between psychiatrists and social workers, I have consulted an unpublished manuscript by Nancy J. Tomes, "The Rise of the Mental Health Professions in the United States, 1900–1970" (in author's possession). For a nuanced analysis of the emergence of social work (and the gender politics that

ensued within the psychiatric realm), see Elizabeth Lunbeck, *The Psychiatric Persuasion: Knowledge, Gender, and Power in Modern America* (Princeton: Princeton University Press, 1994), 35–45.

4. E. E. Southard and Mary C. Jarrett, *The Kingdom of Evils: Psychiatric Social Work Presented in One Hundred Case Histories Together with a Classification of Social Divisions of Evil* (New York: Macmillan, 1922), 262–67.

5. Jean V. Sapir, "Social Work and Alcoholism," *Annals of the American Academy of Political and Social Science* 315 (January 1958), 128. Sapir was director of psychiatric social service at the Connecticut Commission on Alcoholism.

6. Lunbeck, *Psychiatric Persuasion*, 35–45; Tomes, "Rise of the Mental Health Professions," 1–20.

7. Gladys M. Price, "Why I Want a Professional Social Worker on My Clinic Staff," in *Selected Papers from the Sixth Annual Meeting of the National States' Conference on Alcoholism* (Portland, Ore., 1956), 27–31.

8. Margaret L. Lewis, "The Initial Contact with Wives of Alcoholics," *Social Casework* 35, no. 1 (January 1954): 8–14.

9. Sapir, "Social Work and Alcoholism," 129.

10. Margaret B. Bailey, "Alcoholism and Marriage: A Review of Research and Professional Literature," *QJSA*, 22, no. 1 (March 1961): 81–94.

11. Gladys M. Price, "A Study of the Wives of Twenty Alcoholics," *QJSA* 5, no. 4 (March 1945): 623.

12. M. H. Boggs, "The Rise of Social Work in the Treatment of Inebriates," *QJSA* 4, no. 4 (March 1944): 557–67.

13. Samuel Futterman, "Personality Trends in Wives of Alcoholics," *Journal of Psychiatric Social Work* 23 (1953): 37–41.

14. Thelma Whalen, "Wives of Alcoholics: Four Types Observed in a Family Service Agency," *QJSA* 14, no. 4 (December 1953): 632–40.

15. Ibid.

16. On this point, see Margaret B. Bailey, "Alcoholism and Marriage," 81–94.

17. Whalen, "Wives of Alcoholics," 640. There is no evidence that alcoholism experts read Philip Wylie's *Generation of Vipers* (New York: Holt, Rinehart and Winston, 1942), but the cultural trend of Momism was pervasive in the postwar period, striking a nerve among producers of popular culture. Thus most experts were probably exposed to anxious representations of female dominance and masculine weakness even if they did not read Wylie's work.

18. Linda Gordon, *Heroes of Their Own Lives: The Politics and History of Family Violence, Boston, 1880–1960* (New York: Viking, 1988), 208, 280–84; Elizabeth Pleck, *Domestic Tyranny: The Making of Social Policy against Family Violence from Colonial Times to the Present* (New York: Oxford University Press, 1987), 145–63.

19. Sybil M. Baker, "Social Case Work with Inebriates," in *Alcohol, Science, and Society: Twenty-nine Lectures with Discussions as Given at the Yale Summer School of Alcohol Studies* (New Haven: Quarterly Journal of Studies on Alcohol, 1945), 420–21.

20. Joan K. Jackson, personal correspondence with author, June 1997.

21. Joan K. Jackson, "The Adjustment of the Family to the Crisis of Alcoholism," *QJSA* 15, no. 4 (December 1954): 562–86.

22. No doubt Jackson came to this interpretation in part because the women she observed described their situation in strikingly gendered terms *themselves*. Jackson's aim was to record the actual thoughts and behavior of women, not to offer her own abstract theory. But as with any study, the researcher's own assumptions and biases influenced the resulting interpretation. Sociological studies reveal much about the beliefs and actions of "ordinary" people in the past, but only as they were filtered through the interpretive lens of the observer.

23. Ibid., 567–75. All quotations are taken from Jackson's article in the *QJSA*, but she published similar studies in various books and journals, including a special issue on alcoholism in *Annals of the American Academy of Political and Social Sciences* 315 (January 1958): 90–98; *Marriage and Family Living*, 18 (1956): 361–369; and David J. Pittman and Charles R. Snyder, eds., *Society, Culture, and Drinking Patterns* (New York: John Wiley and Sons, 1962).

24. Jackson, "Adjustment of the Family to the Crisis of Alcoholism," 575–82. Psychiatrist Ruth Fox, who became medical director of the National Council on Alcoholism, also described the situation of the alcoholic family in terms of gender reversal: "In many homes the father may indeed have become 'the forgotten man'; mother may have become the ruler of the household. She seems strong, self-reliant and aggressive. Actually she may be unconsciously disappointed that she can no longer lean on her husband for authority and shared responsibility. . . . Unwittingly she may be losing her femininity just as her husband may be losing his masculinity." Quoted in *Living with an Alcoholic with the Help of Al-Anon* (New York: Al-Anon Family Group Headquarters, 1966), 19.

25. Whalen, "Wives of Alcoholics," 641; Jackson, "Adjustment of the Family to the Crisis of Alcoholism," 569–77.

26. Sapir, "Social Work and Alcoholism," 125–32.

27. Experts and commentators from various professional and theoretical backgrounds—not to mention producers of popular culture—shared such assumptions. For a useful overview of postwar family sociology, see Wini Breines, *Young, White, and Miserable: Growing Up Female in the Fifties* (Boston: Beacon Press, 1992), 25–46.

28. Mariana Valverde, "Comment," in "Dialogue: Gender History/Women's History: Is Feminist Scholarship Losing Its Critical Edge?," *Journal of Women's History* 5 (spring 1993): 123.

29. Nancy F. Cott, "Giving Character to Our Whole Civil Polity: Marriage and the Public Order in the Late Nineteenth Century," in *U.S. History as Women's History: New Feminist Essays*, ed. Linda K. Kerber, Alice Kessler-Harris, and Kathryn Kish Sklar (Chapel Hill: University of North Carolina Press, 1995), 111.

30. Price, "Study of the Wives," 623.

31. In 1956, for example, a group of psychiatrists published "Group Therapy of Alcoholics with Concurrent Group Meetings of Their Wives," *QJSA* 17, no. 4 (December 1956): 655–70. Group therapy actually began as a form of marriage

counseling in the 1930s; it mushroomed during World War II due to a shortage of trained therapists for distressed soldiers. After the war it was applied to a broader range of psychological problems, including alcoholism. See Hillel Schwartz, *Never Satisfied: A Cultural History of Diets, Fantasies, and Fat* (New York: Free Press, 1986), 202–6.

32. Although the spouses' groups acquired the name Al-Anon Family Groups in 1951, many local groups continued to use their earlier names, including Seattle's Auxiliary.

33. Sapir, "Social Work and Alcoholism," 129.

34. I do not mean to inscribe a rigid separation between professional/medical authorities and the lay experts of AA and Al-Anon. There was much cross-fertilization of ideas among physicians, social workers, AA founders, and public health advocates. Many individuals were involved in several institutions, including research centers, hospitals, the National Committee for Education on Alcoholism, and AA. It is not my purpose to uncover the linkages and divisions among these organizations or to compare the relative cultural authority wielded by AA versus other agencies. In any case, most Americans were unaware of these internal connections.

35. Mary C. Darrah, *Sister Ignatia: Angel of Alcoholics Anonymous* (Chicago: Loyola University Press, 1992), 116–17.

36. For a general history of Al-Anon written from the perspective of the organization itself, see *First Steps: Al-Anon . . . Thirty-five Years of Beginnings* (New York: Al-Anon Family Group Headquarters, 1986).

37. *AACOA*, 114–15.

38. Undated memorandum, file 9.4, Al-Anon Family Groups Archives, Virginia Beach, Va.

39. "The Family Group of Alcoholics Anonymous," file D 1.6, Al-Anon Archives.

40. *AACOA*, 33.

41. *First Steps*, 64.

42. Cyril Louth, *But for the Grace of God* (New York: Pageant Press, 1956), 107.

43. Correspondence files of Lois Wilson and the Al-Anon Headquarters, file 9.4, 1.10, Al-Anon Archives.

44. Ibid.

45. *First Steps*, 44–64.

46. Memorandum of the Policy Session on Family Groups, Report of the Second General Service Conference of AA, April 1952, reproduced in ibid., 62.

47. *AACOA*, 32–34, 42–47, 97–98.

48. *First Steps*, 87–98, 138–48.

49. *Al-Anon Family Groups* (New York: Al-Anon Family Groups Publications, 1955), 102–3. The Al-Anon Archives in Virginia Beach houses many files of personal sharings typed or handwritten by members from various locales. Thus while members often shared their stories extemporaneously, others prepared their remarks in advance (as suggested in the description of the Personal Story Meeting noted previously).

50. On the intermixing of history and personal narrative in AA, see Norman K.

Denzin, *Hollywood Shot by Shot: Alcoholism in American Cinema* (New York: Aldine de Gruyter, 1991), 228–32.

51. Darrah, *Sister Ignatia*, 127–31.

52. Obituary of Anne Smith, reprinted in *First Steps*, 12.

53. *Lois Remembers: Memoirs of the Co-founder of Al-Anon and the Wife of the Co-founder of Alcoholics Anonymous* (New York: Al-Anon Family Group Headquarters, 1979), 77–80.

54. This is not to suggest that wives in the nineteenth and early twentieth centuries never stayed married to drinking husbands (whether due to love, social custom, economic necessity, an ideological commitment to marriage, or some combination of these factors). My focus, rather, is on the difference between popular norms that gained influence in each era and how those norms affected social and familial responses to chronic drunkenness.

55. *AA*, 117.

56. *Lois Remembers*, 114.

57. On Wilson's "ventriloquism" in writing these chapters in Lois's guise, see also Matthew J. Raphael, *Bill W. and Mr. Wilson: The Legend and Life of A.A.'s Co-founder* (Amherst: University of Massachusetts Press, 2000), 119–20, 128.

58. *Grapevine*, December, April 1948, February 1949. Each of these letters was written by a female spouse. Before Al-Anon launched a newsletter of its own, the *Grapevine* provided a limited outlet for wives to voice their opinions. That the editors of AA's newsletter printed letters from wives suggests their support of the wives' views (although it is impossible to know what letters they elected *not* to publish).

59. *AACOA*, 34.

60. Arlie Hochschild, *The Managed Heart: Commercialization of Human Feeling* (Berkeley: University of California Press, 1983), 1–75.

61. *AA*, 130.

62. *Grapevine*, December 1947.

63. Anonymous letter, "Al-Anon" file, AA Archives, New York, N.Y.

64. Undated Al-Anon memorandum by Lois Wilson, reprinted in *First Steps*, 13.

65. *Lois Remembers*, 91–100.

66. As Hochschild points out, the goals of psychologists and institutions (including hospitals, schools, and churches) often entail influencing how people *feel*: "In times of uncertainty, the expert rises to prominence. Authorities on how a situation ought to be viewed are also authorities on how we should feel. . . . In the matter of what to feel, the social bottom usually looks for guidance to the social top. Authority carries with it a certain mandate over feeling rules" (*Managed Heart*, 75). As an institution organized by lay experts, AA strove to promote sobriety in part by schooling participants in specific techniques of emotion management. To understand fully how AA shaped Americans' perceptions and experiences of alcoholism, we need to unravel the emotional system it laid out for members.

67. *AA*, 124.

68. *Long Beach, California, Press-Telegram*, January 8, 1950, Press Clippings Scrapbooks, AA Archives.

69. Dorothy Hunter, "New Help for Alcoholics: Relatives of Habitual Drinkers Have Found a Novel Way of Dealing with Their Problem," *Coronet*, July 1949 (emphasis in original).

70. *AA*, 131–32.

71. *Grapevine*, May 1945.

72. *AA*, 133–32.

73. *Grapevine*, December 1948.

74. Hochschild, *Managed Heart*, 162–65. On other aspects of women's emotion work, see Micaela di Leonardo, "The Female World of Cards and Holidays: Women, Families, and the Work of Kinship," *Signs* 12 (spring 1987): 440–53.

75. *AA*, 133.

76. "The Alcoholic Husband: A Message to Wives," file 9.4, 1.16, Al-Anon Archives, exact date unknown (file dated 1955–61).

77. *Grapevine*, November 1946.

78. Ibid., April 1948. There is more evidence of wives' criticism and even rejection of AA in the postwar period, but it helps to mine sources *not* produced by the fellowship. In *The Cured Alcoholic: New Concepts in Alcoholism Treatment and Research* (New York: John Day, 1964), for example, outspoken AA critic Arthur Cain wrote that while most wives accepted their husbands' participation in AA, some confessed "that eating, sleeping, and talking AA twenty-four hours a day is almost worse than having an alcoholic husband." One Ohio wife explained that while her husband was no longer a "drunk," he had become a "religious fanatic"; she viewed his AA membership as a "terrible mistake" and found it difficult to support his efforts. See Cain, *Cured Alcoholic*, 67, 95–96.

79. *Grapevine*, December 1946.

80. Margaret B. Bailey, "Al-Anon Groups as an Aid to Wives of Alcoholics," *Social Work* 10, no. 1 (January 1965): 68–74.

81. Hugh Reilly [pseud.], *Easy Does It: The Story of Mac* (New York: P. J. Kenedy, 1950), 201–3.

82. "How to Live Happily Ever After—with an Alcoholic," Personal Sharings File 9.4, 1.2, Al-Anon Archives, exact date unknown (file dated 1946–54).

83. "Help for the Alcoholic at Home," ibid.

84. *How to Live with an Alcoholic Husband*, pamphlet produced by the Triple A Family Group, Tucson, Az., 1954, Printed Matter/Literature file D 1.6, Al-Anon Archives.

85. *Al-Anon Family Groups*, 39.

86. For a recent study of middle-class marriage in postwar America, subtle in its treatment of marital roles and responsibilities, see Jessica Weiss, *To Have and to Hold: Marriage, the Baby Boom, and Social Change* (Chicago: University of Chicago Press, 2000), 15–47.

87. Undated form letter, Al-Anon Headquarters Correspondence File, Al-Anon Archives.

88. Harold Maine, "The Alcoholic and His Women," *Ladies Home Journal*, July 1948, 45.

89. "Research Based on Seattle Al-Anon Members," personal papers of Joan K. Jackson, in author's possession.

90. Letter from Lois Wilson to Harold B., Correspondence Files of Lois Wilson, Al-Anon Archives.

91. Anonymous personal sharing, file 9.4, 1958, Al-Anon Archives.

92. Darrah, *Sister Ignatia*, 120–22, 189–90.

93. Elaine Tyler May, *Homeward Bound: American Families in the Cold War Era* (New York: Basic Books, 1988), 4–8, 183–207, 224.

94. David G. Wittels, "The Post Reports on Divorce," *Saturday Evening Post,* January 21, 1950, 20.

95. Weiss, *To Have and to Hold*, 178–88.

96. May, *Homeward Bound*, 183–207, 224.

97. Joanne Meyerowitz, ed., *Not June Cleaver: Women and Gender in Postwar America, 1945–1960* (Philadelphia: Temple University Press, 1994), esp. the editor's introduction and essay "Beyond the Feminine Mystique: A Reassessment of Postwar Mass Culture," 229–62. Meyerowitz has helped to recast our view of the postwar family, arguing that an unrelenting focus on the white, middle-class, suburban family oversimplifies a more complex historical picture. She and others contend that an emphasis on dominant ideals reproduces the marginalization of men and women whose class, race, ethnicity, or sexuality created different yet equally significant experiences and norms. Yet even for individuals who tried to adhere to prevailing ideals, family life often fell short of their expectations. To her credit Elaine Tyler May recognized sources of discontent and rebellion against dominant ideals. In part because my study focuses primarily on couples who fell within the demographic boundaries of the ideal postwar family (at least in terms of race, class, and ethnicity), I have found that idealized prescriptions structured social and cultural responses to the alcoholic family in profound ways.

98. Eva S. Moskowitz, " 'It's Good to Blow Your Top': Women's Magazines and a Discourse of Discontent, 1945–1965," *Journal of Women's History* 8 (fall 1996): 66–98, and *In Therapy We Trust: America's Obsession with Self-Fulfillment* (Baltimore: Johns Hopkins University Press, 2001).

99. Ellen Herman, *The Romance of American Psychology: Political Culture in the Age of Experts* (Berkeley: University of California Press, 1995), 1–15, 238–41.

100. May, *Homeward Bound*, 14, 27.

101. Susan M. Hartmann, "Prescriptions for Penelope: Literature on Women's Obligations to Returning World War II Veterans," *Women's Studies* 5 (1978): 223–39.

102. *Grapevine*, October 1946.

103. For two recent arguments about contemporary self-help culture along these lines, see Elayne Rapping, *The Culture of Recovery: Making Sense of the Self-Help Movement in Women's Lives* (Boston: Beacon Press, 1996), and Wendy Kaminer, *"I'm Dysfunctional, You're Dysfunctional": The Recovery Movement and Other Self-Help Fashions* (New York: Vintage, 1993).

104. For a perceptive discussion of this issue, see feminist psychologist Janice Haaken's brief historical analysis of Al-Anon in "From Al-Anon to ACOA: Codependence and the Reconstruction of Caregiving," *Signs* 18 (winter 1993): 321–45.

105. Ron Roizen, "How Does the Nation's Alcohol Problem Change from Era to Era? Stalking the Social Logic of Problem-Definition Transformations since

Repeal," in *Altering the American Consciousness: Drugs and Alcohol in American Society*, ed. Sarah W. Tracy and Caroline J. Acker (Amherst: University of Amherst Press, forthcoming).

106. Cott, "Giving Character to Our Whole Civil Polity," 107–10, 121.

107. On the legal and political history of marriage in the United States, see Hendrik Hartog, *Man and Wife in America: A History* (Cambridge, Mass.: Harvard University Press, 2000), and Nancy F. Cott, *Public Vows: A History of Marriage and the Nation* (Cambridge, Mass.: Harvard University Press, 2000).

CHAPTER FIVE

1. William Grimes, *Straight Up or On the Rocks: A Cultural History of American Drink* (New York: Simon and Schuster, 1993), 112–19.

2. Georgio Lolli, *Social Drinking: How to Enjoy Drinking without Being Hurt by It* (Cleveland: World Publishing, 1960), 88–89.

3. Ibid., 90.

4. Bernard DeVoto, *The Hour* (Boston: Houghton Mifflin, 1948), 12–13, 28–29, 57, 75–84.

5. Ibid., 51–60.

6. Lolli, *Social Drinking*, 92.

7. Joseph Lanza, *The Cocktail: The Influence of Spirits on the American Psyche* (New York: Picador, 1995), 102–3.

8. Lolli, *Social Drinking*, 15.

9. *An Alcoholic to His Sons*, as told to Henry Beetle Hough (New York: Simon and Schuster, 1954), 237–39.

10. William H. Whyte Jr., *The Organization Man* (New York: Simon and Schuster, 1956); David Riesman, *The Lonely Crowd* (New Haven: Yale University Press, 1950); John Seeley, R. Alexander Sim, and Elizabeth W. Loosley, *Crestwood Heights* (Toronto: University of Toronto Press, 1956). Wini Breines offers a useful summary and analysis of these books in her *Young, White, and Miserable: Growing Up Female in the Fifties* (Boston: Beacon Press, 1992), 25–30.

11. Stanley Rowland, "Suburbia Buys Religion," *Nation*, July 28, 1956, 78–80, cited in James T. Patterson, *Grand Expectations: The United States, 1945–1974* (New York: Oxford University Press, 1996), 338.

12. John W. Riley and Charles F. Marden, "The Social Pattern of Alcoholic Drinking," *QJSA* 8, no. 2 (September 1947): 265–73. This specific demographic drinking trend went hand in hand with the general increase in the per capita consumption of beverage alcohol, which doubled from .97 gallons in 1934 to 2.00 gallons by 1950. (After 1950 the figure rose gradually over the 1960s and 1970s until it began to decline in 1980; the highest figure between 1950 and 1980 was 2.82 gallons.) These statistics are in Mark Edward Lender and James Kirby Martin, *Drinking in America: A History* (New York: Free Press, 1987), 205–6.

13. Whyte, *Organization Man*, 374–77.

14. Seeley, Sim, and Loosley, *Crestwood Heights*, 300–303.

15. Ibid.

16. Ibid.

17. J. Maurice Trimmer, "How to Refuse a Cocktail," *Christian Century*, April 16, 1947, 489–90.

18. *Fortune*, December 1958, 135.

19. Ibid., December 1950, 151.

20. Ibid., 159.

21. DeVoto, *The Hour*, 12–13, 35.

22. *Fortune*, December 1950, 155.

23. *New Yorker*, December 12, 1959, 134; *Fortune*, November 1953, 179.

24. On the postwar consumption boom, see John Patrick Diggins, *The Proud Decades: America in War and Peace, 1941–1960* (New York: Norton, 1988), 178–91, and Thomas Hine, *Populuxe* (New York: Knopf, 1985), 10–17, 129–31.

25. Elaine Tyler May, *Homeward Bound: American Families in the Cold War Era* (New York; Basic Books, 1988), 16, 164–66.

26. *New Yorker*, December 12, 1959, 95.

27. Eva S. Moskowitz, "'It's Good to Blow Your Top': Women's Magazines and a Discourse of Discontent, 1945–1965," *Journal of Women's History* 8 (fall 1996): 66–98.

28. Seeley, Sim, and Loosley, *Crestwood Heights*, 301.

29. Whyte, *Organization Man*, 353.

30. Michelle Lee McClellan, "Lady Lushes: Women Alcoholics and American Society, 1880–1960" (Ph.D. diss., Stanford University, 1999), 230–33.

31. *Alcoholism and Social Drinking: A Report of the National Planning Conference on Alcoholism and Alcohol Education Held at Seabury House, Greenwich, Connecticut* (New York: National Council, 1956), 4, 15.

32. Robert Straus and Selden D. Bacon, *Drinking in College* (New Haven: Yale University Press, 1953), 46–50. The authors found that students in private, non-sectarian colleges drank the most, while students in public vocational colleges, such as teachers' colleges, drank less. They also surveyed students at public "Southern Negro" colleges, where they found relatively low rates among women (40 percent) and slightly lower rates among men than at private (and generally white) campuses.

33. Ibid., 60–75; Raymond G. McCarthy, ed., *Drinking and Intoxication: Selected Readings in Social Attitudes and Controls* (Glencoe, Ill.: Free Press, 1959), 220–30.

34. McCarthy, *Drinking and Intoxication*, 205–18.

35. Seward Hiltner, *It's Up to You* (New York: Association Press, 1947), 10–12. Hiltner was executive secretary of the Commission on Religion and Health of the Federal Council of the Churches of Christ as well as a member of the editorial board of the *QJSA*. In the mid-1940s he led seminars for ministers at the Yale Summer School on Alcohol Studies.

36. On the alcoholism film, see Norman K. Denzin, *Hollywood Shot by Shot: Alcoholism in American Cinema* (New York: Aldine de Gruyter, 1991), and Robin Room, "Alcoholism and Alcoholics Anonymous in U.S. Films, 1945–1962: The Party Ends for the 'Wet Generations,'" *Journal of Studies on Alcohol* 50, no. 4 (1989):

368–81. On the social problem film more generally, see Peter Roffman and Jim Purdy, *The Hollywood Social Problem Film: Madness, Despair, and Politics from the Depression to the Fifties* (Bloomington: Indiana University Press, 1981).

37. Jackie Byars, *All That Hollywood Allows: Re-reading Gender in 1950s Melodrama* (Chapel Hill: University of North Carolina Press, 1991), 112–21.

38. Denzin, *Hollywood Shot by Shot*, 122.

39. *Come Back, Little Sheba*, produced by Hal B. Wallis (Paramount, 1952). Other films revolving around an alcoholic marriage include *The Country Girl* (1954), *Cat on a Hot Tin Roof* (1958), and *Days of Wine and Roses* (1962). For two different analyses of such films, see Denzin, *Hollywood Shot by Shot*, 95–125, and Denise Herd, "Ideology, Melodrama, and the Changing Role of Alcohol Problems in American Films," *Contemporary Drug Problems* 13 (summer 1986): 213–47.

40. Inge's play was first performed in 1949 at a summer theater in Westport, Connecticut, with Shirley Booth cast as Lola and Sidney Blackmer as Doc. The play continued on Broadway; by most standards used to measure the success of a first play, *Sheba* was a triumph. For critical and historical background on Inge, see R. Baird Shuman, *William Inge* (Boston: Twayne, 1989).

41. Denzin, *Hollywood Shot by Shot*, 124.

42. Ibid., 103.

43. Herd, "Ideology, Melodrama, and the Changing Role of Alcohol Problems in American Films," 213–47; Denzin, *Hollywood Shot by Shot*, 110–24.

44. Denzin, *Hollywood Shot by Shot*, 102.

45. These reviews are cited in ibid., 100–103.

46. For an excellent discussion of the conflicting images and messages regarding female sexuality in the 1950s, see Breines, *Young, White, and Miserable*, 84–126. Breines argues that the postwar dating system was based on careful regulation of heterosexual social life and feminine restraint. The double standard inherent in the puritanical didacticism of American sexual culture made it difficult for young, white, middle-class women (symbolized in the film by Marie Buckholder) to negotiate the puzzling boundary between accepted forms of sexual pleasure (including necking and petting) and tabooed sexual acts, especially premarital intercourse.

47. Denzin, *Hollywood Shot by Shot*, 105.

48. John Cheever, *The Stories of John Cheever* (New York: Ballantine, 1980), 234–48.

49. Ibid., 242.

50. Ibid., 246.

51. The connections between the story and Cheever's own life are striking. In 1953, when "Sorrows of Gin" was first published, Cheever's daughter, Susan, was ten years old, nearly the same age as the character Amy. Indeed, in her recent memoir *Note Found in a Bottle: My Life as a Drinker* (New York: Simon and Schuster, 1999), Susan Cheever notes that "the fictional Amy is as good a portrait of me as anything I can recall" (26). Her father's sensitivity to the psychological effects of growing up in an alcoholic home—so implicit in the story—is fascinating considering Susan's later struggles with alcohol and marital relationships as an adult.

52. John Cheever, *Stories*, 713–25.

53. Ibid., 713 (emphasis in original), 721.

54. Ibid., 720–21.

55. *The Swimmer*, produced by Frank Perry and Roger Lewis (Columbia Pictures, 1968); Lolli, *Social Drinking*, 92.

56. John Cheever, *Stories*, 723.

57. The film generally received poor reviews. As several contemporary critics noted, the difficulties of translating a story rooted in symbolism and allegory onto the screen were substantial. As reviewer Penelope Gilliatt wrote in the *New Yorker*, May 25, 1968, 84–85, "Cheever wrote a story that was a true and dark image of being a middle-class American, but the Perrys' mawkish film seems to be about a sporting kook with a dewy turn of mind who gets overemotional during an all-day swim." Yet the filmmakers did succeed in emphasizing the central role of alcohol in Neddie Merrill's world.

58. Christopher Lehmann-Haupt, "Talk with John Cheever," in *Conversations with John Cheever*, ed. Scott Donaldson (Jackson: University Press of Mississippi, 1987), 39–43; reprinted from the *New York Times Book Review*, April 27, 1969, 42–44.

59. Susan Cheever, *Home before Dark* (Boston: Houghton Mifflin, 1984), 161.

60. John Cheever, *The Journals of John Cheever* (New York: Knopf, 1991), 94, 108–11.

61. Christina Robb, "Cheever's Story," in Donaldson, *Conversations with John Cheever*, 216–17; reprinted from the *Boston Globe Magazine*, July 6, 1980, 11–13, 27–31, 35.

62. Susan Cheever, *Home before Dark*, 155.

63. Quoted in J. W. Savage, "John Cheever: The Long and the Short and the Tall," in Donaldson, *Conversations with John Cheever*, 192–93; reprinted from the *Chicago Tribune Magazine*, April 22, 1979, 30–35.

64. Susan Cheever, *Home before Dark*, 42.

65. On the history of homosexuality, see George Chauncey, *Gay New York: Gender, Urban Culture, and the Making of the Gay Male World, 1890–1940* (New York: Basic Books, 1994); Jonathan Ned Katz, *The Invention of Heterosexuality* (New York: Plume, 1996); and John D'Emilio and Estelle B. Freedman, *Intimate Matters: A History of Sexuality in America* (New York: Harper and Row, 1988), 288–95.

66. On all three writers as closeted homosexuals, see John W. Crowley, "A Charles Jackson Diptych," *Syracuse University Library Associates Courier* 32 (1997): 35–38.

67. John Cheever, *Journals*, 365.

68. Herbert A. Bloch, "Alcohol and American Recreational Life," *American Scholar* 18, no. 1 (January 1949): 54–66.

69. John Kenneth Galbraith, "The Unseemly Economics of Opulence," *Harper's*, January 1952, 58–63 (quote on 61).

70. On the history of this intellectual tradition, see Jackson Lears, *Fables of Abundance: A Cultural History of Advertising in America* (New York: Basic Books, 1994), esp. 254–57, and Daniel Horowitz, *The Morality of Spending: Attitudes toward the Consumer Society in America* (Baltimore: Johns Hopkins University Press, 1985).

71. David Potter, *People of Plenty: Economic Abundance and the American Character* (Chicago: University of Chicago Press, 1955), 103–8, 182, 188.

72. *AACOA*, 274–82.

73. Ibid., 282–83.

74. Father John Doe [pseud.], *Sobriety and Beyond* (Indianapolis: SMT Publishing, 1951), 112–15.

75. Ernest Kurtz, *Not God: A History of Alcoholics Anonymous* (Center City, Minn.: Hazelden, 1979), 208–9.

CONCLUSION

1. For an excellent synthesis of these trends, see Lynn Dumenil, *The Modern Temper: American Culture and Society in the 1920s* (New York: Hill and Wang, 1995).

2. Robin Room, "Alcoholism and Alcoholics Anonymous in U.S. Films, 1945–1962: The Party Ends for the 'Wet Generations,'" *Journal of Studies on Alcohol* 50, no. 4 (1989): 380.

3. The recovery movement is difficult to define precisely. According to Gary Greenberg, who has interpreted recovery books of the 1980s from a theoretical perspective, the phenomenon is neither a political nor a social movement but, rather, "an uprising against an inner state, against the private demons that thrive within a 'diseased' psyche." The word "recovery" once referred primarily to the alcoholic's rehabilitation through the ΛΛ Twelve Step program but has come to connote "the treatment of choice for an enormous range of human suffering" (*The Self on the Shelf: Recovery Books and the Good Life* [Albany: State University of New York Press, 1994], 1). See also Stanton Peele, *The Diseasing of America: Addiction Treatment out of Control* (Lexington, Mass.: Lexington Books, 1989); Wendy Kaminer, *"I'm Dysfunctional, You're Dysfunctional": The Recovery Movement and Other Self-Help Fashions* (New York: Vintage, 1993); Elayne Rapping, *The Culture of Recovery: Making Sense of the Self-Help Movement in Women's Lives* (Boston: Beacon Press, 1996); and Wendy Simonds, *Women and Self-Help Culture: Reading between the Lines* (New Brunswick, N.J.: Rutgers University Press, 1992).

4. Harry Gene Levine, "The Discovery of Addiction: Changing Conceptions of Habitual Drunkenness in America," *Journal of Studies on Alcohol* 39, no. 1 (January 1978): 143–74.

5. Mark Edward Lender and James Kirby Martin, *Drinking in America: A History* (New York: Free Press, 1987), 191–94.

6. Indeed alcoholism, understood metaphorically as a pathological hallmark of a particular era, would eventually face competition from other illnesses according to subsequent epidemiological and social changes. To a great extent during the 1980s alcoholism was subsumed within the broader recovery movement. Also, as unprecedented numbers of Americans became infected with the HIV virus, AIDS came to dominate the nation's public health agenda and cultural landscape. On the troubling metaphorical significance and cultural politics of AIDS, see Susan Sontag, *Illness as Metaphor and AIDS and Its Metaphors* (New York: Anchor Books, 1989).

7. Statistics on the apparent per capita consumption of alcohol beverages can be

found in Lender and Martin, *Drinking in America*, 205–6. On the drug culture of the 1960s, see David Farber, *The Age of Great Dreams: America in the 1960s* (New York: Hill and Wang, 1994), 170–89.

8. Farber, *Age of Great Dreams*, 170–89.

9. Elaine Tyler May, *Homeward Bound: American Families in the Cold War Era* (New York: Basic Books, 1988), 221–22.

10. NOW's charter platform is cited in Farber, *Age of Great Dreams*, 248.

11. On demographic shifts in marital and sexual patterns, see May, *Homeward Bound*, 221–23. The literature on feminism and the women's movement includes Cynthia Harrison, *On Account of Sex: The Politics of Women's Issues, 1945–1968* (Berkeley: University of California Press, 1988), and Alice Echols: *Daring to Be Bad: Radical Feminism in America, 1967–1975* (Minneapolis: University of Minnesota Press, 1989).

12. Janice Haaken, "From Al-Anon to ACOA: Codependence and the Reconstruction of Caregiving," *Signs* 18 (winter 1993): 335.

13. Ibid.; *The Dilemma of the Alcoholic Marriage* (New York: Al-Anon Family Group Headquarters, 1971), 2–3.

14. Haaken, "From Al-Anon to ACOA," 336.

15. Rapping, *Culture of Recovery*, offers the most thorough account of the complex relationship between contemporary therapeutic culture and feminism.

BIBLIOGRAPHY

ARCHIVAL SOURCES

Al-Anon Family Groups Archives, Virginia Beach, Virginia
    Pamphlets and Printed Matter of Al-Anon Family Groups
    Records and Correspondence of Al-Anon Family Groups
Alcoholics Anonymous Archives, New York, New York
    Press Clippings Scrapbooks
    Records and Correspondence of Alcoholics Anonymous

CONTEMPORARY PUBLISHED PRIMARY SOURCES

Magazines

Fortune	*New Yorker*
Life	*Printer's Ink*
Newsweek	*Time*

Newsletters

Family Forum (published by Al-Anon Family Groups)
Grapevine (published by Alcoholics Anonymous)
Science News Letter

Books

Ade, George. *The Old-Time Saloon*. New York: Long and Smith, 1931.
Al-Anon Family Groups. New York: Al-Anon Family Groups Publications, 1955.
Alcoholics Anonymous Comes of Age, by a Co-Founder. New York: Harper and
    Brothers, 1957.
*Alcoholics Anonymous: The Story of How More Than One Hundred Men Have
    Recovered from Alcoholism*. New York: Works Publishing, 1939.
An Alcoholic to His Sons. As told to Henry Beetle Hough. New York: Simon and
    Schuster, 1954.

Allen, Frederick Lewis. *Only Yesterday: An Informal History of the 1920's*. New York: Harper and Row, 1931.

——. *Since Yesterday: The Nineteen Thirties in America*. New York: Harper and Brothers, 1939.

Binkley, Robert C. *Responsible Drinking: A Discreet Inquiry and a Modest Proposal*. New York: Vanguard, 1930.

Boole, Ella. *Give Prohibition Its Chance*. New York: Fleming H. Revell, 1929.

Booth, Evangeline. *Some Have Stopped Drinking*. Westerville, Ohio: American Issue Publishing, 1928.

Bruere, Marthy Bensley. *Does Prohibition Work?* New York: Harper and Brothers, 1927.

Cain, Arthur. *The Cured Alcoholic: New Concepts in Alcoholism Treatment and Research*. New York: John Day, 1964.

Cheever, John. *The Journals of John Cheever*. New York: Knopf, 1991.

——. *The Stories of John Cheever*. New York: Ballantine, 1980.

Cheever, Susan. *Home before Dark*. Boston: Houghton Mifflin, 1984.

——. *Note Found in a Bottle: My Life as a Drinker*. New York: Simon and Schuster, 1999.

Clancy, Jay R. [pseud.]. *Clancy Got Well*. Des Moines, Iowa: McGreevey, 1951.

DeVoto, Bernard. *The Hour*. Boston: Houghton Mifflin, 1948.

The Dilemma of the Alcoholic Marriage. New York: Al-Anon Family Group Headquarters, 1971.

Doe, Father John [pseud.]. *Sobriety and Beyond*. Indianapolis: SMT Publishing, 1955.

Emerson, Haven. *Alcohol: Its Effects on Man*. New York: D. Appleton-Century, 1934.

Feldman, Herman. *Prohibition: Its Economic and Industrial Aspects*. New York: D. Appleton, 1927.

Frederick, Christine. *Selling Mrs. Consumer*. New York: Business Bourse, 1929.

Fullam, Thomas [pseud.]. *Here's to Sobriety: A Plain Approach to Understanding the Compulsive Drinker and His Problems*. New York: Abelard Press, 1950.

Gellman, Irving Peter. *The Sober Alcoholic: An Organizational Analysis of Alcoholics Anonymous*. New Haven: College and University Press, 1964.

Goodman, David. *A Parent's Guide to the Emotional Needs of Children*. New York: Hawthorne Books, 1959.

Haggard, Howard W., and E. M. Jellinek. *Alcohol Explored*. New York: Doubleday, 1942.

Hirsh, Joseph. *The Problem Drinker*. New York: Duell, Sloan and Pearce, 1949.

Komaravsky, Mirra. *The Unemployed Man and His Family: The Effect of Unemployment upon the Status of the Man in Fifty-nine Families*. New York: Dryden Press, 1940.

The Language of the Heart: Bill W.'s Grapevine Writings. New York: AA Grapevine, 1988.

Lewis, Sinclair. *Babbitt*. 1922. Reprint, New York: Penguin, 1992.

Living with an Alcoholic with the Help of Al-Anon. New York: Al-Anon Family Group Headquarters, 1966.

Lois Remembers: Memoirs of the Co-founder of Al-Anon and the Wife of the Co-founder of Alcoholics Anonymous. New York: Al-Anon Family Group Headquarters, 1979.

Lolli, Georgio. *Social Drinking: How To Enjoy Drinking without Being Hurt by It.* Cleveland: World Publishing, 1960.

London, Jack. *John Barleycorn.* New York: Century, 1913.

Louth, Cyril. *But for the Grace of God.* New York: Pageant Press, 1956.

Lovell, Harold W. *Hope and Help for the Alcoholic.* New York: Doubleday, 1951.

Lynd, Robert S., and Helen M. Lynd. *Middletown: A Study in Modern American Culture.* 1929. Reprint, New York: Harcourt, Brace and World, 1956.

McCarthy, Raymond G., ed. *Drinking and Intoxication: Selected Readings in Social Attitudes and Controls.* Glencoe, Ill.: Free Press, 1959.

McCarthy, Raymond G., and Edgar M. Douglas. *Alcohol and Social Responsibility: A New Educational Approach.* New York: Thomas Y. Crowell, 1949.

Menninger, Karl. *Man against Himself.* New York: Harcourt, Brace and World, 1938.

Reilly, Hugh [pseud.]. *Easy Does It: The Story of Mac.* New York: P. J. Kenedy, 1950.

Seeley, John, R. Alexander Sim, and Elizabeth W. Loosley. *Crestwood Heights.* Toronto: University of Toronto Press, 1956.

The Shadow of the Bottle. Washington, D.C.: Review and Herald Publishing, 1925.

Southard, E. E., and Mary C. Jarrett. *The Kingdom of Evils: Psychiatric Social Work Presented in One Hundred Case Histories Together with a Classification of Social Divisions of Evil.* New York: Macmillan, 1922.

Stewart, Mother Eliza A. *Memories of the Crusade.* Chicago: H. J. Smith, 1890.

Straus, Robert, and Selden D. Bacon. *Drinking in College.* New Haven: Yale University Press, 1953.

Strecker, Edward A. *Their Mothers' Sons: The Psychiatrist Examines an American Problem.* Philadelphia: Lippincott, 1946.

Strecker, Edward A., and Francis T. Chambers Jr. *Alcohol: One Man's Meat.* New York: Macmillan, 1938.

Taintor, Eliot [Ruth Fitch Mason and Gregory Mason]. *September Remember.* New York: Prentice Hall, 1945.

Todd, Arthur J. *The Chicago Recreation Survey 1937.* Vol. 2. Chicago: Chicago Recreation Committee, 1938.

Veblen, Thorstein. *Theory of the Leisure Class: An Economic Study of Institutions.* New York: Macmillan, 1899. Reprint, New York: Modern Library, 1934.

Whyte, William H., Jr. *The Organization Man.* New York: Simon and Schuster, 1956.

Willard, Frances. *Glimpses of Fifty Years: The Autobiography of an American Woman.* Chicago: H. J. Smith, 1889.

Willis, George E. *The Bottle Fighters.* New York: Random House, 1963.

Wylie, Philip. *Generation of Vipers.* New York: Holt, Rinehart and Winston, 1942.

Pamphlets

Alcoholism and Social Drinking: A Report of the National Planning Conference on Alcoholism and Alcohol Education Held at Seabury House, Greenwich, Connecticut. New York: National Council, 1956.

Cutten, George Barton. *We Are at War*. Speech delivered at the Northern Baptist Convention, Cleveland, Ohio, May 27, 1942. Philadelphia: n.p., 1942.

Daggett, Mabel Potter. *Why We Prohibit*. Westerville, Ohio: American Issue Publishing, 1924.

Hiltner, Seward. *It's Up to You*. New York: Association Press, 1947.

Johnson, James W. *To Drink or Not to Drink*. N.p., 1930.

Johnson, William. *What Prohibition Has Done for Business*. Reprinted from *Scientific Temperance Journal*, 1920.

Lipsett, Charles H. *The Effect of Repeal on Industrial Recovery*. New York: Atlas, 1935.

McCarthy, Raymond G. *A Manual of Facts and Fancies about Alcohol*. New Haven: Yale Plan Clinic, 1950.

The Prohibition Question Viewed from the Economics and Moral Standpoint. Baltimore: Manufacturer's Record, 1922.

Ross, Edward Alesworth. *Prohibition as the Sociologist Sees It*. Westerville, Ohio: American Issue Publishing, 1921.

Sheppard, Morris. *Present Status of Prohibition in the United States*. Washington, D.C.: Government Printing Office, 1926.

Articles

Abraham, Karl. "The Psychological Relations between Sexuality and Alcoholism." *International Journal of Psycho-Analysis* 7 (January 1926): 2–10.

"Alcoholics Anonymous and the Advertising Man." *Printer's Ink*, September 14, 1945, 98.

"Alcoholics Anonymous: A Uniquely American Phenomenon." *Fortune*, February 1951, 99–100, 138, 141–44.

"The Alcoholic Veteran." *Newsweek*, February 23, 1948, 44–45.

"Alcoholism No Problem When Soldiers Have a Good Time." *Science News Letter*, August 1, 1942, 71.

"Alcoholism Seven Times More Prevalent among Men." *Science News Letter*, January 13, 1945, 22.

Alexander, Jack. "Alcoholics Anonymous: Freed Slaves of Drink, Now They Free Others." *Saturday Evening Post*, March 1, 1941, 9–11.

Bacon, Selden D. "Alcohol and Complex Society." In *Alcohol, Science, and Society: Twenty-nine Lectures with Discussions as Given at the Yale Summer School of Alcohol Studies*, 179–200. New Haven: Quarterly Journal of Studies on Alcohol, 1945.

———. "Excessive Drinking and the Institution of the Family." In *Alcohol, Science, and Society: Twenty-nine Lectures with Discussions as Given at the Yale Summer School of Alcohol Studies*, 223–38. New Haven: Quarterly Journal of Studies on Alcohol, 1945.

———. "A Sociologist Looks at A.A." *Proceedings of the First Annual Alberta Conference on Alcohol Studies*. Edmonton: Alcoholism Foundation of Alberta, 1954.

Bailey, Margaret B. "Alcoholism and Marriage: A Review of Research and Professional Literature." *Quarterly Journal of Studies on Alcohol* 22, no. 1 (March 1961): 81–97.

———. "Al-Anon Groups as an Aid to Wives of Alcoholics." *Social Work* 10, no. 1 (January 1965): 68–74.

Baker, Sybil M. "Social Case Work with Inebriates." In *Alcohol, Science, and Society: Twenty-nine Lectures with Discussions as Given at the Yale Summer School of Alcohol Studies*, 419–35. New Haven: Quarterly Journal of Studies on Alcohol, 1945.

Bales, Robert Freed. "The Therapeutic Role of Alcoholics Anonymous as Seen by a Sociologist." *Quarterly Journal of Studies on Alcohol* 5 (1944): 267–78.

Bloch, Herbert A. "Alcohol and American Recreational Life." *American Scholar* 18, no. 1 (January 1949): 54–66.

Boggs, M. H. "The Rise of Social Work in the Treatment of Inebriates." *Quarterly Journal of Studies on Alcohol* 4, no. 4 (March 1944): 557–67.

Brower, Daniel. "An Opinion Poll on Reactions to *The Lost Weekend.*" *Quarterly Journal of Studies on Alcohol* 1, no. 1 (March 1946): 596–98.

C., Bill. "The Growth and Effectiveness of Alcoholics Anonymous in a Southwestern City, 1945–1962." *Quarterly Journal of Studies on Alcohol* 26, no. 2 (June 1965): 279–84.

Cain, Arthur. "Alcoholics Anonymous: Cult or Cure?" *Harper's*, February 1963, 48–52.

Dollard, John. "Drinking Mores of the Social Classes." In *Alcohol, Science, and Society: Twenty-nine Lectures with Discussions as Given at the Yale Summer School of Alcohol Studies*, 95–104. New Haven: Quarterly Journal of Studies on Alcohol, 1945.

"Drinking Increasing during World War II." *Louisville Times*, March 9, 1944.

Futterman, Samuel. "Personality Trends in Wives of Alcoholics." *Journal of Psychiatric Social Work* 23 (1953): 37–41.

Galbraith, John Kenneth. "The Unseemly Economics of Opulence." *Harper's*, January 1952, 58–63.

Grisedieck, Alvin. "Beer and Brewing in a Nation at War." *Quarterly Journal of Studies on Alcohol* 3, no. 2 (September 1942): 293–301.

Gunther, Max. "Alcohol and Your Job: Do They Mix?" *True*, July 1970.

Haggard, Howard W. "The Physiology of Alcohol." *Yale Review* 35, no. 2 (December 1945): 295–307.

Henderson, Ralph M. "Profile of the Alcoholic." *Proceedings of the First Annual Alberta Conference on Alcohol Studies*. Edmonton: Alcoholism Foundation of Alberta, 1954.

Hewitt, Charles C. "A Personality Study of Alcohol Addiction." *Quarterly Journal of Studies on Alcohol* 4, no. 3 (December 1943): 368–86.

Hoke, Travis. "The Corner Saloon." *American Mercury*, March 1931, 311–15.

Horton, Donald. "The Functions of Alcohol in Primitive Societies." In *Alcohol, Science, and Society: Twenty-nine Lectures with Discussions as Given at the Yale Summer School of Alcohol Studies*, 153–78. New Haven: Quarterly Journal of Studies on Alcohol, 1945.

Hunter, Dorothy. "New Help for Alcoholics: Relatives of Habitual Drinkers Have Found a Novel Way of Dealing with Their Problem." *Coronet*, July 1949.

Jackson, Joan K. "The Adjustment of the Family to the Crisis of Alcoholism." *Quarterly Journal of Studies on Alcohol* 15, no. 4 (December 1954): 562–86.

James, William. "The Moral Equivalent of War." In *Essays on Faith and Morals.* New York: Longmans, Green, 1943.

Jellinek, E. M. "Effects of Alcohol on Psychological Functions." In *Alcohol, Science, and Society: Twenty-nine Lectures with Discussions as Given at the Yale Summer School of Alcohol Studies*, 83–94. New Haven: Quarterly Journal of Studies on Alcohol, 1945.

———. "Phases in Drinking History of Alcoholics." *Quarterly Journal of Studies on Alcohol* 7, no. 1 (June 1946): 1–88.

Kessel, Joseph. *The Road Back: A Report on Alcoholics Anonymous.* Translated by Frances Partridge. New York: Knopf, 1962.

Knight, R. P. "The Psychoanalytic Treatment in a Sanatorium of Chronic Addiction to Alcohol." *Journal of the American Medical Association* 111 (October 15, 1938): 1443–48.

———. "The Psychodynamics of Chronic Alcoholism." *Journal of Nervous and Mental Diseases* 86 (November 1937): 544–45.

Landis, Benson Y. "Some Economic Aspects of Inebriety." In *Alcohol, Science, and Society: Twenty-nine Lectures with Discussions as Given at the Yale Summer School of Alcohol Studies*, 201–22. New Haven: Quarterly Journal of Studies on Alcohol, 1945.

Landis, Carney. "Theories of the Alcoholic Personality." In *Alcohol, Science, and Society: Twenty-nine Lectures with Discussions as Given at the Yale Summer School of Alcohol Studies*, 129–42. New Haven: Quarterly Journal of Studies on Alcohol, 1945.

Levine, Jacob. "The Sexual Adjustment of Alcoholics: A Clinical Study of a Selected Sample." *Quarterly Journal of Studies on Alcohol* 16, no. 4 (December 1955): 675–80.

Lewis, Margaret L. "The Initial Contact with Wives of Alcoholics." *Social Casework* 35, no. 1 (January 1954): 8–14.

Mainec, Harold. "The Alcoholic and His Women." *Ladies Home Journal*, July 1948, 45.

Maxwell, Milton A. "Alcoholics Anonymous: An Interpretation." In *Society, Culture, and Drinking Patterns*, edited by David J. Pittman and Charles R. Snyder. New York: John Wiley and Sons, 1962.

———. "The Washingtonian Movement." *Quarterly Journal of Studies on Alcohol* 11, no. 3 (September 1950): 410–51.

"Mrs. Drunkard." *Newsweek*, March 8, 1948, 22–23.

Murphy, A. J. "Alcohol and Pauperism." In *Alcohol, Science, and Society: Twenty-nine Lectures with Discussions as Given at the Yale Summer School of Alcohol Studies*, 239–50. New Haven: Quarterly Journal of Studies on Alcohol, 1945.

Murphy, Mary Martha. "Values Stressed by Two Social Class Levels at Meetings of Alcoholics Anonymous." *Quarterly Journal of Studies on Alcohol* 14, no. 4 (December 1953): 576–85.

Osborn, Leslie. "New Attitudes toward Alcoholism." *Quarterly Journal of Studies on Alcohol* 12, no. 1 (March 1951): 58–60.

Parkhurst, Genevieve. "Laymen and Alcoholics." *Harper's*, September 1941, 422–29.

"The Plattsburg Idea." *New Republic*, October 9, 1915, 247–49.

Price, Gladys M. "A Study of the Wives of Twenty Alcoholics." *Quarterly Journal of Studies on Alcohol* 5, no. 4 (March 1945): 620–27.

———. "Why I Want a Professional Social Worker on My Clinic Staff." In *Selected Papers from the Sixth Annual Meeting of the National States' Conference on Alcoholism*, 27–31. Portland, Ore., 1956.

"Problem Drinking." *Time*, January 31, 1949, 54.

Riley, John W., and Charles F. Marden. "The Social Pattern of Alcoholic Drinking." *Quarterly Journal of Studies on Alcohol* 8, no. 2 (September 1947): 265–73.

Ritchie, Oscar W. "A Sociohistorical Survey of Alcoholics Anonymous." *Quarterly Journal of Studies on Alcohol* 9, no. 1 (June 1948): 119–56.

Sapir, Jean V. "Social Work and Alcoholism." *Annals of the American Academy of Political and Social Science* 315 (January 1958): 128.

Squires, Fred D. L. *The Truth about Alcohol in This Hour of National Emergency.* Chicago: American Business Men's Research Foundation, 1942.

Straus, Robert. "Alcohol and the Homeless Man." *Quarterly Journal of Studies on Alcohol* 7, no. 3 (December 1946): 360–404.

Strecker, Edward A. "Chronic Alcoholism: A Psychological Survey." *Quarterly Journal of Studies on Alcohol* 1, no. 2 (September 1941): 12–17.

Trimmer, J. Maurice. "How to Refuse a Cocktail." *Christian Century*, April 16, 1947, 489–90.

———. "The Menace of Moderation." *Christian Century*, August 28, 1946, 1037–38.

Wall, J. H. "A Study of Alcoholism in Men." *American Journal of Psychiatry* 92 (1936): 1391.

Warshow, Robert. "Anatomy of a Falsehood." In *The Immediate Experience: Movies, Comics, Theater, and Other Aspects of Popular Culture*, 155–61. Garden City, N.Y.: Doubleday, 1962.

Whalen, Thelma. "Wives of Alcoholics: Four Types Observed in a Family Service Agency." *Quarterly Journal of Studies on Alcohol* 14, no. 4 (December 1953): 632–40.

Wickware, Francis Sill. "Liquor: Current Studies in Medicine and Psychiatry Are Bringing Enlightenment to the 30,000 Year-Old Problem of Drinking." *Life*, May 27, 1946, 66–77.

Films

The Best Years of Our Lives. Produced by Samuel Goldwyn. Metro Goldwyn Mayer, 1946.

Come Back, Little Sheba. Produced by Hal B. Wallis. Paramount, 1952.

Come Fill the Cup. Produced by Henry Blanke. Warner, 1951.

The Country Girl. Produced by William Perlberg. Paramount, 1954.

The Lost Weekend. Produced by Charles Brackett. Paramount, 1945.

Murder at the Vanities. Produced by E. Lloyd Sheldon. Paramount, 1934.

The Swimmer. Produced by Frank Perry and Roger Lewis. Columbia, 1968.
The Thin Man. Produced by Hunt Stromberg. Metro Goldwyn Mayer, 1934.
The Voice in the Mirror. Produced by Gordon Kay. Universal-International, 1958.

SECONDARY SOURCES

Books

Bailey, Beth L. *From Front Porch to Back Seat: Courtship in Twentieth-Century America.* Baltimore: Johns Hopkins University Press, 1988.

Beauchamp, Dan E. *Beyond Alcoholism: Alcohol and Public Health Policy.* Philadelphia: Temple University Press, 1980.

Bederman, Gail. *Manliness and Civilization: A Cultural History of Gender and Race in the United States, 1880–1917.* Chicago: University of Chicago Press, 1995.

Blocker, Jack S., Jr. *American Temperance Movements: Cycles of Reform.* Boston: Twayne, 1989.

Blum, John Morton. *V Was for Victory: Politics and Culture during World War II.* San Diego: Harcourt, Brace, Jovanovich, 1976.

Bordin, Ruth. *Women and Temperance: The Quest for Power and Liberty, 1873–1900.* Philadelphia: Temple University Press, 1981.

Breines, Wini. *Young, White, and Miserable: Growing Up Female in the Fifties.* Boston: Beacon Press, 1992.

Burnham, John. *Bad Habits: Drinking, Smoking, Taking Drugs, Gambling, Sexual Misbehavior, and Swearing in American History.* New York: New York University Press, 1993.

Byars, Jackie. *All That Hollywood Allows: Re-reading Gender in 1950s Melodrama.* Chapel Hill: University of North Carolina Press, 1991.

Chauncey, George. *Gay New York: Gender, Urban Culture, and the Making of the Gay Male World, 1890–1940.* New York: Basic Books, 1994.

Clark, Norman. *Deliver Us from Evil: An Interpretation of American Prohibition.* New York: Norton, 1976.

Coontz, Stephanie. *The Social Origins of Private Life: A History of American Families, 1600–1900.* London: Verso, 1988.

——. *The Way We Never Were: American Families and the Nostalgia Trap.* New York: Basic Books, 1992.

Cott, Nancy F. *Public Vows: A History of Marriage and the Nation.* Cambridge, Mass.: Harvard University Press, 2000.

Cross, Gary. *Time and Money: The Making of Consumer Society.* London: Routledge, 1993.

Crowley, John W. *The White Logic: Alcoholism and Gender in American Modernist Fiction.* Amherst: University of Massachusetts Press, 1994.

Dardis, Tom. *The Thirsty Muse: Alcohol and the American Writer.* New York: Ticknor and Fields, 1989.

Darrah, Mary C. *Sister Ignatia: Angel of Alcoholics Anonymous.* Chicago: Loyola University Press, 1992.

Dawley, Alan. *Struggles for Justice: Social Responsibility and the Liberal State.* Cambridge, Mass.: Harvard University Press, 1991.

de Lauretis, Teresa. *Technologies of Gender: Essays on Theory, Film, and Fiction.* Bloomington: Indiana University Press, 1987.

D'Emilio, John, and Estelle B. Freedman. *Intimate Matters: A History of Sexuality in America.* New York: Harper and Row, 1988.

Demos, John. *Past, Present, and Personal: The Family and the Life Course in American History.* New York: Oxford University Press, 1986.

Denzin, Norman K. *Hollywood Shot by Shot: Alcoholism in American Cinema.* New York: Aldine de Gruyter, 1991.

Diggins, John Patrick. *The Proud Decades: America in War and Peace, 1941–1960.* New York: Norton, 1988.

Donaldson, Scott, ed. *Conversations with John Cheever.* Jackson: University Press of Mississippi, 1987.

Douglas, Ann. *Terrible Honesty: Mongrel Manhattan in the 1920s.* New York: Farrar, Straus and Giroux, 1995.

Dr. Bob and the Good Old-timers: A Biography, with Recollections of Early AA in the Midwest. New York: AA World Services, 1980.

Duis, Perry. *The Saloon: Public Drinking in Chicago and Boston, 1880–1920.* Urbana: University of Illinois Press, 1983.

Dumenil, Lynn. *The Modern Temper: American Culture and Society in the 1920s.* New York: Hill and Wang, 1995.

Echols, Alice. *Daring to Be Bad: Radical Feminism in America, 1967–1975.* Minneapolis: University of Minnesota Press, 1989.

Ehrenreich, Barbara. *The Hearts of Men: American Dreams and the Flight from Commitment.* New York: Anchor Books, 1983.

Ehrenreich, Barbara, and Deirdre English. *"For Her Own Good": 150 Years of the Experts' Advice to Women.* London: Pluto Press, 1979.

Epstein, Barbara L. *The Politics of Domesticity: Women, Evangelism, and Temperance in Nineteenth-Century America.* Middletown, Conn.: Wesleyan University Press, 1981.

Erenberg, Lewis. *Steppin' Out: New York Nightlife and the Transformation of American Culture, 1890–1930.* Westport, Conn.: Greenwood Press, 1981.

Farber, David. *The Age of Great Dreams: America in the 1960s.* New York: Hill and Wang, 1994.

Filstead, William J., Jean J. Rossi, and Mark Keller, eds. *Alcohol and Alcohol Problems: New Thinking and New Directions.* Cambridge, Mass: Ballinger, 1976.

First Steps: Al-Anon . . . Thirty-five Years of Beginnings. New York: Al-Anon Family Group Headquarters, 1986.

Gilmore, Thomas B. *Equivocal Spirits: Alcoholism and Drinking in Twentieth Century-Literature.* Chapel Hill: University of North Carolina Press, 1987.

Ginzberg, Lori D. *Women and the Work of Benevolence: Morality, Politics, and Class in the Nineteenth-Century United States.* New Haven: Yale University Press, 1990.

Gordon, Linda. *Heroes of Their Own Lives: The Politics and History of Family Violence, Boston, 1880–1960.* New York: Viking, 1988.

Gorn, Elliott J. *The Manly Art: Bare-Knuckle Prize-Fighting in America*. Ithaca, N.Y.: Cornell University Press, 1986.

Graebner, William. *The Age of Doubt: American Thought and Culture in the 1940s*. Boston: Twayne, 1991.

Greenberg, Gary. *The Self on the Shelf: Recovery Books and the Good Life*. Albany: State University of New York Press, 1994.

Grimes, William. *Straight Up or On the Rocks: A Cultural History of American Drink*. New York: Simon and Schuster, 1993.

Griswold, Robert. *Fatherhood in America: A History*. New York: Basic Books, 1993.

Gusfield, Joseph R. *Symbolic Crusade*. Urbana: University of Illinois Press, 1963.

Hale, Nathan G. *The Rise and Crisis of Psychoanalysis in the United States: Freud and the Americans, 1917–1985*. New York: Oxford University Press, 1995.

Hamill, Pete. *A Drinking Life*. Boston: Little, Brown, 1994.

Harrison, Cynthia. *On Account of Sex: The Politics of Women's Issues, 1945–1968*. Berkeley: University of California Press, 1988.

Herman, Ellen. *The Romance of American Psychology: Political Culture in the Age of Experts*. Berkeley: University of California Press, 1995.

Hewitt, Nancy. *Women's Activism and Social Change: Rochester, New York, 1822–1872*. Ithaca: Cornell University Press, 1984.

Hine, Thomas. *Populuxe*. New York: Knopf, 1985.

Hochschild, Arlie. *The Managed Heart: Commercialization of Human Feeling*. Berkeley: University of California Press, 1983.

Horowitz, Daniel. *The Morality of Spending: Attitudes toward the Consumer Society in America*. Baltimore: Johns Hopkins University Press, 1985.

Howe, Daniel Walker. *Victorian America*. Philadelphia: University of Pennsylvania Press, 1976.

Hyde, Lewis. *The Gift: Imagination and the Erotic Life of Property*. New York: Vintage, 1979.

Kaminer, Wendy. *"I'm Dysfunctional, You're Dysfunctional": The Recovery Movement and Other Self-Help Fashions*. New York: Vintage, 1993.

Kasson, John F. *Amusing the Million: Coney Island at the Turn of the Century*. New York: Hill and Wang, 1978.

Katz, Alfred H., and Eugene I. Bender. *The Strength in Us: Self-Help Groups in the Modern World*. New York: Franklin Watts, 1976.

Katz, Jonathan Ned. *The Invention of Heterosexuality*. New York: Plume, 1996.

Kerr, K. Austin. *The Politics of Moral Behavior: Prohibition and Drug Abuse*. Reading, Mass.: Addison-Wesley, 1973.

Kozol, Wendy. *Life's America: Family and Nation in Postwar Photojournalism*. Philadelphia: Temple University Press, 1994.

Kunzel, Regina G. *Fallen Women, Problem Girls: Unmarried Mothers and the Professionalization of Social Work, 1890–1945*. New Haven: Yale University Press, 1993.

Kurtz, Ernest. *Not God: A History of Alcoholics Anonymous*. Center City, Minn.: Hazelden, 1979.

Kyvig, David. *Repealing National Prohibition*. Chicago: University of Chicago Press, 1979.

Lanza, Joseph. *The Cocktail: The Influence of Spirits on the American Psyche*. New York: Picador, 1995.

Lasch, Christopher. *The Culture of Narcissism*. New York: Norton, 1978.

Leach, William. *Land of Desire: Merchants, Power, and the Rise of a New American Culture*. New York: Pantheon, 1993.

Lears, Jackson. *Fables of Abundance: A Cultural History of Advertising in America*. New York: Basic Books, 1994.

Lender, Mark Edward, and James Kirby Martin. *Drinking in America: A History*. New York: Free Press, 1987.

Lenson, David. *On Drugs*. Minneapolis: University of Minnesota Press, 1995.

Lunbeck, Elizabeth. *The Psychiatric Persuasion: Knowledge, Gender, and Power in Modern America*. Princeton: Princeton University Press, 1994.

McElvaine, Robert S. *The Great Depression*. New York: Times Books, 1984.

Makela, Klaus, et al. *Alcoholics Anonymous as a Mutual-Help Movement: A Study in Eight Societies*. Madison: University of Wisconsin Press, 1996.

Marchand, Roland. *Advertising the American Dream: Making Way for Modernity*. Berkeley: University of California Press, 1985.

Matthews, Glenna. *"Just a Housewife": The Rise and Fall of Domesticity in America*. New York: Oxford University Press, 1987.

Mauss, Marcel. *The Gift: Forms and Functions of Exchange in Archaic Societies*. Translated by Ian Cunnison. New York: Norton, 1967.

May, Elaine Tyler. *Great Expectations: Marriage and Divorce in Post-Victorian America*. Chicago: University of Chicago Press, 1980.

——. *Homeward Bound: American Families in the Cold War Era*. New York: Basic Books, 1988.

Melosh, Barbara. *Engendering Culture: Manhood and Womanhood in New Deal Public Art and Theater*. Washington, D.C.: Smithsonian Institution Press, 1991.

Meyer, Donald. *The Positive Thinkers*. New York: Doubleday, 1965.

Meyerowitz, Joanne, ed. *Not June Cleaver: Women and Gender in Postwar America, 1945–1960*. Philadelphia: Temple University Press, 1994.

Moskowitz, Eva S. *In Therapy We Trust: America's Obsession with Self-Fulfillment*. Baltimore: Johns Hopkins University Press, 2001.

Murdock, Catherine Gilbert. *Domesticating Drink: Women, Men, and Alcohol in America, 1870–1940*. Baltimore: Johns Hopkins University Press, 1998.

Nasaw, David. *Going Out: The Rise and Fall of Public Amusements*. New York: Basic Books, 1993.

Ohmann, Richard. *Selling Culture: Magazines, Markets, and Class at the Turn of the Century*. New York: Verso, 1996.

O'Reilly, Edmund B. *Sobering Tales: Narratives of Alcoholism and Recovery*. Amherst: University of Massachusetts Press, 1997.

P., Wally. *But, for the Grace of God . . . How Intergroups and Central Offices Carried the Message of Alcoholics Anonymous in the 1940s*. Wheeling, W.Va.: Bishop of Books, 1995.

Palmer, Bryan. *Descent into Discourse: The Reification of Language and the Writing of Social History*. Philadelphia: Temple University Press, 1990.

Parrish, Michael E. *Anxious Decades: America in Prosperity and Depression, 1920–1942*. New York: Norton, 1992.

Patterson, James T. *Grand Expectations: The United States, 1945–1974*. New York: Oxford University Press, 1996.

Peele, Stanton. *The Diseasing of America: Addiction Treatment out of Control*. Lexington, Mass.: Lexington Books, 1989.

Peiss, Kathy. *Cheap Amusements: Working Women and Leisure in Turn-of-the-Century New York*. Philadelphia: Temple University Press, 1986.

Pfister, Joel, and Nancy Schnog, eds. *Inventing the Psychological: Toward a Cultural History of Emotional Life in America*. New Haven: Yale University Press, 1997.

Pleck, Elizabeth. *Domestic Tyranny: The Making of Social Policy against Family Violence from Colonial Times to the Present*. New York: Oxford University Press, 1987.

Powers, Madelon. *Faces along the Bar: Lore and Order in the Workingman's Saloon, 1890–1920*. Chicago: University of Chicago Press, 1998.

Raphael, Matthew J. *Bill. W. and Mr. Wilson: The Legend and Life of A.A.'s Co-Founder*. Amherst: University of Massachusetts Press, 2000.

Rapping, Elayne. *The Culture of Recovery: Making Sense of the Self-Help Movement in Women's Lives*. Boston: Beacon Press, 1996.

Rieff, Philip. *The Triumph of the Therapeutic*. New York: Harper and Row, 1966.

Roffman, Peter, and Jim Purdy. *The Hollywood Social Problem Film: Madness, Despair, and Politics from the Depression to the Fifties*. Bloomington: Indiana University Press, 1981.

Rorabaugh, W. J. *The Alcoholic Republic: An American Tradition*. New York: Oxford University Press, 1979.

Rose, Kenneth D. *American Women and the Repeal of Prohibition*. New York: New York University Press, 1996.

Rosen, Ruth. *The Lost Sisterhood: Prostitution in America, 1900–1918*. Baltimore: Johns Hopkins University Press, 1982.

Rosenzweig, Roy. *Eight Hours for What We Will: Workers and Leisure in an Industrial City, 1870–1920*. New York: Cambridge University Press, 1983.

Rotundo, E. Anthony. *American Manhood: Transformations in Masculinity from the Revolution to the Modern Era*. New York: Basic Books, 1993.

Rumbarger, John J. *Profits, Power, and Prohibition: Alcohol Reform and the Industrialization of America, 1800–1930*. Albany: State University of New York Press, 1989.

Ryan, Mary P. *Cradle of the Middle Class: The Family in Oneida County, New York, 1790–1865*. Cambridge: Cambridge University Press, 1981.

Sagarin, Edward. *Odd Man In: Societies of Deviants in America*. Chicago: Quadrangle Books, 1969.

Scanlon, Jennifer. *Inarticulate Longings: The Ladies' Home Journal, Gender, and the Promises of Consumer Culture*. New York: Routledge, 1995.

Schamel, Charles E. *The Washington Group: Foundations, 1936–1941*. Washington, D.C.: Washington Intergroup Association, 1995.

Scharf, Lois. *To Work and to Wed: Female Employment, Feminism, and the Great Depression*. Westport, Conn.: Greenwood Press, 1980.

Schwartz, Hillel. *Never Satisfied: A Cultural History of Diets, Fantasies, and Fat.* New York: Free Press, 1986.

Scott, Joan W. *Gender and the Politics of History.* New York: Columbia University Press, 1989.

Seidman, Steven. *Romantic Longings: Love in America, 1830–1980.* New York: Routledge, 1991.

Shuman, R. Baird. *William Inge.* Boston: Twayne, 1989.

Silverman, Kaja. *Male Subjectivity at the Margins.* New York: Routledge, 1992.

Simonds, Wendy. *Women and Self-Help Culture: Reading between the Lines.* New Brunswick, N.J.: Rutgers University Press, 1992.

Sinclair, Andrew. *Prohibition: The Era of Excess.* Boston: Little, Brown, 1962.

Sklar, Robert. *Movie-Made America: A Social History of American Movies.* New York: Random House, 1975.

Skocpol, Theda. *Protecting Soldiers and Mothers: The Political Origins of Social Policy in the United States.* Cambridge, Mass.: Harvard University Press, 1992.

Sontag, Susan. *Illness as Metaphor.* New York: Farrar, Straus and Giroux, 1978.

——. *Illness as Metaphor and AIDS and Its Metaphors.* New York: Anchor Books, 1989.

Stage, Sarah. *Female Complaints: Lydia Pinkham and the Business of Women's Medicine.* New York: Norton, 1979.

Stasz, Clarice. *American Dreamers: Charmian and Jack London.* New York: St. Martin's Press, 1988.

Stevenson, Louise L. *The Victorian Homefront: American Thought and Culture, 1860–1880.* New York: Twayne, 1991.

Stivers, Richard. *A Hair of the Dog: Irish Drinking and American Stereotype.* University Park: Pennsylvania State University Press, 1976.

Strasser, Susan. *Satisfaction Guaranteed: The Making of an American Mass Market.* New York: Pantheon, 1989.

Susman, Warren. *Culture as History: The Transformation of American Society in the Twentieth Century.* New York: Pantheon, 1984.

Thomsen, Robert. *Bill W.* New York: Harper and Row, 1975.

Toch, Hans. *The Social Psychology of Social Movements.* Indianapolis: Bobbs-Merrill, 1965.

Todd, Ellen Wiley. *The "New Woman" Revised: Painting and Gender Politics on Fourteenth Street.* Berkeley: University of California Press, 1993.

Townsend, Kim. *Manhood at Harvard: William James and Others.* New York: Norton, 1996.

Tuttle, William M., Jr. *"Daddy's Gone to War": The Second World War in the Lives of America's Children.* New York: Oxford University Press, 1993.

Tyrrell, Ian. *Sobering Up: From Temperance to Prohibition in Antebellum America, 1800–1860.* Westport, Conn.: Greenwood Press, 1979.

Waits, William B. *The Modern Christmas in America: A Cultural History of Gift Giving.* New York: New York University Press, 1993.

Weiss, Jessica. *To Have and to Hold: Marriage, the Baby Boom, and Social Change.* Chicago: University of Chicago Press, 2000.

White, William L. *Slaying the Dragon: The History of Addiction Treatment and Recovery in America*. Bloomington, Ill.: Chestnut Health Systems, 1998.

Wiener, Carolyn L. *The Politics of Alcoholism: Building an Arena around a Social Problem*. New Brunswick, N.J.: Transaction Press, 1981.

Zelizer, Viviana. *Pricing the Priceless Child: The Changing Social Value of Children*. New York: Basic Books, 1985.

Articles

Aaron, Paul, and David Musto. "Temperance and Prohibition in America: A Historical Overview." In *Alcohol and Public Policy: Beyond the Shadow of Prohibition*, edited by Mark H. Moore and Dean R. Gerstein. Washington, D.C.: National Academy Press, 1981.

Antze, Paul. "Symbolic Action in Alcoholics Anonymous." In *Constructive Drinking: Perspectives on Drink from Anthropology*, edited by Mary Douglas. Cambridge: Cambridge University Press, 1987.

Baumohl, Jim, and Robin Room. "Inebriety, Doctors, and the State: Alcoholism Treatment Institutions before 1940." In *Recent Developments in Alcoholism*, edited by Mark Galanter, vol. 5. New York: Plenum, 1987.

Benson, Susan Porter. "Living on the Margin: Working-Class Marriages and Family Survival Strategies in the United States, 1919–1941." In *The Sex of Things: Gender and Consumption in Historical Perspective*, edited by Victoria de Grazia. Berkeley: University of California Press, 1996.

Collier, Jane, Michelle Z. Rosaldo, and Sylvia Yanagisako. "Is There a Family? New Anthropological Views." In *Rethinking the Family: Some Feminist Questions*, edited by Barrie Thorne and Marilyn Yalom. New York: Longman, 1982.

Cott, Nancy F. "Giving Character to Our Whole Civil Polity: Marriage and the Public Order in the Late Nineteenth Century." In *U.S. History as Women's History: New Feminist Essays*, edited by Linda K. Kerber, Alice Kessler-Harris, and Kathryn Kish Sklar. Chapel Hill: University of North Carolina Press, 1995.

———. "On Men's History and Women's History." In *Meanings for Manhood: Constructions of Masculinity in Victorian America*, edited by Mark C. Carnes and Clyde Griffen. Chicago: University of Chicago Press, 1990.

di Leonardo, Micaela. "The Female World of Cards and Holidays: Women, Families, and the Work of Kinship." *Signs* 12 (spring 1987): 440–53.

Eby, Clare Virginia. "Babbitt as Veblenian Critique of Manliness." *American Studies* 34, no. 2 (fall 1993): 5–19.

Ehrenreich, Barbara, and John Ehrenreich. "The Professional-Managerial Class." In *Between Labor and Capital*, edited by Pat Walker. Boston: South End Press, 1970.

Erenberg, Lewis. "From New York to Middletown: Repeal and the Legitimization of Nightlife in the Great Depression." *American Quarterly* 38 (winter 1986): 761–78.

Gerber, David A. "Heroes and Misfits: The Troubled Social Reintegration of Disabled Veterans in *The Best Years of Our Lives*." *American Quarterly* 46 (December 1994): 545–74.

Griffen, Clyde. "Reconstructing Masculinity from the Evangelical Revival to the Waning of Progressivism: A Speculative Synthesis." In *Meanings for Manhood: Constructions of Masculinity in Victorian America*, edited by Mark C. Carnes and Clyde Griffen. Chicago: University of Chicago Press, 1990.

Haaken, Janice. "From Al-Anon to ACOA: Codependence and the Reconstruction of Caregiving." *Signs* 18 (winter 1993): 321–45.

Hartmann, Susan M. "Prescriptions for Penelope: Literature on Women's Obligations to Returning World War II Veterans." *Women's Studies* 5 (1978): 223–39.

Herd, Denise. "Ideology, Melodrama, and the Changing Role of Alcohol Problems in American Films." *Contemporary Drug Problems* 13 (summer 1986): 213–47.

Kingsdale, Jon M. "The 'Poor Man's Club': Social Functions of the Urban Working-Class Saloon." *American Quarterly* 24 (October 1975): 472–89.

Kunzel, Regina G. "Pulp Fictions and Problem Girls: Reading and Rewriting Single Pregnancy in the Postwar United States." *American Historical Review* 100 (December 1995): 1465–87.

Kyvig, David. "Women against Prohibition." *American Quarterly* 28 (winter 1976): 465–82.

Lears, T. J. Jackson. "From Salvation to Self-Realization: Advertising and the Therapeutic Roots of the Consumer Culture, 1880–1930." In *The Culture of Consumption: Critical Essays in American History, 1880–1980*, edited by Richard Wightman Fox and T. J. Jackson Lears. New York: Pantheon, 1983.

Levine, Harry Gene. "The Discovery of Addiction: Changing Conceptions of Habitual Drunkenness in America." *Journal of Studies on Alcohol*, 39, no. 1 (January 1978): 143–74.

———. "Temperance and Women in the Nineteenth-Century United States." In *Alcohol and Drug Problems in Women*, edited by Oriana J. Kalant. New York: Plenum, 1980.

Lynch, Katherine A. "The Family and the History of Public Life." *Journal of Interdisciplinary History* 24, no. 4 (spring 1994): 665–84.

Marsh, Margaret. "From Separation to Togetherness: The Social Construction of Domestic Space in American Suburbs, 1840–1915." *Journal of American History* 76 (September 1989): 506–27.

———. "Suburban Men and Masculine Domesticity, 1870–1915." *American Quarterly* 40 (June 1988): 165–86.

Mick, David Glen. "Self-Gifts." In *Gift Giving: A Research Anthology*, edited by Cele Otnes and Richard F. Beltramini. Bowling Green, Ohio: Bowling Green University Press, 1996.

Moore, John Hammond. "The Cocktail: Our Contribution to Humanity's Salvation." *Virginia Quarterly Review* 56 (1980): 336–44.

Moskowitz, Eva S. " 'It's Good to Blow Your Top': Women's Magazines and a Discourse of Discontent, 1945–1965." *Journal of Women's History* 8 (fall 1996): 66–98.

O'Reilly, Edmund B. "Bill's Story: Form and Meaning in A.A. Recovery

Narratives." In *The Serpent in the Cup: Temperance in American Literature*, edited
by David S. Reynolds and Debra J. Rosenthal. Amherst: University of
Massachusetts Press, 1997.

Pfister, Joel. "On Conceptualizing the Cultural History of Emotional and
Psychological Life in America." In *Inventing the Psychological: Toward a Cultural
History of Emotional Life in America*, edited by Joel Pfister and Nancy Schnog.
New Haven: Yale University Press, 1997.

Powers, Madelon. "Decay from Within: The Inevitable Doom of the American
Saloon." In *Drinking: Behavior and Belief in Modern History*, edited by Susanna
Barrows and Robin Room. Berkeley: University of California Press, 1993.

Roizen, Ron. "How Does the Nation's Alcohol Problem Change from Era to Era?
Stalking the Social Logic of Problem-Definition Transformations since Repeal."
In *Altering the American Consciousness: Drugs and Alcohol in American Society*,
edited by Sarah W. Tracy and Caroline J. Acker. Amherst: University of Amherst
Press, forthcoming.

Room, Robin. "Alcoholism and Alcoholics Anonymous in U.S. Films, 1945–1962:
The Party Ends for the 'Wet Generations.'" *Journal of Studies on Alcohol* 50, no. 4
(1989): 368–81.

——. "The Movies and the Wettening of America: The Media as Amplifiers of
Cultural Change." *British Journal of Addiction* 83 (1988): 11–18.

Rosen, Ruth. "The Female Generation Gap: Daughters of the Fifties and the
Origins of Contemporary American Feminism." In *U.S. History as Women's
History: New Feminist Essays*, edited by Linda K. Kerber, Alice Kessler-Harris,
and Kathryn Kish Sklar. Chapel Hill: University of North Carolina Press, 1995.

Rubin, Jay L. "The Wet War: American Liquor Control, 1941–1945." In *Alcohol,
Reform, and Society: The Liquor Issue in Social Context*, edited by Jack S. Blocker.
Westport, Conn.: Greenwood Press, 1979.

Sanchez-Eppler, Karen. "Temperance in the Bed of a Child: Incest and Social
Order in Nineteenth-Century America." *American Quarterly* 47 (March 1995):
1–33.

Scott, Joan W. "Deconstructing Equality-versus-Difference; Or, the Uses of
Poststructuralist Theory for Feminism." *Feminist Studies* 14 (spring 1988):
33–50.

——. "The Evidence of Experience." *Critical Inquiry* 17 (summer 1991): 773–97.

"Sociological Aspects of the Disease Concept of Alcoholism." In *Research Advances
in Alcohol and Drug Problems*, edited by Robert J. Gibbens and Reginald G.
Smart, vol. 7. New York: Plenum, 1983.

Susman, Warren. "Did Success Spoil the United States? Dual Representations in
Postwar America." In *Recasting America: Culture and Politics in the Age of Cold
War*, edited by Lary May. Chicago: University of Chicago Press, 1989.

Tarbell, Ida. "Ladies at the Bar." *Liberty*, July 26, 1930, 6–10.

Valverde, Mariana. "Comment," in "Dialogue: Gender History/Women's History:
Is Feminist Scholarship Losing Its Critical Edge?" *Journal of Women's History* 5
(spring 1993): 123.

Westbrook, Robert B. "Fighting for the American Family." In *The Power of Culture: Critical Essays in American History*, edited by Richard W. Fox and T. J. Jackson Lears. Chicago: University of Chicago Press, 1993.

———. "I Want a Girl, Just Like the Girl That Married Harry James: American Women and the Problem of Political Obligation in World War II." *American Quarterly* 42 (December 1990): 587–614.

Yanagisako, Sylvia. "Family and Household: The Analysis of Domestic Groups." *American Review of Anthropology* 8 (1979): 186–98.

Dissertations

Allen, Holly. "Fallen Women and Forgotten Men: Gendered Concepts of Community, Home, and Nation, 1932–1945." Ph.D. diss., Yale University, 1996.

Dirks, Jacqueline K. "Righteous Goods: Women's Production, Reform Publicity, and the National Consumers' League, 1891–1919." Ph.D. diss., Yale University, 1996.

Ellis, Leonard. "Men among Men: An Exploration of All-Male Relationships in Victorian America." Ph.D. diss., Columbia University, 1982.

Johnson, Bruce Holley. "The Alcoholism Movement in America: A Study in Cultural Innovation." Ph.D. diss., University of Illinois, 1973.

McClellan, Michelle Lee. "Lady Lushes: Women Alcoholics and American Society, 1880–1960." Ph.D. diss., Stanford University, 1999.

McFadden, Margaret. "Anything Goes: Gender and Knowledge in the Comic Popular Culture of the 1930s." Ph.D. diss., Yale University, 1996.

Murdock, Catherine Gilbert. "Domesticating Drink: Women and Alcohol in Prohibition America, 1870–1940." Ph.D. diss., University of Pennsylvania, 1995.

Roizen, Ron. "The American Discovery of Alcoholism, 1933–1939." Ph.D. diss., University of California, Berkeley, 1991.

Room, Robin. "Governing Images of Alcohol and Drug Problems: The Structure, Sources, and Sequels of Conceptualizations of Intractable Problems." Ph.D. diss., University of California, Berkeley, 1978.

Rotskoff, Lori E. "Sober Husbands and Supportive Wives: Gendered Cultures of Drink and Sobriety in Post–World War II America." Ph.D. diss., Yale University, 1999.

Tracy, Sarah W. "The Foxborough Experiment: Medicalizing Inebriety at the Massachusetts Hospital for Dipsomaniacs and Inebriates, 1833–1919." Ph.D. diss., University of Pennsylvania, 1992.

Unpublished Papers

Chavigny, Katherine A. "Reforming Drunkards in Nineteenth-Century America: A Religious Therapeutic Tradition." Paper delivered at the conference "Historical Perspectives on Alcohol and Drug Use in American Society." College of Physicians and Surgeons, May 1997.

Tomes, Nancy J. "The Rise of the Mental Health Professions in the United States, 1900–1970."

Tracy, Sarah W. "Therapeutic and Civic Ideals in the Rehabilitation of Inebriates: The Evolution of State Hospital Care for Habitual Drunkards in Massachusetts, 1890–1920." Paper delivered at the conference "Historical Perspectives on Alcohol and Drug Use in American Society." College of Physicians and Surgeons, May 1997.

INDEX

Abraham, Karl, 69–70, 80, 259 (n. 49)
Abstinence, 12, 25, 27–28, 36–37, 39–40, 60
Adult Children of Alcoholics (ACOA), 241
Advertisements: of alcoholic beverages, 41–42, 50–52, 55–56, 58, 201–6, 208, 253 (n. 81)
Advertising: profession of, 56–57, 99–100, 231
African Americans, 10, 119–21
AIDS, 280 (n. 6)
Akron, Ohio, 105, 114, 116, 122, 162–64, 185
Al-Anon Family Groups: attitudes of AA men toward, 164–66; in contemporary society, 237; effects of feminism on, 240–41; founding of, 3–4, 15, 161–67; and marital ideology, 15, 173–90; public relations efforts of, 168; role of, in postwar society, 190–93. *See also* Smith, Anne; Wilson, Lois B.
Alateen, 13
Alcohol consumption: rates of, 38, 62, 89, 237, 239, 276 (n. 12)
Alcohol education, 207–10
Alcoholic beverage industries. *See* Beer industry; Liquor industry
Alcoholic culture: definition of, 210–11
Alcoholics Anonymous: 3–4, 14, 66, 70, 104; clubhouses of, 123–26; criticism of, 264 (n. 13), 274 (n. 78); as depicted in film, 131–32, 212–13, 217; early membership of, 107–8, 114–22;

effectiveness of, 109; founding of, 105–6, 236; and masculinity, 111, 114–18, 122–48; as middle-class organization, 110, 121, 148; oral narratives in, 139–41; racial composition of, 110, 118–21; as social network, 122–26; sponsorship in, 129–31, 135; wives' groups within, 161–71; women in, 115–18. *See also* Al-Anon Family Groups; Self-help movement; Smith, Robert H., Twelve Steps; Wilson, Bill
Alcoholics Anonymous Comes of Age (Wilson), 163, 265 (n. 22)
Alcoholics Anonymous: The Story of How More Than One Hundred Men Have Recovered from Alcoholism ("Big Book"), 117–18, 127, 129, 139, 141–47, 171–73, 177–79, 257 (n. 23)
Alcoholic to His Sons, An (Hough), 142–43
Alcoholism movement, 2, 10, 65–67, 69, 104, 149–50, 211, 244 (n. 5), 256 (n. 12)
Alcoholism paradigm, 2, 63–70, 108–9, 113, 120, 192–93, 226, 236. *See also* Alcoholism movement
Alcohol: One Man's Meat (Chambers and Strecker), 71
Alcohol, Science, and Society, 69
Allen, Frederick Lewis, 40–41
American Journal of Inebriety, 69
American Magazine, 41
American Scholar, 52, 64, 67
Andrews, Dana, 93
Anne B., 167

Drunkard's wife: symbol of, 28–29

Drunkenness, 24, 39, 81, 206–7

Drys. *See* Temperance movement; Temperance reformers

Ebby T., 127, 130

Egan, Richard, 131

Ehrenreich, Barbara, 81

Eighteenth Amendment. *See* Prohibition amendment

Emotional sobriety, 174, 236

Emotion management, 101, 174–81, 205, 217, 236, 241–42, 262 (n. 94), 273 (n. 66)

Familialism, new, 6–7

Family: definition of, 6, 245 (n. 11)

Family Forum, 173

Farber, David, 238–39

Feeling rules. *See* Emotion management

Feminine Mystique, The (Friedan), 240

Femininity. *See* Womanhood

Feminism, 29–30, 191–92, 240–41

Films: "alcoholism films," 86–87, 211–12, 216, 260 (n. 63), 268 (n. 69); censorship of, 42–43; depictions of Alcoholics Anonymous in, 131–32. *See also names of individual films*

"Forgotten man," 35–36, 46, 110. *See also* Great Depression

Fortune, 56, 114, 202

Freudian theory, 70–80, 154–56, 215. *See also* Psychiatrists

Friedan, Betty, 240

Galbraith, John Kenneth, 230

Gender: and alcoholism rates, 4, 67–69; definition of, 112, 244 (n. 9); identification, process of, 75–76; ideologies of, 5, 7, 15–6, 17. *See also* Manhood; Womanhood

Gender formation, 12, 112–13, 159, 162, 193, 244 (n. 9)

Generation of Vipers (Wylie), 76, 270 (n. 17)

Gerber, David, 92–93, 96, 98

"G.I. Bill," 188

Gift exchange: and Alcoholics Anonymous, 128–33; at Christmas, 58, 202; within marriage, 179–81; rituals of, 74; treating as, 20

Gordon, Anna, 27

Graebner, William, 91, 147

Grapevine, 116–20, 122–26, 133, 137, 140, 173–77, 180, 189, 265 (n. 22), 273 (n. 58)

Great Depression, 6–7, 14, 34–36, 42–47, 54–55, 70, 105, 110, 147

Grimes, William, 194, 196

Haaken, Janice, 191, 240–41

Haggard, Howard, 68, 73

Hamill, Pete, 53–54, 208

Hammett, Dashiel, 43

Hartmann, Susan, 188

Hays Production Code, 42–43

Henrietta D., 163

Herman, Ellen, 188

Heterosexuality, 78–80. *See also* Sexuality

Heterosocial drinking. *See* Social drinking

Hitler, Adolf, 51

Hochschild, Arlie, 174, 179, 262 (n. 94), 273 (n. 66)

Home before Dark (Susan Cheever), 224

Homosexuality, 78–80, 88, 226–27, 259 (n. 49)

Hope and Help for the Alcoholic (Lovell), 76

Hoover, Herbert, 35

Hough, Henry Beetle, 57, 99, 143, 197–98

Hour, The (DeVoto), 196–97

Housebreaker of Shady Hill, The (John Cheever), 218

Hyde, Lewis, 128–29

Ignatia, Sister Mary, 115, 185–86
I'll Cry Tomorrow (film), 131
Immigrants, 10, 23
Inge, William, 212, 218, 227, 278 (n. 40)

Jackson, Charles, 87–88, 123, 218, 227, 261 (n. 64)
Jackson, Joan K., 157–61, 184, 271 (n. 22)
James, William, 108, 134–35
Jellinek, E. M., 66–69, 73, 82–83, 102, 151, 195, 225, 256 (n. 12)
John Barleycorn (London), 17–23, 25, 27, 31, 74, 78, 88, 218, 225, 227
Johnson, Bruce Holley, 65, 90

Kantor, MacKinley, 262 (n. 87)
Kingdom of Evils (Southard and Jarrett), 151
Knight, Robert P., 77, 79
Kurtz, Ernest, 108, 118, 120, 126, 233, 263 (n. 5)

Ladies Home Journal, 184
Lancaster, Burt, 131, 212, 223
Lanza, Joseph, 44–45, 197
Leach, William, 99
Leisure: commercialization of, 38–39, 54–55, 228–29
Lewis, Sinclair, 99
Life, 42, 50, 61–64, 204, 253 (n. 81)
Liquor industry, 37, 41, 44, 47–49, 51, 66, 201
Lolli, Georgio, 195–97, 223
London, Jack, 17–23, 25–28, 53–55, 225
Lost Weekend, The (film), 86–93, 97, 101–2, 104, 107, 123, 146, 149, 211–12, 216
Lowry, Malcolm, 87
Loy, Myrna, 43, 94, 103
Lunbeck, Elizabeth, 5, 79, 112

McCarthy, Raymond, 78, 82
Man against Himself (Menninger), 71
Manhood: 5, 15, 52; and Alcoholics Anonymous, 111–48; "dissolute manhood," 17–18, 79, 84, 143–36, 147–48; and middle-class drinkers, 24–25; and New Deal, 46–47; and Prohibition, 30–31; "respectable manhood," 18, 25, 31–34, 79, 84, 144, 147–48; and saloon culture, 18–23; and social drinking, 59–60, 77. *See also* Breadwinning; Gender; Gender formation; Sober manhood
Mann, Marty, 66, 86, 115
March, Fredric, 93, 98
Marijuana, 238
Marriage: normative conventions of, 12, 176–85, 193; companionate, 32, 245 (n. 13). *See also* Al-Anon Family Groups; Emotion management; Wives
Marriage rate, 239
Martinis. *See* Cocktail culture; Three-martini lunch
Masculine domesticity, 31–33, 112
Masculinity. *See* Gender; Manhood
Materialism. *See* Consumer culture
May, Elaine Tyler, 7, 187, 190, 205, 275 (n. 97)
Mayo, Virginia, 94
Medicalization: of alcoholism, 63–67, 86, 90, 244 (n. 3). *See also* Alcoholism paradigm
Menninger, Karl, 71, 80
Menninger clinic, 71, 77
Mental health experts. *See* Psychiatrists; Social workers
Meyerowitz, Joanne, 275 (n. 97)
Middle classes: drinking styles among, 10–11, 23–25, 47, 57, 89, 194, 204; and family ideals, 33–34. *See also* Class affiliation; Manhood; Professional-managerial class
Military. *See* Armed services
Milland, Ray, 87
Moderation: concept of, 49, 60
"Momism," 76–77, 79, 155–56, 259 (n. 41), 270 (n. 17)
"Moral Equivalent of War," 134

Moskowitz, Eva, 187
Murder at the Vanities (film), 45
Mutual help movement, 106, 234. *See also* Self-help movement

National Committee for Education on Alcoholism (NCEA), 66, 115, 272 (n. 34)
National Council of Catholic Women, 186
National Organization for Women, 240
New Deal, 46. *See also* Great Depression
Newsweek, 67, 86, 215
New York City, 57, 107, 120, 122–23, 125, 127, 165–66, 265 (n. 27)
New Yorker, 203–4, 206, 218, 221
New York Times, 41, 70, 215
Nixon, Richard, 205
Nurturance, 8

O'Donnell, Cathy, 93
O'Reilly, Edmund, 139, 245 (n. 11)
Organization Man (Whyte), 198
Ossining, N.Y., 224
Oxford Group, 127, 175, 130

Park Forest, Ill., 198–99
People of Plenty (Potter), 231
Pfister, Joel, 11, 109
Physicians, 65, 70, 150. *See also* Medicalization; Psychiatrists
Plattsburgh, N.Y., 137, 268 (n. 80)
Pleck, Elizabeth, 29, 56
Potter, David, 231
Powell, William, 43
Price, Gladys, 152–53, 160
Professional-managerial class, 11, 56–58, 89, 99–100, 110
Prohibition amendment, 1, 25–26, 34, 38–39, 67, 235. *See also* Temperance movement
Prohibitionists. *See* Temperance reformers

Prohibition movement. *See* Temperance movement
Psychiatrists, 2, 4–5, 22, 65–66, 69–71, 73–80, 84–85, 102, 150–52, 176, 188. *See also* Freudian theory; Social workers
Psychoanalysis. *See* Freudian theory

Quarterly Journal of Studies on Alcohol, 69, 153

Race: and alcoholism, 10, 118–21
Rapping, Elayne, 110
Recovery movement, 236–37. *See also* Self-help movement; Twelve Step program
Reformers. *See* Temperance reformers
Repeal amendment, 34–36, 40
Repeal movement, 34–37, 39–40, 49, 253 (n. 77)
Roizen, Ron, 66
Room, Robin, 66, 110
Roosevelt, Franklin Delano, 35–36, 39–40
Rush, Benjamin, 65, 243 (n. 3)
Russell, Harold, 92

Sabin, Pauline Morton, 39–40, 103
Saloons, 17–23, 30, 79; after repeal, 53–55
Saturday Evening Post, 107, 186
Schnog, Nancy, 109
Seeley, John, 198–201, 230
Self-help movement, 14, 106, 192, 234, 236–37, 247 (n. 29)
September Remember (Taintor), 100
Servicemen's Readjustment Act. *See* "G.I. Bill"
Sexuality, 216, 239, 278 (n. 46). *See also* Heterosexuality; Homosexuality
Silkworth, William D., 106
Skid-row alcoholics, 81
Smith, Anne, 105, 162–64, 166, 169–73, 181, 185–86
Smith, Bernard B., 231–33

U.S. History as Women's History: New Feminist Essays, edited by Linda K. Kerber, Alice Kessler-Harris, and Kathryn Kish Sklar (1995)

Common Sense and a Little Fire: Women and Working-Class Politics in the United States, 1900–1965, by Annelise Orleck (1995)

How Am I to Be Heard?: Letters of Lillian Smith, edited by Margaret Rose Gladney (1993)

Entitled to Power: Farm Women and Technology, 1913–1963, by Katherine Jellison (1993)

Revising Life: Sylvia Plath's Ariel Poems, by Susan R. Van Dyne (1993)

Made From This Earth: American Women and Nature, by Vera Norwood (1993)

Unruly Women: The Politics of Social and Sexual Control in the Old South, by Victoria E. Bynum (1992)

The Work of Self-Representation: Lyric Poetry in Colonial New England, by Ivy Schweitzer (1991)

Labor and Desire: Women's Revolutionary Fiction in Depression America, by Paula Rabinowitz (1991)

Community of Suffering and Struggle: Women, Men, and the Labor Move

ment in Minneapolis, 1915–1945, by Elizabeth Faue (1991)

All That Hollywood Allows: Re-reading Gender in 1950s Melodrama, by Jackie Byars (1991)

Doing Literary Business: American Women Writers in the Nineteenth Century, by Susan Coultrap-McQuin (1990)

Ladies, Women, and Wenches: Choice and Constraint in Antebellum Charleston and Boston, by Jane H. Pease and William H. Pease (1990)

The Secret Eye: The Journal of Ella Gertrude Clanton Thomas, 1848–1889, edited by Virginia Ingraham Burr, with an introduction by Nell Irvin Painter (1990)

Second Stories: The Politics of Language, Form, and Gender in Early American Fictions, by Cynthia S. Jordan (1989)

Within the Plantation Household: Black and White Women of the Old South, by Elizabeth Fox-Genovese (1988)

The Limits of Sisterhood: The Beecher Sisters on Women's Rights and Woman's Sphere, by Jeanne Boydston, Mary Kelley, and Anne Margolis (1988)